A
DICTIONARY
OF
MUSICAL QUOTATIONS

A
DICTIONARY
OF
MUSICAL QUOTATIONS

Compiled by
Ian Crofton and Donald Fraser

SCHIRMER BOOKS
A Division of Macmillan, Inc.
New York

Schirmer Books
A Division of Macmillan, Inc.
866 Third Avenue, New York, N.Y. 10022

First American Edition 1985

Library of Congress Catalog Card Number: 85-5051
printing number
1 2 3 4 5 6 7 8 9 10

Library of Congress Cataloging in Publication Data
Crofton, Ian.
A dictionary of musical quotations.
Includes indexes.
1. Music—Quotations, maxims, etc. I. Fraser,
David. II. Title.
ML66.C86   1985   780   85-5051
ISBN 0-02-906530-5

Typeset by Leaper & Gard Ltd, Bristol, England
Printed and bound in Great Britain

For Alison and Karen
who put up with us

PREFACE

This book is designed both as a work of reference and as a book for reading and dipping into. We have collected more than three thousand notable, often celebrated, utterances by and about music and musicians. We have considered music in its many aspects — from historical and social, to technical and psychological — and we have also tried to cover a wide range of kinds of music, though there is a stress on traditional 'classical' music and its exponents.

Although the book is not an anthology, we have included a number of longer quotations, sometimes because these constitute a kind of manifesto by a musician, and sometimes because a good point has required many words to achieve its full impact. It will be clear that the most celebrated composers have attracted the greatest number of interesting quotations, though they have not always been the most prolific in quotable verbal statements themselves.

The quotations are arranged in a single alphabetical sequence of topics and composers. Some of the topics have cross-references to other headings where further related quotations may be found. The quotations under each heading are generally ordered chronologically according to date of utterance; for composers, we begin with the subject's own statements, and these are followed by quotations about the subject by other speakers. (With 'Conductors', the arrangement is alphabetical, and with 'Stars', by date of birth.)

Our referencing system is straightforward. We have generally given the date of first publication of the source work, except where the date of a translation has seemed more useful or accessible. For names of musicians, we have followed the conventions of *The Concise Oxford Dictionary of Music* (3rd edition, OUP, 1980).

There are two indexes: the first consists of the authors and speakers of quotations; the second, the subject index, consists of significant keywords, linked to a short identifying phrase, from the quotations. This can be used (a) to find the exact form and source of a half-remembered quotation, or (b) to search for quotations on topics of interest which do not have full headings to themselves, or (c) to lead to further references to individuals who have headings of their own.

Ian Crofton
Donald Fraser

Glasgow

CONTENTS

THE QUOTATIONS

ACADEMIES AND ACADEMICISM

See also EDUCATION.

1 Music resembles poetry; in each
Are nameless graces which no methods teach,
And which a master-hand alone can reach.

Alexander Pope, *An Essay on Criticism* (1711)

2 It is often by seeing and hearing musical works
(operas and other good musical compositions),
rather than by rules, that taste is formed.

Jean-Philippe Rameau, *Le nouveau Système de musique théorique* (1726)

3 And grant that a man read all the books of
music that ever were wrote, I shall not allow
that music is or can be understood out of them,
no more than the taste of meats out of cookish
receipt books.

Roger North, *The Musicall Gramarian* (1728)

4 [Refusing an honorary degree from Oxford]
Should I have had to spend my money in order
to be like those idiots? Never in this world!

George Frideric Handel, quoted in Rolland, *Essays on Music* (1948), 'Handel'

5 Perhaps it may be expected by some, that I
should say somewhat concerning Rules for
Composition; to these I answer that Nature is
the best Dictator, for all the hard, dry, studied
Rules that ever were prescribed, will not enable
a person to form an air.

William Billings, quoted in Wooldridge, *Charles Ives* (1974)

6 If an idea strikes me as beautiful and
satisfactory to the ear and heart, I would far
rather overlook a grammatical error than
sacrifice what is beautiful to mere pedantic
trifling.

Joseph Haydn, quoted in Nohl, *Life of Haydn* (1883)

7 [Of his entry for the Prix de Rome] I will be
lavish in redundancies, because they are the
forms to which the great masters adhered, and
one must not do better than the great masters.

Hector Berlioz, Letter to Humbert Ferrand, 1827

8 Nothing is more futile than theorizing about
music. No doubt there are laws, mathematically
strict laws, but these laws are not music; they
are only its conditions. . . . The essence of music
is revelation.

Heinrich Heine, *Letters on the French Stage* (1837)

9 How can inspired form in music be
scientifically differentiated from empty form?

Eduard Hanslick, quoted in Gall, *Johannes Brahms* (1961)

10 Can't you listen to chords without knowing
their names?

Claude Debussy, remark to fellow students at the
Conservatoire, quoted in *La Revue musicale*, 1926

11 Nothing but ceremonies and deans, all solemn-
faced and apparently incapable of speaking
anything but Latin. When it dawned upon me
that they were talking to me, I felt as if I were
drowning in hot water, so ashamed was I that I
could not understand them. However, when all
is said and done, that *Stabat Mater* of mine is
more than just Latin.

Antonín Dvořák, on receiving his honorary doctorate
of music from Cambridge University in 1891, quoted
in Michl, *Reminiscences*

12 The fact is, there are no rules, and there never
were any rules, and there never will be any
rules of musical composition except rules of
thumb; and thumbs vary in length, like ears.

George Bernard Shaw, *Music in London, 1890-1894* (1931)

13 [Of the Prix de Rome] It continues to exist with
that deplorable obstinacy which distinguishes
absurd ideas.

Claude Debussy, *Monsieur Croche, antidilettante* (1921)

14 There are nine and sixty ways of constructing
tribal lays,
And — every — single — one — of — them —
is — right!

Rudyard Kipling, 'In the Neolithic Age'

15 All those lily-pad Doctors of Music.

Charles Ives, quoted in Wooldridge, *Charles Ives* (1974)

16 Theory amounts to a registering of what has
been accomplished (often without set purpose)
by men bigger than their book knowledge.

Arthur William Foote, quoted in Ewen, *American Composers* (1982)

17 One tries to pin down on humble paper the
sweetest kisses of Frau Musica and — when
one thinks one has conjured up a vision of
eternal bliss — what do these blockheads hear?
Not music, but just notes, bars, dynamics,
forms and suchlike trivialities.

Paul Hindemith, Letter to Emmy Ronnefeldt, 1917,
during his time at the Frankfurt Conservatorium

1 You can't teach a young musician to compose any more than you can teach a delicate plant to grow, but you can guide him a little by putting a stick in here and a stick in there.

Frederick Delius, quoted in Fenby, *Delius as I knew him* (1936)

2 The best textbook for teaching composition is ... Walter de la Mare's *Peacock Pie*.

Gustav Holst, quoted in Holst, *Holst* (1974)

3 Very musical, but forbidden.

Nadia Boulanger, comment on students' exercises, quoted in Kendall, *The Tender Tyrant: Nadia Boulanger* (1976)

4 The tyranny of technique in part blinds us, whilst analysis that is too anatomical makes us lukewarm. It is of course excellent if, over and above this analysis, there is an impassioned love of music and thought, an impassioned love of life and the ardent desire not to lose any of the beauty spread around us in indescribable profusion.

Nadia Boulanger, quoted in Kendall, *The Tender Tyrant: Nadia Boulanger* (1976)

5 Imagine Pharaoh's dream interpreted successively by Joseph, by the Egyptian soothsayers, by Freud, by Rivers, by Adler, by Jung, by Wohlgemuth: it would 'say' a great many different things. Not nearly so many, however, as the Fifth Symphony has been made to say in the verbiage of its analysts.

Aldous Huxley, *Music at Night* (1931)

6 A musicologist is a man who can read music but can't hear it.

Sir Thomas Beecham, quoted in Atkins and Newman, *Beecham Stories* (1978)

7 My God, how can anyone ever be a *master* of music?

Paul Hindemith, on the title of 'Master of Music', quoted in Skelton, *Paul Hindemith* (1975)

8 Law, every law, has a chilling effect, and music has so much warmth anyhow, stable warmth, cow warmth, I'd like to say, that she can stand all sorts of regulated cooling off — she has even asked for it.
(Leverkühn)

Thomas Mann, *Doctor Faustus* (1947); trans. Lowe-Porter

9 They are so proud to know something, these old professors whose job it is in all corners of the globe to disgust students with music, and who are the more proud of their art as it is the more inconvenient and difficult to apply.

Arthur Honegger, *I am a Composer* (1951)

10 Academicism results when the reasons for the rule change, but not the rule.

Igor Stravinsky, *Conversations with Stravinksy* (1958)

11 Which is more musical, a truck passing by a factory or a truck passing by a music school?

John Cage, *Silence* (1961), 'Communication' (lecture)

ACCOMPANIMENT

12 It is difficult to say whether accompanist or soloist deserves greater credit ... Nevertheless, the soloist takes all the bravos to himself and gives no credit to his accompanist. But he is right, for he knows that ignorant custom directs these bravos to him alone.

Carl Philipp Emanuel Bach, *Essay on the True Art of Playing Keyboard Instruments* (1753-62)

13 Poor accompanists are admittedly numerous enough, but there are very few good ones, for today everyone wants to be the soloist.

Leopold Mozart, *Versuch einer gründlichen Violinschule* (1756)

14 Am I Too Loud?

Gerald Moore, title of autobiography (1962)

THE ACCORDION

15 Accordion, n. An instrument with the sentiments of an assassin.

Ambrose Bierce, *The Devil's Dictionary* (1911)

16 The vile belchings of lunatic accordions.

Arthur Honegger, *I am a Composer* (1951)

THE AEOLIAN HARP

17 The breeze warbles, and the mute still air
Is Music slumbering on her instrument.

Samuel Taylor Coleridge, 'The Aeolian Harp' (1795)

18 Make me thy lyre, even as the forest is:
What if the leaves are falling like its own?
The tumult of thy mighty harmonies

Will take from both a deep, autumnal tone,
Sweet though in sadness.

Percy Bysshe Shelley, 'Ode to the West Wind' (1819)

ALEATORY MUSIC

19 By temperament I cannot toss a coin ... Chance must be very well controlled. *Il y a suffisamment d'inconnu.* [There is already enough unknown.]

Pierre Boulez, Letter to John Cage

20 Composing ... is simply a series of musical decisions, the most basic being the decision to make decisions.

Larry Austin, quoted in Ewen, *American Composers* (1982)

AMATEURS

21 *Etiam singulorum fatigatio quamlibet se rudi modulatione solatur.*

Even when alone, men comfort their weariness
with song, however unskilled.

Quintilian, *De Institutione Oratoria*

1   Yet do we daily observe that when any shall
    sing a treble to an instrument, the standers by
    will be offering at an inward part out of their
    own nature, and, true or false, out it must,
    though to the perverting of the whole harmony.

    Thomas Campion, *The First Booke of Ayres* (c. 1613)

2   Swans sing before they die — 'twere no bad
              thing
    Should certain persons die before they sing.

    Samuel Taylor Coleridge, 'Epigram on a Volunteer
    Singer'

3   Though there seemed no chance of her
    [Catherine] throwing a whole party into
    raptures by a prelude on the pianoforte of her
    own composition, she could listen to other
    people's performance with very little fatigue.

    Jane Austen, *Northanger Abbey* (pub. 1818)

4   There is delight in singing, tho' none hear
    beside the singer.

    Walter Savage Landor, 'To Robert Browning'

5   It is not unjust to define amateur concerts by
    saying that the music performed at them seems
    to have been composed to make those who
    render it happy and drive those who listen to
    despair.

    Adolphe Adam, *Souvenirs d'un musicien* (1857)

6   We were none of us musical, though Miss
    Jenkyns beat time, out of time, by way of
    appearing to be so.

    Elizabeth Gaskell, *Cranford* (1851-3)

7   We never see a young lady, surrounded by
    eight or ten bachelors, take off her gloves, and
    seat herself at the piano, but we shudder . . .
    Who knows how many men may be killed dead
    on the spot by the first crash!

    Douglas Jerrold, *Cakes and Ale* (1852), 'The Preacher
    Parrot'

8   A vile beastly rottenheaded foolbegotten
    brazenthroated pernicious piggish screaming,
    tearing, roaring, perplexing, splitmecrackle,
    crashmecriggle insane ass of a woman is
    practising howling below-stairs with a brute of
    a singing master so horribly that my head is
    nearly off.

    Edward Lear, Letter to Lady Strachey, 1859

9   Hell is full of musical amateurs. Music is the
    brandy of the damned.
    (Don Juan)

    George Bernard Shaw, *Man and Superman*, III (1903)

AMERICA

10 I hear America singing, the varied carols I hear.

    Walt Whitman, *Leaves of Grass* (1855)

11 The future music of this country [America]
    must be founded on what are called the Negro
    melodies.

    Antonín Dvořák, interview in *The New York Herald*

12 Syncopation is in the soul of every true
    American.

    Irving Berlin, quoted in Whitcomb, *After the Ball* (1972)

13 I am trying to do something for the future of
    American music, which today has no class
    whatsoever and is mere barbaric mouthing.

    Jerome Kern, quoted in *The New York Times*, 1920

14 The role of music and art is to nourish and
    sustain people. The day of American leadership
    has dawned and it is necessary for us to
    become spiritual leaders.

    John Alden Carpenter, quoted in Ewen, *American
    Composers* (1982)

15 Jazz is the result of the energy stored up in
    America.

    George Gershwin, quoted in Morgenstern, *Composers
    on Music* (1958)

16 The Real American Folk Song is a Rag.

    Ira Gershwin, title of song

17 Jazz I regard as an American folk music; not the
    only one, but a very powerful one which is
    probably in the blood and feeling of the
    American people more than any other style of
    folk music.

    George Gershwin, 'The Relation of Jazz to American
    Music' (1933)

18 The way to write American music is simple. All
    you have to do is be an American and then
    write any kind of music you wish.

    Virgil Thomson, quoted in Machlis, *Introduction to
    Contemporary Music* (1963)

19 Is the Dust Bowl more American than, say, a
    corner in the Boston Athenaeum?

    Walter Piston, quoted in Machlis, *Introduction to
    Contemporary Music* (1963)

20 The composer cannot afford the wild-goose
    chase of trying to be more American than he is.

    Walter Piston, quoted in Ewen, *American Composers*
    (1982)

21 If there is a national American form of song it is
    the blues.

    Russell Ames, *The Story of American Folk Song* (1955)

22 We hear too much music . . . Until we have a
    great listening public, and not just a passively
    hearing one, we will never be a musically
    cultured nation.

    Leonard Bernstein, *The Infinite Variety of Music* (1966)

1 In Vienna people listen and know about style —
in America they listen with their heart.
Ljuba Welitsch, quoted in Jacobson, *Reverberations*
(1975)

2 We are not an aria country. We are a song
country.
Alan Jay Lerner, quoted in Palmer, *All You Need Is Love*
(1976)

ANTHEIL

3 [His aim] to warn the age in which I am living
of the simultaneous beauty and danger of its
unconscious mechanistic philosophy.
George Antheil, quoted in Ewen, *American Composers*
(1982)

4 Bad Boy of Music
George Antheil, title of autobiography (1945)

ANTI-MUSIC

See also PRO-MUSIC.

5 All the daughters of musick shall be brought
low.
Ecclesiastes 12:4

6 Much music marreth men's manners.
Galen, quoted in Ascham, *Toxophilus* (1545)

7 Can a minstrel be saved? No; minstrels are
ministers of Satan. They laugh now, but God
shall laugh at them on the last day.
Honorius of Autun, quoted in Raynor, *Social History of
Music* (1972)

8 Karolles, wrastlings, or sumer games,
Whoso every haunteth any swich shames
In cherche, other in cherchyerd,
Of sacrilege he may be aferd:
Of enterludes of singing,
Or tabor bete or other pypinge —
Whyle the prest stondeth at masse.
Richard Rolle (early 14th century), quoted in Lee,
Music of the People (1970)

9 Gif there by onie that . . . ar bairdes [bards] . . .
and gif onie sic be funden, that they be put in
the king's waird, or in his irons for their
trespasses, . . . that their eares be nailed to the
trone [pillory], or till ane uther tree, and their
eare cutted off, and banished the cuntrie — and
gif thereafter they be funden again, that they be
hanged.
Act of the Scottish Parliament, 1449

10 Schaw now quhat kynd of soundis musicall
Is maist semand to vailyeand cheveleris.
As the thondrand blast of trumpat bellicall
The spretis of men to hardy curage steris,
So syngyng, fydlyng, and piping not efferis
For men of honour nor of hye estate.
Becaus it spoutis swete venome in thair eris

And makis thair myndis al effeminate.
John Bellenden (early 16th century)

11 He who despises music, as do all the fanatics,
does not please me. Music is a gift of God, not a
gift of men.
Martin Luther, quoted in Headington, *Bodley Head
History of Western Music* (1974)

12 I believe music . . . together with many other
vanities is meet for women, and peradventure
for some also that have the likeness of men, but
not for them that be men indeed; who ought
not with such delicacies to womanish their
minds.
(Lord Gaspar)
Baldassare Castiglione, *The Booke of the Courtyer*
(1528); trans. Hoby (1561)

13 Much music marreth men's manners, sayeth
Galen, although some men will say that it doth
not so but rather recreateth and maketh quick a
man's mind, yet me think by reason it doth as
honey doth to a man's stomach, which at first
receiveth it well, but afterward it maketh it
unfit to abide any good strong nourishing meat,
or else any wholesome sharp and quick drink.
Roger Ascham, *Toxophilus* (1545)

14 I had rather be a kitten and cry mew
Than one of those same metre balladmongers,
I had rather hear a brazen canstick turned
Or a dry wheel grate on the axletree.
(Hotspur)
William Shakespeare, *Henry IV, Part One*, III.i

15 The man that hath no music in himself,
Nor is not moved with concord of sweet
    sounds,
Is fit for treasons, stratagems and spoils;
The motions of his spirit are dull as night,
And his affections dark as Erebus:
Let no such man be trusted. Mark the music.
(Lorenzo)
William Shakespeare, *The Merchant of Venice*, V.i

16   He [Cassius] loves no plays —
As thou dost, Antony — he hears no music,
Seldom he smiles . . .
(Julius Caesar)
William Shakespeare, *Julius Caesar*, I.ii

17 *Clown:* . . . the General so likes your music that
he desires you, of all loves, to make no more
noise with it.
First Musician: Well, sir, we will not.
Clown: If you have any music that may not be
heard, to't again, but, as they say, to hear music
the General does not greatly care.
William Shakespeare, *Othello*, III.i

18 *All:* The music, ho!
Enter Mardian the Eunuch
Cleopatra: Let it alone; let's to billiards.
William Shakespeare, *Antony and Cleopatra*, II.v

1 Who loves not music and the heavenly muse,
   That man God hates.

   John Dowland, commendatory poem to Sir William
   Leighton's *Teares or Lamentations of a Sorrowfull Soule*
   (1614)

2 That which is always accompanied with
   effeminate lust-provoking music is doubtless
   inexpedient and unlawful unto Christians.

   William Prynne, *Histriomastix* (1632)

3   Their lean and flashy songs
   Grate on their scrannel pipes of wretched
      straw.

   John Milton, 'Lycidas' (1637)

4 Give the piper a penny to play, and twopence
   to leave off.

   Thomas Fuller, *Gnomologia* (pub. 1732)

5 You make as good music as a wheelbarrow.

   Thomas Fuller, *Gnomologia* (pub. 1732)

6 I was moved also to cry out against all sorts of
   music.

   George Fox, Journal, 1649

7 Though the entertainments of music are very
   engaging; though they make a great discovery
   of the soul; and show it capable of strange
   diversities of pleasure: yet to have our passion
   lie at the mercy of a little minstrelsy; to be
   fiddled out of our reason and sobriety; to have
   our courage depend upon a drum, or our
   devotions upon an organ, is a sign we are not
   as great as we might be.

   Jeremy Collier, *An Essay of Musick* (1702)

8 [In the Commonwealth period] Many chose
   rather to fiddle at home, than to go out and be
   knocked on the head abroad.

   Roger North, *Memoires of Musicke* (pub. 1846)

9 A taste of sculpture and painting is in my mind
   as becoming as a taste of fiddling and piping is
   unbecoming a man of fashion. The former is
   connected with history and poetry, the latter,
   with nothing that I know of but bad company.

   Lord Chesterfield, Letter to his son, 1749

10 True philosophy — but there is no treating the
   subject whilst my uncle Toby is whistling
   Lillabullero.

   Laurence Sterne, *Tristram Shandy* (1760-67)

11 [Of *The Beggar's Opera*] There is in it such a
   labefactation of all principles as may be injurious
   to morality.

   Samuel Johnson, quoted in Boswell, *Life* (1791)

12 Of all noises I think music the least
   disagreeable.

   Samuel Johnson, quoted in *The Morning Chronicle*,
   1816

13 Tonight he said, that, 'if he had learnt music, he
   should have been afraid he would have done
   nothing else but play. It was a method of
   employing the mind, without the labour of
   thinking at all, and with some applause from a
   man's self.'

   Samuel Johnson, quoted in Boswell, *Journal of a Tour to
   the Hebrides* (1785)

14 In the judgment of Reason music has less worth
   than any other of the beautiful arts.

   Immanuel Kant, *Critique of Judgment* (1790)

15 I have sat through an Italian Opera, till, for
   sheer pain, and inexplicable anguish, I have
   rushed out into the noisiest places of the
   crowded streets, to solace myself with sounds
   which I was not obliged to follow, and get rid of
   the distracting torment of endless, fruitless,
   barren attention!

   Charles Lamb, *Essays of Elia* (1820-23), 'A Chapter on
   Ears'

16 A carpenter's hammer, in a warm summer
   noon, will fret me into more than midsummer
   madness. But those unconnected, unset sounds
   are nothing to the measured malice of music.

   Charles Lamb, *Essays of Elia* (1820-3), 'A Chapter on
   Ears'

17 I even think that sentimentally I am disposed to
   harmony. But organically I am incapable of a
   tune.

   Charles Lamb, *Essays of Elia* (1820-23), 'A Chapter on
   Ears'

18 Some cry up Haydn, some Mozart,
   Just as the whim bites. For my part,
   I do not care a farthing candle
   For either of them, nor for Handel.

   Charles Lamb, 'To William Ayrton'

19 Music, indeed! Give me a mother singing to her
   clean and fat and rosy baby.

   William Cobbett, *Advice to Young Men* (1830)

20 Let a man try the very uttermost to *speak* what
   he means, before singing is had recourse to.

   Thomas Carlyle, Journal, 1843

21 Music is the most disagreeable and the most
   widely beloved of all noises.

   Théophile Gautier, in *Le Figaro*, 1863

22 I only know two tunes. One of them is Yankee
   Doodle, and the other isn't.

   Ulysses S. Grant, attr.

23 Music sweeps by me as a messenger
   Carrying a message that is not for me.

   George Eliot, *The Spanish Gypsy*, III (1868)

24 Stuffing birds or playing stringed instruments
   is an elegant pastime, and a resource to the idle,
   but it is not education.

   Cardinal Newman, 'The Idea of a University Defined'
   (1873)

1 Her [Pauline Viardot-Garcia's] parties are rigidly musical and to me, therefore rigidly boresome . . . I stood the other night on my legs for three hours . . . in a suffocating room, listening to an interminable fiddling, with the only consolation that Gustav Doré, standing beside me, seemed as bored as myself.

Henry James, Letter to his father, 1876

2 I shall hate sweet music my whole life long.

Algernon Swinburne, 'The Triumph of Time'

3 Musical people are so very unreasonable. They always want one to be perfectly dumb at the very moment when one is longing to be absolutely deaf.

Oscar Wilde, An Ideal Husband, II (1895)

4 [After a musical evening] I must tell you how I dislike it all . . . Beethoven is nonsense, Pushkin and Lermontov also.

Leo Tolstoy, in 1900, quoted in Bertensson and Leyda, Sergei Rachmaninoff (1965)

5 I can't listen to music too often . . . it affects my nerves.

V.I. Lenin, quoted in Bowers, Skriabin (1969)

6 Oh some are fond of fiddles, and a song well
     sung,
And some are all for music for to lilt upon the
     tongue;
But mouths were made for tankards, and for
     sucking at the bung,
Says the old bold mate of Henry Morgan.

John Masefield, 'Captain Stratton's Fancy'

7 The truth is that there comes a time
When we can mourn no more over music
That is so much motionless sound.

Wallace Stevens, 'Sad Strains of a Gay Waltz' (1935)

8 The effect of rock 'n' roll on young people is to turn them into devil-worshippers; to stimulate self-expression through sex; to provoke lawlessness, impair nervous stability, and destroy the sanctity of marriage.

Rev. Albert Carter in 1956, quoted in Rogers, Rock 'n' Roll (1982)

9 He has Van Gogh's ear for music.

Orson Welles, attr. (also to others)

10 There is no such thing as an unmusical person.

Hans Werner Henze, Music and Politics (1982), 'Does Music have to be Political?' (1969)

11 Music is no different than opium. Music affects the human mind in a way that makes people think of nothing but music and sensual matters . . . Music is a treason to the country, a treason to our youth, and we should cut out all this music and replace it with something instructive.

Ayatollah Khomeini, Speech (1979)

APOLLO

12 Wilt thou have music? Hark — Apollo plays
And twenty caged nightingales do sing.
(Lord)

William Shakespeare, The Taming of the Shrew, Induction, ii

13   . . . as sweet and musical
As bright Apollo's lute, strung with his hair.
(Berowne)

William Shakespeare, Love's Labour's Lost, IV.iii

14 What music will be in him when Hector has knocked out his brains, I know not — but I am sure none, unless the fiddler Apollo get his sinews to make catlings on.
(Thersites)

William Shakespeare, Troilus and Cressida, III.iii

15 Musical as is Apollo's lute.

John Milton, Comus (1634)

16 Yea, is not even Apollo, with hair and
     harpstring of gold,
A bitter God to follow, a beautiful God to
     behold?
I am sick of singing . . .

Algernon Charles Swinburne, 'Hymn to Proserpine'

APPLAUSE

17 It is as fat and fulsome to my ear
As howling after music.
(Olivia)

William Shakespeare, Twelfth Night, V.i

18 People applaud a prima donna as they do the feats of the strong man at a fair. The sensations are painfully disagreeable, hard to endure, but one is so glad when it is all over that one cannot help rejoicing.

Jean-Jacques Rousseau, La Nouvelle Héloïse (1761)

19 A great deal of noise . . . is always appropriate at the end of an act. The more noise the better, and the shorter the better, so that the audience has no time to cool down with their applause.

Wolfgang Amadeus Mozart, Letter, 1781

20 The custom of showing one's pleasure at beautiful music by immediately following it with an ugly noise.

Percy Scholes, The Oxford Companion to Music (1955)

21 [On refusing to play encores] Applause is a receipt, not a bill.

Artur Schnabel, quoted in Kolodin, The Musical Life (1958)

22 The one thing I hate at the Met is the note in the programme that the public is requested not to interrupt the music with applause.

Placido Domingo, in 1972, quoted in Jacobson, Reverberations (1975)

ARNE

1　Arne had kept bad company: he had written for vulgar singers and hearers too long to be able to comport himself properly at the opera-house, in the first circle of taste and fashion.

Charles Burney, *A General History of Music* (1776-89)

2　It is probable that not a notion of duty ever occurred to Dr Arne, so happy was his self-complacency in the fertility of his invention and the ease of his compositions, and so dazzled by the brilliancy of his success in his powers of melody — which, in truth, for the English stage, were in sweetness and variety unrivalled.

Fanny Burney, quoted in Langley, *Doctor Arne* (1938)

3　But many days have past since last my heart
Was warm'd luxuriously by divine Mozart,
By Arne delighted, or by Handel madden'd,
Or by the song of Erin pierced and sadden'd.

John Keats, 'Epistle to Charles Cowden Clarke' (1816)

4　A jealous and self-seeking tradesman.

G.E.P. Arkwright, in *The Musical Gazette*, 1902

ATONALITY

See also AVANT-GARDE, DISSONANCE.

5　[Of his String Quartet No. 2 of 1908] The overwhelming multitude of dissonances cannot be balanced any longer by occasional returns to such tonal triads as represent a key. It seemed inadequate to force a movement into the Procrustean bed of tonality without supporting it by harmonic progressions that pertain to it.

Arnold Schoenberg, quoted in Reich, *Arnold Schoenberg* (1971)

6　The tyrannical rule of the major-minor keys.

Béla Bartók, quoted in Machlis, *Introduction to Contemporary Music* (1963)

7　There are today a considerable number of composers who issue works that they call atonal. Doubtless these composers see in their freedom from tonality a liberty that will lift their art to the infinity of time and space. Apart from the fact that I consider it impossible to abolish the inherent characteristics of the medium, I do not believe that liberty is achieved by substituting mere variety for the principle of natural order.

Paul Hindemith, *The Craft of Musical Composition* (1937)

8　Every composer of the better sort carries within himself a canon of the forbidden, the self-forbidding, which by degrees includes all the possibilities of tonality, in other words all traditional music.
(Leverkühn's 'Document')

Thomas Mann, *Doctor Faustus* (1947); trans. Lowe-Porter

9　Atonality is simply the maintenance of an ambiguous tonal state of affairs. It is the denial of harmony as a structural means. The problem of a composer in a musical world in this state is to supply another structural means, just as in a bombed-out city the opportunity to build again exists. This way one finds courage and a sense of necessity.

John Cage, *Silence* (1961), 'Forerunners of Modern Music' (1949)

10　We can no longer tolerate this fetishism of tonality, which has been a burden on entire generations of musicians.

Arthur Honegger, *I am a Composer* (1951)

11　Atonality is against nature. There is a centre to everything that exists. The planets have the sun, the moon, the earth ... All music with a centre is tonal. Music without a centre is fine for a moment or two, but it soon sounds all the same.

Alan Hovhaness, quoted in Ewen, *American Composers* (1982)

12　The bourgeois capitalistic world is tonal; that of love (unhappiness, despair) atonal.

Hans Werner Henze, speaking of his *Boulevard Solitude*, in *Music and Politics* (1982), 'German music in the 1940s and 1950s'

13　The European structure, based on tonality, would not admit noises or pitches outside the major and minor scale, and was incorrect.

John Cage, interview in *The Observer Magazine*, 1982

AUDIENCE

See also APPLAUSE.

14　Gentle and noble are their tempers framed,
That can be quickened with perfumes and sounds.

George Chapman, *Ovid's Banquet of Sense* (1595)

15　A song that is well and artificially made cannot be well perceived nor understood at the first hearing, but the oftener you shall hear it, the better cause of liking you will discover, and commonly that song is best esteemed with which our ears are best acquainted.

William Byrd, *Psalmes, Songs, and Sonnets* (1611)

16　[Asked by a talkative audience why he stopped playing] I was only afraid I interrupted business.

Arcangelo Corelli, quoted in Cibber, *Apology* (1740)

17　It is the custom of this country [England], when a lady or gentleman happens to sing, for the company to sit as mute and motionless as statues.

Oliver Goldsmith, *The Citizen of the World* (1762)

18　With respect to EXCELLENCE OF STYLE AND COMPOSITION, it may be perhaps be said that to practised ears the most pleasing Music is such as has the merit of novelty, added to refinement, and ingenious contrivance; and to the ignorant, such as is most familiar and common.

Charles Burney, *A General History of Music* (1772-89)

1 True music is for the ear alone; a fine voice is the most universal thing that can be figured ... Accordingly he always used to shut his eyes while hearing music; thereby to concentrate his whole being on the single pure enjoyment of the ear.

Johann Wolfgang von Goethe, *Wilhelm Meister* (1795-6)

2 During this terzetto, the Reverend Mr Portpipe fell asleep, and accompanied the performance with rather a deeper bass than was generally deemed harmonious.

Thomas Love Peacock, *Melincourt* (1817)

3 'Brave Galuppi! that was music! good alike at grave and gay!
I can always leave off talking, when I hear a master play.'

Robert Browning, 'A Toccata of Galuppi's'

4 The Public doesn't *want* to be asked to work: it doesn't seek to understand: it wants to *feel*, and to *feel immediately*.

Charles Gounod, Letter to Mme Charles Rhoné, 1862

5 *Le bourgeois ruminant dans sa stalle serrée.*
The bourgeois ruminating in his crowded stall.

Camille Saint-Saëns, Sonnet, describing the typical member of an audience

6 It is a matter of long experience that people always expect something very definite, and it is just as true that they get from us something entirely different.

Johannes Brahms, Letter to Simrock

7 I like Wagner's music better than anybody's. It is so loud that one can talk the whole time without other people hearing what one says.

Oscar Wilde, *The Picture of Dorian Gray* (1891)

8 If one plays good music people don't listen, and if one plays bad music people don't talk.

Oscar Wilde, *The Importance of Being Earnest*, III (1899)

9 The best kind of audience ... all that is required to rouse its enthusiasm is a graceful attitude or a romantically waved lock of hair.

Claude Debussy, quoted in Bonavia, *Musicians on Music* (1956)

10 People don't very much like things that are beautiful — they are so far from their nasty little minds.

Claude Debussy, Letter to Pierre Louÿs, 1900

11 I am quite convinced that there has to be a

barrier between the public and a great work of art.

Ferruccio Busoni, Letter to Gisella Selden-Goth, 1918

12 A man responds or fails to respond to certain music by virtue not only of what the music is, but of what he is.

Ernest Newman, *A Musical Critic's Holiday* (1925)

13 Great art presupposes the alert mind of the educated listener.

Arnold Schoenberg, *Memories and Commentaries* (1960)

14 People in the underworld, dope fiends and gun men, invariably are music lovers and, if not, they are affected by it.

George Gershwin, 'The Composer in the Machine Age' (1930)

15 Those who maintain that they only enjoy music to the full with their eyes shut do not hear better than when they have them open, but the absence of visual distractions enables them to abandon themselves to the reveries induced by the lullaby of its sounds, and that is really what they prefer to the music itself.

Igor Stravinsky, *Chronicles of My Life* (1936)

16 I think when an audience doesn't go to sleep, they think the style is wrong.

Wilhelm Furtwängler, Remark at press conference, quoted in Jacobson, *Reverberations* (1975)

17 It is to be regretted that in general so little relationship exists between the producers and the consumers of music.

Paul Hindemith, quoted in Machlis, *Introduction to Contemporary Music* (1963)

18 How then would the perfect musician exercise his art? He would take his horse (answered a Chinese musician) and ride to a mountain far away from houses and men. There he would play his instrument and sing for his own enlightenment.

Paul Hindemith, *A Composer's World* (1952)

19 A composer knows his work as a woodsman knows a path he has traced and retraced, while a listener is confronted by the same work as one is in the woods by a plant he has never seen before.

John Cage, *Silence* (1961), 'Experimental Music' (1957)

20 The composer would do himself and his music an immediate and eventual service by total, resolute and voluntary withdrawal from this public world to one of private performance and electronic media, with its very real possibility of complete elimination of the public and social aspects of musical composition.

Milton Babbitt, quoted in Ewen, *American Composers* (1982)

1   Audiences have kept me alive.

Judy Garland, quoted in Palmer, *All You Need Is Love* (1976)

2   I've got no talent, still sing flat as a table. I'm a sort of human spaniel. People come to see what I'm like. I make them feel, I exhaust them, I destroy them.

Johnnie Ray, quoted in Palmer, *All You Need Is Love* (1976)

3   I know two kinds of audience only — one coughing and one not coughing.

Artur Schnabel, *My Life and Music* (1961)

4   I never understood the need for a 'live' audience. My music, because of its extreme quietude, would be happiest with a dead one.

Igor Stravinsky, quoted in *London Magazine*, 1967

5   The current state of music presents a variety of solutions in search of a problem, the problem being to find somebody left to listen.

Ned Rorem, *Music from Inside Out* (1967)

6   Pop music is ultimately a show, a circus. You've got to hit the audience with it. Punch them in the stomach, and kick them on the floor.

Peter Townshend, quoted in Palmer, *Born Under a Bad Sign* (1970)

7   We don't play to be seen. I'm addicted to music, not audiences.

Miles Davis, in 1970, quoted in Roberts, *Black Music of Two Worlds* (1973)

8   [Of a woman who 'didn't understand' a performance] It took me twenty years' study and practice to work up to what I wanted to play in this performance. How can she expect to listen five minutes and understand it?

Miles Davis, quoted in Collier, *Jazz* (1975)

9   Why doesn't anybody go to concerts any more? ... because the halls are full of people like you! ... Half asleep, nodding and smiling, farting through their dentures, hawking and spitting into paper bags, dreaming up ever more ingenious plots against their children ... just a nice background murmur of wheezing, belching, intestinal gurgles, scratching, sucking, croaking, an entire opera house crammed full of them ... and you know what they're *all* listening to, Säure? eh? They're all listening to Rossini! Sitting there drooling away to some medley of predictable little tunes, leaning forward elbows on knees muttering, 'C'mon, c'mon then Rossini, let's get all this pretentious fanfare stuff out of the way, let's get on to the *real good tunes!*' Behavior as shameless as eating a whole jar of peanut butter at one sitting. (Gustav)

Thomas Pynchon, *Gravity's Rainbow* (1973)

10 Is it not a prime function of the composer to influence, and indeed educate, habits of listening?

Hans Werner Henze, *Music and Politics* (1982), 'German music in the 1940s and 1950s'

AVANT-GARDE

See also ALEATORY MUSIC, ATONALITY, DISSONANCE, ELECTRONIC MUSIC, FUTURISM, TWELVE-NOTE MUSIC.

11 Music was chaste and modest so long as it was played on simpler instruments, but since it has come to be played in a variety of manners and confusedly, it has lost the mode of gravity and virtue and fallen almost to baseness.

Boethius, *De Consolatione Philosophiae*

12 Now on some hollow tree the owl, shrill chorister of the night, hoots forth some notes which might charm the ears of some modern connoisseurs in music.

Henry Fielding, *Tom Jones* (1749)

13 Art demands of us that we shall not stand still.

Ludwig van Beethoven, quoted in Scott, *Beethoven* (1934)

14 Your genius is centuries in advance, and at the present time there is scarcely one hearer who would be sufficiently enlightened to enjoy the full beauty of this music.

Prince Galitsin, Letter to Beethoven, 1824

15 Wagner is the Marat of music, and Berlioz is its Robespierre.

A. Gasperini, in *Le Siècle*, 1858

16 Music, which today is in the full vigour of its youth, is emancipated, free: it does what it likes ... New needs of the mind, the heart and the aural sense necessitate new attempts and even, in certain cases, the abolition of ancient laws.

Hector Berlioz, *A travers chants* (1862)

17 The composer who stumbles in taking a step forward is worth more attention than the composer who shows us how easily he can step backwards.

Ernest Reyer, in 1872, quoted in Dean, *Bizet* (1975)

18 There is no sign of music changing at all. A dissonant chord would almost cause a revolution.

Claude Debussy, Letter to Emile Baron, 1887

19 [Of Schoenberg] He is young and perhaps he is right. Maybe my ear is not sensitive enough.

Gustav Mahler, quoted in Lebrecht, *Discord* (1982)

20 This is the first time in sixty years anyone has dared insult me!

The Comtesse de Pourtalès, at the première of *The Rite of Spring* in 1913, quoted in Lebrecht, *Discord* (1982)

1 What shocks people today will not shock them tomorrow, which is equivalent to saying that one can get accustomed to anything . . . How is it that people will not understand that there are things to which *one must not* become accustomed?

Camille Saint-Saëns, *Germanophilie* (1916)

2 When a work of art appears to be in advance of its period, it is really the period that has lagged behind the work of art.

Jean Cocteau, *Le Coq et l'arlequin* (1918)

3 There is no such thing as new music; there are only new musicians.

Paul Dukas, quoted in Myers, *Modern French Music* (1971)

4 Modern music is as dangerous as cocaine.

Pietro Mascagni, interview, 1927

5 Only the developing composer can compose for the developing listener.

Arnold Schoenberg, quoted in Walker, *Anatomy of Musical Criticism* (1966)

6 It's up to you whether you want to be on this side of the barricades or that one.

Arnold Schoenberg, remark to Rudolf Serkin, quoted in Jacobson, *Reverberations* (1975)

7 The great men of music close periods; they do not inaugurate them. The pioneer work, the finding of new paths, is left to smaller men.

Ralph Vaughan Williams, *National Music* (1934)

8 Not until the turn of the century did the outlines of the new world discovered in *Tristan* begin to take shape. Music reacted to it as a human body to an injected serum, which it at first strives to exclude as a poison, and only afterwards learns to accept as necessary and even wholesome.

Paul Hindemith, *The Craft of Musical Composition* (1937)

9 Two of the untamed spirits of the present age, Arthur Bliss and Constant Lambert.

Neville Cardus, in *The Manchester Guardian*, 1938

10 Nothing matures or grows old more rapidly than music. The brilliant audacity of one generation declines into the sober commonplace of another.

Sir Thomas Beecham, *A Mingled Chime* (1944)

11 The key to the understanding of contemporary music lies in repeated hearing: one must hear it till it sounds familiar.

Roger Sessions, *The Musical Experience* (1950)

12 [Of 'modern' music] Three farts and a raspberry, orchestrated.

Sir John Barbirolli, quoted in Kennedy, *Barbirolli, Conductor Laureate* (1971)

13 Composing's one thing, performing's another, listening's a third. What can they have to do with one another?

John Cage, *Silence* (1961), 'Experimental Music: Doctrine' (1955)

14 What we know as modern music is the noise made by deluded speculators picking through the slagpile.

Henry Pleasants, *The Agony of Modern Music* (1955)

15 Art is constantly in danger and must incessantly be re-invented, to ward off the encroachment of mechanical processes.

Hans Werner Henze, *Music and Politics* (1982), 'The Message of Music' (1959)

16 I occasionally play works by contemporary composers and for two reasons. First, to discourage the composer from writing any more, and secondly to remind myself how much I appreciate Beethoven.

Jascha Heifetz, in *Life*, 1961

17 Its function [that of the avant-garde] is, like fashion, self-destructive so that it can be replaced by a new collection.

Pierre Boulez, in 1969, quoted in Jacobson, *Reverberations* (1975)

18 Categories of the establishment and the avant-garde makes no sense anymore . . . We are living in a blotter society which absorbs everything.

Pierre Boulez, in 1969, quoted in Jacobson, *Reverberations* (1975)

19 It is fortunate that to assert itself in music, a new generation does not need to destroy the works of its ancestors. It is sufficient to let them gather dust on the shelves of the library.

Ernst Křenek, *Horizons Circled* (1974)

20 I remember seeing, a few years ago, a newspaper report about one of the international music festivals headlined: 'So-and-so Festival — No New Breakthrough'.

Ernst Křenek, *Horizons Circled* (1974)

21 In traditional music everything depends on your having something to say and on saying it in a perfectly fused way, with form and content balancing one another. It seemed to me there was no sense in doing that unless you were being understood. Yet no one was being understood at that time. Each composer worked in a different way and no two composers understood what each other said. Sometimes, when I wrote a sad piece, half the audience would laugh. So I moved away from the concept of understanding to the concept of direct experience.

John Cage, quoted in Peyser, *Boulez* (1976)

1   *Bitonality* . . . a way of making one's music seem
    more 'modern' than it really is.

    Antony Hopkins, *Downbeat Music Guide* (1977)

2   Now we have schools of music like schools of
    fish.

    John Corigliano, quoted in Ewen, *American Composers*
    (1982)

C.P.E. BACH

3   Dissonances are generally played more loudly
    and consonances more softly, because the
    former stimulate and exacerbate the emotions,
    while the latter calm them.

    Carl Philipp Emanuel Bach, *Essay* (1753)

4   [Of C.P.E. Bach performing] His eyes were
    fixed, his under lip fell, and drops of
    effervescence distilled from his countenance.

    Charles Burney, *The Present State of Music in Germany*
    (1773)

5   [C.P.E.] Bach is the father, we the children.

    Joseph Haydn, quoted in Headington, *Bodley Head
    History of Western Music* (1974)

6   I have only a few examples of [Carl Philipp]
    Emanuel Bach's compositions for the clavier;
    and yet some of them should certainly be in the
    possession of every true artist.

    Ludwig van Beethoven, Letter to Christoph Breitkopf,
    1809

J.S. BACH

7   I have always kept one end in view, namely,
    with all good will to conduct a well regulated
    church music to the honour of God.

    Johann Sebastian Bach, Letter to the Mühlhausen
    Council, 1708

8   For the glory of the most high God alone,
    And for my neighbour to learn from.

    Johann Sebastian Bach, Epigraph to the *Little Organ
    Book* (1717)

9   I was obliged to work hard. Whoever is equally
    industrious will succeed just as well.

    Johann Sebastian Bach, quoted in Forkel, *Über Johann
    Sebastian Bachs Leben, Kunst und Kunstwerke* (1802)

10 This can only be the devil or Bach himself!

    A village organist, on finding Bach playing on his
    organ, quoted in Geiringer, *The Bach Family* (1954)

11 If Bach continues to play in this way, the organ
    will be ruined in two years, or most of the
    congregation will be deaf.

    Member of the Arnstadt Council, in 1705, quoted in
    Geiringer, *The Bach Family* (1954)

12 His composition [the cantata *Jesus nahm zu sich
    die Zwölfe*] was much praised by those who like

this kind of music.

    A Hamburg newspaper, in 1723, quoted in Neuman,
    Bach (1961)

13 [On appointing Bach as cantor at Leipzig,
    Graupner having refused the post] Since the
    best cannot be had, one must take the next
    best.

    Mayor Abraham Platz, in 1723, quoted in Neuman,
    Bach (1961)

14 Rhythm is in his every limb, he takes in all the
    harmonies by his subtle ear and utters all the
    different parts through the medium of his own
    mouth. Great admirer as I am of antiquity in
    other respects, I yet deem this Bach of mine to
    comprise in himself many Orpheuses and
    twenty Arions.

    Johann Mathias Gesner, Commentary on Quintilian's
    De Institutio Oratoria (*c.* 1730)

15 'Tis said, when Orpheus used to pluck the
        strings
    The forest creatures meekly to him came,
    But when our own Bach's music richly rings,
    He puts great Orpheus himself to shame.

    Anon., in a Dresden newspaper, 1731, quoted in
    Neuman, *Bach* (1961); trans. de Haan

16 [Bach] judges the difficulties of his music
    according to his fingers. His compositions,
    therefore, are difficult to perform, as he
    demands that singers and instrumentalists
    perform with their throats and instruments the
    same feats he can perform on the clavier. This,
    of course, is impossible.

    Johann Adolf Scheiber, in *Der critische Musicus*, 1737

17 This great man would be the admiration of
    whole nations if he had more amenity, if he did
    not take away the natural element in his pieces
    by giving them a turgid and confused style, and
    if he did not darken their beauty by an excess of
    art.

    Johann Adolf Scheiber, in *Der critische Musicus*, 1737

18 Lamented Bach! Your touch upon the organ's
        keys
    Long since has earned you company among the
        great,
    And what your quill upon the music-sheet has
        writ
    Has filled hearts with delight, though some did
        envy seize.

    Georg Philipp Telemann, Sonnet; trans. de Hann

19 He, who possessed the most profound
    knowledge of all the contrapuntal arts (and
    even artifices) understood how to make art
    subservient to beauty.

    C.P.E. Bach, attr., quoted in Geiringer, *The Bach
    Family* (1954)

20 [If] Sebastian Bach and his admirable son
    Emanuel . . . had been fortunately employed to

compose for the stage and public of great capitals ... they would doubtless have simplified their style more to the level of their judges ... [and] by writing in a style more popular, and generally intelligible and pleasing, would have extended their fame.

Charles Burney, *A General History of Music* (1776-89)

1 It is as though eternal harmony were conversing with itself, as it may have happened in God's bosom shortly before He created the world.

Johann Wolfgang von Goethe, on hearing Bach's organ works, quoted in Geiringer, *The Bach Family* (1954)

2 The immortal god of harmony.

Ludwig van Beethoven. Letter to Christoph Breitkopf, 1801

3 Not Brook [*Bach* is German for 'brook'] but Sea should be his name.

Ludwig van Beethoven, quoted in Neuman, *Bach* (1961)

4 In the execution of his own pieces he generally took the time very brisk, but contrived, besides this briskness, to introduce so much variety in his performance that under his hand every piece was, as it were, like a discourse.

Johann Nikolaus Forkel, *Über Johann Sebastian Bachs Leben, Kunst und Kunstwerke* (1802)

5 Johann Sebastian Bach has done everything completely, he was a man through and through.

Franz Schubert, Diary, 1832

6 Bach is a colossus of Rhodes, beneath whom all musicians pass and will continue to pass. Mozart is the most beautiful, Rossini the most brilliant, but Bach is the most comprehensive: he has said all there is to say.

Charles Gounod, in *Le Figaro*, 1891

7 Bach belongs not to the past, but to the future — perhaps the near future.

George Bernard Shaw, quoted in Graf, *Composer and Critic* (1947)

8 A benevolent god, to whom musicians should offer a prayer before setting to work so that they may be preserved from mediocrity.

Claude Debussy, quoted in Lockspeiser, *Debussy* (1963)

9 With my prying nose I dipped into all composers, and found that the houses they erected were stable in the exact proportion that Bach was used in the foundation.

James Huneker, *Old Fogy* (1913)

10 Bach almost persuades me to be a Christian.

Roger Fry, quoted in Woolf, *Roger Fry* (1940)

11 Too much counterpoint — and what is worse, Protestant counterpoint.

Sir Thomas Beecham, quoted in Atkins and Newman, *Beecham Stories* (1978)

12 The closer the performing conditions for Sebastian Bach's concerted music are approximated to those of early eighteenth century provincial Germany, the more that music sounds like twentieth-century American swing.

Virgil Thomson, *The Art of Judging Music* (1948)

13 Unaccompanied Bach is for me one of the severest hardships of the calling of the musical critic. It is probably good, even jolly to play, but to have to listen to it is worse than breaking stones.

Neville Cardus, *The Delights of Music* (1966)

14 When one of them [Nadia Boulanger's students] had the temerity to point out that what J.S. Bach did all the time in his music was what the student was being criticised for, she retorted: 'He can, but you cannot.'

Alan Kendall, *The Tender Tyrant: Nadia Boulanger* (1976)

THE BAGPIPES

15 *Falstaff:* ... 'Sblood, I am as melancholy as a gib cat or a lugged bear.
Prince Henry: Or an old lion or a lover's lute.
Falstaff: Yea, or the drone of a Lincolnshire bagpipe.

William Shakespeare, *Henry IV, Part One*, I.ii

16 ... others, when the bagpipe sings i' the nose, Cannot contain their urine.
(Shylock)

William Shakespeare, *The Merchant of Venice*, IV.i

17 Twelve Highlanders and a bagpipe make a rebellion.

Proverb, cited by Sir Walter Scott, quoted in Collinson, *The Bagpipe* (1975)

18 Plant, what are you then? Your leafs
Mind me o' the pipes lood drone
— And a' your purple tops
Are the pirly-wirly notes
That gang staggerin' owre them as they groan.

Hugh MacDiarmid, *A Drunk Man Looks at the Thistle* (1926)

19 The bagpipes — they are screaming and they are sorrowful.
There is a wail in their merriment, and cruelty in their triumph.
They rise and fall like a weight swung in the air at the end of a string.

Hugh MacDiarmid, 'Bagpipe Music' (1943)

1   ... I got to try the bagpipes. It was like trying to blow an octopus.

James Galway, *An Autobiography* (1978)

BALAKIREV

2   It has always been a terrible thing for me that if you compose something there is no means of hearing it other than at a concert. This is like relating the most precious secrets of one's soul to police officials.

Mily Balakirev, Letter to Stassov, 1863

3   In time he will be a second Glinka.

Mikhail Glinka, quoted in Garden, *Balakirev* (1967)

4   Balakirev's personality is the strongest in the whole group ... His talent is amazing, but various fatal drawbacks have helped to extinguish it ... In spite of his wonderful gifts, he has done a lot of harm ... He is the inventor of all the theories of this extraordinary circle, in which are to be found so many undeveloped, incorrectly developed, or prematurely decayed talents.

Pyotr Ilyich Tchaikovsky, Letter to Nadezhda von Meck, 1877

THE BANJO

5   The banjo's categorical gut.

Wallace Stevens, 'The Comedian as the Letter C' (1924)

BARBER

6   I have always believed that I need a circumference of silence. As to what happens when I compose, I really haven't the faintest idea.

Samuel Barber, quoted in Ewen, *American Composers* (1982)

7   Most composers bore me because most composers are boring.

Samuel Barber, quoted in Ewen, *American Composers* (1982)

BAROQUE MUSIC

8   Some say, compared with Bononcini,
That Mynheer Handel's but a ninny;
Others aver that he to Handel
Is scarcely fit to hold a candle;
Strange! that such dispute should be
'Twixt Tweedeldum and Tweedeldee!

John Byrom, Epigram

9   There exists a common fallacy that all music of the first half of the eighteenth century not written by Bach was written by Handel.

Percy M. Young, *Handel* (1947)

10   An ersatz form of the *Brandenburg* Concertos.

Pierre Boulez, in 1969, quoted in Jacobson, *Reverberations* (1975)

11   Muzak for the intelligensia.

Anon., *c.* 1970

BARTÓK

12   For my own part, all my life, in every sphere, always and in every way, I shall have one objective: the good of Hungary and the Hungarian nation.

Béla Bartók, Letter to his family, 1903

13   I prophesy, I have a foreknowledge, that this spiritual loneliness is to be my destiny.

Béla Bartók, Letter to his mother, 1905

14   If I ever crossed myself, it would signify 'In the name of Nature, Art and Science'.

Béla Bartók, Letter to Stefi Geyer, 1907

15   Mr Nielsen, do you think my music is modern enough?

Béla Bartók, remark to Carl Nielsen in 1920, quoted in Simpson, *Carl Nielsen* (1952)

16   The extremes of variation, which is so characteristic of our folk music, is at the same time the expression of my own nature.

Béla Bartók, in 1927, quoted in Ujfalussy, *Béla Bartók* (1971)

17   My own idea ... of which I have been fully conscious since I found myself as a composer — is the brotherhood of peoples, brotherhood despite all wars and conflicts. I try — to the best of my ability — to serve this idea in my music.

Béla Bartók, Letter to Octavian Beu, 1931

18   The composer does not use genuine peasant melodies, but devises instead something imitating a peasant melody.

Béla Bartók, quoted in Ujfalussy, *Béla Bartók* (1971)

19   [Of the String Quartet No. 1] The return to life of a man who has reached the shores of nothingness.

Zoltán Kodály, in *La Revue musicale*, 1921

20   The piano becomes a machine, the orchestra a machine workshop, and all this in the service of brutal, crudely materialistic noise, and all signifying a kind of Hungarian-Russian-Bolshevik machine art.

Julius Korngold, reviewing a performance of Bartók's Piano Concerto No. 1, in *Die Neue Freie Presse*, 1927

21   Bartók's name ... stands for the principle of and the demand for regeneration stemming from the people, both in art and in politics.

Zoltán Kodály, Address (1956)

1 He not only never wears his heart on his sleeve;
   he seems to have deposited it in some bank
   vault.

   Colin Wilson, *Brandy of the Damned* (1964)

THE BASSOON

2 The Wedding-Guest here beat his breast,
   For he heard the loud bassoon.

   Samuel Taylor Coleridge, 'The Rime of the Ancient
   Mariner' (1798)

3   The wind,
   Tempestuous clarion, with heavy cry,
   Came bluntly thundering, more terrible
   Than the revenge of music on bassoons.

   Wallace Stevens, 'The Comedian as the Letter C'
   (1924)

4 It is a bass instrument without proper bass
   strength, oddly weak in sound, bleating,
   burlesque.

   Thomas Mann, *Doctor Faustus* (1947); trans. Lowe-
   Porter

THE BEATLES

5 We are more popular than Jesus now.

   John Lennon, interview in *The Evening Standard*, 1966

6 People think The Beatles know what's going on.
   We don't. We're just doing it.

   John Lennon, quoted in Doney, *Lennon and McCartney*
   (1981)

7 The dream is over. It's just the same only I'm
   thirty and a lot of people have got long hair,
   that's all.

   John Lennon, in 1970, quoted in Wenner, *Lennon
   Remembers* (1972)

8 Nothing happened in the Sixties except that we
   all dressed up.

   John Lennon, quoted in Green, *The Book of Rock Quotes*
   (1982)

9 I think the main point of the situation is that
   those pieces of plastic we did are still some of
   the finest pieces of plastic around.

   Ringo Starr, quoted in Green, *The Book of Rock Quotes*
   (1982)

10 I *still* don't know what *Sergeant Pepper* was
   about. We always thought of ourselves as just
   happy little song writers ... Unfortunately it
   gets more important than that after you've been
   to America, and got knighted.

   Paul McCartney, quoted in Palmer, *All You Need Is
   Love* (1976)

11 [On his first visit to the Cavern to hear The
   Beatles] Dark, damp and smelly. I regretted my
   decision immediately, the noise was deafening.

   Brian Epstein, Diary, 1961

12 The outstanding English composers of 1963.

   William Mann, in *The Times*, 1963

13 [Of The Beatles' music] The voice of 80,000
   crumbling houses and 30,000 people on the
   dole.

   The Daily Worker, *c.* 1964

14 The Beatles are now my secret weapon.

   Lord Home, then Sir Alec Douglas-Home, PM, in 1964,
   quoted in Green, *the Book of Rock Quotes* (1982)

15 The Beatles cult can be the very shot in the arm
   that the Church needs today.

   Rev. Ronald Gibbons, quoted in Palmer, *All You Need
   Is Love* (1976)

16 The Beatles? They're a passing phase,
   symptoms of the uncertainty of the times and
   the confusion about us.

   Billy Graham, quoted in Palmer, *All You Need Is Love*
   (1976)

17 [On seeing The Beatles at Abbey Road Studios]
   Is that the Fuzzy Wuzzies? because we'd better
   close the door — in case they *charge*.

   Sir John Barbirolli, quoted in Kennedy, *Barbirolli,
   Conductor Laureate* (1971)

18 The Beatles are turning awfully funny, aren't
   they?

   Elizabeth II, attr. remark to Sir Joseph Lockwood,
   chairman of EMI, *c.* 1967, quoted in Doney, *Lennon and
   McCartney* (1981)

19 A Beatles record is shorter and cleverer than a
   Henze opera.

   Pierre Boulez, attr.

BEETHOVEN

20 *Power* is the moral principle of those who excel
   others, and it is also mine.

   Ludwig van Beethoven, Letter to Freiherr Zmeskall
   von Domanowecz, 1798

21 Music is a higher revelation than all wisdom
   and philosophy, it is the wine of a new
   procreation, and I am Bacchus who presses out
   this glorious wine for men and makes them
   drunk with the spirit.

   Ludwig van Beethoven, quoted in Scott, *Beethoven*
   (1934)

22 [On hearing the Funeral March from Päer's
   Achilles] I must compose that!

   Ludwig van Beethoven, quoted in Walker, *Anatomy of
   Musical Criticism* (1966)

23 [Of J.S. Bach] My heart ... beats sincerely for
   the sublime and magnificent art of that first
   father of harmony.

   Ludwig van Beethoven, Letter to Hofmeister, 1801

24 [Of some of his friends] Instruments on which I
   play when I please.

   Ludwig van Beethoven, Letter to Karl Amenda, 1801

1   I will seize Fate by the throat; it shall certainly
    not bend and crush me completely.
    Ludwig van Beethoven, Letter to F.G. Wegeler, 1801

2   I must confess that I live a miserable life . . . I
    live entirely in my music.
    Ludwig van Beethoven, Letter to F.G. Wegeler, 1801

3   I was on the point of putting an end to my life
    — The only thing that held me back was *my art*.
    For indeed it seemed to me impossible to leave
    this world before I had produced all the works
    that I felt the urge to compose; and thus I have
    dragged on this miserable existence.
    Ludwig van Beethoven, 'Heiligenstadt Testament',
    1802

4   Oh Providence — do but grant me one day *of
    pure joy* — For so long now the inner echo of
    real joy has been unknown to me — Oh when
    — oh when, Almighty God — shall I be able to
    hear and feel this echo again in the temple of
    Nature and in contact with humanity — Never?
    — No! — Oh, that would be too hard.
    Ludwig van Beethoven, Postscript to the 'Heiligenstadt
    Testament', 1802

5   [When asked to explain the meaning of the
    Sonata in D Minor, Op. 31 no. 2, and the
    Appassionata Sonata] Read Shakespeare's
    Tempest.
    Ludwig van Beethoven, quoted in Scott, *Beethoven*
    (1934)

6   I could not compose operas like *Don Giovanni*
    and *Figaro*. I hold them both in aversion. I could
    not have chosen such subjects; they are too
    frivolous for me.
    Ludwig van Beethoven, quoted in *Beethoven:
    Impressions of Contemporaries* (1927)

7   Let your deafness no longer be a secret — even
    in art.
    Ludwig van Beethoven, written on a page of sketches
    for the Rasumovsky Quartets, *c.* 1805

8   When I composed that, I was conscious of
    being inspired by God Almighty. Do you think I
    can consider your puny little fiddle when He
    speaks to me?
    Ludwig van Beethoven, remark to the violinist
    Schuppanzigh, who had complained of the difficulty
    of playing a certain passage, quoted in Hopkins, *Music
    all around me* (1967)

9   Prince, what you are, you are by the accident of
    birth; what I am, I am of myself. There are and
    there will be thousands of princes. There is only
    one Beethoven.
    Ludwig van Beethoven, Letter to Prince Lichnowsky,
    1806

10 [On hearing his own Variations in C Minor,
    WoO 80] That nonsense by me? O Beethoven,
    what an ass you were!
    Ludwig van Beethoven, quoted in Scott, *Beethoven*
    (1934)

11 You may be a man no longer, not for yourself,
    only for others, for you there is no longer
    happiness except in yourself, in your art — O
    God, give me strength to conquer myself,
    nothing must chain me to life.
    Ludwig van Beethoven, Journal, 1812

12 When writing for the public, one undoubtedly
    writes most beautifully — and also rapidly.
    Ludwig van Beethoven, Journal, 1813

13 I am not in the habit of altering my
    compositions once they are finished. I have
    never done this, for I hold firmly that the
    slightest change alters the character of the
    composition.
    Ludwig van Beethoven, Letter, 1813

14 [Of *Fidelio*] My crown of martyrdom.
    Ludwig van Beethoven, quoted in Scott, *Beethoven*
    (1934)

15 I carry my thoughts about me for a long time,
    before I write them down. Meanwhile my
    memory is so tenacious that I am sure never to
    forget, not even in years, a theme that has once
    occurred to me. I change many things, discard
    and try again until I am satisfied. Then,
    however, there begins in my head the
    development in every direction and, insomuch
    as I know exactly what I want, the fundamental
    idea never deserts me — it arises before me,
    grows — I see and hear the picture in all its
    extent and dimensions stand before my mind
    like a cast, and there remains for me nothing
    but the labour of writing it down, which is
    quickly accomplished when I have the time, for
    I sometimes take up other work, but never to
    the confusion of one with the other.
    Ludwig van Beethoven, Letter to Louis Schlösser,
    1823

16 I still hope to create a few great works and then
    like an old child to finish my earthly course
    somewhere among kind people.
    Ludwig van Beethoven, Letter to F.G. Wegeler, 1826

17 *Muss es sein? Es muss sein! Es muss sein!*
    Must it be? It must be! It must be!
    Ludwig van Beethoven, comment written below the
    opening phrases of the finale of his String Quartet in F
    Major, Op 135 (his last work)

18 Strange, I feel as if up to now I had written no
    more than a few notes.
    Ludwig van Beethoven, words on his deathbed

19 *Plaudite, amici, comedia finita est.* Applaud, my
    friends, the comedy is over.
    Ludwig van Beethoven, words on his deathbed,
    quoting the dying Augustus

1   I shall hear in heaven.
    Ludwig van Beethoven, attr. last words

2   They are burying the general of the musicians.
    Unknown old woman at Beethoven's funeral, quoted
    in Scott, *Beethoven* (1934)

3   [Of the sixteen-year-old Beethoven] Keep your
    eyes on him; some day he will give the world
    something to talk about.
    Wolfgang Amadeus Mozart, in 1787, quoted in Scott,
    Beethoven (1934)

4   The Great Mogul.
    Joseph Haydn, quoted in Headington, *The Bodley Head
    History of Western Music* (1974)

5   You make upon me the impression of a man
    who has several heads, several hearts and
    several souls.
    Joseph Haydn, remark to Beethoven, quoted in Scott,
    Beethoven (1934)

6   He is no man; he's a devil. He will play me and
    all of us to death. And how he improvises!
    Joseph Gelinek, in *c.* 1795, quoted in Scott, *Beethoven*
    (1934)

7   A more self-contained, energetic, sincere artist I
    never saw.
    Johann Wolfgang von Goethe, quoted in Scott,
    Beethoven (1934)

8   His talent amazed me; unfortunately he is an
    utterly untamed personality, not altogether in
    the wrong in holding the world to be
    detestable, but who does not make it any the
    more enjoyable either for himself or others by
    his attitude.
    Johann Wolfgang von Goethe, quoted in Scott,
    Beethoven (1934)

9   [After the first performance of Beethoven's
    Eroica Symphony] The symphony would be all
    the better — it lasts a whole hour — if
    Beethoven could reconcile himself to making
    some cuts in it and to bringing to the score
    more light, clarity, and unity.
    Allgemeine musikalische Zeitung, 1805

10 The haughty beauty, Beethoven
    Muzio Clementi, Letter to F.W. Collard, 1807

11 [On hearing Beethoven's Mass in C Major] But
    my dear Beethoven, what is this you have done
    now?
    Prince Esterházy, quoted in Scott, *Beethoven* (1934)

12 [Of Beethoven's Symphony No. 5] How big it is
    — quite wild! Enough to bring the house about
    one's ears!
    Johann Wolfgang von Goethe, attr. by Mendelssohn

13 [Of Beethoven's Symphony No. 5] Ouf! Let me
    get out; I must have air. It's incredible!
    Marvellous! It has so upset and bewildered me
    that when I wanted to put on my hat, *I couldn't*

find my head. . . . One ought not to write music
like that.
Jean François Le Sueur, quoted in Berlioz, *Memoirs*
(1865)

14 The extravagances of Beethoven's genius have
    reached the *ne plus ultra* in the Seventh
    Symphony, and he is quite ripe for the
    madhouse.
    Carl Maria von Weber, quoted in Hughes and Van
    Thal, *The Music Lover's Companion* (1971)

15 Beethoven's genius was once attributed by
    Schubert to what he termed his 'superb
    coolness under the fire of creative fantasy'.
    Aaron Copland, quoted in Ewen, *American Composers*
    (1982)

16 [Of Beethoven's *Pastoral* Symphony] This is no
    question of gaily dressed shepherds . . . it is a
    matter of nature in her simple truth.
    Hector Berlioz, Essay

17 Nature would burst should she attempt to
    produce nothing save Beethovens.
    Robert Schumann, quoted in Walker (ed.), *Robert
    Schumann: the Man and his Music* (1972)

18 To us musicians the work of Beethoven
    parallels the pillars of smoke and fire which led
    the Israelites through the desert.
    Franz Liszt, Letter to Wilhelm von Lenz, 1852

19 *Une fleur entre deux abîmes*. A flower between
    two abysses.
    Franz Liszt, of the middle movement of Beethoven's
    Moonlight Sonata, quoted in Tovey, *Beethoven* (1944)

20 [Of the late quartets of Beethoven] The polluted
    source from which have sprung the evil
    musicians of modern Germany, the Liszts,
    Wagners, Schumanns, not to mention
    Mendelssohn in certain equivocal details of his
    style.
    Pierre Scudo, in 1862, quoted in Dean, *Bizet* (1975)

21 [Of Beethoven's Symphony No. 9] The fourth
    movement is, in my opinion, so monstrous and
    tasteless and, in its grasp of Schiller's *Ode*, so
    trivial that I cannot understand how a genius
    like Beethoven could have written it.
    Louis Spohr, *Autobiography* (1865)

22 The first of Beethoven's compositions *are*
    music; in his last compositions Beethoven *makes*
    music.
    Eduard Hanslick, quoted in Graf, *Composer and Critic*
    (1947)

23 Beethoven's music is music about music.
    Friedrich Nietzsche, *Human All-too-Human* (1878)

24 Beethoven always sounds to me like the
    upsetting of bags of nails, with here and there
    an also dropped hammer.
    John Ruskin, Letter, 1881

1   One is prompted to believe not that he had the
    idea first and then expressed it, but that it often
    came in the process of finding the expression.

    Sir George Grove, *Beethoven and his Nine Symphonies*
    (1906)

2   It will be generally admitted that Beethoven's
    Fifth Symphony is the most sublime noise that
    has ever penetrated into the ear of man. . . . You
    are bound to admit that such a noise is cheap at
    two shillings. It is cheap, even if you hear it in
    the Queen's Hall, dreariest music-room in
    London, though not as dreary as the Free Trade
    Hall, Manchester.

    E.M. Forster, *Howard's End* (1910)

3   Here [in Beethoven's sketches for the *Eroica
    Symphony*], more than anywhere else, do we
    get the curious feeling that in his greatest
    works Beethoven was 'possessed' — the mere
    human instrument through which a vast
    musical design realised itself in all its
    marvellous logic . . . We have the conviction
    that his mind did not proceed from the
    particular to the whole, but began, in some
    curious way, with the whole and then worked
    back to the particular . . . The long and painful
    search for the themes was simply an effort, not
    to find workable atoms out of which he could
    construct a musical edifice according to the
    conventions of symphonic form, but to reduce
    an already existing nebula, in which the edifice
    was implicit, to the atom, and then, by the
    orderly arrangement of these atoms, to make
    the implicit explicit.

    Ernest Newman, *The Unconscious Beethoven* (1927)

4   [Of the slow movement of the Rasumovsky
    Quartet in C Major] There is here a remote and
    frozen anguish, wailing over some implacable
    destiny. This is hardly human suffering; it is
    more like a memory from some ancient and
    starless night of the soul.

    J.W.N. Sullivan, *Beethoven: his Spiritual Development*
    (1927)

5   It is a peculiarity of Beethoven that he can use
    the words 'best' and 'noblest' without making
    an intelligent man laugh up his sleeve . . . The
    very words 'good', 'noble', 'spiritual', 'sublime',
    have all become in our time synonymous with
    humbug. In Beethoven's music they take on a
    new and tremendous significance and not all
    the corrosive acid of the most powerful intellect
    and the profoundest scepticism can burn
    through them into any leaden substratum. They
    are gold throughout.

    W.J. Turner, *Beethoven: The Search for Reality* (1927)

6   Beethoven's last quartets are not the
    justification of modern music, but modern
    music has reached the point at which it justifies
    the quartets.

    Marion M. Scott, *Beethoven* (1934)

7   [Of Beethoven] Music was getting along so
    nicely before 'le grand Sourd'.

    Maurice Ravel quoted in *Revue internationale de
    musique*, 1938

8   Even Beethoven thumped the tub; the Ninth
    Symphony was composed by a kind of Mr
    Gladstone of music.

    Sir Thomas Beecham, quoted in Atkins and Newman,
    Beecham Stories (1978)

9   Or like a Beethovian semitonal modulation to a
            wildly remote key,
    As in the Allegretto where what happens with
            a sudden jump of seven sharps,
    And feels like the sunrise gilding the peak of
            the Dent Blanche
    While the Arolla valley is still in cloud.

    Hugh MacDiarmid, *The Kind of Poetry I Want* (1943)

10 [Of Beethoven's Sonata in C Minor, Op 111] An
    ego painfully isolated in the absolute, isolated
    too from sense by the loss of his hearing; lonely
    prince of a realm of spirits, from whom now
    only a chilling breath issued to terrify his most
    willing contemporaries, standing as they did
    aghast at these communications of which only
    at moments, only by exception, they could
    understand anything at all.
    (Kretschmar)

    Thomas Mann, *Doctor Faustus* (1947); trans. Lowe-
    Porter

11 Untouched, untransformed by the subjective,
    convention often appeared in the late works, in
    a baldness, one might say exhaustiveness, an
    abandonment of self, with an effect more
    majestic and awful than any reckless plunge
    into the personal.
    (Kretschmar)

    Thomas Mann, *Doctor Faustus* (1947); trans. Lowe-
    Porter

12 That the affirmative gestures of the reprise in
    some of Beethoven's greatest symphonies
    assume the force of crushing repression, of an
    authoritarian 'That's how it is' . . . this is the
    tribute Beethoven was forced to pay to the
    ideological character whose spell extends even
    to the most sublime music ever to mean
    freedom by continued un-freedom.

    T.W. Adorno, *Introduction to the Sociology of Music*
    (1959)

13 He reminds me of a man driving the car with
    the handbrake on, but stubbornly refusing to
    stop, even though there is a strong smell of
    burning rubber.

    Colin Wilson, *Brandy of the Damned* (1964)

14 I'm not so much for Beethoven *qua* Beethoven
    . . . but as he represents the German dialectic,
    the incorporation of more and more notes into
    the scale, culminating in dodecaphonic
    democracy, where all the notes get an equal

hearing. Beethoven was one of the architects of musical freedom — he submitted to the demands of history, despite his deafness. (Gustav)

Thomas Pynchon, *Gravity's Rainbow* (1973)

BELLS

1 We have heard the chimes at midnight, Master Shallow.
(Falstaff)

William Shakespeare, *Henry IV, Part 1*, III.ii

2 [Of English change-ringing] They are vastly fond of great noises that fill the air, such as the firing of cannon, drums, and the ringing of bells, so that in London it is common for a number of them when drunk to go up into some belfry and ring the bells for hours together.

Paul Hentzner, in 1598, quoted in Rye, *England as Seen by Foreigners* (1865)

3 [Of the passing bell] This moody music of impartial death.

Francis Quarles, *Mors Tua*, 'Pentelogia'

4 Bells, the poor man's only music.

Samuel Taylor Coleridge, 'Frost at Midnight'

5 Bells, the music nighest bordering upon heaven.

Charles Lamb, *Essays of Elia* (1820-23)

6 Keeping time, time, time,
    In a sort of Runic rhyme,
To the tintinnabulation that so musically wells
    From the bells, bells, bells, bells.

Edgar Allan Poe, 'The Bells'

7 The mellow lin-lan-lone of evening bells.

Alfred, Lord Tennyson, 'Far-Far-Away'

8 Gay bells or sad, they bring you memories
Of half-forgotten innocent old places.

W.B. Yeats, 'The Dedication to a Book of Stories selected from the Irish Novelists' (1893)

9 He was a rationalist, but he had to confess that he liked the ringing of church bells.

Anton Chekhov, *Note Book* (trans. 1921)

BERG

10 I declare firmly and decisively the great importance which sensuality has for everything spiritual. Only through an understanding of sensuality, only through a profound insight into the 'depths of mankind' (or should it rather be 'heights of mankind'?) does one arrive at the true idea of the human psyche.

Alban Berg, Letter to Frida Semler Seabury

11 I owe it to you and *you alone. You composed* it and I only write it down.

Alban Berg, Letter to his wife Helene, 1922, referring to the D minor interlude in the last act of *Wozzeck*

12 When I compose I always feel I am like Beethoven; only afterwards do I become aware that at best I am only Bizet.

Alban Berg, quoted in Adorno, *Alban Berg* (1968)

13 Now the difficulty [in writing *Lulu*] is ... to work the music, which is conditioned by *musical laws*, into the Wedekind text which is determined by *dialectical laws*, make the two coincide and span over it the powerful arc of the action.

Alban Berg, Letter to Webern, 1931

14 The best music always results from ecstasies of logic.

Alban Berg, quoted in *The New York Times Magazine*, 1975

15 [Of Berg's Twelve Piano Variations] No theme but twelve variations on it.

Unnamed critic, in 1908, quoted in Reich, *The Life and Work of Alban Berg* (1963)

16 Berg's music is diluted with Schoenberg, who in spite of his name is no more beautiful than his pupil.

Olin Downes, quoted in Hughes and Van Thal, *The Music Lover's Companion* (1971)

17 Lulu's last victim.

Helene Berg, referring to her husband, Letter to Heinsheiner, 1937

18 [His love] affairs formed a part of his creative apparatus.

T.W. Adorno, quoted in Carner, *Alban Berg* (1983)

19 The Puccini of twelve-note music.

Unnamed critic, quoted in Carner, *Alban Berg* (1983)

BERLIN

20 He doesn't attempt to stuff the public's ears with pseudo-original ultra-modernism, but he honestly absorbs the vibrations emanating from the people, manners and life of his time, and in turn, gives these impressions back to the world — simplified — clarified — glorified.

Jerome Kern, Letter to Alexander Woolcott

21 Irving just loves hits. He has no sophistication about it — he just loves hits.

Oscar Hammerstein II, quoted in Freedland, *Irving Berlin* (1974)

BERLIOZ

22 My life is to me a deeply interesting romance.

Hector Berlioz, Letter to Humbert Ferrand, 1833

1   People have asked why the author made his hero go into Hungary. He did so because he wishes to compose a piece of instrumental music whose theme is Hungarian.
    Hector Berlioz, Preface to *The Damnation of Faust* (1846)

2   I am for the music which you yourself call *free*. Yes, free and wild and sovereign; I want it to conquer everything, to assimilate everything to itself.
    Hector Berlioz, Letter, 1856

3   If I were threatened with the destruction of all my works but one, I would beg mercy for the *Messe des morts*.
    Hector Berlioz, Letter to Humbert Ferrand, 1867

4   [On hearing music he admired] My arteries quiver violently; tears ... indicate only a condition which may be intensified. If the further stage is reached, muscles contract spasmodically; limbs tremble; feet and hands grow quite numb ... I cannot see perfectly; I am giddy and half-fainting.
    Hector Berlioz, Essay

5   [On hearing music he disliked] I blush as though ashamed ... observing me, one might imagine that I had received an unpardonable affront ... my entire organism strives to reject the impressions received.
    Hector Berlioz, Essay

6   There is one god — Bach — and Mendelssohn is his prophet.
    Hector Berlioz, quoted in Elliot, *Berlioz* (1967)

7   [Of his role as a critic] I want to *work*, and I have to *toil* in order to live.
    Hector Berlioz, quoted in Elliot, *Berlioz* (1967)

8   Life is nothing; death is no better. Worlds die as we die. All is emptiness.
    Hector Berlioz, quoted in Elliot, *Berlioz* (1967)

9   He is an immense nightingale, a lark as great as an eagle ... the music causes me to dream of fabulous empires filled with fabulous sins.
    Heinrich Heine, quoted in Elliot, *Berlioz* (1967)

10 Berlioz composes by splashing his pen over the manuscript and leaving the issue to chance.
    Frederick Chopin, quoted in Elliot, *Berlioz* (1967)

11 [Of Berlioz's *Symphonie fantastique*] What a good thing it isn't music.
    Gioacchino Rossini, attr.

12 Berlioz is a regular freak, without a vestige of talent.
    Felix Mendelssohn, Letter, 1831

13 Miss Smithson was married last week, in Paris, to Derlioz [*sic*], the musical composer. We trust this marriage will insure the happiness of an amiable young woman, as well as secure us against her reappearance on the English boards.
    The Court Journal, 1833

14 [Of Berlioz's overture *Les Francs Juges*] His orchestration is such ... an incongruous mess, that one ought to wash one's hands after handling one of his scores.
    Felix Mendelssohn, Letter, 1834

15 [Referring to Berlioz] Everybody composes as well as he can.
    Felix Mendelssohn, quoted in Wagner, 'On Poetry and Composition'; to which Wagner added, in reference to Brahms: 'The evil only starts when one attempts to compose better than one can.'

16 [Of Berlioz's *Symphonie fantastique*] I believe that Berlioz, when a young student of medicine, never dissected the head of a handsome murderer with greater unwillingness than I feel in analysing his first movement.
    Robert Schumann, in *Neue Zeitschrift*, 1835

17 Berlioz does not try to be pleasing and elegant; what he hates, he grasps fiercely by the hair; what he loves, he almost crushes in his fervour.
    Robert Schumann, quoted in Walker (ed.), *Robert Schumann: the Man and his Music* (1972)

18 Cold, unsympathetic and querulous.
    Clara Schumann, quoted in Elliot, *Berlioz* (1967)

19 The savage, who whips himself into a fury by the rubbing together of two stones, makes music of the kind written by M. Berlioz.
    Pietro Scudo, in *Revue des deux mondes*, c. 1840

20 Berlioz ... had genius without talent.
    Georges Bizet, quoted in Dean, *Bizet* (1975)

21 The thinker, Beethoven, and the super-thinker, Berlioz.
    Modest Mussorgsky, quoted in Elliot, *Berlioz* (1967)

22 [Of Berlioz's music] Often rough on one's ears.
    Johannes Brahms, quoted in Elliot, *Berlioz* (1967)

23 Devilishly smart.
    Richard Wagner, quoted in Elliot, *Berlioz* (1967)

24 [Berlioz has] no love in him — which is the solution of the disheartening enigma of his nature.
    Richard Wagner, quoted in Elliot, *Berlioz* (1967)

25 *He*: A wonderful man is Berlioz.
    She: Oh, charming! So original! I hope he'll write many more symphonies.
    He (with a vague idea that Berlioz is no more): Yes, yes. He was a Russian, wasn't he?
    Punch, c. 1880

26 Up to a comparatively recent time it was the fashion to speak of Berlioz as a charlatan, a madman, or both.
    Birmingham Daily Post, 1882

1   A monster. He is not a musician at all. He
    creates the illusion of music by means
    borrowed from literature and painting. Besides,
    there is, as far as I can see, little that is French
    in him.
    Claude Debussy, quoted in Lockspeiser, *Debussy*
    (1963)

2   The early ideas of Berlioz seem to bear the same
    relation to those of ordinary men as a gas does
    to a solid or liquid; the moment they are
    liberated they try to diffuse themselves through
    as much space as they can.
    Ernest Newman, *Berlioz, Romantic and Classic*,
    Heyworth (ed.) (1972)

3   The worst musician among the musical
    geniuses.
    Maurice Ravel, quoted in Headington, *The Bodley Head
    History of Western Music* (1974)

4   His love of dramatic realism embarrassed the
    quality of his musical ideas.
    Neville Cardus, in *The Manchester Guardian*, 1936

5   [Of the finale of the *Symphonie fantastique*] It is
    pictorialism run riot and, as music, ugly and
    unpleasant.
    J.H. Elliot, *Berlioz* (1967)

6   *Lélio, ou le Retour à la vie* must be the craziest
    work ever sketched out by a composer not
    actually insane.
    J.H. Elliot, *Berlioz* (1967)

BERNSTEIN

7   It would be nice to hear someone accidentally
    whistle something of mine, somewhere, just
    once.
    Leonard Bernstein, *The Joy of Music* (1960)

8   I have two answers to everything and one
    answer to nothing.
    Leonard Bernstein, *The Infinite Variety of Music* (1966)

9   Any composer's writing is the sum of himself,
    of all his roots and influences. I have deep
    roots, each different from one another ... I can
    only hope it adds up to something you could
    call universal.
    Leonard Bernstein, quoted in Ewen, *American
    Composers* (1982)

10 Mr Bernstein is a born entertainer of a superior
    sort.
    Donal Henehan, in *The New York Times*, 1980

BIRDSONG

11 By them shall the fowls of the air have their
    habitation, which sing among the branches.
    Psalms 104:12

12 And smale foweles maken melodye.
    Geoffrey Chaucer, *The Canterbury Tales*, General
    Prologue

13 What bird so sings, yet does so wail?
    O 'tis the ravish'd nightingale.
    Jug, jug, jug, jug, tereu, she cries,
    And still her woes at midnight rise.
    John Lyly, *Campaspe*, V.i (1584)

14 By shallow rivers, to whose falls
    Melodious birds sing madrigals.
    Christopher Marlowe, 'The Passionate Shepherd to
    His Love'

15 Spring, the sweet spring, is the year's pleasant
                king; ...
    Cold doth not sting, the pretty birds do sing;
    Cuckoo, jug-jug, pu-we, to̅-witta-woo.
    Thomas Nashe, *Summer's last Will and Testament*,
    'Spring' (1592)

16 Crave the tuneful nightingale to help you with
                her lay,
    The ousel and the throstlecock, chief music of
                our May.
    Michael Drayton, *The Shepherd's Garland* (1593)

17 The merry cuckoo, messenger of Spring,
    His trumpet shrill hath thrice already sounded.
    Edmund Spenser, *Amoretti* (1595)

18 It is the lark that sings so out of tune,
    Straining harsh discords and unpleasing
                sharps.
    (Juliet)
    William Shakespeare, *Romeo and Juliet*, III.v

19   He makes a swanlike end,
    Fading in music.
    (Portia)
    William Shakespeare, *The Merchant of Venice*, III.ii

20 The crow doth sing as sweetly as the lark
    When neither is attended, and I think
    The nightingale, if she should sing by day
    When every goose is cackling, would be
                thought
    No better a musician than the wren.
    (Portia)
    William Shakespeare, *The Merchant of Venice*, V.i

21 As it fell upon a day
    In the merry month of May ...
    Everything did banish moan,
    Save the nightingale alone.
    She, poor bird, as all forlorn,
    Lean'd her breast up-till a thorn,
    And there sung the dolefull'st ditty
    That to hear it was great pity.
    Fie, fie, fie, now would she cry;
    Tereu, Tereu, by and by.
    Richard Barnfield, 'An Ode' (1599); also attr.
    Shakespeare

1   Our cage
We make a choir, as doth the prisoned bird,
And sing our bondage freely.
(Arviragus)
William Shakespeare, *Cymbeline*, III.iii

2   Sweet bird, that shunn'st the noise of folly,
Most musical, most melancholy!
John Milton, 'Il Penseroso' (1632)

3   The nightingale does sit so late,
And studying all the summer night,
Her matchless songs does meditate.
Andrew Marvell, 'The Mower to the Glowworms'

4   I value my garden more for being full of
blackbirds than of cherries, and very frankly
give them fruit for their songs.
Joseph Addison, in *The Spectator*, 1712

5   [The nightingale] The sober-suited songstress.
James Thomson, *The Seasons* (1728), 'Summer'

6   Books! 'tis a dull and endless strife:
Come, hear the woodland linnet,
How sweet his music! on my life,
There's more of wisdom in it.
William Wordsworth, 'The Tables Turned'

7   O cuckoo! Shall I call thee bird,
Or but a wandering voice?
William Wordsworth, 'To the Cuckoo'

8   Where the nightingale doth sing
Not a senseless, tranced thing,
But divine melodious truth.
John Keats, 'Ode'

9   Thou wast not born for death, immortal Bird!
No hungry generations tread thee down;
The voice I hear this passing night was heard
In ancient days by emperor and clown:
Perhaps the self-same song that found a path
Through the sad heart of Ruth, when, sick for
          home,
She stood in tears amid the alien corn;
The same that oft-times hath
Charm'd magic casements, opening on the
          foam
Of perilous seas, in faery lands forlorn.
John Keats, 'Ode to a Nightingale' (1819)

10   Hail to thee, blithe Spirit!
      Bird thou never wert,
That from Heaven, or near it,
      Pourest thy full heart
In profuse strains of unpremeditated art.
Percy Bysshe Shelley, 'To a Skylark' (1819)

11   And singing still dost soar, and soaring ever
          singest.
Percy Bysshe Shelley, 'To a Skylark' (1819)

12   That's the wise thrush; he sings each song
          twice over,

Lest you think he never could recapture
The first fine careless rapture!
Robert Browning, 'Home-Thoughts, from Abroad'

13   And drown'd in yonder living blue
The lark becomes a sightless song.
Alfred, Lord Tennyson, *In Memoriam A.H.H.* (1850)

14   The music soars within the little lark,
And the lark soars.
Elizabeth Barrett Browning, *Aurora Leigh* (1857)

15   Say, has some wet bird-haunted English lawn
Lent it the music of its trees at dawn?
Matthew Arnold, 'Parting'

16   You must hear the bird's song without
attempting to render it into nouns and verbs.
Ralph Waldo Emerson, *Society and Solitude*, 'Works
and Days' (1870)

17   Pussy said to the Owl, 'You elegant fowl!
      How charmingly sweet you sing!'
Edward Lear, *Nonsense Songs* (1871), 'The Owl and the
Pussy-Cat'

18   [Of birds] Do you hear them? How they sing!
They are the real masters.
Antonín Dvořák, quoted in Fidler, *Recollections of
Antonín Dvořák* (1910-11)

19   As for the perennially cited nightingale, his
musical knowledge makes his most ignorant
auditors shrug. Not only is his voice not placed,
but he has absolutely no knowledge of clefs,
tonality, modality or measure.
Erik Satie, *Memoirs of an Amnesiac* (1914)

20   She says, 'I am content when wakened birds,
Before they fly, test the reality
Of misty fields, by their sweet questionings.'
Wallace Stevens, 'Sunday Morning'

21   Deer walk upon our mountains, and the quail
Whistle about us their spontaneous cries.
Wallace Stevens, 'Sunday Morning'

22   . . . Yet there the nightingale
Filled all the desert with inviolable voice
And still she cried, and still the world pursues,
'Jug Jug' to dirty ears.
T.S. Eliot, *The Waste Land* (1922)

23   I do not know which to prefer,
The beauty of inflections
Or the beauty of innuendoes,
The blackbird whistling
Or just after.
Wallace Stevens, 'Thirteen Ways of Looking at a
Blackbird'

24   A passionately niggling nightingale.
Wallace Stevens, 'The Comedian as the Letter C'

25   Nightingales sing badly.
Jean Cocteau, attr.

1 And hear the pleasant cuckoo, loud and
        long —
The simple bird that thinks two notes a song.
W.H. Davies, 'April's Charms'

2 They sang, but had nor human tunes nor
        words,
Though all was done in common as before;

They had changed their throats and had the
        throats of birds.
W.B. Yeats, 'Cuchulain Comforted' (1939)

3 I doubt that one can find in any human music,
however inspired, melodies and rhythms that
have the sovereign freedom of bird song.
Olivier Messiaen, quoted in Headington, *The Bodley
Head History of Western Music* (1974)

4 Among the artistic hierarchy, birds are
probably the greatest musicians to inhabit our
planet.
Olivier Messiaen, quoted in Johnson, *Messiaen* (1975)

BIZET

5 I want to do nothing *chic*, I want to have *ideas*
before beginning a piece.
Georges Bizet, Letter to Gounod, 1858

6 I have become a little perfection.
Georges Bizet, quoted in Dean, *Bizet* (1975)

7 Let us have fantasy, boldness, unexpectedness,
enchantment — above all, tenderness,
morbidezza!
Georges Bizet, Letter to Edmond Galabert

8 I am not made for the symphony; I need the
theatre, I can do nothing without it.
Georges Bizet, quoted in Dean, *Bizet* (1975)

9 *Auber*: I've heard your work. It's very good.
Bizet: I accept your praise, but I do not
reciprocate it. |Auber makes a face] A private
soldier may receive the praises of a marshal of
France; he does not return them.
Quoted in Dean, *Bizet* (1975)

10 Take the Spanish airs and mine out of the
score, and there remains nothing to Bizet's
credit but the sauce that masks the fish.
Charles Gounod, at the first performance of Bizet's
Carmen, 1875, quoted in Dean, *Bizet* (1975)

11 In *Carmen* the composer has made up his mind
to show us how learned he is, with the result
that he is often dull and obscure.
Léon Escudier, in 1875, quoted in Dean, *Bizet* (1975)

12 |*Carmen*] This inferno of ridiculous and
uninteresting corruption.
Oscar Comettant, in *Le Siècle*, 1875

13 |Of *Carmen*] This music is wicked, refined,
fantastic, and yet it retains a popular appeal.
Frederick Nietzsche, quoted in Headington, *The Bodley
Head History of Western Music* (1974)

BLACK MUSIC

See also BLUES, JAZZ, RACISM, RAGTIME.

14 In the Negro melodies of America I find all that
is needed for a great and noble school of music.
Antonín Dvořák, interview in *The New York Herald*

15 Happily works the dusky figure while he and
his companions sing.
Odum and Johnson, *The Negro and His Songs* (1925)

16 |Of *Porgy and Bess*] The times are here to
debunk Gershwin's lampblack Negroisms.
Duke Ellington, in 1935, quoted in Schwartz, *Gershwin*
(1973)

17 I don't write jazz, I write Negro folk music.
Duke Ellington, quoted in Jewell, *Duke* (1977)

18 No white man ever had the blues.
Leadbelly, quoted in Berendt, *The Jazz Book* (1976)

19 If I could find a white man who had the Negro
sound and the Negro feel, I could make a
million dollars.
Sam Phillips, record producer, quoted in Hopkins,
Elvis (1974)

20 After emancipation . . . all those people who
had been slaves, they needed the music [jazz]
more than ever now; it was like they were
trying to find out in this music what they were
supposed to do with this freedom.
Sidney Bechet, *Treat it Gentle* (1960)

21 When a Negro musician or dancer swings the
blues . . . he is making an affirmative and hence
exemplary and heroic response to that which
André Malraux describes as *la condition humaine*
. . . The blues idiom becomes survival
technique, esthetic equipment for living.
Albert Murray, *The Omni-Americans* (1969)

22 I don't like the word jazz that white folks
dropped on us.
Miles Davis, quoted in *Down Beat*, 1970

23 If you get rich singing badly about society, you
can't really sing badly about it any more . . . For
black people, it was always easier to be a
failure. And in this way, their music has been
preserved.
LeRoi Jones, quoted in Palmer, *All You Need Is Love*
(1976)

24 I'd much rather have any American coloured
group singing one of our songs than us. 'Cause
they do it better.
Paul McCartney, quoted in Palmer, *All You Need Is
Love* (1976)

1 The blues originated behind the mule, but
there's no race in it; no reason why a white boy
shouldn't play blues just as good as a black
boy.

Bukka White, quoted in Palmer, *All You Need Is Love*
(1976)

2 [Of The Supremes] With lacquered wigs and
blasted smiles, they ensured ... that the
emasculation of black music would be finally
completed.

Tony Palmer, *All You need Is Love* (1976)

BLISS

3 There is only a little of the spider about me,
spinning his own web from his inner being. I
am more of a magpie type. I need what Henry
James calls a 'trouvaille' or a 'donnée'.

Arthur Bliss, *As I Remember* (1970)

4 Visits to the studios of painters act as a greater
incentive to work than any amount of talk with
my fellow musicians. In looking at the struggle
for realised form in a sculptor's or painter's
work I find something that instructs me in my
own art.

Arthur Bliss, *As I Remember* (1970)

5 He who cannot write anything beautiful falls
back on the bizarre.

Charles Villiers Stanford, remark on student MS of
Arthur Bliss, quoted in Bliss, *As I Remember* (1970)

6 I felt that a sensibility of an older world, almost
lost in this stark ignorant age, was experiencing
the present, and bringing to it something which
hardly anyone seems to have any more.

Kathleen Raine, Letter to Arthur Bliss, after hearing
his *Beatitudes*

BLOCH

7 I aspire to write Jewish music not for the sake
of self-advertisement, but because it is the only
way in which I can produce music of vitality ...
It is the Jewish soul that interests me, the
complex, glowing, agitated soul that I feel
vibrating through the Bible.

Ernest Bloch, *c.* 1912, quoted in Ewen, *American
Composers* (1982)

8 Only that art can live which is an active
manifestation of the life of the people. It must
be a necessary and essential portion of that life,
and not a luxury.

Ernest Bloch, 'Man and Music' (1917)

9 When art ... becomes an expression of a
philosophy of life, it is no longer a luxury ... It
is a storm that carries one away, unites all men
in a unit of solidarity, shakes them to the

bottom of their souls, waking them to the
greatest problems of their common destiny.

Ernest Bloch, quoted in Ewen, *American Composers*
(1982)

THE BLUES

See also BLACK MUSIC

10 The Devil's music.

Anon., traditional

11 *Blues:* an American dance stemming from the
Foxtrot, the speed of which it reduced and into
which it brought a deliberately contrived dismal
atmosphere.

Eric Blom, *Everyman's Dictionary of Music* (1947)

12 She [Bessie Smith] once said to me ... 'You're
gonna sing "Blacksnake Blues" for me real
good tonight or I'm gonna break your neck.'
She was a wonderful woman.

Victoria Spivey, quoted in Palmer, *All You Need Is Love*
(1976)

13 She [Billie Holliday] doesn't need any horns.
She sounds like one, anyway.

Miles Davis, quoted in Hentoff, *Jazz is* (1978)

14 Jazz is not music but a style. Blues is music.

Lieutenant George Lee, quoted in Palmer, *All You Need
Is Love* (1976)

15 All blues singers are great liars.

Memphis Slim, quoted in Palmer, *All You Need Is Love*
(1976)

BORODIN

16 Music is a pastime, a relaxation from more
serious occupations.

Alexander Borodin, Letter to V.A. Krylov, 1867

17 I am a composer in search of oblivion; and I'm
always slightly ashamed to admit that I
compose.

Alexander Borodin, Letter to Lydia Karmalina

18 [Borodin] never had much brains and
overstepped his mark.

Nadezhda von Meck, quoted in Lockspeiser, *Debussy*
(1963)

BOULANGER

19 [Of her own music] *Pas mauvaise, mais inutile.*
Not bad, but useless.

Nadia Boulanger, quoted in Kendall, *The Tender
Tyrant: Nadia Boulanger* (1976)

20 Legend credits every US town with two things
— a five-and-dime and a Boulanger pupil.

Virgil Thomson, quoted in Kendall, *The Tender Tyrant:
Nadia Boulanger* (1976)

BOULEZ

1 Schoenberg is dead.

Pierre Boulez, title of essay (1951)

2 Music should be a collective magic and hysteria.

Pierre Boulez, quoted in Machlis, *Introduction to Contemporary Music* (1963)

3 As a revolutionary I'm very Leninistic. I'm all for the efficiency of the revolution, by going to the important organizations to change the sense of them and to convince them by my existence.

Pierre Boulez, in 1969, quoted in Jacobson, *Reverberations* (1975)

4 [Of his compositions] Just listen with the vastness of the world in mind. You can't fail to get the message.

Pierre Boulez, quoted in Jacobson, *Reverberations* (1975)

5 For me that is the definition of a great work — a landscape painted so well that the artist disappears in it.

Pierre Boulez, quoted in Peyser, *Boulez* (1976)

6 It was like Descartes' 'Cogito, ergo sum.' I momentarily suppressed inheritance. I started from the fact that I was thinking and went on to construct a musical language from scratch.

Pierre Boulez, quoted in Peyser, *Boulez* (1976)

7 [Of Boulez' *Marteau sans maître*] Webern sounding like Debussy.

Heinrich Strobel, quoted in Myers, *Modern French Music* (1971)

8 [Of Boulez' *Pli Selon Pli*] Pretty monotonous and monotonously pretty.

Igor Stravinsky, attr. by Robert Craft, quoted in Peyser, *Boulez* (1976)

9 Boulez is a great composer. He is also a very intelligent man. He understands all the changes and they make him suffer. There are people who go unperturbed through change. Like Bach. Like Richard Strauss. But Boulez cannot. He thinks that advancing the language is all. He feels he must be in the advance guard and he doesn't like what is happening there.

Olivier Messiaen, quoted in Peyser, *Boulez* (1976)

10 Pierre is a hen that hatches slowly.

Virgil Thomson, quoted in Peyser, *Boulez* (1976)

11 Pierre has the mind of an expert. With that kind of mind you can only deal with the past. You can't be an expert in the unknown.

John Cage, quoted in Peyser, *Boulez* (1976)

BRAHMS

12 When I feel the urge to compose, I begin by appealing directly to my Maker and I first ask Him the three most important questions pertaining to our life here in this world — whence, wherefore, whither.

Johannes Brahms, quoted in Hopkins, *Music all around me* (1967)

13 My [first] symphony is long and not exactly amiable.

Johannes Brahms, Letter to Carl Reinecke

14 [Of his Symphony No. 2] Whether or not I have a pretty symphony I do not know; I will have to ask some wiser people.

Johannes Brahms, Letter to Theodor Billroth

15 The musicians play my new work [the Symphony No. 2] here with crêpe round their arms, because it sounds so mournful. It will be printed on black-edged paper.

Johannes Brahms, Letter to Elizabeth von Herzogenberg, 1878

16 [Of some of his late piano music] Even one listener is too many.

Johannes Brahms, attr.

17 My things really are written with an appalling lack of practicability!

Johannes Brahms, Letter to Joachim

18 [On being asked to play his Piano Quintet with the Joachim Quartet] Under absolutely no circumstances! Even if you were four lovely, lovable loves instead of being serious and dignified gentlemen!

Johannes Brahms, Letter to Joachim, 1896

19 [Of his *Four Serious Songs*] Ungodly ditties.

Johannes Brahms, Letter to Mandyczewski, 1896

20 I once told Wagner himself that I was the best Wagnerian of our time.

Johannes Brahms, quoted in Specht, *Johannes Brahms* (1928)

21 [Leaving a party] I beg a thousand pardons if there should be anyone here whom I have not insulted tonight!

Johannes Brahms, quoted in Specht, *Johannes Brahms* (1928)

22 I felt . . . that one day there must suddenly emerge the one who would be chosen to express the most exalted spirit of the times in an ideal manner, one who would not bring us mastery in gradual developmental stages but who, like Minerva, would spring fully armed from the head of Jove. And he has arrived — a youth at whose cradle the graces and heroes of old stood guard. His name is Johannes Brahms.

Robert Schumann in *Neue Zeitschrift*, 1844

23 [Of Brahms's piano sonatas] Veiled symphonies.

Robert Schumann, in *Neue Zeitschrift*, 1844

1   I believe Johannes to be the true Apostle, who
will also write Revelations.
Robert Schumann, Letter to Joachim

2   Brahms has . . . a nature which can develop to
its fullest bloom only in the most perfect
seclusion; pure as diamond, soft as snow . . .
Joseph Joachim, quoted in Gall, *Johannes Brahms* (1961)

3   Brahms has two personalities: one
predominantly of childlike genius . . . and the
other of demoniac cunning which, with an icy
surface, suddenly breaks forth in a pedantic,
prosaic compulsion to dominate.
Joseph Joachim, quoted in Gall, *Johannes Brahms* (1961)

4   When Brahms is in extra good spirits, he sings
'The grave is my joy'.
Hellmesberger, contemporary concertmaster of the
Vienna Philharmonic Orchestra, quoted in Gall,
Johannes Brahms (1961)

5   For the drawing room he is not graceful
enough, for the concert hall not fiery enough;
for the countryside he is not primitive enough,
for the city not cultured enough. I have but
little faith in such natures.
Anton Rubinstein, Letter to Liszt

6   Is that foggy turbidity of brooding reflection
which frequently beclouds his latest creations
the precursor of penetrating sunlight or of still
denser, more inhospitable dusk?
Eduard Hanslick, in 1862, quoted in Gall, *Johannes
Brahms* (1961)

7   In a newspaper column Hanslick once quipped
about Brahms, who had sprouted a beard
during his summer vacation, saying that his
original face was just as hard to recognise as
the theme in many of his variations.
Hans Gall, *Johannes Brahms* (1961)

8   He seemed to lack liveliness, so that in our
meetings he was often scarcely noticed.
Richard Wagner, *Memoirs* (1875)

9   Mr Johannes Brahms once was good enough to
play some piece with serious variations for me,
from which I could tell that he is not a joker,
and which I considered quite acceptable.
Richard Wagner, 'On Conducting'; the piece referred
to is the Variations and Fugue on a theme of Handel

10 [Of Brahms's *German Requiem*] Schumann's
Last Thought.
Richard Wagner, 'On Poetry and Composition'

11 [Of Brahms] I know of some famous composers
who in their concert masquerades choose the
disguise of a cabaret singer one day [*Liebeslieder
waltzes*], the hallelujah periwig of Handel the
next [*Song of Triumph*], the dress of a Jewish
csárdás fiddler another time [*Hungarian Dances*],
and then again the guise of a highly respectable
symphonic composer dressed up as a Number

Ten [von Bülow had described Brahms's First
Symphony as Beethoven's Tenth].
Richard Wagner, 'On Poetry and Composition'

12 [Referring to Brahms] The evil only starts when
one attempts to compose better than one can.
Richard Wagner, 'On Poetry and Composition';
Wagner had just quoted Mendelssohn's comment on
Berlioz: 'Everybody composes as well as he can.'

13 I have played over the music of that scoundrel
Brahms. What a giftless bastard!
Pyiotr Ilyich Tchaikovsky, Diary, 1886

14 *Er kann nicht jubeln.*
He can't exult.
Hugo Wolf, quoted by Cardus in *The Manchester
Guardian*, 1935

15 Brahms's *Tragic Overture* brings to mind the
entry of a ghost in a Shakespearean drama,
startling the murderer by its presence but
invisible to all others. We do not know whom
Brahms has murdered in his *Tragic Overture*.
Hugo Wolf, quoted in Lebrecht, *Discord* (1982)

16 [Of Brahms's Piano Concerto No. 2] Anyone
who can gulp down this concerto with appetite
can face a famine without concern. It may be
taken for granted that his digestive system is
enviable and, in a famine, will function
splendidly on the nutritive equivalent of
window panes, corks, stove-pipes and the like.
Hugo Wolf, quoted in Lebrecht, *Discord* (1982)

17 Brahms's *Requiem* has not the true funeral
relish: it is so execrably and ponderously dull
that the very flattest of funerals would seem
like a ballet, or at least a *danse macabre*, after it.
George Bernard Shaw, *The World*, 1892

18 His *Requiem* is patiently borne only by the
corpse.
George Bernard Shaw, in *The Star*, 1892

19 The Leviathan Maunderer.
George Bernard Shaw, in *The Star*, 1892

20 [Of Brahms's music] It is a verbosity which
outfaces its commonplaceness by dint of sheer
magnitude.
George Bernard Shaw, in *The Star*, 1892

21 Too much beer and beard.
Paul Dukas, quoted in Demuth, *Vincent d'Indy* (1951)

22 [Of Brahms's music] I was able to admire its
workmanship and construction and to derive
the same type of enjoyment from it that a
physician may experience in laying bare the
musculature of a well-grown corpse. If,
however, I tried to submit to a spontaneous
impression, I would experience that paralysing
disillusion which would befall the physician

who had the temerity to try to bring the corpse
back to life.

Felix Weingartner, quoted in Gall, *Johannes Brahms*
(1961)

1 A landscape, torn by mists and clouds, in which
I can see ruins of old churches, as well as of
Greek temples — that is Brahms.

Edvard Grieg, Letter to Henry T. Finck, 1900

2 Brahms, for all his grumbling and grizzling, had
never guessed what it felt like to be suspected
of stealing an umbrella.

E.M. Forster, *Howard's End* (1910)

3 Brahms . . . was a musical sensualist with
intellectual affectations, and succeeded only as
an incoherent voluptuary, too fundamentally
addleheaded to make anything great out of the
delicious musical luxuries he produced.

George Bernard Shaw, in *Music and Letters*, 1920

4 He was always the musician of conscience; he
had too much conscience, as a fact — which
accounts for his many tedious stretches of
'joinery', confidently put forward as
development passages.

Neville Cardus, in *The Manchester Guardian*, 1939

5 Benjamin Britten claims that he plays through
'the whole of Brahms' at intervals to see
whether Brahms is really as bad as he thought,
and ends by discovering that he is actually
much worse.

Colin Wilson, *Brandy of the Damned* (1964)

6 In the presence of overwhelming spiritual ideas
Brahms is often either comfortable or, for want
of a vivid idea, merely professional.

Neville Cardus, *The Delights of Music* (1966)

BRASS

See also individual instruments.

7 With horns and trumpets now to madness
swell,
Now sink in sorrows with a tolling bell.

Alexander Pope, *The Dunciad* (1728)

8 Never encourage the brass, except with a curt
glance, in order to give an important entrance
cue.

Richard Strauss, 'Ten Golden Rules Inscribed in the
Album of a Young Conductor' (1927)

9 If you think that the brass is not blowing loud
enough, mute it by a couple of degrees.

Richard Strauss, 'Ten Golden Rules Inscribed in the
Album of a Young Conductor' (1927)

BRASS BANDS

10 [Of a village brass band contest] A musical
prize fight.

Title of story in *All the Year Round*

11 Some day the Press will awake to the fact,
already known abroad and to some few of us in
England, that the living centre of music in
Great Britain is not London but somewhere
farther north.

Edward Elgar, in 1903, quoted in Bainbridge, *Brass
Triumphant* (1980)

12 Armies of men . . . have been turned to a better
life by first hearing the sounds of a Salvation
Army band. The next time you hear a Salvation
Army band, no matter how humble, take off
your hat.

John Philip Sousa, quoted in Bainbridge, *Brass
Triumphant* (1980)

13 The brass band contest is the one and only
successful rival to the football match in the
affections of a certain section of the British
public . . . Its home is in an English Bohemia
which lies between the Trent and the Tweed.

George Millar, *The Military Band* (1912)

BRITTEN

14 I've come to the conclusion that I must have a
very clever subconscious.

Benjamin Britten, in 1952, quoted in Headington,
Britten (1981)

15 [Of the composition of *The Turn of the Screw*]
Like squeezing toothpaste out of a tube that's
nearly finished.

Benjamin Britten, quoted in Headington, *Britten* (1981)

16 I do not easily think in words, because words
are not my medium . . . I also have a very real
dread of becoming one of those artists who *talk*.
I believe so strongly that it is dangerous for
artists to *talk*.

Benjamin Britten, Speech of acceptance of an
Honorary Doctorate at Hull University, 1962

17 I remember the first time I tried [composing]
the result looked rather like the Forth Bridge.

Benjamin Britten, in *The Sunday Telegraph*, 1964

18 When [Frank] Bridge played questionable
chords across the room at me and asked if that
was what I had meant, I would retort, 'Yes it
is', and he'd grunt back, 'Well, it oughtn't to
be.'

Benjamin Britten, in *The Sunday Telegraph*, 1964

19 One day I'll be able to relax a bit, and try and
become a good composer.

Benjamin Britten, Letter to Imogen Holst, 1968

20 [Of the Piano Concerto] Mr Britten's cleverness,
of which he has frequently been told, has got
the better of him and led him into all sorts of
errors, the worst of which are errors of taste.

William McNaught, in *The Musical Times*, 1938

21 [Of *Albert Herring*] Mr Britten is still pursuing
his old problem of seeing how much

indigestible material he can dissolve in music ... the result is a charade.

The Times, 1947

1   To sit in Orford Church, where I had spent so many hours of my childhood dutifully waiting some spark of divine fire, and then to receive it at last in the performance of *Noye's Fludde*, was an overwhelming experience.

Lord Kenneth Clark, quoted in Headington, *Britten* (1981)

2   If wind and water could write music, it would sound like Ben's.

Yehudi Menuhin, quoted in Headington, *Britten* (1981)

3   So much *heart* — such *Russianness*.

Mstislav Rostropovich, quoted in Headington, *Britten* (1981)

4   There is no reason ... why innocence should not be a valid theme for music; but to dwell on it for thirty years argues a certain arrested development.

Colin Wilson, *Brandy of the Damned* (1964)

5   The piercing benediction of his music.

Geoffrey Grigson, in *The Times*, 1976

6   [Of the *War Requiem*] I think he [Britten] felt the easy success was an outrage and an invasion of privacy. Every creative artist who goes before the public takes something private with him, something vulnerable that can be crushed and wounded, only with Ben it turned out sometimes to have been too private a risk.

Lord Harewood, *The Tongs and the Bones* (1981)

BRUCH

7   [On hearing a hurdy-gurdy man in the street] Listen, Bruch, this fellow has gotten hold of your *Arminius*.

Johannes Brahms, referring to Bruch's new oratorio, quoted in Gall, *Johannes Brahms* (1961)

8   [Of Bruch's violin concertos] Pussycats.

Neville Cardus, in *The Manchester Guardian*, 1938

BRUCKNER

9   [Of his Symphony No. 1] *Das kecke Beserl*. The saucy little besom.

Anton Bruckner, quoted in Watson, *Bruckner* (1975)

10 The sixth [symphony] is the cheekiest.

Anton Bruckner, quoted in Watson, *Bruckner* (1975)

11 I will present to him [God] the score of my *Te Deum*, and he will judge me mercifully.

Anton Bruckner, quoted in Watson, *Bruckner* (1975)

12 [Of Bruckner's Symphony No. 2] Very nice.

Richard Wagner, quoted in Bruckner, Letter to Hans von Wolzogen, 1884

13 Bruckner! He is my man!

Richard Wagner, quoted in Watson, *Bruckner* (1975)

14 [Of Bruckner's Symphony No. 3] A vision of Beethoven's Ninth becoming friendly with Wagner's Valkyries and finishing up trampled under their hooves.

Eduard Hanslick, quoted in Watson, *Bruckner* (1975)

15 'Look!' Brahms exclaimed, pointing to the first pages of the score [of Bruckner's Symphony No. 4]. 'Here this man composes as though he were a Schubert.' Brahms then indicated the unisons and the chromatic passages in the closing section and said: 'Then he suddenly remembers that he is a Wagnerian, and everything goes to the devil.'

Hans Gall, *Johannes Brahms* (1961)

16 [Of Bruckner's symphonies] Symphonic boa-constrictors.

Johannes Brahms, quoted in Specht, *Johannes Brahms* (1928)

17 [Of Bruckner's symphonies] A swindle that will be forgotten in a few years.

Johannes Brahms, quoted in Watson, *Bruckner* (1975)

18 [Of Bruckner's Symphony No. 7] The work is a failure. It may be beautiful in twenty-five years; it is not beautiful now.

H.E. Krehbiel, in *The New York Tribune*, 1886

19 [Of Bruckner's Symphony No. 7] It comes from the Nibelungen and goes to the devil.

Max Kalbeck (Brahms's official biographer), quoted in Watson, *Bruckner* (1975)

20 [Of Bruckner's symphonies] The anti-musical ravings of a half-wit.

Hans von Bülow, Letter, 1888

21 [Of Bruckner's Symphony No. 8] It is not impossible that the future belongs to this nightmarish Katzenjammer style, a future which we therefore do not envy.

Eduard Hanslick, in *Neue Freie Presse*, 1892

22 One single cymbal clash by Bruckner is worth all the four symphonies of Brahms with the serenades thrown in.

Hugo Wolf, quoted in Watson, *Bruckner* (1975)

THE BUGLE

23 Blow, bugle, blow, set the wild echoes flying,
    Blow, bugle; answer, echoes, dying, dying, dying.

Alfred, Lord Tennyson, *The Princess*, IV

BULL

1 Lo, where doth pace in order
A braver Bull, than did Europa carry.

Anon., *Parthenia, or the Maydenhead of the first musicke
that ever was printed for the Virginalls* (1612)

BUSONI

2 Music was born free, and to win freedom is its
destiny.

Ferruccio Busoni, quoted in Machlis, *Introduction to
Contemporary Music* (1963)

3 I want to attain the unknown! What I already
know is boundless. But I want to go even
further. The final word still eludes me.

Ferruccio Busoni, *Der mächtige Zauberer* (1905)

4 I hardly play with my hands any more. This
way of playing is equally effective whatever the
piece.

Ferruccio Busoni, Letter to Gerda Busoni, 1906

5 First there has to be the *idea*, then *inspiration*
follows, or if it does not one goes in search of it,
and finally there is the *realisation* . . . In my case,
I usually make my musical discoveries while
out walking in the street, preferably in a lively
part of the town and in the evening. The
realisation happens at home, when I have a free
morning.

Ferruccio Busoni, in *Der Konzertsaal*, 1907

6 In matters concerning art my feelings are those
of an autocrat.

Ferruccio Busoni, Letter to Gisella Selden-Goth, 1918

7 . . . youth and high spirits, qualities which for
me are inseparable from the art of music.

Ferruccio Busoni, Letter to Heinrich Burkard, 1923

8 He could conceive wonderful things in music;
unfortunately he could not consistently turn
them into music.

Neville Cardus, in *The Manchester Guardian*, 1937

BYRD

9 [Referring to Byrd] There be some English
songs lately set forth by a great Master of
Music, which for skill and sweetness may
content the most curious.

Nicholas Yonge, *Musica Transalpina* (1588)

10 List to that sweet recorder;
How daintily this Byrd his notes doth vary,
As if he were the Nightingale's own brother!

Anon., in *Parthenia, or the Maydenhead of the first
musicke that was ever printed for the Virginalls* (1612)

11 *Birde, suos iactet si Musa Britanna clientes
Signiferum turmis te creet illa suis.*
If the British muse should hold a review of her
followers, she would appoint you, master Byrd,
as standard-bearer of her squadrons.

Robert Dow, comment on one of the part-books he
prepared for Christ Church, Oxford

12 For motets and music of piety and devotion as
well as for the honour of our nation, as the
merit of the man, I prefer above all our Phoenix
Mr William Byrd, whom in that kind I know not
whether any may equal.

Henry Peacham, *The Compleat Gentleman* (1622)

CAGE

13 Until I die there will be sounds. And they will
continue following after my death. One need
not fear about the future of music.

John Cage, *Silence* (1961), 'Experimental Music' (1957)

14 And what is the purpose of writing music? . . .
simply a way to wake up to the very life we're
living, which is so excellent once one gets one's
mind and one's desires out of its way and lets it
act of its own accord.

John Cage, *Silence* (1961), 'Experimental Music' (1957)

15 When later I heard modern music, I took, like a
duck to water, to all the modern intervals: the
sevenths, the seconds, the tritone, and the
fourth. I liked Bach too about this time, but I
didn't like the sound of the thirds and sixths.

John Cage, *Silence* (1961), 'Lecture on Nothing' (1959)

16 nothing is accomplished by writing a piece of
         music
nothing is accomplished by hearing a piece of
         music
nothing is accomplished by playing a piece of
         music

John Cage, *Silence* (1961)

17 I thought I could never compose socially
important music. Only if I could *invent*
something new, then would I be useful to
society.

John Cage, quoted in Peyser, *Boulez* (1976)

18 Schoenberg said I would never be able to
compose, because I had no ear for music; and
it's true that I don't hear the relationships of
tonality and harmony. He said: 'You always
come to a wall and you won't be able to go
through.' I said, well then, I'll beat my head
against that wall; and I quite literally began
hitting things; and developed a music of
percussion that involved noises.

John Cage, interview in *The Observer Magazine*, 1982

19 My music liberates because I give people the
chance to change their minds in the way I've
changed mine. I don't want to police them.

John Cage, interview in *The Observer Magazine*, 1982

1 He is not a composer, but an inventor — of genius.

Arnold Schoenberg, quoted in Yates, *Twentieth Century Music* (1968)

2 I do not believe in ghosts, astrology, palmistry, John Cage, love or God.

Gore Vidal, *Two Sisters* (1970)

3 He was refreshing but not very bright. His freshness came from an absence of knowledge.

Pierre Boulez, quoted in Peyser, *Boulez* (1976)

CARTER

4 I am a radical, having a nature that leads me to perpetual revolt.

Elliott Carter, in *c.* 1939, quoted in Ewen, *American Composers* (1982)

5 I'm always concerned with context — with preceding and succeeding ideas. Making things that go along, changing in very slight degrees, bit by bit. Or dealing with things that change abruptly. And making all this *significant*.

Elliott Carter, quoted in Ewen, *American Composers* (1982)

CASTRATI

6 *Cleopatra:* Thou, eunuch Mardian.
 Mardian: What's your
   Highness' pleasure?
 Cleopatra: Not to hear thee sing. I take no
   pleasure
In aught an eunuch has.

William Shakespeare, *Antony and Cleopatra*, I.v

7 Who can endure to hear one of the rough old Romans squeaking through the mouth of an eunuch, especially when they [composers] may choose a subject out of courts where eunuchs are really actors, or represent by them any of the soft Asiatic monarchs?

Joseph Addison, *Remarks on Several Parts of Italy* (1705)

8 In walking with singers, especially castrati, the composer will always place himself at their left and keep one step behind, hat in hand, remembering that the lowest of them is, in the operas, at least a general, a captain of the king's forces, of the queen's forces, etc.

Benedetto Marcello, *Il teatro alla moda* (1720)

9 One God, one Farinelli!

Lady Bingley, shouted at the opera, 1734, quoted in Young, *Handel* (1947)

10 But never shall a truly British age
Bear a vile race of eunuchs on the stage:
The boasted work's called National in vain,
If one Italian voice pollute the strain.

Charles Churchill, *The Rosciad* (1761), commenting on Arne's use of Italian singers

ST CECILIA

11 Orpheus could lead the savage race;
 And trees uprooted left their place,
  Sequacious of the lyre:
But bright Cecilia rais'd the wonder high'r:
When to her organ vocal breath was giv'n,
An angel heard, and straight appear'd
  Mistaking earth for heaven.

John Dryden, 'A Song for St Cecilia's Day' (1687)

12 Of Orpheus now no more let poets tell,
 To bright Cecilia greater pow'r is giv'n;
  His numbers rais'd a shade from Hell,
  Hers lift the soul to Heav'n.

Alexander Pope, 'Ode for Musick, on St Cecilia's Day' (*c.* 1708)

13 In a garden shady this holy lady
With reverent cadence and subtle psalm,
Like a black swan as death came on
Poured forth her song in perfect calm:
And by ocean's margin this innocent virgin
Constructed an organ to enlarge her prayer,
And notes tremendous from her great engine
Thundered out on the Roman air.

Blonde Aphrodite rose up excited,
Moved to delight by the melody . . .

W.H. Auden, 'Anthem for St Cecilia's Day', set to music by Benjamin Britten as *Hymn to St Cecilia* (1942)

14 Blessed Cecilia, appear in visions
To all musicians, appear and inspire:
Translated Daughter, come down and startle
Composing mortals with immortal fire.

W.H. Auden, 'Anthem for St Cecilia's Day', set to music by Benjamin Britten as *Hymn to St Cecilia* (1942)

THE CELLO

15 You have between your legs the most sensitive instrument known to man, and all you can do is to sit there and scratch it.

Sir Thomas Beecham, attr. remark to a woman cellist

16 . . . the wasp-in-the-window effect which most times we have to put up with whenever a 'cellist gets to work.

Neville Cardus, in *The Manchester Guardian*, 1939

17 The cello is like a beautiful woman who has not grown older, but younger with time, more slender, more supple, more graceful.

Pablo Casals, in *Time*, 1957

CHAMBER MUSIC

18 [Of quartets] You listen to four sensible persons conversing, you profit from their discourse, and you get to know the peculiar properties of their several instruments.

Johann Wolfgang von Goethe, Letter, quoted in Barzun (ed.), *Pleasures of Music* (1977)

1 Most string quartets [as ensembles] have a basement and an attic, and the lift is not working.

Neville Cardus, *The Delights of Music* (1966)

2 The significance of chamber music is that in dealing with the intimate it can attain to the ineffable. Chamber music conceives itself as a world of sound that has external boundaries but no internal ones.

Hans Werner Henze, *Music and Politics* (1982) 'Instrumental Composition' (1963)

CHERUBINI

3 *Napoleon:* My dear Cherubini, you are certainly an excellent musician; but really your music is so noisy and complicated, that I can make nothing of it.
Cherubini: My dear general, you are certainly an excellent soldier; but, in regard to music, you must excuse me if I don't think it necessary to adapt my compositions to your comprehension.

Quoted in Bellasis, *Cherubini* (1874)

4 True art is imperishable and the true artist feels heartfelt pleasure in grand works of genius, and that is what enchants me when I hear a new composition of yours; in fact I take greater interest in it than in my own; in short, I love and honour you.

Ludwig van Beethoven, Letter to Cherubini, 1823

5 [In his *Communion Prelude* Cherubini] plumbed the mystic depths of Christian meditation.

Hector Berlioz, quoted in Elliot, *Berlioz* (1967)

6 The learned lucubrations of Cherubini.

Vincent d'Indy, quoted in Demuth, *Vincent d'Indy* (1951)

CHOPIN

7 I'm a revolutionary, money means nothing to me.

Fryderyk Chopin, in 1833, quoted in Hedley, *Chopin* (1947)

8 We are two old cembalos on which time and circumstances have played out their wretched trills ... The *table d'harmonie* is perfect, only the strings have snapped and some of the pegs are missing.

Fryderyk Chopin, Letter to Juljan Fontana, 1848

9 Bach is like an astronomer who, with the help of ciphers, finds the most wonderful stars ... Beethoven embraced the universe with the power of his spirit ... I do not climb so high. A long time ago I decided that my universe will be the soul and heart of man.

Fryderyk Chopin, Letter to Delphine Potocka

10 Nothing is more odious than music without hidden meaning.

Fryderyk Chopin, quoted in *Le Courrier musical*, 1910

11 Remember! Never forget that we in Poland love you ... in foreign lands they may appreciate and reward you better, but they cannot love you more.

Konstancja Gladkowska, writing in Chopin's album in 1830. After her marriage in 1832, Chopin added 'Oh yes they can!'

12 He is the truest artist I have ever met.

Eugène Delacroix, quoted in Hedley, *Chopin* (1947)

13 Once at the piano Chopin played until he was exhausted. In the grip of a disease that knows no mercy, dark rings appeared around his eyes, a feverish brightness lit up his face, his lips turned to a vivid red and his breath came in short gasps. He felt, we felt, that something of his life was flowing away with the music; he would not stop and we had not the strength to stop him. The fever which consumed him took possession of us all!

Ernest Legouvé, quoted in Hedley, *Chopin* (1947)

14 If one holds Field's charming romances before a distorting concave mirror, so that every delicate expression becomes coarse, one gets Chopin's work.

Ludwig Rellstab, quoted in Hedley, *Chopin* (1947)

15 I was glad to be once again with a thorough musician, not one of those half-virtuosos and half-classics who would like to combine in music the honours of virtue and the pleasures of vice.

Felix Mendelssohn, in 1835, quoted in Hedley, *Chopin* (1947)

16 Hats off, gentlemen, a genius!

Robert Schumann, quoted in Pleasants (ed.), *The Musical World of Robert Schumann* (1965)

17 Let one imagine that an Aeolian harp had all the scales and that an artist's hand had mingled them together in all kinds of fantastic decorations, but in such a way that you could always hear a deeper fundamental tone and a softly singing melody — there you have something of a picture of his playing.

Robert Schumann, quoted in Hedley, *Chopin* (1947)

18 He was dying all his life.

Hector Berlioz, quoted in Elliot, *Berlioz* (1967)

19 A composer for the right hand.

Richard Wagner, quoted in Cardus, *The Delights of Music* (1966)

20 After playing Chopin, I feel as if I had been weeping over sins that I had never committed, and mourning over tragedies that were not my own.

Oscar Wilde, *The Critic as Artist* (1891)

1   We have been, let us say, to hear the latest Pole
    Transmit the Preludes, through his hair and
        fingertips.

    T.S. Eliot, 'Portrait of a Lady'

2   The modern virtuosi ... ride the piano over his
    music as though in brisk and masterful control
    of a Rolls-Royce. Chopin in our time has been
    streamlined.

    Neville Cardus, in *The Manchester Guardian*, 1935

3   I love the angelic in his figure, which reminds
    me of Shelley: the peculiarly and very
    mysteriously veiled, unapproachable,
    withdrawing, unadventurous flavour of his
    being, that not wanting to know, that rejection
    of material experience, the sublime incest of his
    fantastically delicate and seductive art.
    (Leverkühn)

    Thomas Mann, *Doctor Faustus* (1947); trans. Lowe-
    Porter

4   Compared with Berlioz, Chopin was a morbidly
    sentimental flea by the side of a roaring lion.

    J.W. Davison, quoted in Elliot, *Berlioz* (1967)

CHURCH MUSIC

See also HEAVENLY MUSIC, RELIGION.

5   O clap your hands together, all ye people:
    O sing unto God with the voice of melody.

    Psalms 47:1 (version in the Book of Common Prayer)

6   O come, let us sing unto the Lord; let us make a
    joyful noise to the rock of our salvation.
    Let us come before his presence with
    thanksgiving, and make a joyful noise unto him
    with psalms.

    Psalms 95:1-2

7   How greatly did I weep in thy hymns and
    canticles, deeply moved by the voices of thy
    sweet-speaking church!

    St Augustine, *Confessions*

8   Athanasius Bishop of Alexandria ... caused the
    reader of the psalm to sound it forth with so
    little warbling of the voice, as that it was nearer
    to speaking, than to singing.

    St Augustine, *Confessions*

9   When it happens that I am moved more by the
    music than by the words which it accompanies,
    I confess that I am guilty of a grave sin.

    St Augustine, *Confessions*

10 Psalmody unites those who disagree, makes
    friends of those at odds, brings together those
    who are out of charity with one another. Who
    could retain a grievance against the man with
    whom he had joined in singing before God?

    St Ambrose, quoted in Routley, *The Church and Music*
    (1950)

11 Sing to God, not with the voice, but with the
    heart. ... Although a man be *kakophonos*, to use
    a common expression, if he have good works,
    he is a sweet singer before God.

    St Jerome, Commentary on Ephesians

12 [The Holy Spirit] blended the delight of melody
    with doctrines [in the Psalms] in order that
    through the pleasantness and softness of the
    sound we might unawares receive what was
    useful in the words, according to the practice of
    wise physicians, who, when they give the more
    bitter draughts to the sick, often smear the rim
    of the cup with honey.

    St Basil the Great, Homily on the First Psalm

13 Whence hath the Church so many organs and
    musical instruments? To what purpose, I pray
    you, is that terrible blowing of bellows,
    expressing rather the cracks of thunder, than
    the sweetness of a voice?

    Aelred, Abbot of Rievaulx, in *c.* 1160, quoted in
    Prynne, *Histriomastix* (1632)

14 We do not mean to prohibit the use of harmony
    occasionally on festive days ... We approve
    such harmony as follows the melody at the
    intervals, for example, of the octave, fifth, and
    fourth, and such harmony as may be supported
    by the simple chant of the church; but we
    prescribe this condition, that the integrity of the
    chant itself remain undamaged, and that no
    well-established piece of music is altered as
    under this authority.

    Pope John XXII, Edict, 1325

15 Modern church music is so constructed that the
    congregation cannot hear one distinct word.

    Desiderius Erasmus, in the early 16th century, quoted
    in Lee, *Music of the People* (1970)

16 I am not of the opinion that all the arts shall be
    crushed to earth and perish through the
    Gospel, as some bigoted persons pretend, but
    would willingly see them all, and especially
    music, servants of Him who gave and created
    them.

    Martin Luther, Foreword to the *Wittenberg Gesangbuch*
    (1524)

17 In truth we know by experience that song has
    great force and vigour to move and inflame the
    hearts of men to invoke and praise God with a
    more vehement and ardent zeal.

    Jean Calvin, *The Geneva Psalter* (1543)

18 [Of his translation of the Litany] In mine
    opinion the song, that shall be made thereunto,
    would not be full of notes, but, as nearly as may
    be, for every syllable a note, so that it may be
    sung distinctly and devoutly.

    Archbishop Cranmer, Letter to Henry VIII, quoted in
    Phillips, *The Singing Church* (1968)

19 We have decided to follow the example of the

prophets and the fathers of the church and write German hymns for the German people.

Martin Luther, *Table Talk* (pub. 1566)

1 Their tossing to and fro of psalms and sentences is like tennis play, whereto God is called to judge who can do best and be most gallant in his worship.

Robert Browne, *A True and Short Declaration* (1583)

2 I would I were a weaver, I could sing psalms or anything.
(Falstaff)

William Shakespeare, *Henry IV, Part One*, II.iv

3 For even as among artisans it is shameful in a craftsman to make a rude piece of work from some precious material, so indeed to sacred words in which the praises of God and of the Heavenly host are sung, none but some celestial harmony (so far as our powers avail) will be proper.

William Byrd, Dedication to *Gradualia* (1605-7)

4 The common singing-men in cathedral churches are a bad society, and yet a company of good fellows, that roar deep in the choir, deeper in the tavern.

John Earle, *Microcosmographie* (1628)

5 Choristers bellow the tenor, as it were oxen; bark a counterpart, as it were a kennel of dogs; roar out a treble, as it were a sort of bulls; and grunt out a bass, as it were a number of hogs.

William Prynne, *Histriomastix* (1632)

6 There let the pealing organ blow,
To the full voic'd choir below,
In service high, and anthems clear,
As may with sweetness, through mine ear,
Dissolve me into ecstasies,
And bring all Heav'n before mine eyes.

John Milton, 'Il Penseroso' (1632)

7 Let all the world in ev'ry corner sing
    My God and King.
The Church and psalms must shout,
No door can keep them out:
But above all, the heart
Must bear the longest part.

George Herbert, *The Temple* (1633), 'Antiphon'

8 The fineness which a hymn or psalm affords
Is when the soul unto the lines accords.

George Herbert, 'A True Hymn'

9 That the music used in cathedrals and collegiate churches be framed with less curiosity; and that no hymns or anthems be used where ditties are framed by private men, but such as are contained in the Holy Scriptures, or in our liturgy or prayers, or have public allowance.

Committee of the Long Parliament, Report, 1641

10 Whosoever is harmonically composed delights in harmony; which makes me much distrust the symmetry of those heads which declaim against all church music.

Sir Thomas Browne, *Religio Medici* (1642)

11 In quires and places where they sing.

The Book of Common Prayer (1662)

12 Instead of the ancient, grave, and solemn wind music accompanying the organ, was introduced a concert of twenty-four violins between every pause, after the French fantastical light way, better suiting a tavern or playhouse than a church.

John Evelyn, Diary, 1662

13 Right glad I was when music was lately shut out of our churches, on what default of hers I may not enquire, it hath since been harboured and welcomed in the halls, parlours and chambers of the primest persons of this nation.

Thomas Fuller, *The Worthies of England* (1662)

14 [George Herbert] would say that 'his time spent in prayer, and cathedral music, elevated his soul, and was his Heaven upon Earth'.

Izaak Walton, *Life of Herbert* (1670)

15 The use of musical instruments may also add some little advantages to singing, but they are more apt to change religion into air and fancies, and take some of its simplicity, and are not so fitted for edification.

Jeremy Taylor, *Ductor Dubitantium* (1676)

16 [Of Charles II] His Majesty, who was a brisk and airy prince, coming to the throne in the flower and vigour of his age, was soon, if I may so say, tired with the grave and solemn way, and ordered the composers of his chapel to add symphonies etc. with instruments to their anthems.

Thomas Tudway, quoted in Westrup, *Purcell* (1968)

17   As some to church repair,
Not for the doctrine, but the music there.

Alexander Pope, *Essay on Criticism* (1711)

18 The music of the church must be expressive . . . The passions of opera are cold in comparison to those of our church music.

J. Bonnet, *Histoire de la musique* (1725)

19 Light quirks of music, broken and unev'n,
Make the soul dance upon a jig to Heaven.

Alexander Pope, *Epistle to Lord Burlington* (1731)

20 Listed into the cause of sin,
Why should a good be evil?
Music, alas! too long has been
Pressed to obey the Devil.
Drunken, or lewd, or light, the lay
Flower to the soul's undoing;

Widened and strewed with flowers the way
Down to eternal ruin.

Charles Wesley, *The True Use of Music* (1749)

1 Where through the long-drawn aisle and fretted
       vault
   The pealing anthem swells the note of praise.

   Thomas Gray, 'Elegy Written in a Country
   Churchyard' (1750)

2 The most High has a decided taste for vocal
   music, provided it be lugubrious and gloomy
   enough.

   Voltaire, *Dictionnaire philosophique* (1764)

3 I would earnestly entreat those who sing ill, not
   to sing at all, at least in the church.

   James Beattie, *On the Improvement of Psalmody in
   Scotland* (1778)

4 Why should the devil have all the good tunes?

   Rev. Rowland Hill, Sermon, quoted in Broome, *Rev.
   Rowland Hill*

5 At the thought of God [my] heart leapt for joy,
   and [I] could not help [my] music's doing the
   same.

   Joseph Haydn, apologising for the cheerfulness of his
   masses, quoted in Hughes, *Haydn* (1970)

6 [Of cathedral music] No coat of varnish can do
   for a picture what the exquisitely reverberating
   qualities can do for music. And then the organ.
   What a multitude of sins does that cover!

   Samuel Wesley, 'A Few Words on Cathedral Music'
   (1849)

7 There's a certain Slant of light,
   Winter Afternoons —
   That oppresses like the Heft
   Of Cathedral Tunes —

   Emily Dickinson, 'There's a certain Slant of light'

8 I am as fond of fine music and handsome
   buildings as Milton was, or Cromwell, or
   Bunyan; but if I found that they were becoming
   the instruments of a systematic idolatry of
   sensuousness, I would hold it good
   statemanship to blow every cathedral in the
   world to pieces with dynamite, organ and all,
   without the least heed to the screams of the art
   critics and cultured voluptuaries.

   George Bernard Shaw, Preface to *Plays for Puritans*
   (1901)

9 One ought not to sing in churches anything
   except plainsong in unison.

   Gabriel Fauré, in *Le Monde musicale*, 1904

10 Music in England was ruined by *Hymns Ancient
   and Modern*.

   Edward Elgar, quoted in Redwood (ed.), *An Elgar
   Companion* (1982)

11 The world, the flesh, and the devil lurk in the
   larynx of the soprano or alto, and her place is

before the footlights, not as a vocal staircase to
paradise.

James Huneker, *Ivory Apes and Peacocks* (1915)

12 'Tis Summer Time on Bredon,
       And now the farmers swear;
   The cattle rise and listen
       In valleys far and near,
       And blush at what they hear.

   But when the mists in autumn
       On Bredon top are thick,
   The happy hymns of farmers
       Go up from fold and rick,
       The cattle then are sick.

   Hugh Kingsmill, 'Two Poems after A.E. Housman'

13 In spite of myself, the insidious mastery of song
   Betrays me back, till the heart of me weeps
       to belong
   To the old Sunday evenings at home, with
       winter outside
   And hymns in the cosy parlour, the tinkling
       piano our guide.

   D.H. Lawrence, 'Piano'

14 [Of plainsong] I see no mystery in it; just
   dullness.

   Frederick Delius, quoted in Fenby, *Delius as I knew him*
   (1936)

15 [On editing a hymnbook] Two years of close
   association with some of the best (as well as
   some of the worst) tunes in the world was a
   better musical education than any amount of
   sonatas and fugues.

   Ralph Vaughan Williams, quoted in Machlis,
   Introduction to Contemporary Music (1963)

16 Sing on with hymns uproarious,
   Ye humble and aloof.

   John Betjeman, 'Hymn'

17 [Of his *Mass*] The Credo is the longest
   movement. There is much to believe.

   Igor Stravinsky, quoted in Machlis, *Introduction to
   Contemporary Music* (1963)

18 The Church knew what the Psalmist knew:
   Music praises God. Music is well or better able
   to praise Him than the building of the church
   and all its decoration; it is the Church's greatest
   ornament.

   Igor Stravinsky, *Conversations with Stravinsky* (1958)

THE CLARINET

19 The clarinet is suited to the expression of
   sorrow, and even when it plays a merry air
   there is a suggestion of sadness about it. If I
   were to dance in a prison, I should wish to do
   so to the accompaniment of a clarinet.

   André Grétry, *Memoirs*

20 The many-keyed clarinet, which can sound so
   ghostly in the deep chalumeau register but

higher up can gleam in silvery blossoming harmony.

Thomas Mann, *Doctor Faustus* (1947); trans. Lowe-Porter

1 [The sound of the clarinet] Leering cacherination.

Isaac Goldberg, *Tin Pan Alley* (1930)

CLASS

See also POLITICS.

2 The excellence of music is to be measured by pleasure. But the pleasure must not be that of chance persons; the fairest music is that which delights the best and best-educated, and especially that which delights the one man who is pre-eminent in virtue and education.

Plato, *Laws*

3 A gentleman, playing or singing in a common audience appaireth his estimation, the people forgetting reverence when they behold him in the similitude of a common servant or minstrel.

Sir Thomas Elyot, *The Boke of the Governour* (1531)

4 Ben Wallington ... did sing a most excellent bass, and yet a poor fellow, a working goldsmith, that goes without gloves to his hands.

Samuel Pepys, Diary, 1667

5 If you love music, hear it; go to operas, concerts, and pay fiddlers to play to you; but I insist upon your neither piping nor fiddling yourself. It puts a gentleman in a very frivolous, contemptible light.

Lord Chesterfield, Letter to his son, 1749

6 And tuned, to please a peasant's ear,
The harp a king had loved to hear.

Sir Walter Scott, *The Lay of the Last Minstrel* (1805)

7 I consider music as a very innocent diversion, and perfectly compatible with the profession of a clergyman.

Jane Austen, *Pride and Prejudice* (1813)

8 [After *A Life for the Tsar* had been described as 'music for coachmen'] This is good and even just, for coachmen are more sensible than gentlemen.

Mikhail Glinka, *Memoirs*

9 [Of one of Chopin's private concerts] A splendid fête where simplicity was wedded to grace and elegance, and good taste served as a pedestal to wealth.

La France musicale, 1842

10 If no collection of Church Music is to be found in the family library ... it needs little reasoning to discover that ... this must produce a

deleterious influence upon the grade of society immediately inferior.

Anon., *A Plea for the Cultivation of Sacred Music by the Upper Classes* (1850)

11 The music-hall singer attends a series
Of masses, fugues and 'ops'
    By Bach, interwoven
    With Spohr and Beethoven,
At classical Monday Pops.

W.S. Gilbert, *The Mikado* (1885)

12 The professional musician, as such, can have no special status whatever, because he may be anything, from an ex-drummer boy to an artist and philosopher of world-wide reputation.

George Bernard Shaw, in *The World*, 1893

13 Unusual rhythmic combinations and syncopations have been so extensively used by high-class composers that it is not possible for coon song composers to invent anything along these lines.

The Musician, 1901

14 [Of Beethoven's Symphony No. 5] All sorts and conditions are satisfied by it.

E.M. Forster, *Howard's End* (1910)

15 ... the fairest, alas bygone, days of art when a prince stood as a protector before an artist, showing the rabble that art, a matter for princes, is beyond the judgement of common people.

Arnold Schoenberg, Letter to Prince von Fürstenberg, 1924

16 The appalling popularity of music.

Constant Lambert, title of chapter in *Music Ho!* (1934)

17 Furtwängler was once told in Berlin that the people in the back seats were complaining that they could not hear some of his soft passages. 'It does not matter,' he said, 'they do not pay so much.'

Neville Cardus, in *The Manchester Guardian*, 1935

18 The masses, their senses still sound and unadulterated, must be introduced to musical culture.

Zoltán Kodály, 'What is Hungarian in Music?' (1939)

19 The ideal method of broadcasting throughout this country would be to have three separate channels ... For the Calibans, there would be a third service, 'the dirt track', a continual stream of noise and nonsense put on by untouchables with the use of records.

Arthur Bliss, 'Music Policy' (1941)

20 A distinguished British historian ... declares that solo singing is favoured in an aristocratic society and communal or choral in a democratic.

Sir Thomas Beecham, *A Mingled Chime* (1944)

1 There is a belief . . . that the intelligent and enthusiastic music-lover is not to be found in the stalls and boxes but in the pit and gallery . . . This comfortable article of faith has no foundation in fact, my own experience being in the contrary direction.

Sir Thomas Beecham, *A Mingled Chime* (1944)

2 The national culture of music of every people rests on a healthy relationship between folk music and composed music.

Only the music which has sprung from the ancient musical traditions of a people can reach the masses of that people.

Zoltán Kodály, programme note, 1950

3 In music the social standpoint which an individual occupies is not directly translated into tone language.

T.W. Adorno, *Introduction to the Sociology of Music* (1959)

4 Will people in the cheaper seats clap your hands? All the rest of you, if you'll just rattle your jewellery . . .

John Lennon, at the Royal Command Performance, 1963

5 The bourgeois artist, or one who feels himself to be socially secure, tends to disintegrate the material at his disposal while he is creating, whereas the alienated one, the outlaw, puts all his energy into achieving the opposite with the same material, namely to try to integrate himself at all costs.

Hans Werner Henze, *Music and Politics* (1982) 'The Bourgeois Artist' (1964)

CLASSICISM

6 [The style of Haydn] sometimes pleases by its spirit and a wild luxuriancy . . . but possesses too little of the elegance and pathetic expression of music to remain long in the public taste.

John Gregory, *The State and Faculties of Man* (1766)

7 Passions, whether violent or not, must never be expressed in such a way as to disgust, and . . . music, even in the most terrible situations, must never offend the ear.

Wolfgang Amadeus Mozart, Letter, 1782, concerning *Die Entführung aus dem Serail*

8 Haydn, Mozart and Beethoven developed a new art, whose origins first appear in the middle of the eighteenth century.

E.T.A. Hoffmann, in 1814, quoted in Rosen, *The Classical Style* (1971)

9 Form is something created through a thousand years of exertions by the most outstanding masters, and yet no disciple can ever be too eager to appropriate it. It would be a foolish conceit of badly misunderstood originality if

everyone searched and groped around in his own way for something which is already perfected.

Johann Peter Eckermann, 'Contributions to Poetry', quoted by Brahms in his commonplace book

10 Classicism is health, romanticism is sickness.

Johann Wolfgang von Goethe, *Converstions with Eckermann* (1827)

11 The classical tradition is nothing more or less than the Italian tradition.

Edward J. Dent, in 1913, quoted in Sadie (ed.), *New Grove Dictionary* (1980)

12 Until Schumann, Chopin, and Wagner came along to break it up, basic fun in music (from 1730 to well past 1840) consisted mostly in making new restrictions and keeping them . . . It would not be too far-fetched to compare this particular classic period to a man balancing first a single walking stick, then adding a plate, then a vase of flowers, and then a whole table.

George Antheil, *Bad Boy of Music* (1945)

COMPOSERS AND COMPOSING

See also INSPIRATION, TRADITION AND ORIGINALITY.

13 Let us now praise famous men . . .
Such as found out musical tunes, and recited verses in writing:
Rich men furnished with ability, living peaceably in their habitations.

Ecclesiasticus 44:1/5

14 He koude songes make and well endite.

Geoffrey Chaucer, *The Canterbury Tales*, General Prologue

15 [Of his youthful compositions] I thought then that everything was all right if only the paper was chock-full of notes.

Joseph Haydn, quoted in Hughes, *Haydn* (1970)

16 Perhaps it may turn out a sang,
Perhaps turn out a sermon.

Robert Burns, 'Epistle to a Young Friend' (1786)

17 In order to be a great composer, one needs an enormous amount of knowledge, which . . . one does not acquire from listening only to other people's work, but even more from listening to one's own.

Fryderyk Chopin, Letter to Joseph Eisner, 1831

18 The distractions and unsettled nature of the virtuoso life are opposed to and injure lofty research and productiveness, which require happiness and complete isolation from the world.

Robert Schumann, in *Neue Zeitschrift*

19 Among all artists, travel is the least profitable for musicians. Our great composers always

have dwelt quietly in one and the same place, for example, Bach, Haydn, Beethoven, although a view of the Alps or of Sicily might not have harmed them.

Robert Schumann, *Collected Writings* (pub. 1891)

1   Consider it well: each tone of our scale in itself
        is nought;
    It is everywhere in the world — loud, soft, and
        all is said:
    Give it to me to use! I mix it with two in my
        thought:
    And, there! Ye have heard and seen: consider
        and bow the head!

Robert Browning, 'Abt Vogler'

2   To have a lovely thought is nothing so remarkable. A thought comes of itself and if it is fine and great it is not our merit. But to carry out a thought well and make something great of it, that is the most difficult thing, that is, in fact — art!

Antonín Dvořák, quoted in Šourek (ed.), *Antonín Dvořák: Letters and Reminiscences* (1954)

3   A beginner must not think about originality: if he has it in his nature, it will come out. Let the imagination run, and criticise it for *yourself*, after it has its fling.

Charles Villiers Stanford, quoted in Holst, *Holst* (1974)

4   Every German military bandmaster knows, but . . . unfortunately artist-composers don't know, the difference between [instrumental] virtuoso-difficulties and impossibilities.

Nikolay Rimsky-Korsakov, quoted in Abraham, *Rimsky-Korsakov* (1945)

5   I like to look on the composer's vocation as the old troubadours or bards did. In those days it was no disgrace to a man to be turned on to step in front of an army and inspire the people with a song.

Edward Elgar, quoted in *The Strand Magazine*, 1904

6   It is the best of trades, to make songs, and the second best to sing them.

Hilaire Belloc, *On Everything* (1909)

7   What distinguishes genius from talent is condensation, which is related to brevity, but not identical with it.

Alfred Einstein, *Greatness in Music* (trans. 1941)

8   The belief in technique as the only means of salvation must be suppressed, the striving toward truth furthered.

Arnold Schoenberg, 'Problem of Art Instruction' (1911)

9   [Of repetition]. Never do what a copyist can do!

Arnold Schoenberg, quoted in Machlis, *Introduction to Contemporary Music* (1963)

10 The mark of genius is the ability to complete a whole work rapidly.

Arnold Schoenberg, remark to Peter Yates, quoted in Yates, *Twentieth Century Music* (1968)

11 When I'm composing, I feel just like a mathematician.

Gustav Holst, quoted in Holst, *Holst* (1974)

12 Do not take up music unless you would rather die than not do so.

Nadia Boulanger, quoted in Kendall, *The Tender Tyrant: Nadia Boulanger* (1976)

13 *Il faut savoir ce qu'on veut.* You must know what you want.

Nadia Boulanger, advice to young composers, quoted in Kendall, *The Tender Tyrant: Nadia Boulanger* (1976)

14 To be a composer and not a musician is a tragedy; it is to have genius and not talent.

Nadia Boulanger, quoted in Kendall, *The Tender Tyrant: Nadia Boulanger* (1976)

15 Music, as long as it exists, will always take its departure from the major triad and return to it. The musician cannot escape it any more than the painter his primary colours or the architect his three dimensions.

Paul Hindemith, *The Craft of Musical Composition* (1937)

16 The initiated know that most of the music that is produced every day represents everything except the composer: memory, cheap compilation, mental indolence, habit, imitation, and above all the obstinacy of the tones themselves.

Paul Hindemith, *The Craft of Musical Composition* (1937)

17 Composition is like a big arch: it begins with unconsciously inventing and then adding technique, and then forgetting technique and inventing consciously, developing the technique almost unconsciously.

Paul Hindemith, quoted in Skelton, *Paul Hindemith* (1975)

18 As a man grows more mature, it seems that he has a greater longing to be more economical with his means, in order to achieve simplicity.

Béla Bartók, interview in *The Etude*, 1941

19 We have a duty towards music, namely, to invent it . . . Invention presupposes imagination but should not be confused with it. For the act of invention implies the necessity of a lucky find and of achieving full realisation of this find.

Igor Stravinsky, *Poetics of Music* (1947)

20 The material of music is sound and silence. Integrating these is composing.

John Cage, *Silence* (1961), 'Forerunners of Modern Music' (1949)

1 The contemporary composer is ... a sort of intruder who persists in stubbornly trying to impose himself at a banquet to which he has not been invited.

Arthur Honegger, *I am a Composer* (1951)

2 It is clear that the first specification for a composer is to be dead.

Arthur Honegger, *I am a Composer* (1951)

3 Composing is not a profession. It is a mania — a harmless madness.

Arthur Honegger, *I am a Composer* (1951)

4 There are composers who write difficult music with ease, and others who write a facile music with difficulty.

Georges Auric, quoted in Honneger, *I am a Composer* (1951)

5 Form is the balance between tension and relaxation.

Ernst Toch, quoted in Machlis, *Introduction to Contemporary Music* (1963)

6 Composing is a very different thing from writing tunes ... composition *lives* in its development.

Leonard Bernstein, *The Joy of Music* (1960)

7 All the others [painters and poets] translate ...
Only your notes are pure contraption,
Only your song is an absolute gift.

W.H. Auden, 'The Composer'

8 The abundance of technical means allows the heart to expand freely.

Olivier Messiaen, quoted in Shapiro, *An Encyclopedia of Quotations about Music* (1978)

9 I believe that an artist *should* be part of his community, *should* work for it, and be used *by* it. Over the last hundred years this has become rarer and rarer and the artist and community have both suffered as a result.

Benjamin Britten, Speech on acceptance of the Freedom of Aldeburgh, 1962

10 There is no creation save in the unforeseen as it becomes necessity.

Pierre Boulez, quoted in Machlis, *Introduction to Contemporary Music* (1963)

11 Each new piece is the first you have ever written.

Hans Werner Henze, *Music and Politics* (1982), 'Music as a Means of Resistance' (1963)

12 Composers do not often hear the music that is being played; it only serves as an impulse for something quite different — for the creation of music that only lives in their imagination. It is a sort of schizophrenia — we are listening to something and at the same time creating something else.

Witold Lutosławski, quoted in Stucky, *Lutosławski and his Music* (1981)

13 Composition is like writing a letter to a stranger. I don't hear things in my head, nor do I have inspiration. Nor is it right, as some people have said, that because I use chance operations my music is written not by me, but by God. I doubt whether God, say he existed, would take the trouble to write my music.

John Cage, interview in *The Observer Magazine*, 1982

14 There is one question that a composer ought always to ask of the music he is writing: Is this music that I want to hear and that I could not otherwise hear?

Edward Cone, quoted in Ewen, *American Composers* (1982)

15 A composer should be able to use what he knows about music in an instinctive manner, flying by the seat of his pants.

Donald Erb, quoted in Ewen, *American Composers* (1982)

16 Composing is fun because it makes things happen.

Andrew Welsh Imbrie, quoted in Ewen, *American Composers* (1982)

THE CONCERTO

17 The conductor's job in the presentation of a concerto may be likened to that of a driver of a team of horses which is drawing a single chariot (or any other vehicle, from a chariot to a hearse to a dustbin, according to who has composed the music).

Neville Cardus, in *The Manchester Guardian*, 1938

18 *Cadenza:* The orchestra's favourite part of a solo concerto, when they can get on with reading *Playboy*, *Autocar*, etc. while the soloist sweats it out alone ... Traditionally [cadenzas] would end with a prolonged trill, the nearest musical equivalent to an alarm-clock, its purpose being to rouse the orchestra from slumber — the ones who have nothing to read, that is.

Antony Hopkins, *Downbeat Music Guide* (1977)

CONCERTS

See also APPLAUSE, AUDIENCE.

19 A concert of music in a banquet of wine is as a signet of carbuncle set in gold. As a signet of an emerald set in a work of gold, so is the melody of music with pleasant wine.

Ecclesiasticus 32:5-6

20 *Wilding:* I am a great admirer —
Friendall: Of everything in petticoats.
Wilding: Of these musical entertainments; I am very musical, and love any call that brings the women together.

Thomas Southerne, *The Wives' Excuse* (1691)

1   The lewd trebles squeak nothing but bawdy,
    and the basses roar blasphemy.

    William Congreve, *The Way of the World*, V.v, (1700),
    referring to 'profane music-meetings'

2   Mr Arne ... intends, between the acts of his
    serenatas, operas, and other musical
    performances, to intermix comic interludes ...
    intended to give relief to that grave attention
    necessary to be kept up in serious
    performances.

    Dublin newspaper announcement, quoted in *The
    Musical Antiquary*, 1910

3   [Of the public concerts in York Buildings,
    London] Now a consort, then a lutenist, then a
    violino solo, then flutes, then a song, and so
    piece after piece, the time sliding away, while
    the masters blundered and swore in shifting
    places, and one might perceive that they
    performed ill out of spite to one another.

    Roger North, *Memoirs of Musick* (pub. 1846)

4   Of the ladies that sparkle at a musical
    performance, a very small number has any
    quick sensibility of harmonious sounds. But
    every one that goes has the pleasure of being
    supposed to be pleased with a refined
    amusement, and of hoping to be numbered
    among the votaresses of harmony.

    Samuel Johnson, *The Idler*, 1758

5   Nor cold, nor stern, my soul! Yet I detest
       These scented rooms, where to a gaudy
          throng,
    Heaves the proud harlot her distended breast
       In intricacies of laborious song.

    Samuel Taylor Coleridge, 'Lines composed in a
    Concert-Room'

6   Because I have no ear for music, at the Concert
    of the Quintette Club, it looked to me as if the
    performers were crazy, and all the audience
    were making-believe crazy, in order to soothe
    the lunatics and keep them amused.

    Ralph Waldo Emerson, Journal, 1861

7   [Sign over a piano] Please do not shoot the
    pianist. He is doing his best.

    Oscar Wilde, *Impressions of America* (1883)

8   If one hears bad music, it is one's duty to
    drown it by one's conversation.

    Oscar Wilde, *The Picture of Dorian Gray* (1891)

9   I paid a shilling for my programme. The editor
    informs me with the law of libel in its present
    unsatisfactory condition, I must not call this a
    fraud, a cheat, a swindle, an imposition, an
    exorbitance, or even an overcharge.

    George Bernard Shaw, quoted in Graf, *Composer and
    Critic* (1947)

10 To know whether you are enjoying a piece of
    music or not you must see whether you find

yourself looking at the advertisements of Pears'
soap at the end of the programme.

Samuel Butler, *Note-Books* (1912)

11 Music should either be done in a church or in
    someone's home.

    Gustav Holst, quoted in Holst, *Holst* (1974)

12 Man and boy we have all been going to the
    Hallé concerts these many years (and man and
    boy we have all been listening to the same
    music).

    Neville Cardus, in *The Manchester Gardian*, 1938

13 The great tragedy of our age: the more
    numerous the concerts, the less music is
    understood.

    Arthur Honegger, *I am a Composer* (1951)

14 No one any longer listens to 'music'; they come
    to view the performance of a famous conductor
    or a celebrated pianist. And that, as we know,
    comes nearer the domain of sport than art.

    Arthur Honegger, *I am a Composer* (1951)

CONDUCTING

15 There are no good or bad orchestras, only good
    and bad conductors.

    Oral tradition

16 The baton makes no sound.

    Oral tradition

17 The more time is beaten the less it is kept; and
    it is certain that when the measure is broken,
    the fury of the musical general, or director,
    increasing with the disorder and confusion of
    his troops, he becomes more violent, and his
    strokes and gesticulations more ridiculous in
    proportion to their disorder.

    Jean-Jaques Rousseau, attr. by Burney

18 The real task of the conductor consists, in my
    opinion, in making himself ostensibly quasi-
    useless. We are pilots, not drillmasters.

    Franz Liszt, 'A Letter on Conducting' (1853)

19 The conductor is nothing more than the driver
    of the coach engaged by the composer. He
    should stop at every request or quicken the
    pace according to the fare's orders. Otherwise
    the composer is entitled to get out and complete
    the journey on foot.

    Charles Gounod, quoted in Harding, *Gounod* (1973)

20 You must have the score in your head, not your
    head in the score.

    Hans von Bülow, remark to Richard Strauss, quoted in
    Schönberg, *The Great Conductors* (1967)

21 Conducting is a black art.

    Nikolay Rimsky-Korsakov, *Chronicles of My Musical
    Life* (1909)

1   It's easy. All you have to do is waggle a stick.
    Sir Thomas Beecham, remark to his 10-year-old sister,
    quoted in Reid, *Thomas Beecham* (1961)

2   Never let the horns and woodwinds out of your
    sight; if you can hear them at all, they are too
    loud.
    Richard Strauss, 'Ten Golden Rules Inscribed in the
    Album of a Young Conductor' (1927)

3   You must not perspire while conducting; only
    the public must get warm.
    Richard Strauss, 'Ten Golden Rules Inscribed in the
    Album of a Young Conductor' (1927)

4   It is the most wonderful of all sensations that
    any man can conceive. It really oughtn't to be
    allowed.
    Eugene Goossens, quoted in Nichols, *Are They the
    Same at Home?* (1927)

5   The baton is always in C major.
    José Iturbi, quoted in Gattey, *Peacocks on the Podium*
    (1982)

6   The secret of a persuasive manner is an
    elasticity of control, so exercised as to give the
    impression that the iron bonds of rhythm are
    never for a moment seriously loosened.
    Sir Thomas Beecham, *A Mingled Chime* (1944)

7   For a fine performance only two things are
    necessary: the maximum of virility coupled
    with the maximum of delicacy.
    Sir Thomas Beecham, quoted in Atkins and Newman,
    Beecham Stories (1978)

8   Now you take a symphony, something by
    Britten, and put it in the hands of some old cat
    with no finesse, and you get the worst noise
    you ever heard.
    Duke Ellington, quoted in Jewell, *Duke* (1977)

9   He should rely on gestures more than words. It
    often happens that a conductor begins to talk
    when gestures fail him, and then becomes
    accustomed to his own chatter.
    Nikolai Malko, *A Certain Art* (1966)

10 When you get lost, and you will, everybody
    does at one time or other, just make some
    elegant vague motion and we'll put it all to
    rights quickly enough.
    Barry Tuckwell, remark to André Previn, quoted in
    Gattey, *Peacocks on the Podium* (1982)

11 Today, conducting is a question of ego: a lot of
    people believe they are actually playing the
    music.
    Daniel Barenboim, in 1968, quoted in Jacobson,
    Reverberations (1975)

12 The listener is only a reflection of the orchestra
    and a work in performance is built like a
    telescope. The focus is the work, and a
    conjunction of mirrors is used to magnify —
    first the conductor is mirrored by the orchestra,
    then the orchestra is mirrored by the audience.
    Pierre Boulez, in 1969, quoted in Jacobson,
    Reverberations (1975)

13 'Great' conductors, like 'great' actors, soon
    become unable to play anything but
    themselves.
    Igor Stravinsky, *Themes and Conclusions* (1972)

14 Conducting is semaphoring, after all.
    Igor Stravinsky, *Themes and Conclusions* (1972)

15 Conductors are still the lapdogs of musical life.
    Igor Stravinsky, *Themes and Conclusions* (1972)

16 In the performance you have to *be* the
    composer: 'This is *my* music, part of my body
    — it belongs to *me*.'
    Carlo Maria Giulini, quoted in Jacobson,
    Reverberations (1975)

17 No wise conductor tries to outdo that bunch of
    professional comics which is the average
    symphony orchestra.
    Jack Brymer, *From Where I Sit* (1979)

18 Why is anyone who adopts successfully this
    strange form of extroversion regarded instantly
    as being of so much greater moment than he
    was last week, when he was just a player?
    Jack Brymer, *From Where I Sit* (1979)

CONDUCTORS

19 You're singing about Angels and Archangels,
    not Gold Flake and Players.
    Sir John Barbirolli, remark to chorus, quoted in
    Kennedy, *Barbirolli, Conductor Laureate* (1971)

20 You're not bank clerks on a Sunday outing,
    you're souls sizzling in hell.
    Sir John Barbirolli, remark to chorus, quoted in
    Kennedy, *Barbirolli, Conductor Laureate* (1971)

21 Hark! the herald angels sing!
    Beecham's pills are just the thing.
    Two for a woman, one for a child . . .
    Peace on Earth and mercy mild!
    Sir Thomas Beecham, quoted in Atkins and Newman,
    Beecham Stories (1978)

22 [Of the Royal Philharmonic Orchestra] I have
    the finest players in England. They are so good
    that they refuse to play under anybody except
    me.
    Sir Thomas Beecham, in 1946, quoted in Reid, *Thomas
    Beecham* (1961)

23 [To a tenor singing Walther in *The
    Mastersingers*] Observing your grave, deliberate
    motion, I was reminded, Mr ——, of that
    estimable quadruped, the hedgehog.
    Sir Thomas Beecham, quoted in Reid, *Thomas Beecham*
    (1961)

1   *Fritz Reiner:* I wanted to thank you for a
    wonderful night with Mozart and Beecham.
    Beecham: Why drag in Mozart?

    Quoted in Reid, *Thomas Beecham* (1961)

2   I am not the greatest conductor in this country.
    On the other hand I'm better than any damned
    foreigner.

    Sir Thomas Beecham, quoted in Atkins and Newman,
    Beecham Stories (1978)

3   At a rehearsal I let the orchestra play as they
    like. At the concert I make them play as *I* like.

    Sir Thomas Beecham, quoted in Cardus, *Sir Thomas
    Beecham* (1961)

4   [On hearing his 70th birthday telegrams]
    Nothing from Mozart?

    Sir Thomas Beecham, quoted in Cardus, *Sir Thomas
    Beecham* (1961)

5   [On hearing Beecham conduct *Petrushka*]
    *Comme l'orchestre dirige bien Monsieur Beecham çe
    soir.* How well the orchestra conducts Mr
    Beecham tonight.

    Vaslav Nijinsky, quoted in Reid, *Thomas Beecham*
    (1961)

6   There are some people who slap you in the face
    and ask for half a crown. Sir Thomas slaps you
    in the face and asks for a five pound note.

    Sir Hugh Allen, then Director of the Royal College of
    Music, quoted in Reid, *Thomas Beecham* (1961)

7   On one occasion he [Beecham] achieved the
    best square-cut I have seen since Macartney
    retired. But he should try to get nearer to the
    ball and over it, while making his leg-glance.

    Neville Cardus, in *The Manchester Guardian*, 1938

8   [Of Beecham] Any guy who can turn up fifteen
    minutes late for an air show sponsored by
    Kellogg's Corn Flakes and just explain on the
    air that he had lost a collar button in the hotel is
    the man for me!

    Unnamed American musician, quoted in Brymer, *From
    Where I Sit* (1979)

9   [Of Beecham] A pompous little duckarsed
    bandmaster who stood against everything
    creative in the art of his time.
    ('G.P.')

    John Fowles, *The Collector* (1963)

10 Beecham was like a man who drinks and
    swears for six days of the week, then goes to
    church and prays with genuine devotion on
    Sunday.

    Colin Wilson, *Brandy of the Damned* (1964)

11 [Of Leonard Bernstein] He uses music as an
    accompaniment to his conducting.

    Oscar Levant, *Memoirs of an Amnesiac* (1965)

12 The only way to land a big job [in music] in the
    United States is to proclaim arrogantly that you

would never stoop to take it.

    Pierre Boulez, quoted in Peyser, *Boulez* (1976)

13 I have always maintained that I as an executant
    am not, and have no right to be, a critic of any
    kind, even to the extent of having preferences
    and favourites. I consider it is my job to make
    the best of whatever is put before me once I
    have agreed to conduct the work. I am often
    asked which is my favourite Beethoven or
    Brahms symphony, and I can only answer that
    my favourite is the one that I am at the moment
    performing, or studying, the one that is
    uppermost in my mind.

    Sir Adrian Boult, *My Own Trumpet* (1973)

14 [Of Karajan] A kind of musical Malcolm
    Sargent.

    Sir Thomas Beecham, quoted in Atkins and Newman,
    Beecham Stories (1978)

15 This is where von Karajan was born. Oh, by the
    way, Mozart was born here too.

    Salzburg oral tradition, quoted in Galway, *An
    Autobiography* (1978)

16 When there is no trouble in a theatre, I make it!

    Erich Kleiber, quoted in Harewood, *The Tongs and the
    Bones* (1981)

17 *Friend:* What a number of distinguished
    conductors have died this year [1954] —
    Clemens Krauss, Wilhelm Fürtwangler, Jasha
    Horenstein . . .
    Klemperer: Ja, it's been a good year, hasn't it?

    Quoted in Gattey, *Peacocks on the Podium* (1982)

18 In my day, Furtwängler and Bruno Walter and
    Kleiber and I *hated* each other. It was more
    healthy.

    Otto Klemperer, quoted in Harewood, *The Tongs and
    the Bones* (1981)

19 Klemperer sat at the piano like an evil spirit,
    thumping on it with long hands like tigers'
    claws, dragging my terrified voice into the fiery
    vortex of his fanatical will.

    Lotte Lehmann, *Wings of Song* (trans. 1938)

20 [Of conducting] The important thing is that one
    should let the orchestra breathe.

    Otto Klemperer, in 1973, quoted in Green, *Dictionary
    of Contemporary Quotations* (1982)

21 Ven my stick touches the air, you play.

    Serge Koussevitzky, quoted in Gattey, *Peacocks on the
    Podium* (1982)

22 [Of Koussevitsky] That Russian boor.

    Arturo Toscanini, attr.

23 [Of Mengelberg] That revolting red Dutchman.

    Paul Hindemith, Letter to Emmy Ronnefeldt, 1917

1 [Of Nikisch] His virtuosity seems to make him forget the claims of good taste.

Claude Debussy, quoted in Bonavia, *Musicians on Music* (1956)

2 I once mentioned Nikisch in one of our conversations, and the maestro [Felix Mottl] immediately said, 'Well, his technique is immense, but here', and he indicated his heart, 'nothing'.

Nikolai Malko, *A Certain Art* (1966)

3 [Of Richter] The generalissimo of deceit.

Anton Bruckner, in 1877, quoted in Watson, *Bruckner* 1975)

4 [Of Richter] For him, all music which was not German was foreign.

Charles Villiers Stanford, *Interludes* (1922)

5 These damned foreign importations! Take Richter. He could conduct five works, no more.

Sir Thomas Beecham, quoted in Reid, *Thomas Beecham* (1961)

6 Some people tell me that they *saw* me conduct somewhere. Apparently they listen with their eyes rather than their ears.

Leopold Stokowski, quoted in Jacobson, *Reverberations* (1975)

7 [Of Stokowski] He is a very fine man I am sure and interested in many things — but not, I think, in music.

Jean Sibelius, quoted in Gattey, *Peacocks on the Podium* (1982)

8 I also went ... to see and hear Stokowski. I use the word 'see', for to watch was to add to the drama of the concert. The whole evening was like a great theatrical production.

Arthur Bliss, *As I Remember* (1970)

9 I love music more than my own convenience. Actually I love it more than myself — but it is vastly more loveable than I.

George Szell, quoted in *Newsweek*, 1963

10 I am a pig.

Arturo Toscanini, remark to Sir John Barbirolli, 1940

11 [During a stormy rehearsal] After I die I am coming back to earth as the doorkeeper of a bordello. And I won't let a one of you in.

Arturo Toscanini, quoted in Lebrecht, *Discord* (1982)

12 [Of Toscanini] It was as though we were listening to music in the teeth of a wind.

Neville Cardus, in *The Manchester Guardian*, 1939

13 [Of a performance of Beethoven's *Pastoral Symphony*] Toscanini took us a country walk, true; but I could not escape the feeling that we must never dally uselessly, and that not far away a resplendent car throbbed as it waited for our return to a more austere environment.

Neville Cardus, in *The Manchester Guardian*, 1939

14 [Of Toscanini] He builds the form of Beethoven consummately, moulds nobly the architecture of the temple; but Oh for some time and place for communion within!

Neville Cardus, in *The Manchester Guardian*, 1939

15 [Of Toscanini] He combined the jealousy of Furtwängler and the vanity of Koussevitzky with the musical insensitivity of neither.

David Wooldridge, *Conductor's World* (1970)

16 [Of Bruno Walter] The end of his baton is like a cradle in which he rocks me.

Lotte Lehmann, quoted in Gattey, *Peacocks on the Podium* (1982)

17 [Of Weingartner] A conscientious gardener.

Claude Debussy, quoted in Gattey, *Peacocks on the Podium* (1982)

18 [Of Weingartner] He is seldom disturbed from a calm physical balance; his laundry-bill probably disappoints those who attend to the weekly linen of most of the other conductors.

Neville Cardus, in *The Manchester Guardian*, 1939

COPLAND

19 The whole problem can be stated quite simply by asking, 'Is there a meaning to music?' My answer to that would be, 'Yes.' And 'Can you state in so many words what the meaning is?' My answer to that would be, 'No.'

Aaron Copland, *What to Listen for in Music* (1939)

20 Music that is born complex is not inherently better or worse than music that is born simple.

Aaron Copland, quoted in Jacobson, *Reverberations* (1975)

21 [Of aiming to appeal to a wider public] I felt that it was worth the effort to see if I couldn't say what I had to say in the simplest possible terms.

Aaron Copland, quoted in Kendall, *The Tender Tyrant* (1976)

22 The melody is generally what the piece is about.

Aaron Copland, attr.

23 [After conducting a performance of Copland's Symphony for Organ and Orchestra] If a young man at the age of twenty-three can write a symphony like that, in five years he will be ready to commit murder.

Walter Damrosch, in 1925, quoted in Machlis, *Introduction to Contemporary Music* (1963)

24 An extremely facile, skilful and sophisticated musician.

Ernst Křenek, *Musik im goldenen Westen* (1949)

CORELLI

1 I never met with any man that suffered his passions to hurry him away so much whilst he was playing on the violin as the famous Arcangelo Corelli, whose eyes will sometimes turn as red as fire.

François Raguenet, *Comparison between the French and Italian Music* (1709)

2 Corelli's excellence consists in the chastity of his composition.

John Gregory, *The State and Faculties of Man* (1766)

THE CORNET

3 What can yield a tone so like an eunuch's voice as a true cornet pipe?

Roger North, *The Musicall Gramarian* (1728)

COUNTERPOINT

4 A canon is a rule showing the purpose of the composer behind a certain obscurity.

Johannes Tinctoris, *Dictionary of Musical Terms* (c. 1475)

5 Pricksong is a fair music ... But to sing to the lute is much better, because all the sweetness consisteth in one alone, and a man is much more heedful and understandeth better the feat manner, and the air or vein of it when ears are not busied in hearing more than one voice.

Baldassare Castiglione, *The Booke of the Courtyer* (1528); trans. Hoby (1561)

6 It would seem a sin to the contrapuntists of today ... if all the parts were heard to beat at the same time with the same notes, with the same syllables of the verse, and with the same longs and shorts; the more they make the parts move, the more artful they think they are.

Giovanni de'Bardi, *Discourse on Ancient Music and Good Singing* (c. 1580)

7 Why cause words to be sung by four or five voices so that they cannot be distinguished, when the Ancients aroused the strongest passions by means of a single voice supported by a lyre? We must renounce counterpoint and different kinds of instruments and return to primitive simplicity.

Vincenzo Galilei, *Dialogo della musica antica e della moderna* (1581)

8 You know that my pretensions to musical taste, are merely a few of Nature's instincts, untaught and untutored by Art. — For this reason, many musical compositions, particularly when much of the merit lies in Counterpoint, however they may transport & ravish the ears of you, connoisseurs, affect my simple lug no otherwise than merely as melodious Din.

Robert Burns, Letter, 1792

9 To make a fugue requires no particular skill ... But the fancy wishes to insert its privileges, and today a new and really poetical element must be introduced into the traditional form.

Ludwig van Beethoven, quoted in Scott, *Beethoven* (1934)

10 So your fugue broadens and thickens,
Greatens and deepens and lengthens,
Till one exclaims — 'But where's the music, the dickens?'

Robert Browning, 'Master Hughes of Saxe-Gotha'

11 Counterpoint can be the nastiest thing in music.

Claude Debussy, Letter to Vasnier, 1885

12 Counterpoint isn't genius, only a means to an end. And it's given me plenty of trouble.

Anton Bruckner, Letter to Franz Bayer, 1893

13 I prophesy that in music melody will triumph over all other compositional techniques: universal polyphony as the end-product of melodic writing, the mother of harmony, and bearer of the idea.

Ferruccio Busoni, Conclusion to his edition of *The Well-Tempered Clavier* (1915)

14 [Of the Paris Conservatory] The wailing notes of sopranos and tenors, the rattling of pianos, the blasts of trumpets and trombones, the arpeggios of clarinets, all uniting to form that ultra-polyphony which some of our composers have tried to attain — but without success.

Camille Saint-Saëns, *Musical Memories* (trans. 1919)

15 Since Bach we have lost the habit of being able to pursue two voices of equal importance; coordination has been replaced by subordination. We concentrate our attention upon notes sounded below one another and are immediately searching for triads if groups of notes are sounded simultaneously. But music, melodious in its essence, is not to be listened to in this way. If we succeed in surveying a larger area with our glance, that is to say, if we hear horizontally, the grating dissonance comes to an end at once.

Zoltán Kodály, in *La Revue musicale* (1921)

16 The whole of life that still remained in him
Dwindled to one sound strumming in his ear,
Ubiquitous concussion, slap and sigh,
Polyphony beyond his baton's thrust.

Wallace Stevens, 'The Comedian as the Letter C' (1924)

17 Counterpoint is my real home.

Igor Stravinsky, quoted in Machlis, *Introduction to Contemporary Music* (1963)

18 *Canon:* ... Not to be confused with the ones required in the 1812 Overture which are spelt differently and which lack contrapuntal interest.

Antony Hopkins, *Downbeat Music Guide* (1977)

1   There is an old saying that fugues are the type of music in which the voices come in one by one while the audience goes out one by one but there is no statistical evidence to support this; audiences have been known to leave in droves.

Antony Hopkins, *Downbeat Music Guide* (1977)

COUNTRY AND WESTERN

2   Them bandits have beat up mah mother, ravished mah girl, burned down mah house, killed mah best friend and stolen mah prize cattle. Ah'm gonna git 'em if'n it's the last thing ah do — but first, folks, ah'm gonna sing ya a little song.

Gene Autry, in probably apocryphal cowboy movie, quoted in Sheldon and Goldblatt, *Country Music Story* (1966)

3   I know all the songs that the cowboys know
'Bout the big corral where the dogies go
'Cos I learned them all from the radio
Yippee Ki O Ki Ay.

Johnny Mercer, 'I'm an Old Cowhand'

4   You got to have smelt a lot of mule manure before you can sing like a hillbilly.

Hank Williams, quoted in *Rolling Stone* (1969)

5   Convicts are the best audiences I ever played for.

Johnny Cash, attr.

6   When people hear that music, they get a feeling that they belong to the music and the music belongs to them.

'Cousin' Minnie Pearl, quoted in Palmer, *All You Need Is Love* (1976)

COUPERIN

7   One might venture to say that in many things music ... has its prose and its poetry.

François Couperin, *L'Art de toucher le clavecin* (1716)

8   I declare in all good faith that I am more pleased with what moves me than with what astonishes me.

François Couperin, *L'Art de toucher le clavecin* (1716)

9   [Of such pieces as 'La Majesteuse', 'L'Auguste', etc.] I have always had one object in composing these pieces; different occasions supplied me with them: in this way the titles match the ideas that I had. I will dispense with giving an account of them. Nevertheless, as, among the titles, there are those which appear to flatter me, it is as well to warn that pieces which carry such titles are of the nature of portraits that I have sometimes found forming themselves beneath my fingers, and that the majority of these conceited titles are rather given to the

admirable originals whom I have wished to represent than to the copies that I have made.

François Couperin, *L'Art de toucher le clavecin* (1716)

10   The Italian style and the French style have for long divided the Republic of Music in France. For my part, I have always valued those works which have merit, without regard for their composer or country of origin.

François Couperin, *Les goûts réunis* (1724)

11   As hardly anyone has composed more than myself ... I hope that my family will find in my wallet something to make them regret my passing.

François Couperin, Preface to *Pièces de clavecin*, Bk. 4 (1730)

COWELL

12   I believe a composer must forge his own forms out of the many influences that play upon him and never close his ears to any part of the world of sound ... For myself I have always wanted to live in the whole world of music.

Henry Cowell, quoted in Ewen, *American Composers* (1982)

CRITICS AND CRITICISM

13   A review, however favourable, can be ridiculous at the same time if the critic lacks average intelligence, as is not seldom the case.

Franz Schubert, Letter, 1825

14   An ear for music is a very different thing from a taste for music. I have no ear for music whatever; I could not sing an air to save my life; but I have the intensest delight in music, and can detect good from bad.

Samuel Taylor Coleridge, *Table-Talk* (1835)

15   [Of bad critics] They ply their saws, and timber and proud oaks are reduced to sawdust.

Robert Schumann, quoted in Graf, *Composer and Critic* (1947)

16   Even the most hard-hearted critic sometimes feels an urge to *praise*.

Robert Schumann, quoted in Walker (ed.), *Robert Schumann: the Man and his Music* (1972)

17   [Of critics] Music sets nightingales to singing of love; it sets pugdogs to yapping.

Robert Schumann, quoted in Graf, *Composer and Critic* (1947)

18   There is so much talk about music, and yet so little is said. For my part, I believe that words do not suffice for such a purpose, and if I found they did suffice I would finally have nothing more to do with music.

Felix Mendelssohn, Letter to Souchay

1 The immoral profession of musical criticism must be abolished.

Richard Wagner, 'Project for Organizing a National Theatre' (1848)

2 [Of critics] Poor devils! Where do they come from? At what age are they sent to the slaughter house? What is done with their bones? Where do such animals pasture in the daytime? Do they have females, and young? How many of them handled the brush before being reduced to the broom?

Hector Berlioz, Les Grotesques de la musique (1859)

3 You regret that the laws do not permit the assassination of certain musicians? But they certainly do permit it, and the divine laws order it ... Try to be in the camp of the assassins; there is no middle way between that and the camp of the victims.

Charles Gounod, Letter to Bizet

4 Never attach too much importance to the judgement of musicians ... They are prejudiced without knowing it, and it blinds them.

Georges Bizet, Letter to Antoine Choudens, 1866

5 When I wish to annihilate, then I do annihilate.

Eduard Hanslick, quoted in Watson, Bruckner (1975)

6 With him [Hanslick] one cannot fight. One can only approach him with petitions.

Anton Bruckner, Letter to J.A. Vergeiner

7 [Refusing to comment on a book about music] In the matter of music, and works dealing with music, I have no faith in my own judgement any more than in that of others. Think of the views expressed by Weber, Schumann or Mendelssohn concerning Rossini, Meyerbeer and others, and tell me whether there is any reason to believe in a composer's opinion.

Giuseppe Verdi, Letter, 1883

8 [Accused of an unjust criticism] No doubt I was unjust; who am I that I should be just?

George Bernard Shaw, quoted in Graf, Composer and Critic (1947)

9 [Of criticism] The most useless occupation in the world.

Giacomo Puccini, attr.

10 Critics love mediocrity.

Giacomo Puccini, attr.

11 The lot of critics is to be remembered by what they failed to understand.

George Moore, Impressions and Opinions (1891)

12 I have hitherto nearly always fared badly with the so-called critics. Where there was sympathy there was no comprehension, and for so-called comprehension without sympathy I do not give a penny.

Edvard Grieg, Letter to Henry T. Finck, 1900

13 Criticism ... too often takes the form of brilliant variations on the theme of: 'You're wrong because you didn't do as I did'; or 'You're talented and I'm not; that can't go on.'

Claude Debussy, in La Revue blanche, 1901

14 Hardly does a composer appear than people start devoting essays to him and weighing his music down with ambitious definitions. They do far greater harm than even the fiercest detractors could do.

Claude Debussy, quoted in Calvocoressi, Musicians' Gallery (1933)

15 [Letter replying to a critic] I am sitting in the smallest room of my house. I have your review before me. In a moment it will be behind me.

Max Reger, quoted in Slonimsky, Lexicon of Musical Invective (1969)

16 She [Zuleika] was one of the people who say: 'I don't know anything about music, but I know what I like.' ... People who say it are never tired of saying it.

Max Beerbohm, Zuleika Dobson (1911)

17 Last year, I gave several lectures on 'Intelligence and Musicality in Animals'. Today, I shall speak to you about 'Intelligence and Musicality in Critics'. The subject is very similar.

Erik Satie, Lecture, 'In Praise of Critics' (1918)

18 Monsier et cher ami:
Vous n'êtes qu'un cul, mais un cul sans musique.
Dear sir and friend, not only are you an arse, you're an unmusical arse.

Erik Satie, Postcard to the critic Jean Poueigh

19 I consider criticism absolutely useless; indeed, I should even say injurious ... Criticism as a rule is the opinion some gentleman or another has of a work. How should such an opinion be of any use to art?

Vincent d'Indy, quoted in Kendall, The Tender Tyrant (1976)

20 Pay no attention to what the critics say; no statue has ever been put up to a critic.

Jean Sibelius, attr.

21 Contemporary judgements are sound enough on Second Bests; but when it comes to Bests, they acclaim ephemerals as immortals, and simultaneously denounce immortals as pestilent charlatans.

George Bernard Shaw, in Music and Letters, 1920

22 The critical faculty is as important, as necessary, as divine, as the imaginative one: it is impossible to overrate the real critic.

Gustav Holst, quoted in Holst, Holst (1974)

23 [Critics] Misbegotten abortions.

Ralph Vaughan Williams, Letter to Holst, 1930

1 The general and musical culture shown in Hanslick's writings represents one of the unlovelier forms of parasitism; that which, having the wealth to collect *objets d'art* and the birth and education to talk amusingly, does not itself attempt a stroke of artistic work, does not dream of revising a first impression, experiences the fine art entirely as the pleasures of a gentleman, and then pronounces judgement as if the expression of its opinion were a benefit and a duty to society.

Donald Tovey, *Essays in Musical Analysis* (1935)

2 Hubermann's playing was possessed; it transcended ordinary violin values. Somebody was heard to remark that the tone here and there became thin. And somebody will get to heaven one day and remark that an angel's halo is not on straight.

Neville Cardus, in *The Manchester Guardian*, 1936

3 Verbal communication about music is impossible except among musicians.

Virgil Thomson, *The State of Music* (1939)

4 Nobody is ever patently right about music.

Virgil Thomson, quoted in Barzun (ed.), *Pleasures of Music* (1977)

5 The trouble with music critics is that so often they have the score in their hands and not in their heads.

Sir Thomas Beecham, quoted in Atkins and Newman, *Beecham Stories* (1978). See 38:21.

6 Please don't call it false modesty if I say that perhaps something was achieved, but that it is not I who deserves the credit. The credit must go to my opponents. It was they who really helped me.

Arnold Schoenberg, quoted in Stuckenschmidt, *Arnold Schoenberg* (1957)

7 I have just read your review of Margaret's concert ... Some day I hope to meet you. When that happens, you'll need a new nose, a lot of beefsteak for black eyes and perhaps a supporter below.

Harry S. Truman, Letter to Paul Hume, music critic of *The Washington Post*, 1950, with reference to Hume's unkind review of Truman's daughter's vocal prowess

8 If a literary man puts together two words about music, one of them will be wrong.

Aaron Copland, quoted in *The Penguin Dictionary of Modern Quotations* (1980)

9 Nothing pleases the composer so much as to have people disagree as to the movements of his piece that they liked best. If there is enough disagreement, it means that everyone liked something best — which is just what the composer wants to hear. The fact that this might include parts that no one liked never seems to matter.

Aaron Copland, quoted in Kendall, *The Tender Tyrant* (1976)

10 There's only two ways to sum up music: either it's good or it's bad. If it's good you don't mess about with it; you just enjoy it.

Louis Armstrong, quoted in Shapiro, *An Encyclopedia of Quotations about Music* (1978)

11 How can we possibly tell what contemporary music is, since now we're not listening to it, we're listening to a lecture about it.

John Cage, *Silence* (1961), 'Communication' (lecture)

12 If the music doesn't say it, how can words *say* it for the music?

John Coltrane, quoted in Hentoff, *Jazz is* (1978)

13 The hardest of all the arts to speak of is music, because music has no meaning to speak of.

Ned Rorem, *Music from Inside Out* (1967)

DANCE

14 A time to weep, and a time to laugh; a time to mourn, and a time to dance.

Ecclesiastes 3:4

15 We have piped unto you, and ye have not danced.

St Matthew 11:17

16 A dance is a measured pace, as a verse is a measured speech.

Francis Bacon, *Advancement of Learning* (1605)

17   Kind are her answers,
But her performance keeps no day;
    Breaks time, as dancers
From their own music when they stray.

Thomas Campion, *Third Book of Airs*

18 He that lives in hope danceth without music.

George Herbert, *Outlandish Proverbs* (1610)

19 Music has charms, we all may find,
Ingratiate deeply with the mind.
When art does sound's high power advance,
To music's pipe the passions dance;
Motions unwill'd its powers have shown,
Tarantulated by a tune.

Matthew Green, *The Spleen* (1737)

20 There's threesome reels, there's foursome reels,
    There's hornpipes and strathspeys, man,
But ae the best dance e'er cam to the Land
    Was, the de'il's awa wi' th'Exciseman.

Robert Burns, 'The De'il's awa wi' th'Exciseman'

21 Imperial waltz; imported from the Rhine
(Famed for the growth of pedigrees and wine)
Long be thine import from all duty free,
And hock itself be less esteem'd than thee.

Lord Byron, 'The Waltz'

1 When Alexander takes his ragtime band to
   France
   He'll capture every Hun, and take them one by
   one.
   Those ragtime tunes will put the Germans in a
   trance;
   They'll throw their guns away, Hip Hooray!
   And start right in to dance.

   Alfred Bryan, Cliff Hess and Edgar Leslie, Rag (c. 1917)

2 Music begins to atrophy when it departs too far
   from the dance ... poetry begins to atrophy
   when it gets too far from music.

   Ezra Pound, *ABC of Reading* (1934), Warning

3 O body swayed to music, O brightening glance,
   How can we know the dancer from the dance?

   W.B. Yeats, 'Among School Children' (1928)

4 Ballet is not a musical form.

   Arnold Schoenberg, quoted in Stravinsky, *Dialogues*
   (1963)

5 Dance, dance, for the figure is easy,
       The tune is catching and will not stop;
   Dance till the stars come down from the rafters;
   Dance, dance, dance till you drop.

   W.H. Auden, 'Death's Echo'

6 At the still point of the turning world. Neither
       flesh nor fleshless;
   Neither from nor towards; at the still point,
       there the dance is,
   But neither arrest nor movement.

   T.S. Eliot, *Four Quartets*, 'Burnt Norton'

7 The trouble with nude dancing is that not
   everything stops when the music stops.

   Robert Helpman, comment on *Oh! Calcutta!*, quoted in
   Fraser, *Collins Concise Dictionary of Quotations* (1983)

DAVID

8 And it came to pass when the evil spirit from
   God was upon Saul that David took up a harp
   and played with his hand; so that Saul was
   refreshed and was well and the evil spirit
   departed from him.

   1 Samuel 16:23

9 David ... the sweet psalmist of Israel.

   2 Samuel 23:1

10 King David and King Solomon
       Led merry, merry lives,
   With many, many lady friends
       And many, many wives;
   But when old age crept over them,
       With many, many qualms,
   King Solomon wrote the Proverbs
       And King David wrote the Psalms.

   James Ball Naylor, 'David and Solomon'

DEATH

11 Is it not fine to dance and sing
   When the bells of death do ring.

   Anon., quoted in Lee, *Music of the People* (1970)

12   Her clothes spread wide,
   And, mermaid-like, awhile they bore her up,
   Which time she chanted snatches of old tunes,
   As one incapable of her own distress.
   (Gertrude, speaking of Ophelia's suicide)

   William Shakespeare, *Hamlet*, IV.vii

13   I will play the swan,
   And die in music.
   (Emilia)

   William Shakespeare, *Othello*, V.ii

14 Cause the musicians play me that sad note
   I named my knell, whilst I sit meditating
   On that celestial harmony I go to.
   (Queen Katharine)

   William Shakespeare, *Henry VIII*, IV.ii

15 Three merry boys, and three merry boys,
   And three merry boys are we,
   As ever did sing in a hempen string
   Under the Gallows-Tree.

   John Fletcher, *The Bloody Brother*, III.ii

16 He [Orpheus] sung, and Hell consented
       To hear the Poet's pray'r;
   Stern Proserpine relented,
       And gave him back the Fair.
           Thus song could prevail
           O'er Death and o'er Hell.

   Alexander Pope, 'Ode for Musick, on St Cecilia's Day'
   (c. 1708)

17 Let me have music dying, and I seek
   No more delight.

   John Keats, *Endymion* (1818)

18 Now more than ever seems it rich to die,
       To cease upon the midnight with no pain,
           While thou art pouring forth thy soul
               abroad
           In such an ecstasy!
       Still wouldst thou sing, and I have ears in
               vain —
       To thy high requiem become a sod.

   John Keats, 'Ode to a Nightingale' (1819)

19 Let me die eating ortolans to the sound of soft
   music!

   Benjamin Disraeli, *The Young Duke* (1831)

20 What is life but a series of preludes to that
   unknown song whose first solemn note is
   sounded by death?

   Franz Liszt, Preface to *Les Préludes* (revised version,
   1854)

21 He is dead, the sweet musician!
   He the sweetest of all singers!
   He has gone from us forever,

He has moved a little nearer
To the Master of all music,
To the Master of all singing!
O my brother, Chibiabos!

Henry Wadsworth Longfellow, *The Song of Hiawatha*
(1855), 'Hiawatha's Lamentation'

1   Art is long, and Time is fleeting,
      And our hearts, though stout and brave,
    Still, like muffled drums, are beating
      Funeral marches to the grave.

Henry Wadsworth Longfellow, 'A Psalm of Life'

2   When I am dead, my dearest,
      Sing no sad songs for me.

Christina Rossetti, Song, 'When I am Dead'

3   But wheesht! — Whatna music is this,
    While the win's haud their breath?
    — *The Moon has a wunnerfu' finger*
    For the back-lill o' Death!

Hugh MacDiarmid, 'Prelude to Moon Music' (1925)
(back-lill — thumb-hole on bagpipe chanter)

4   Now I'll have *eine kleine Pause*.

Kathleen Ferrier, shortly before her death, quoted in
Moore, *Am I Too Loud?* (1962)

5   And at the end I see: the great harmony is
    death. To effect it, we must die. In life it has no
    place.

Paul Hindemith, *Die Harmonie der Welt* (1957)

6   The music is all. People should die for it. People
    are dying for everything else, so why not the
    music?

Lou Reed, quoted in Green, *The Book of Rock Quotes*
(1982)

DEBUSSY

7   [Émile Réty, registrar of the Paris
    Conservatoire] said one day: 'So you imagine
    that dissonant chords do not have to be
    resolved? What rule do you follow?' 'Mon
    plaisir!' Debussy replied.

Quoted in *La Revue musicale*, 1962; often quoted as 'My
rule is what I like.'

8   [On winning the Prix de Rome] All my pleasure
    vanished. I saw in a flash the boredom, the
    vexations inevitably incident to the slightest
    official recognition. Besides, I felt I was no
    longer free.

Claude Debussy, *Monsieur Croche, antidilettante* (1921)

9   I don't know if I'm big enough to do what I
    have in mind.

Claude Debussy, Letter to Vasnier, 1885

10 The colour of my soul is iron-grey and sad bats
    wheel about the steeple of my dreams.

Claude Debussy, Letter to Chausson, 1894

11 I wish to write down my musical dreams in a
    spirit of utter self-detachment. I wish to sing of
    my interior visions with the naïve candour of a
    child.

Claude Debussy, quoted in Vallas, *Debussy* (1926)

12 Any sounds in any combination and in any
    succession are henceforth free to be used in a
    musical continuity.

Claude Debussy, quoted in Cage, *Silence* (1961)

13 A century of aeroplanes deserves its own
    music. As there are no precedents, I must create
    anew.

Claude Debussy, in *La Revue S.I.M.*, 1913

14 I am just an old romantic, who has chucked all
    desire for success out of the window.

Claude Debussy, quoted in Lockspeiser, *Debussy*
(1963)

15 Claude Debussy, if he's not making music, has
    no reason for existing.

Claude Debussy, Letter to Jacques Durand, during
World War I

16 [Of Debussy as a student] He doesn't like the
    piano much, but he does like music.

Antoine-François Marmontel, quoted in Lockspeiser,
Debussy (1963)

17 [Of Debussy's music] *C'est de la musique sur les
    pointes d'aiguilles.* It's music on the points of
    needles.

César Franck, quoted in Lockspeiser, *Debussy* (1963)

18 *Sylvain d'haleine première,*
      Si ta flûte a réussi
    Ouïs toute lumière
      Qu'y soufflera Debussy.
    [literally] Sylvan creature of the first breath, if
    your flute has succeeded, hearken to all light
    which Debussy will breath into it.

Stéphane Mallarmé, lines written on a copy of
Debussy's *Prélude à l'après-midi d'un faune*

19 *Je deviendrais vite aphone,*
      Si j'allais en étourdi
    M'égosiller comme un faune
      Fêtant son après-midi.
    I would soon lose my voice if I went round
    roaring vacuously like a faun celebrating its
    afternoon.

Camille Saint-Saëns, *Rimes familières*, referring to
Debussy's *Prélude à l'après-midi d'un faune*

20 [Of *Prélude à l'après-midi d'un faune*] It is like a
    beautiful sunset; it fades as one looks at it.

Ferruccio Busoni, quoted in Lockspeiser, *Debussy*
(1963)

21 If that was music, I have never understood
    what music was.

Gabriel Fauré, after the premier of Debussy's *Pelléas et
Mélisande*, 1902, quoted in Orledge, *Gabriel Fauré*
(1979)

1 [Of Debussy's music] Better not listen to it; you risk getting used to it, and then you would end by liking it.

Nikolay Rimsky-Korsakov, quoted in Stravinsky, *Chronicles of my Life* (1936)

2 [Of *La Mer*] By dint of looking through the end of his lorgnette, Debussy gives us the impression not of the ocean but of the basin at the Tuileries Gardens ... The audience seemed rather disappointed; they expected the ocean, something big, something colossal, but they were served instead some agitated water in a saucer.

Louis Schneider, in *Gil Blas*, 1905

3 [Of *La Mer*] For perfect enjoyment of this music there is no attitude of mind more to be recommended than the passive, unintelligent rumination of the typical amateur of the mid-Victorian era.

The Times, 1908

4 This great painter of dreams.

Romain Rolland, quoted in Machlis, *Introduction to Contemporary Music* (1963)

5 Debussy has always remained my favourite composer after Mozart. I could not do without his music. It is my oxygen.

Francis Poulenc, quoted in Bernac, *Francis Poulenc* (1977)

6 Stravinsky scared the daylights out of Claude Debussy.

Virgil Thomson, quoted in Stravinsky, *Themes and Conclusions* (1972)

DEFINITIONS OF MUSIC

7 Mathematics is music for the mind; music is mathematics for the soul.

Anon., quoted in Shapiro, *An Encyclopedia of Quotations about Music* (1978)

8   *O laborum*
Dulce lenimen medicumque.
O sweet and healing balm of troubles.

Horace, *Odes*, I, 32

9 ... the most liberal art, and the noblest among the mathematical arts, namely divine music.

Johannes Tinctoris, Dedication to *Dictionary of Musical Terms* (c. 1475)

10 Music is made up of a large number of individual sounds, and is either a single melody or a partsong.

Johannes Tinctoris, *Dictionary of Musical Terms* (c. 1475)

11 Music is that skill consisting of performance in singing and playing, and it is threefold, namely harmonic, organal, and rhythmical. Harmonic music is that which is performed by the human voice. Organal music is that which is made by instruments which produce sound by wind. Rhythmical music is that which is made by instruments which render the sound by touch.

Johannes Tinctoris, *Dictionary of Musical Terms* (. 1475)

12 Music is the medicine of a troubled mind.

Walter Haddon, *Lucubrationes Poemata* (1567), 'Musica'

13 Plato defines melody to consist of harmony, number and words: harmony naked of itself, words the ornament of harmony, number the common friend and uniter of them both.

John Dowland, *The First Booke of Songes* (1597)

14 Nor is he a stranger to poetry, which is music in words; nor to music, which is poetry in sound.

Thomas Fuller, *The Holy State* (1642)

15 Music is nothing else but wild sounds civilised into time and tune.

Thomas Fuller, *History of the Worthies of England* (1662), 'Musicians'

16 Music is a kind of counting performed by the mind without knowing that it is counting.

G.W. Leibniz, *The Monadology* (1714)

17 MUSIC is an innocent luxury, unnecessary, indeed, to our existence, but a great improvement and gratification of the sense of hearing. It consists, at present, of MELODY, TIME, CONSONANCE, and DISSONANCE.

Charles Burney, *A General History of Music* (1776-89)

18 A method of employing the mind without the labour of thinking at all.

Samuel Johnson, quoted by Boswell, *Journal of a Tour to the Hebrides* (1785)

19 It is the only sensual pleasure without vice.

Samuel Johnson, quoted in Hawkins, *Johnsoniana* (1787)

20 Music is the moonlight in the gloomy night of life.

Jean Paul, *Titan* (1800-3)

21 Music ... is an invisible dance, as dancing is silent music.

Jean Paul, *Levana* (1807)

22 Music is the one incorporeal entrance into the higher world of knowledge which comprehends mankind but which mankind cannot comprehend.

Ludwig van Beethoven, quoted by Bettina von Arnim, Letter to Goethe, 1810

23 Music is the occult metaphysical exercise of a soul not knowing that it philosophises.

Arthur Schopenhauer, quoted in Shapiro, *An Encyclopedia of Quotations about Music* (1978)

24 Music is a sublime art precisely because, unable to imitate reality, it rises above ordinary nature

into an ideal world, and with celestial harmony moves the earthly passions.

Gioacchino Rossini, quoted in Zanolini, *Biografia di Gioacchino Rossini* (1875)

1   The only reality in music is the state of mind which it induces in the listener.

Stendhal, *Life of Rossini* (1824)

2   A distinguished philosopher spoke of architecture as *frozen* music, and his assertion caused many to shake their heads. We believe this really beautiful idea could not be better reintroduced than by calling architecture *silent* music.

Johann Wolfgang von Goethe, *Conversations with Eckermann* (1827)

3   Music is something innate and internal, which needs little nourishment from without, and no experience drawn from life.

Johann Wolfgang von Goethe, Letter, 1831

4   Who is there that, in logical words, can express the effect music has on us? A kind of inarticulate unfathomable speech, which leads us to the edge of the Infinite and lets us for moments gaze into that.

Thomas Carlyle, *On Heroes, Hero-Worship, and the Heroic in History* (1841)

5   Music is well said to be the speech of angels.

Thomas Carlyle, 'The Opera'

6   Music is the crystallisation of sound.

Henry David Thoreau, Journal, 1841

7   Music means itself.

Eduard Hanslick, *The Beautiful in Music* (1854)

8   All music is what awakes from you when you are reminded by the instruments,
It is not the violins and the cornets, it is not the oboe nor the beating drums, nor the score of the baritone singer singing his sweet romanza, nor that of the men's chorus, nor that of the women's chorus.
It is nearer and farther than they.

Walt Whitman, 'A Song for Occupations'

9   Music is the poor man's Parnassus.

Ralph Waldo Emerson, *Letters and Social Aims* (1876), 'Poetry and Imagination'

10   Music is another planet.

Alphonse Daudet, quoted in Mencken, *Dictionary of Quotations* (1942)

11   Music is not a science any more than poetry is. It is a sublime instinct, like genius of all kinds.

Ouida, quoted in Shapiro, *An Encyclopedia of Quotations about Music* (1978)

12   Music tells no truths.

P.J. Bailey, *Festus* (1889)

13   A quality
Which music sometimes has, being the Art
Which is most nigh to tears and memory.

Oscar Wilde, 'The Burden of Itys'

14   Music is the arithmetic of sounds as optics is the geometry of light.

Claude Debussy, quoted in *The Penguin Dictionary of Modern Quotations* (1980)

15   What most people relish is hardly music; it is rather a drowsy reverie relieved by nervous thrills.

George Santayana, *Life of Reason* (1905-6)

16   Music is the art of thinking with sounds.

Jules Combarieu, quoted in Dent, *Mozart's Operas* (1913)

17   Music, being identical with heaven, isn't a thing of momentary thrills ... It's a condition of eternity.

Gustav Holst, Letter to W.G. Whittaker, 1914

18   Music is another lady that talks charmingly and says nothing.

Austin O'Malley, *Keystones of Thought* (1914)

19   Music is a sort of dream architecture which passes in filmy clouds and disappears into nothingness.

Percy Scholes, *The Listener's Guide to Music* (1919)

20   Music — that no one knows what it is — and the less he knows he knows what it is the nearer it is to music — probably

Charles Ives, 'Epitaph for David Twichell' (1924)

21   Music? It is the half-articulate art, the dubious, the irresponsible, the insensible. (Settembrini)

Thomas Mann, *The Magic Mountain* (1924)

22   Music is natural law as related to the sense of hearing.

Anton von Webern, *The Path to the New Music* (pub. 1960)

23   Servant and master am I: servant of those dead, and master of those living. Through my spirit immortals speak the message that makes the world weep and laugh, and wonder and worship ... For I am the instrument of God. I am Music.

Unknown, spoken by Walter Damrosch, and quoted in *The International Musician*, 1928

24   How can music ever be a mere intellectual speculation or a series of curious combinations of sound that can be classified like the articles of a grocer's shop? Music is an outburst of the soul.

Frederick Delius, quoted in Fenby, *Delius as I knew him* (1936)

1   Music
Which can be made anywhere, is invisible,
And does not smell.

W.H. Auden, 'In Praise of Limestone'

2   All music is nothing more than a succession of
impulses that converge towards a definite point
of repose.

Igor Stravinsky, quoted in Machlis, *Introduction to
Contemporary Music* (1963)

3   If this word 'music' is sacred and reserved for
eighteenth and nineteenth-century instruments,
we can substitute a more meaningful term:
organisation of sound.

John Cage, *Silence* (1961), 'The Future of Music: Credo'
(1937)

4   The plain fact is that music *per se* means
nothing; it is sheer sound.

Sir Thomas Beecham, *A Mingled Chime* (1944)

5   Music is a beautiful opiate, if you don't take it
too seriously.

Henry Miller, *The Air-Conditioned Nightmare* (1945)

6   'It's a Rum Go!'

Ralph Vaughan Williams, on being asked what he
thought about music, quoted in Wintle and Kenin, *The
Dictionary of Biographical Quotations* (1978)

7   Music turns the equivocal into a system.
(Leverkühn)

Thomas Mann, *Doctor Faustus* (1947); trans. Lowe-
Porter

8   Music has always seemed to me personally a
magic marriage between theology and the so
diverting mathematic.
(Leverkühn)

Thomas Mann, *Doctor Faustus* (1947); trans. Lowe-
Porter

9   A gay modulating anguish, rather like music.

Christopher Fry, *The Lady's Not For Burning* (1948)

10   Geometry in time.

Arthur Honegger, *I am a Composer* (1951)

11   I want the musical work not to be that series of
compartments which one must inevitably visit
one after the other. I try to think of it as a
domain in which, in some manner, one can
choose one's own direction.

Pierre Boulez, in *La nouvelle revue française*, 1954

12   Music . . . is as far from being abstract as is a
language, a death, a love. The mere fact that it
is endlessly invented, wrested from the
material, that through it something is snatched
from fleeting time as it rushes by, that
something is preserved, that in the
concretisation of time a longing is expressed
and fulfilled — all this prohibits the use of the
word 'abstract'.

Hans Werner Henze, *Music and Politics* (1982), 'Signs' (1955)

13   Music is the best means we have of digesting
time.

W.H. Auden, quoted in Craft, *Stravinsky: Chronicle of a
Friendship* (1972)

14   Music is a complex of activities, ideas and
objects that are patterned into culturally
meaningful sounds recognised to exist on a
level different from secular communication.

Anon., quoted in Merriam, *The Anthropology of Music*
(1964)

15   In its urgency to become sound, in its haste to
come into the world, to make itself manifest,
music by its very nature tends to make
manifestos superfluous.

Hans Werner Henze, *Music and Politics* (1982), 'Music
as a Means of Resistance' (1963)

16   Music is a fluid architecture of sound.

Roy Ellsworth Harris, quoted in Ewen, *American
Composers* (1982)

17   Music is a safe kind of high.

Jimi Hendrix, quoted in Green, *The Book of Rock Quotes*
(1982)

18   A piece of music is simply a chunk of time you
are paying attention to with your ears.

Barney Sanford Childs, quoted in Ewen, *American
Composers* (1982)

19   Music is work.

John Cage, *Empty Words* (1980)

20   Music is . . . well I *know* it's better than working
in Ford's.

Ian Dury, quoted in Green, *The Book of Rock Quotes*
(1982)

21   You just pick a chord, go twang, and you've got
music.

Sid Vicious, quoted in Green, *The Book of Rock Quotes*
(1982)

DELIUS

22   It is only that which cannot be expressed
otherwise that is worth expressing in music.

Frederick Delius, 'At the Crossroads' (1920)

23   So long as I can enjoy the taste of my food and
drink and hear the sound of my music, I want
to live . . . I have seen the best of the earth and
done everything that is worth doing.

Frederick Delius, quoted in Fenby, *Delius as I knew him*
(1936)

24   You'll never convince me that music will be any
good until it gets rid of the Jesus element. It has
paralysed music all along.

Frederick Delius, quoted in Fenby, *Delius as I knew him*
(1936)

25   There is only one real happiness in life, and that
is the happiness of creating.

Frederick Delius, quoted in Fenby, *Delius as I knew him*
(1936)

1   One can't define form in so many words, but if
    I was asked I should say that it was nothing
    more than imparting spiritual unity to one's
    thought.

    Frederick Delius, quoted in Fenby, *Delius as I knew him*
    (1936)

2   Music to rock the convalescents of the rich
    neighbourhoods.

    Claude Debussy, quoted in Lockspeiser, *Debussy*
    (1963)

3   I never dreamt that anyone except myself was
    writing such good music.

    Richard Strauss, quoted in Redwood (ed.) *An Elgar
    Companion* (1976)

4   'What is flying like?' he [Delius] asked. 'Well,' I
    answered, 'to put it poetically, it is not unlike
    your life and my life. The rising from the
    ground was a little difficult . . . When once you
    have reached the height it is very different.
    There is a delightful feeling of elation in sailing
    through gold and silver clouds. It is, Delius,
    rather like your music — a little intangible
    sometimes, but always very beautiful. I should
    have liked to stay there for ever. The descent is
    like our old age — peaceful, even serene.'

    Edward Elgar, in *The Daily Telegraph*, 1933

5   [Of Delius's *Appalachia*] What should have been
    evident at first hearing was the remotely alien
    sound of it, a note in English music stranger
    than any heard for over two hundred years.

    Sir Thomas Beecham, *A Mingled Chime* (1944)

6   His entire philosophy of life was based upon an
    ultra-Nietzschean conception of the individual
    . . . This, of course, means that Frederick from
    the Anglo-Saxon point of view must be
    reckoned a supreme and complete egoist, and
    such he was, unquestionably.

    Sir Thomas Beecham, *A Mingled Chime* (1944)

7   In Delius the apples of decadence have turned
    slightly more rotten.

    Colin Wilson, *Brandy of the Damned* (1964)

8   The musical equivalent of blancmange.

    Bernard Levin, *Enthusiasms* (1983)

DISEASE

9   The sound of the flute will cure epilepsy and
    sciatic gout.

    Theophrastus

10 Ismenias the Theban, when the torments of
    sciatica were troubling a number of Boeotians,
    is reported to have rid them of all their
    afflictions by his melodies.

    Boethius, *De Institutione Musica*

11 And I, of ladies most deject and wretched,
    That sucked the honey of his music vows,

Now see that noble and most sovereign reason,
Like sweet bells jangled, out of tune and harsh.
(Ophelia)

William Shakespeare, *Hamlet*, III.i

12 Theophrastus right well prophesied, that
    diseases were either procured by music, or
    mitigated.

    Robert Burton, *Anatomy of Melancholy* (1621)

13 Many times the sound of a trumpet on a
    sudden, bells ringing, a carman's whistle, a boy
    singing some ballad tune early in the street,
    alters, revives, recreates a restless patient that
    cannot sleep in the night, etc.

    Robert Burton, *Anatomy of Melancholy* (1621)

14 [Music] is an enemy to melancholy and
    dejection of the mind, which St Chrysostom
    truly called the Devil's bath; yea, a curer of
    some diseases — in Apulia in Italy and
    thereabouts it is most certain that those who
    are stung with the tarantula are cured only by
    music.

    Henry Peacham, *The Compleat Gentleman* (1622)

15 Music helps not the toothache.

    George Herbert, *Jacula Prudentum* (1640)

16 Music exalts each joy, allays each grief,
    Expels diseases, softens every pain,
    Subdues the rage of poison, and the plague.

    John Armstrong, *The Art of Preserving Health* (1744)

DISSONANCE

See also HARMONY.

17 *Concordia discors.* Harmony in discord.

    Horace, *Epistles*, I, xii

18 *Discors concordia.* Discordant harmony.

    Ovid, *Metamorphoses*, I

19 A dissonance is a combination of different
    sounds that by nature is displeasing to the ears.

    Johannes Tinctoris, *Dictionary of Musical Terms* (c.
    1475)

20 So discord oft in music makes the sweeter lay.

    Edmund Spenser, *The Faerie Queene*, III (1589)

21 How irksome is this music to my heart.
    When such strings jar, what hope of harmony?
    (Henry)

    William Shakespeare, *Henry VI, Part Two* II.i

22 Melodious discord, heavenly tune harsh
        sounding,
    Ear's deep sweet music, and heart's deep
        sore wounding.

    William Shakespeare, *Venus and Adonis* (1593)

23   I never heard
    So musical a discord, such sweet thunder.
    (Hippolyta)

    William Shakespeare, *A Midsummer Night's Dream*, IV.i

1 Drive far off the bar'brous dissonance
Of Bacchus and his revellers.
John Milton, *Paradise Lost*, VII

2 Discords make the sweetest airs,
And curses are a sort of prayers.
Samuel Butler, *Hudibras* (1678)

3 All discord, harmony not understood.
Alexander Pope, *Essay on Man* (1732-4)

4 [Discord] occasions a momentary distress to the
ear, which remains unsatisfied, and even
uneasy, till it hears something better . . . the ear
must be satisfied at last.
Charles Burney, *Present State of Music in France and
Italy* (1771)

5 I am convinced that provided the ear be at
length made amends, there are few dissonances
too strong for it.
Charles Burney, *Present State of Music in France and
Italy* (1771)

6 DISSONANCE . . . is the DOLCE PICCANTE of Music,
and operates on the ear as a poignant sauce on
the palate: it is a zest, without which the
auditory sense would be as much cloyed as the
appetite, if it had nothing to feed on but sweets.
Charles Burney, *A General History of Music* (1776-89)

7 No sound is dissonant which tells of Life.
Samuel Taylor Coleridge, 'This Lime-Tree Bower my
Prison'

8 There is nothing stable in the world; uproar's
your only music.
John Keats, Letter to George and Tom Keats, 1818

9 Why rushed the discords in but that harmony
should be prized?
Robert Browning, 'Abt Vogler'

10 [Of an anthem by Gibbons] The composer has
fallen into the error of attempting to represent
the antagonism of the ideas of Life and Death
by the use of discords utterly intolerable to
modern ears.
Frederick Ouseley, *A Collection of the Sacred
Compositions of Orlando Gibbons* (1873)

11 Every dissonance doesn't have to resolve if it
doesn't happen to feel like it, any more than
every horse should have its tail bobbed just
because it's the prevailing fashion.
George Ives, remark to his son Charles, quoted in
Wooldridge, *Charles Ives* (1974)

12 [Of discords] *Le régal de l'ouïe*. A feast for the
ear.
Claude Debussy, quoted in *La Revue musicale*, 1926

13 Dissonances are only the more remote
consonances.
Arnold Schoenberg, quoted in Machlis, *Introduction to
Contemporary Music* (1963)

14 Dissonances are more difficult to comprehend
than consonance. Therefore the battle about
them goes on throughout history.
Arnold Schoenberg, quoted in Machlis, *Introduction to
Contemporary Music* (1963)

15 Whereas, in the past, the point of disagreement
has been between dissonance and consonance,
it will be, in the immediate future, between
noise and so-called music sounds.
John Cage, *Silence* (1961), 'The Future of Music: Credo'
(1937)

16 What distinguishes dissonances from
consonances is not a greater or lesser degree of
beauty, but a greater or lesser degree of
comprehensibility.
Arnold Schoenberg, *Style and Idea* (1951)

17 [In Wagner's music] All energy is now invested
in dissonance; by comparison the individual
resolutions become ever thinner, mere optional
decor or restorative asseveration. Tension
becomes the fundamental organizing principle
to the degree that the negation of the negation,
the utter cancelling out of the debt of each
dissonance, is as in some gigantic credit system
indefinitely postponed.
T.W Adorno, *Versuch über Wagner* (1952)

18 Disharmony, to paraphrase Bergson's
statement about disorder, is simply a harmony
to which many are unaccustomed.
John Cage, *Silence* (1961), 'Experimental Music' (1957)

DISTANT MUSIC

19 The still sweet fall of music far away.
Thomas Campbell, *The Pleasures of Hope* (1799)

20   Sweetest melodies
Are those by distance made more sweet.
William Wordsworth, 'Personal Talk' (1807)

21 And music, too — dear music! that can touch
Beyond all else the soul that loves it much —
Now heard far off, so far as but to seem
Like the faint, exquisite music of a dream.
Thomas Moore, *Lalla Rookh*, 'The Veiled Prophet of
Khorassan' (1817)

22 O hark, O hear! how thin and clear,
    And thinner, clearer, farther going!
O sweet and far from cliff and scar
    The horns of Elfland faintly blowing!
Alfred, Lord Tennyson, *The Princess* (1847)

DONIZETTI

23 My heyday is over, and another must take my
place. The world wants something new. Others
have ceded their places to us and we must cede
ours to still others . . . I am more than happy to
give mine to people of talent like Verdi.
Gaetano Donizetti, Letter to Giuseppina Appiani, 1844

1 [Of Donizetti's *La Favorita*] I only heard two acts. Marionette stage-music!

Robert Schumann, *Operatic Note-Book*, 1847

2 [At the first performance of Donizetti's *Anna Bolena*] I wallowed in rapture.

Mikhail Glinka, *Memoirs*

THE DOUBLE BASS

3 A dangerous rogue-elephant.

Charles Villiers Stanford, quoted in Hughes and Van Thal, *The Music Lover's Companion* (1971)

4 With bass players ... national differences are greater ... The Germans are very much the Herr Professors; the Americans often the muscular ball-players; while the English tend to treat the whole matter as a joke, referring to their chosen instrument usually as 'the Dog House' and being perfectly ready to concede the superior importance of any other instrument, apart from the 'cello.

Jack Brymer, *From Where I Sit* (1979)

DOWLAND

5 What time and diligence I have bestowed in the search of music, what travel in foreign countries, what success and estimation even among strangers I have found, I leave to the report of others.

John Dowland, *The First Booke of Songes* (1597)

6 *Semper Dowland Semper Dolens*. Always Dowland, always sad.

John Dowland, title of pavan for solo lute

7 *Dolande misero surripis mentem mihi,*
Excorsque cordae pectus impulsae premunt.
Quis tibi deorum tam potenti numine
Digitos trementes dirigit is inter deos
Magnos oportet principem obtineat locum ...
At O beate siste divinas manus,
Iam iam parumper siste divinas manus,
Liquescit anima, quam cave exugas mihi.
O Dowland, unawares thou stealest my poor mind, the strings thou pluckest quite overwhelm my breast. The god who with such divine power directs thy trembling fingers, among the great gods he should hold the leading place ... But O thou blest one, stay thy divine hands; now, now, for a moment stay thy divine hands. My soul dissolves, draw it not from me quite.

Thomas Campion, *Poemata* (1595)

8 Dowland to thee is dear, whose heavenly touch Upon the lute doth ravish human sense.

Richard Barnfield, Sonnet, published in *The Passionate Pilgrim* (1599)

9 For, as an old, rude, rotten tuneless kit, If famous Dowland deign to finger it, Makes sweeter music than the choicest lute In the gross handling of a clownish brute.

Joshua Sylvester, verse in his translation of *The Divine Weekes and Workes* of Guillaume de Saluste du Bartas (1605-6)

10 He was the rarest musician that his age did behold ... it is questionable whether he excelled in vocal or instrumental music.

Thomas Fuller, *The History of the Worthies of England* (1662)

DRUMS AND PERCUSSION

See also MARTIAL MUSIC

11 There is no instrument the sound of which proclaims such vast internal satisfaction as the drum.

George Meredith, *Sandra Belloni* (1886)

12 A gasconade of drums.

Wallace Stevens, 'The Comedian as the Letter C' (1924)

13 The percussion and the bass ... function as a central heating system.

Igor Stravinsky, quoted in Lee, *Music of the People* (1970)

14 A drum is a woman

Duke Ellington, quoted in Wilmer, *Jazz People* (1977)

15 You're not supposed to *rape* the drums, you make love to them as far as I'm concerned.

Billy Higgins, quoted in Wilmer, *Jazz People* (1977)

16 Then there was the terrible moment when Muir Matheson once asked one of the percussion players to 'give that thing a good bang three bars before C'. It was a cymbal, I think, and Jimmy [Bradshaw] didn't like it being insulted. 'Mister Matheson,' he said. 'It isn't a thingg — it's a cymball; and he dusn't bangg it — he *draws* the *toan* out of it!'

Jack Brymer, *From Where I Sit* (1979)

DVOŘÁK

17 What have either of us to do with politics? Let's be happy that we can dedicate our services to art.

Antonín Dvořák, Letter to his publisher Simrock, 1885

18 I am just an ordinary Czech musician.

Antonín Dvořák, Letter, 1886

19 I compose only for my own pleasure.

Antonín Dvořák, Letter to Simrock, 1893

20 I have composed too much.

Antonín Dvořák, Letter to Sibelius

21 You do write a bit hastily.

Johannes Brahms, Letter to Dvořák

1 The composer, after long groping, has found the right path to the temple of independent Slavonic art.

Ludovic Procházka, reviewing *King and Collier* in *Dalibor*, 1874

2 Next to Brahms, the most God-gifted composer of the present day.

Hans von Bülow, Letter to Dvořák, 1877

3 There may be people who are serious enough to find this opera comic, just as there are people comical enough to take Brahms' symphonies seriously.

Hugo Wolf, reviewing *The Peasant a Rogue* in 1885

4 A composer by the grace of God.

Hans Richter, Letter to Dvořák, 1887

5 [Of Dvořák's *Requiem*] When I hear Dvořák's weird chords on muted cornets (patent Margate Pier echo attachment), finishing with a gruesome ding on the tamtam, I feel exactly as I should if he held up a skull with a lighted candle inside to awe me ... But the public ... loves everything connected with a funeral.

George Bernard Shaw, *Music in London 1890-4* (1931)

6 I should be glad if something occurred to me as a main idea that occurs to Dvořák only by the way.

Johannes Brahms, quoted in Šourek (ed.), *Antonín Dvořák: Letters and Reminiscences* (1954)

7 Why on earth didn't I know that one could write a violincello concerto like this? If I had only known, I would have written one long ago!

Johannes Brahms, after reading the score of Dvořák's cello concerto, quoted in Robertson, *Dvořák* (1964)

8 [Of Dvořák's piano pieces] Curiously coloured scarlet music.

Oscar Wilde, quoted in Robertson, *Dvořák* (1964)

9 You know the feeling when somebody takes the word out of your mouth before you have time to form it? That was always my experience in Dvořák's company. In him his person and his work were interchangeable. And then his melodies were as if he had taken them from my heart. Such a bond nothing on earth can sever.

Leoš Janáček, *Recollections of Antonín Dvořák* (1910-11)

10 Old Borax ... was as mild-mannered a musical pirate as ever scuttled a pupil's counterpoint.

James Huneker, *Variations on a Theme* (1922)

11 There are composers for whom music is an instrument for the expression of their poetic or philosophical ideas or of their Titanism. On the other hand there are composers who are themselves the instruments of music and saturated with its beauty. The former express through music what touches them, the latter change to music what they touch. Among these

latter are the geniuses Haydn, Mozart and Schubert and ... Dvořák.

Vítězslav Novák, quoted in Šourek (ed.), *Antonín Dvořák: Letters and Reminiscences* (1954)

12 Our national style is something far deeper than his sonorous exoticism.

František Bartoš, quoted in Robertson, *Dvořák* (1964)

DYLAN

13 My records are selling and I'm making money, but it makes me think I'm not doin' right.

Bob Dylan, quoted in *Life*, 1964

14 I'm just as good a singer as Caruso ... I hit all those notes and I can hold my breath three times as long if I want to.

Bob Dylan, in documentary film *Don't Look Back* (1965)

15 Folk music destroyed itself.

Bob Dylan, in 1965 (after he had gone electric), quoted in Gross and Alexander, *Bob Dylan*

16 I don't believe you — you're a liar.

Bob Dylan, at the 1966 Albert Hall concert, in response to a member of the audience who had shouted 'Judas'

17 It's always lonely where I am.

Bob Dylan, in 1966, quoted in Shelton, *No Direction Home* (1983)

18 They're just songs. Songs that are transparent so you can see every bit through them.

Bob Dylan, quoted in Green, *The Book of Rock Quotes* (1982)

19 Bob Dylan doesn't know his ethnic musicology.

Graffito in New York subway, *c.* 1964

20 A young neurotic.

Joan Baez, quoted in Gross and Alexander, *Bob Dylan* (1978)

21 We have an America that in Bob Dylan's phrase is busy being born, not busy dying.

Jimmy Carter, Inaugural Address, 1977

22 There's so many sides to Dylan, he's round.

Unnamed friend, quoted in Shelton, *No Direction Home* (1983)

EDUCATION

See also ACADEMIES AND ACADEMICISM, PRACTICE.

23 Education in music is most sovereign, because more than anything else rhythm and harmony find their way to the inmost soul and take strongest hold upon it, bringing with them and imparting grace, if one is rightly trained.

Plato, *Republic*

24 It seems there are two arts which I would say some god gave to mankind, music and gymnastics for the service of the high-spirited

principle and the love of knowledge in them —
not for the soul and body except incidentally,
but for the harmonious adjustment of these two
principles by the proper degree of tension and
relaxation of each.

Plato, *Republic*

1   It is not easy to determine the nature of music,
or why anyone should have a knowledge of it.

Aristotle, *Politics*

2   Music has the power of producing a certain
effect on the moral character of the soul, and if
it has the power to do this, it is clear that the
young must be directed to music and must be
educated in it.

Aristotle, *Politics*

3   Artificial instruments are not fit to be applied to
the use of disciplines.

Aristotle; trans. Taylor, *Ductor Dubitantium* (1676)

4   The Spartans were indignant at Timotheus the
Milesian, because by complicating music he had
harmed the minds of the boys whom he had
taken as pupils and had turned them from the
modesty of virtue, and because he had
perverted harmony, which he found modest,
into the chromatic genius, which is more
effeminate.

Boethius, *De Institutione Musica*

5   I always loved music; whoso has skill in this art
is of a good temperament, fitted for all things.
We must teach music in schools; a schoolmaster
ought to have skill in music, or I would not
regard him; neither should we ordain young
men as preachers unless they have been well
exercised in music.

Martin Luther, *Table-Talk* (pub. 1566)

6   To teach men's sons and daughters on the
virginal and viol, it is as harmless a calling as
any man can follow.

Solomon Eccles, *A Musick-Lector* (1667)

7   At the beginning of children's study I actually
keep the key of the instrument on which I am
instructing them as a precautionary measure, so
that in my absence they cannot spoil in a
moment what I have so carefully set in three-
quarters of an hour.

François Couperin, *L'Art de toucher le clavecin* (1716)

8   'Dumb keyboards' have been invented; practice
on them for a while in order to see that they are
worthless. Dumb people cannot teach us to
speak.

Robert Schumann, quoted in Wolff (ed.), *On Music and
Musicians* (1946)

9   They laughed when I sat down at the piano. But
when I started to play!

John Caples, Advertisement for U.S. School of Music,
1925

10   [To George Gershwin, on refusing him as a
pupil] You would only lose the spontaneous
quality of your melody, and end by writing bad
Ravel.

Maurice Ravel, quoted in Kendall, *The Tender Tyrant*
(1976)

11   Nadia Boulanger told me this way she has of
deciding who to accept for students. Those who
have no talent, and those who have no money;
these are not acceptable. There are those who
have talent but no money. These she accepts.
Those who have little talent but much money
she also accepts. But those who have much
talent and much money she says she never
gets.

Roy Harris, quoted in Kendall, *The Tender Tyrant*
(1976)

12   We have to establish already in schoolchildren
the belief that music belongs to everyone and
is, with a little effort, available to everyone.

Zoltán Kodály, Lecture, 1946

13   If you study with me, you might as well write
like me. If you have anything to say, it will
come out.

Paul Hindemith, quoted in Skelton, *Paul Hindemith*
(1975)

14   When I give advice to my pupils, I tell them
they can do one of three things:
(a) accept it blindly — bad!
(b) reject it blindly — bad, but not so bad!
(c) think over a third course for themselves —
good!

Ralph Vaughan Williams, Letter to Arthur Bliss, 1958

15   Learning music by reading about it is like
making love by mail.

Isaac Stern, quoted in Ayre, *The Wit of Music* (1966)

EFFECTS OF MUSIC

See also DISEASE, MARTIAL MUSIC,
MELANCHOLY, SLEEP.

GENERAL

16   That which colours the mind is a raga.

Sanskrit proverb, quoted in Shankar, *My Music, My
Life* (1969)

17   The business of music should in some measure
lead to the love of the beautiful.

Plato, *Republic*

18   Music is a part of us, and either ennobles or
degrades our behaviour.

Boethius, *De Institutione Musica*

19   Though music oft hath such a charm
To make bad good, and good provoke to harm.
(Duke Vincentio)

William Shakespeare, *Measure for Measure*, IV.i

1 Generally music feedeth that disposition of the spirits which it findeth.

Francis Bacon, *Sylva Sylvarum* (1627)

2 Such sweet compulsions doth in music lie.

John Milton, *Arcades* (c. 1633)

3 Begin to charm, and as thou strok'st mine ears
With thy enchantment, melt me into tears.
Then let thy active hand scud o'er thy lyre:
And make my spirits frantic with the fire.
That done, sink down into a silv'ry strain,
And make me smooth as balm and oil again.

Robert Herrick, 'To Music'

4 One and the same thing can at the same time be good, bad, and indifferent, for example, music is good to the melancholy, bad to those who mourn, and neither good nor bad to the deaf.

Baruch Spinoza, *Ethics* (pub. 1677)

5 The manner of the conveyance of sounds, which is as it were the basis of music, is unintelligible. For what can be more strange, than that the rubbing of a little *Hair* and *Cat-Gut* together, should make such a mighty alteration in a man that sits at a distance?

Jeremy Collier, *An Essay of Musick* (1702)

6 Music the fiercest grief can charm,
And Fate's severest rage disarm:
Music can soften pain to ease,
And make despair and madness please:
Our joys below it can improve,
And antedate the bliss above.

Alexander Pope, 'Ode for Musick, on St Cecilia's Day' (c. 1708)

7 But would you sing, and rival Orpheus' strain,
The wond'ring forests soon should dance again;
The moving mountains hear the powerful call,
And headlong streams hang list'ning in their fall!

Alexander Pope, *Pastorals*, 'Summer' (1709)

8 The peculiar quality of music to raise the sociable and happy passions, and to subdue the contrary ones.

Charles Avison, *An Essay on Musical Expression* (1752)

9 There is in souls a sympathy with sounds,
And, as the mind is pitch'd, the ear is pleas'd
With melting airs, or martial brisk, or grave:
Some chord in unison with what we hear
Is touch'd within us, and the heart replies.

William Cowper, *The Task*, VI (1785)

10 O Music! Reverberation from a distant world of harmony! Sigh of the angel within us! When the word is speechless, and the embrace, and the eye, and the tear; when our dumb hearts lie lonely behind the ironwork of our breasts — then it is Thou alone through whom they call to one another in their dungeons and through whom, in their desert habitation, they unite their distant sighs!

Jean Paul, quoted by Liszt, Essay on Berlioz (1855)

11 Music revives the recollection it would appease.

Madame de Stael, *Corinne* (1807)

12 Who is there that, in logical words, can express the effect music has on us? A kind of inarticulate unfathomable speech, which leads us to the edge of the Infinite and lets us for moments gaze into that.

Thomas Carlyle, *On Heroes, Hero-Worship, and the Heroic in History* (1841)

13 Such sweet
Soft notes as yet musician's cunning
Never gave the enraptured air.

Robert Browning, 'The Pied Piper of Hamelin' (1845)

14 When I hear music, I fear no danger. I am invulnerable. I see no foe. I am related to the earliest times, and to the latest.

H.D. Thoreau, *Journal*, 1857

15 Who hears music, feels his solitude
Peopled at once.

Robert Browning, *Balaustion's Adventure* (1871)

16 My objections to Wagner's music are physiological — why disguise them as usual behind aesthetic formulas? Aesthetics is nothing else than applied physiology. I base myself upon fact ... when I say that I breathe with difficulty as soon as Wagner's music begins to act upon me.

Friedrich Nietzsche, quoted in Barzun (ed.), *Pleasures of Music* (1977)

17 I can fancy a man who had led a perfectly commonplace life, hearing by chance some curious piece of music, and suddenly, discovering that his soul, without his being conscious of it, had passed through terrible experiences, and known fearful joys, or wild romantic loves, or great renunciations.

Oscar Wilde, *The Critic as Artist* (1891)

18 When music sounds, all that I was I am
Ere to the haunt of brooding dust I came.

Walter de la Mare, 'Music'

19 Music sets up a certain vibration which unquestionably results in a physical reaction. Eventually the proper vibration for every person will be found and utilised. I like to think of music as an emotional science.

George Gershwin, quoted in Morgenstern, *Composers on Music* (1958)

20 The sense of music is a primal thing in mankind, and a tremendous force, either for good or evil.

Arthur Bliss, 'Music Policy' (1941)

1   The reactions music evokes are not feelings,
    but they are the images, memories of feelings.
    Paul Hindemith, *A Composer's World* (1952)

2   You can't mess with people's heads, that's for
    sure. But that's what music's all about,
    messing with people's heads.
    Jimi Hendrix, quoted in Shapiro, *An Encyclopedia of
    Quotations about Music* (1978)

SEDATION

3   Indulged in to excess, music emasculates
    instead of invigorating the mind.
    Plato, *Republic*

4   [On music at Homeric banquets] This was the
    accepted custom, first in order that every one
    who felt impelled to get drunk and stuff
    himself might have music to cure his violence
    and intemperance, and secondly, because
    music appeases surliness; for, by stripping off
    a man's gloominess, it produces good temper
    and gladness becoming to a gentleman.
    Athenaeus, *Sophists at Dinner*

5   *Enervant animos citharae, lotosque, lyraeque.*
    Lutes, flutes and lyres enervate the mind.
    Ovid, *Remedia Amoris*

6   How valuable a thing music is, and how useful
    for checking the mad impulses of the mind.
    Richard Mulcaster, 'For the Music of Thomas Tallis
    and William Byrd' (1575)

7   For do but note a wild and wanton herd
    Or race of youthful and unhandled colts
    Fetching mad bounds, bellowing and neighing
             loud,
    Which is the hot condition of their blood —
    If they but hear perchance a trumpet sound,
    Or any air of music touch their ears,
    You shall perceive them make a mutual stand,
    Their savage eyes turned to a modest gaze
    By the sweet power of music. Therefore the
             poet
    Did feign that Orpheus drew trees, stones and
             floods,
    Since nought so stockish, hard and full of rage
    But music for the time doth change his nature.
    (Lorenzo)
    William Shakespeare, *The Merchant of Venice*, V.i

8   An admirable musician! O, she will sing the
    savageness out of a bear.
    (Othello)
    William Shakespeare, *Othello*, IV.i

9   This music crept by me upon the waters,
    Allaying both their fury and my passion
    With its sweet air.
    (Ferdinand)
    William Shakespeare, *The Tempest*, I.ii

10 A solemn air, and the best comforter
    To an unsettled fancy, cure thy brains,
    Now useless, boiled within thy skull.
    (Prospero)
    William Shakespeare, *The Tempest*, V.i

11 Music's the cordial of a troubled breast,
    The softest remedy that grief can find;
    The gentle spell that charms our care to rest
    And calms the ruffled passions of the mind.
        Music does all our joys refine,
        And gives the relish to our wine.
    John Oldham, 'An Ode on St Cecilia's Day' (1683)

12 Music hath charms to soothe a savage breast,
    To soften rocks, or bend a knotted oak.
    (Almeira)
    William Congreve, *The Mourning Bride*, I.i (1696-7),
    opening lines

13 Music alone with sudden charms can bind
    The wand'ring sense, and calm the troubled
             mind.
    William Congreve, 'Hymn to Harmony'

14 By music, minds an equal temper know,
        Not swell too high, nor sink too low.
    Alexander Pope, 'Ode for Musick, on St Cecilia's Day'
    (*c.* 1708)

15 Music has charms alone for peaceful minds.
    Alexander Pope, 'Sappho to Phaon' (1712)

16 Music's force can tame the furious beast:
    Can make the wolf or foaming boar restrain
    His rage; the lion drop his crested mane
    Attentive to the song.
    Matthew Prior, *Solomon, or the Vanity of Human Wishes*
    (1718)

17 Music might tame and civilise wild beasts, but
    'tis evident it never yet could tame and civilise
    musicians.
    John Gay, *Polly* (1729)

18 Is there a heart that music cannot melt?
    Alas! how is that rugged heart forlorn!
    James Beattie, *The Minstrel* (1771)

19 And the night shall be filled with music,
    And the cares, that infest the day,
    Shall fold their tents, like the Arabs,
    And as silently steal away.
    Henry Wadsworth Longfellow, 'The Day is Done'

20 Music — makes a people's disposition more
    gentle; e.g. 'The Marseillaise'.
    Gustave Flaubert, *Dictionary of Received Ideas* (pub.
    1913)

21 The law ... ought to employ your music ... in
    order to lead hardened criminals to repentance.
    No one could resist it ... and the day is not far
    distant, in these times of humanitarian ideas,

when similar psychological methods will be used to soften the hearts of the vicious.

Pope Pius IX, after hearing Liszt play in 1862, quoted in Wohl, *Franz Liszt* (trans. 1887)

1 People who make music together cannot be enemies, at least while the music lasts.

Paul Hindemith, quoted in Shapiro, *An Encyclopedia of Quotations about Music* (1978)

2 Most people use music as a couch . . . But serious music was never meant to be used as a soporific.

Aaron Copland, in *The New York Times*, 1949

STIMULATION

3 Awake up, my glory; awake, psaltery and harp: I myself will awake early.

Psalms 57:8; cf. the version in the Book of Common Prayer: 'Awake up, my glory; awake, lute and harp: I myself will wake right early.'

4 Music is a science that would have us laugh and sing and dance.

Guillaume de Machaut, quoted in Shapiro, *An Encyclopedia of Quotations about Music* (1978)

5 This music mads me, let it sound no more —
For though it have holp madmen to their wits,
In me it seems it will make wise men mad.
(Richard)

William Shakespeare, *Richard II*, V.v

6 No mirth without music.

Robert Burton, *Anatomy of Melancholy* (1621)

7 [Music] cures all irksomeness and heaviness of the soul. Labouring men that sing to their work can tell as much, and so can soldiers when they go to fight, whom terror of death cannot so much affright as the sound of trumpet, drum, fife, and suchlike music animates.

Robert Burton, *Anatomy of Melancholy* (1621)

8 ⠀⠀⠀⠀Timotheus, to his breathing Flute,
⠀⠀⠀⠀⠀⠀And sounding Lyre,
Could swell the Soul to rage, or kindle soft
⠀⠀⠀Desire.

John Dryden, 'Alexander's Feast' (1697)

9 Music religious heats inspires,
⠀⠀It wakes the soul, and lifts it high,
And wings it with sublime desires,
⠀⠀And fits it to bespeak the Deity.

Joseph Addison, 'A Song for St Cecilia's Day'

10 And learn, my sons, the wondrous power of
⠀⠀Noise,
To move, to raise, to ravish ev'ry heart.

Alexander Pope, *The Dunciad*, II (1728)

11 Music hath two ends, first to please the sense, and that is done by the pure dulcor of harmony . . . and secondly to move the affections or excite passion. And that is done by measures of time joined with the former. And it must be granted that pure impulse artificially acted and continued hath great power to excite men to act but not to think . . . The melody is only to add to the diversion.

Roger North, *The Musicall Gramarian* (1728)

12 There's no passion in the human soul
But finds its food in music.

George Lillo, *Fatal Curiosity*, I.ii (1736)

13 Thus music, either by imitating these various sounds (of nature) in due subordination to the laws of air and harmony, or by any other method of association, bringing the objects of our passions before us (especially where those objects are determined, and made as it were visibly, and intimately present to the imagination by the help of words) does naturally raise a variety of passions in the human breast, similar to the sounds which are expressed.

Charles Avison, *An Essay on Musical Expression* (1752)

14 Music should strike fire from a man.

Ludwig van Beethoven, quoted in Scott, *Beethoven* (1934)

15 Is not music the mysterious language of a distant realm of spirits, whose lovely sounds re-echo in our soul and awaken a higher, because more intensive, life? All the passions, arrayed in shining and resplendent armour, vie with each other, and ultimately merge in an indescribable longing that fills our breasts. This is the heavenly effect of instrumental music.

E.T.A. Hoffmann, 'The Poet and the Composer' (1816)

16 Good music never tires me, nor sends me to sleep. I feel physically refreshed and strengthened by it, as Milton says he did.

Samuel Taylor Coleridge, *Table-Talk* (1835)

17 In an age of neurasthenics, music, like everything else, must be a stimulant, must be alcoholic, aphrodisiac, or it is no good.

Frederick Delius, 'At the Crossroads' (1920)

ELECTRONIC MUSIC

18 We have also sound-houses, where we practise and demonstrate all sounds and their generation. We have harmonies which you have not, of quarter-sounds and lesser slides of sounds . . . We represent small sounds as great and deep; likewise great sounds, extenuate and sharp; we make divers tremblings and warblings of sounds and letters, and the voices and notes of beasts and birds.

Francis Bacon, *New Atlantis* (1627)

19 What we want is an instrument that will give us a continuous sound at any pitch. The composer

and the electrician will have to labour together to get it.

Edgar Varèse, in 1922, quoted in Machlis, *Introduction to Contemporary Music* (1963)

1 Electrical instruments . . . will make available for musical purposes any and all sounds that can be heard.

John Cage, *Silence* (1961), 'The Future of Music: Credo (1937)

2 Nothing indicates that electric mechanical instruments cannot eventually render high qualities of touch which have heretofore been man's privilege . . . The precision obtainable by electro-mechanical means is incomparably greater than that achieved by men.

Carlos Chavez, *Toward a New Music* (1937)

3 It is by rules and compasses that the Greeks discovered geometry — musicians might do well to be inspired by their example.

Pierre Schaeffer, in 1960, quoted in Ernst, *The Evolution of Electronic Music* (1977)

4 Electric guitars are an abomination, whoever heard of an electric violin? An electric cello? Or for that matter an electric singer?

Andres Segovia, quoted in *The Beatles, Words without Music* (1968)

5 Electronic music has liberated the inner world, for one knows that there is nothing to be seen outside oneself and that there can be no sense in asking with what and by what means the sounds and acoustical forms are produced . . . The inner world is as true as the outer.

Karlheinz Stockhausen, quoted in Wörner, *Stockhausen: Life and Work* (1973)

6 The electronic medium, earlier denounced as a mechanistic degradation of music, lends itself to a kind of controlled compositional improvisation much more readily than the realm of live sound because the composer can mould the sound material while he is creating it.

Ernst Křenek, *Horizons Circled* (1974)

7 The synthesiser world opens the door to musical infinity.

John McLaughlin, quoted in *Time*, 1975

ELGAR

8 My idea is that there is music in the air, music all around us, the world is full of it and you simply take as much as you require.

Edward Elgar, quoted in Buckley, *Sir Edward Elgar* (1904)

9 I take no more interest in music . . . The secret of happiness for an artist when he grows old is to have a passion that can take the place of his

art. I have discovered the joy that diatoms can give me.

Edward Elgar, remark to Compton Mackenzie in 1921, quoted in *The Gramophone*, 1957

10 Look out for this man's music; he has something to say and knows how to say it.

Hubert Parry, remark after hearing the first performance of *Enigma Variations*, 1899

11 [Of *The Dream of Gerontius*] Holy water in a German beer barrel.

George Moore, quoted in Cardus, *The Delights of Music* (1966)

12 [Of *The Dream of Gerontius*] Stinking of incense.

Charles Villiers Stanford, quoted in *The Elgar Society Newsletter*, 1978

13 Edward Elgar, the figure head of music in England, is a composer whose rank it is neither prudent nor indeed possible to determine. Either it is one so high that only time and posterity can confer it, or else he is one of the Seven Humbugs of Christendom.

George Bernard Shaw, in *Music and Letters*, 1920

14 Elgar . . . might have been a great composer if he had thrown all that religious paraphernalia overboard. *Gerontius* is a nauseating work . . .

Frederick Delius, quoted in Fenby, *Delius as I knew him* (1936)

5 The first Progressivist in English music.

Richard Strauss, quoted in *The Musical Times*, 1931

16 I feel that Elgar's music is usually either opening something or closing something institutional; we have in Elgar the Laureate rather than the poet.

Neville Cardus, in *The Radio Times*, 1931

17 Elgar's task has been less to innovate than to complete, not to make a new musical language but to distil what may prove to be the last drop of expression out of the old.

Ernest Newman, in *The Sunday Times*, 1934

18 [Of the Symphony No. 2] A lengthy, pompous, bourgeois sort of thing; it reflects the complacency and stodginess of the era of the anti-macassar and pork-pie bonnets.

Olin Downes, in *The New York Times*, 1939

19 Elgar might have been a great composer if he had not been such a perfect gentleman.

Cecil Gray, quoted in Machlis, *Introduction to Contemporary Music* (1963)

20 None of his successors, compared with him, is more than a tinker working on the Forth Bridge.

Neville Cardus, in *The Manchester Guardian*, 1939

21 [Of *Falstaff*] There are occasions in the work when we feel that this is a Falstaff who has spent as much time in Worcester Cathedral, blowing himself out to a bladder with singing

of anthems, as he has in lying on benches after noon.

Neville Cardus, in *The Manchester Guardian*, 1939

1 He strays with a dangerous ease to the borderline of a military rodomontade that is hardly distinguishable from the commonplace and the vulgar.

Sir Thomas Beecham, *A Mingled Chime* (1944)

2 Elgar's music is like the façade of Euston Station.

Sir Thomas Beecham, quoted in Reid, *Thomas Beecham* (1961)

3 [Of *The Dream of Gerontius*] My son, that is a sublime masterpiece.

Pope Pius XIII, remark to Sir John Barbirolli, quoted in Kennedy, *Barbirolli, Conductor Laureate* (1971)

4 I know that Elgar is not manic enough to be Russian, not witty or *pointilliste* enough to be French, not harmonically simple enough to be Italian and not stodgy enough to be German. We arrive at his Englishry by pure elimination.

Anthony Burgess, in *The Observer*, 1983

ELLINGTON

5 When it sounds good, it *is* good.

Duke Ellington, programme notes to *Such Sweet Thunder* (1957); the saying was common among jazz musicians

6 Somehow I suspect that if Shakespeare were alive today, he might be a jazz fan himself.

Duke Ellington, programme notes to *Such Sweet Thunder* (1957)

7 Bach and myself write with the individual performer in mind.

Duke Ellington, quoted in Jewell, *Duke* (1977)

8 A Harlem Dionysus drunk on bad bootleg liquor.

Ernest Newman, quoted in Jewell, *Duke* (1977)

9 Do I think of Charles Mingus as a disciple of my school? Well, that's what *he* says.

Duke Ellington, quoted in Jewell, *Duke* (1977)

ENGLAND

10 *Thaer waes hearpan sweg, swutel sang scopes.* There [in England] was the sound of the harp, the clear song of the minstrel.

Beowulf (late 10th century)

11 The English could lay claim to the best-looking and most musical people, and to the best tables of any people.

Desiderius Erasmus, *The Praise of Folly* (1509)

12 ... I was trained up in the English court, Where being but young I framed to the harp

Many an English ditty lovely well,
And gave the tongue a helpful ornament.
(Glendower)

William Shakespeare, *Henry IV, Part One*, III.i

13 I willingly, to avoid tediousness, forbear to speak of the worth and excellency of the rest of our English composers ... inferior to none other in the world (how much soever the Italian attributes to himself) for depth of skill and richness of conceit.

Henry Peacham, *The Compleat Gentleman* (1622)

14 I cannot forbear thinking that the cat-call is originally a piece of English music. Its resemblance to the voice of some of our British songsters, as well as the use of it, which is peculiar to our nation, confirms me in this opinion.

Joseph Addison, in *The Spectator*, 1712

15 The Italians exalt music; the French enliven it; the Germans strive after it; and the English pay for it well. The Italians serve music; the French make it into a companion; the Germans anatomize it, and the English compel it to serve them.

Johann Mattheson, *Das Neu-eröffnete Orchestre* (1713)

16 What the English like is something they can beat time to, something that hits them straight on the drum of the ear.

George Frideric Handel, quoted in Schmid, *C.W. von Gluck* (1854)

17 Our composers have run all their concertos into little else than tedious divisions.

Charles Avison, *An Essay on Musical Expression* (1752)

18 Scarcely had we lost Arne when Irish jigs usurped the musical domain. These having had their day, it was difficult to find a substitute, and now music is decidely nowhere.

Charles Dibdin, quoted in Langley, *Doctor Arne* (1938)

19 Those who know my compositions say: — 'Play me your second Sigh — I like your Bells very much.' And every observation finishes with 'leik [sic] water', meaning that my music flows like water. I have not yet played to any English-woman without her saying to me 'leik water'!!

Fryderyk Chopin, Letter, 1848

20 The English are a good, warm-hearted and music-loving nation and it is well known that once they take a liking to someone, they remain faithful to him.

Antonín Dvořák, Letter to Velebín Urbánek, 1884

21 The English do not love music, they respect it.

Antonín Dvořák, in 1896, quoted in Robertson, *Dvořák* (1964)

1   These great men [Stanford, Parry and
    Mackenzie] seem to be busily employed in
    performing one another's works. No-one else
    will.

    Edward Elgar, Letter to A.J. Jaeger, 1898

2   At every one of those concerts in England you
    will find rows of weary people who are there,
    not because they really like classical music, but
    because they think they ought to like it.

    George Bernard Shaw, *Man and Superman*, III (1903)

3   English singers cannot sing. There is only one I
    know who can walk on the stage with any
    grace. The others come on like a duck in a
    thunderstorm.

    Sir Thomas Beecham, Speech at the Manchester Royal
    College of Music, 1914

4   Music is not the natural means of expression
    for the Englishman to the same extent as it is
    for the Italian. He regards it as something
    higher than a mere vehicle of the emotions and
    passions; and this explains why in England
    music remained in a subordinate position to
    drama.

    Alfred Einstein, *A Short History of Music* (1917)

5   The worst of musical criticism in this country is
    that there is so much of it.

    Edward Elgar, quoted in Cumberland, *Set Down in
    Malice* (1919)

6   To rhapsodise is one thing Englishmen *cannot*
    do.

    Edward Elgar, quoted in *The Elgar Society Newsletter*,
    1978

7   The precise and practical English realise that it
    is useless to go on searching [for greatness in
    music] since they have never yet found it.

    Jean Jules Aimable Roger-Ducasse, in *La Revue
    musicale*, 1922

8   English music? Did you say English music?
    Well, I've never heard of any!

    Frederick Delius, quoted in Fenby, *Delius as I knew him*
    (1936)

9   In England you can earn your living by writing
    stuff that wouldn't be listened to in Germany.

    Frederick Delius, quoted in Reid, *Thomas Beecham*
    (1961)

10 The average English Faust possesses less poise
    and charm of gesture than the average lift-boy
    of Prague, Vienna, or Paris.

    Neville Cardus, in *The Manchester Guardian*, 1938

11 Our best conductors . . . usually reveal the
    Englishman's view that music is mainly a thing
    that can be whistled.

    Neville Cardus, in *The Manchester Guardian*, 1939

12 If a German or an Austrian, a Czech or a
    Bashibazouk, had composed *Gerontius*, the

whole world would have by now admitted its
qualities.

Neville Cardus, in *The Manchester Guardian*, 1939

13 There were many who found admirable this
    steady refusal of the British public to traffic
    seriously with art or artists until either had
    been sealed seventy times seven with the
    blessing of every other nation. Why, they
    asked, waste time, money, and, what is far
    more prodigal, brainwork on discovering merit
    for ourselves, when others appear only too
    willing to relieve us of the trouble and
    responsibility? Surely a people which has
    secured such predominance in the world has
    the right to insist that all things which are
    presented for its approval should first pass
    through the testing furnace of foreign opinion.

    Sir Thomas Beecham, *A Mingled Chime* (1944)

14 British music is in a state of perpetual promise.
    It might almost be said to be one long
    promissory note.

    Sir Thomas Beecham, quoted in Atkins and Newman,
    Beecham Stories (1978)

15 The British may not like music, but they
    absolutely love the noise it makes.

    Sir Thomas Beecham, quoted in Atkins and Newman,
    Beecham Stories (1978)

16 Why do we have to have all these third-rate
    foreign conductors around — when we have so
    many second-rate ones of our own?

    Sir Thomas Beecham, quoted in Ayre, *The Wit of Music*
    (1966)

17 It was part of Handel's misfortune, and part too
    of his glory, that his music should readily have
    become an integral part of an Englishman's
    religion.

    Percy M. Young, *Handel* (1947)

18 The average English critic is a don *manqué*,
    hopelessly parochial when not teutonophile,
    over whose desk must surely hang the motto
    (presumably in Gothic lettering) 'Above all no
    enthusiasm'.

    Constant Lambert, in *Opera*, 1950

19 Much English music has the insipid flavour of
    the BBC Variety Orchestra playing an
    arrangement of a nursery tune.

    Colin Wilson, *Brandy of the Damned* (1964)

20 England swings like a pendulum do.

    Roger Miller, Song (1965)

EXPRESSION

See also INTELLECT AND FEELING, PROGRAMME
MUSIC.

21 Sing unto the Lord with the harp; with the
    harp, and the voice of a psalm.
    With trumpets and sound of cornet make a

joyful noise before the Lord, the King.

Psalms 98:5-6; cf. the version in the Book of Common Prayer: 'Praise the Lord upon the harp: sing to the harp with a psalm of thanksgiving. With trumpets also, and shawms: O shew yourselves joyful before the Lord the King.'

1 All their music [in Utopia], both that they play upon instruments, and that they sing with man's voice, doth so resemble and expresses natural affections; the sound and tune is so applied and made agreeable to the thing; that whether it be a prayer, or else a ditty of gladness, of patience, of trouble, of mourning, or of anger, the fashion of the melody doth so represent the meaning of the thing, that it doth wonderfully move, stir, pierce and enflame the hearers' minds.

Sir Thomas More, *Utopia* (1516); trans. Robynson (1551)

2 [Of madrigals] If therefore you will compose in this kind you must possess yourself with an amorous humour (for in no composition shall you prove admirable except you put on, and possess yourself wholly with that vein wherein you compose).

Thomas Morley, *A Plaine and Easie Introduction to Practicalle Musicke* (1597)

3 Can doleful notes to measured accents set
Express unmeasured griefs which time forget?
No, let chromatic tunes, harsh without ground,
Be sullen music for a tuneless heart.

John Danyel, Song (1606)

4 Come, woeful Orpheus, with thy charming lyre
And tune thy voice unto thy skilful wire.
Some strange chromatic notes do you devise
That best with mournful accents sympathise.
Of sourest sharps and uncouth flats make
    choice
And I'll thereto compassionate my voice.

Anon., in Byrd's *Psalmes, Songs and Sonnets* (1611)

5 The composer is culpable who, for the sake of a low and trifling imitation, deserts the beauties of expression.

Charles Avison, *An Essay on Musical Expression* (1752)

6 A musician cannot move others unless he himself is moved.

Carl Philipp Emmanuel Bach, *Essay* (1753)

7 The lack of expression is perhaps the greatest enormity of all. I should prefer music to say something other than it should, rather than it should say nothing at all.

Jean-Jacques Rousseau, *Dictionary of Music* (1767)

8 All music which depicts nothing is nothing but noise.

Jean d'Alembert, quoted in Mellers, *François Couperin* (1950)

9 The music, yearning like a God in pain.

John Keats, 'The Eve of St Agnes' (1819)

10 Music never expresses the phenomenon, but only the inner nature, the in-itself of all phenomena, the will itself.

Arthur Schopenhauer, *The World as Will and Idea* (1819)

11 Music stands quite alone. It is cut off from all the other arts ... It does not express a particular and definite joy, sorrow, anguish, horror, delight or mood of peace, but joy, sorrow, anguish, horror, delight, peace of mind *themselves*, in the abstract, in their essential nature, without accessories, and therefore without their customary motives. Yet it enables us to grasp and share them fully in this quintessence.

Arthur Schopenhauer, *The World as Will and Idea* (1819)

12 [Of the cavatina of his String quartet in B Flat Major, Op 130] Never did music of mine make so deep an impression upon me, even the remembrance of the emotions it aroused always costs me a tear.

Ludwig van Beethoven, quoted in Scott, *Beethoven* (1934)

13 If you ask me what I was thinking of when I wrote it [one of the *Songs Without Words*], I would say: just the song as it stands ... Only the song can say the same thing, can arouse the same feelings in one person as in another, a feeling which is not expressed, however, by the same words.

Felix Mendelssohn, Letter to Souchay

14 The song that we hear with our ears is only the song that is sung in our hearts.

Ouida, 'Ariadne'

15 I shall always prefer a subject where, somehow, action is sacrificed to feeling. It seems to me that music thus becomes more human and real.

Claude Debussy, Letter to Vasnier, 1885

16 Music will express any emotion, base or lofty. She is absolutely unmoral.

George Bernard Shaw, *Music in London, 1890-94* (1931)

17 I don't play accurately — anyone can play accurately — but I play with wonderful expression. As far as the piano is concerned, sentiment is my forte. I keep science for Life. (Algernon Moncrieff)

Oscar Wilde, *The Importance of Being Earnest*, I (1895)

18 [Music's ultimate goal] The expression of human sensibility, through technique being absorbed in an artistic totality.

Ferruccio Busoni, Conclusion to his edition of *The Well-Tempered Clavier* (1915)

19 It is only that which cannot be expressed otherwise that is worth expressing in music.

Frederick Delius, 'At the Crossroads' (1920)

1 Just as my fingers on these keys
Make music, so the selfsame sounds
On my spirit make a music too.

Music is feeling, then, not sound;
And thus it is that what I feel,
Here in this room, desiring you,

Thinking of your blue-shadowed silk,
Is music.

Wallace Stevens, 'Peter Quince at the Clavier' (1924)

2 It is . . . likely an artist's work will express the
opposite of his life . . . The object of art is to fill
up what is missing in the artist's experience.

Romain Rolland, quoted in Orledge, *Gabriel Fauré*
(1979)

3 I cannot conceive of music that expresses
absolutely nothing.

Béla Bartók, quoted in Machlis, *Introduction to
Contemporary Music* (1963)

4 They said, 'You have a blue guitar,
You do not play things as they are.'

The man replied, 'Things as they are
Are changed upon the blue guitar.'

And they said then, 'But play, you must,
A tune beyond us, yet ourselves,

A tune upon the blue guitar
Of things exactly as they are.'

Wallace Stevens, *The Man with the Blue Guitar* (1937)

5 Music, we are told [by 'the higher criticism'],
should be listened to *qua* music — which is as
though a young lover were told to look at a
starlit sky *qua* astronomy, or at his beloved *qua*
anatomy.

Neville Cardus, in *The Manchester Guardian*, 1938

6 The historical movement of the musical
material has turned against the self-contained
work . . . The pretence of feeling as a
compositional work of art, the self-satisfied
pretence of music itself, has become impossible
and no longer to be preserved — I mean the
perennial notion that prescribed and formalised
elements shall be introduced as though they
were the inviolable necessity of the single case
. . . For four hundred years all great music has
found its satisfaction in pretending that this
unity has been accomplished without a break
. . . The inclusion of expression in the general
appeasement is the innermost principle of
musical pretence.
(Leverkühn's 'Document')

Thomas Mann, *Doctor Faustus* (1947); trans. Lowe-
Porter

7 Music cannot express the composer's feelings
. . . If the composer thinks he is expressing his
own feelings, we have to accuse him of a lack of
observation. Here is what he really does: he
knows by experience that certain patterns of
tone-setting correspond with certain emotional
reactions on the listener's part. Writing these
patterns frequently and finding his
observations confirmed, in anticipating the
listener's reactions he believes himself to be in
the same mental situation. From here it is a
very small step to the further conviction that he
himself is not only reproducing the feelings of
other individuals, but is actually having these
same feelings, being obsessed by them
whenever he thinks he needs them, and being
urged to express them with each stroke of his
ever-ready pen.

Paul Hindemith, *A Composer's World* (1952)

8 Music is your own experience, your thoughts,
your wisdom. If you don't live it, it won't come
out of your horn.

Charlie Parker, quoted in Stearns, *The Story of Jazz*
(1956)

9 If you can't sing it, you can't play it. When I'm
improvising, I'm singing in my mind. I sing
what I feel and then try to reproduce it on the
horn.

Mutt Carey, quoted in Shapiro and Hentoff, *Hear Me
Talkin' to Ya* (1955)

10 Emotion takes place in the person who has it.
And sounds, when allowed to be themselves,
do not require that those who hear them do so
unfeelingly.

John Cage, *Silence* (1961), 'Experimental Music' (1957)

11 I feel a need to give an image to an ineffable
experience of my inner life. I feel the inner life
as something that is essentially fluid in
consistency. The process, which may be rapid
or slow, is one of giving articulation to this fluid
experience, and appears in successive stages.

Michael Tippett, quoted in Schafer, *British Composers
in Interview* (1963)

12 I get an audience involved because I'm involved
myself — if the song is a lament at the loss of
love, I get an ache in my gut . . . I cry out the
loneliness.

Frank Sinatra, quoted in Whitcomb, *After the Ball*
(1972)

13 Jazz has always been a man telling the truth
about himself.

Quincy Jones, quoted in Kendall, *The Tender Tyrant:
Nadia Boulanger* (1976)

FALLA

14 The music has no pretensions to being
descriptive; it is merely expressive.

Manuel de Falla, on his *Nights in the Gardens of Spain*,
quoted in Trend, *Manuel de Falla* (1929)

15 The excellence of natural Andalusian melody is
revealed by the fact that it is the only music

continuously and abundantly used by foreign composers.

Manuel de Falla, 'Cante Jondo' (1922)

1 The Spanish Gershwin.

George Gershwin, quoted in Schwartz, *Gershwin* (1973)

FAURÉ

2 It has been said that my *Requiem* does not express the fear of death and someone has called it a lullaby of death. But it is thus that I see death: as a happy deliverance, an aspiration towards happiness above . . .

Gabriel Fauré, quoted in *Comoedia*, 1954

3 To express that which is within you with sincerity, in the clearest and most *perfect* manner, would seem to me always the ultimate goal of art.

Gabriel Fauré, Letter to Mme de Chaumont-Quitry, 1898

4 For me . . . music exists to elevate us as far as possible above everyday existence.

Gabriel Fauré, Letter to his son Philippe, 1908

5 Do not try to be a genius in every bar.

Gabriel Fauré, advice to students, quoted in Honegger, *I am a Composer* (1951)

6 The artist should love life and show us that it is beautiful; without him, we might doubt it.

Gabriel Fauré, quoted in Mellers, *Studies in Contemporary Music* (1947)

7 I have been reserved all my life . . . and have only been able to let myself go in certain situations.

Gabriel Fauré, Letter to his wife Marie, 1921

8 I not only admire, adore and venerate your music, I have been and still am in love with it.

Marcel Proust, Letter to Fauré, 1897

9 [Fauré's music] A mixture of lechery and litanies.

Marcel Proust, quoted in *Musical Quarterly*, 1924

10 The play of the graceful, fleeting lines described by Fauré's music may be compared to the gesture of a beautiful woman without either suffering from comparison.

Claude Debussy, in *Gil Blas*, 1903

11 Without noise or fuss or meaningless gestures, he pointed the way towards marvellous musical horizons overflowing with freshness and light.

Albert Roussel, in *Comoedia*, 1924

12 With age I must admit that Fauré is a very great musician, but his *Requiem* makes me lose faith, and it is a real penance for me to hear it. It is

one of the few things I hate in music.

Francis Poulenc, quoted in Orledge, *Gabriel Fauré* (1979)

13 [Of Fauré's music] It never browbeats or bludgeons the listener into submission; it speaks, and in so doing either makes its point or leaves the listener cold.

Alan Kendall, *The Tender Tyrant: Nadia Boulanger* (1976)

FELDMAN

14 Now that things are so simple, there's so much to do.

Morton Feldman, remark to John Cage, quoted in Yates, *Twentieth Century Music* (1968)

FILM MUSIC

15 You ain't heard nothin' yet.

Al Jolson, in *The Jazz Singer* (film, 1927)

16 A film is a composition and the musical composer is an integral part of the design.

H.G. Wells, Letter to Arthur Bliss, 1934, concerning Bliss's music for *The Shape of Things to Come*

17 In the last resort film music should be judged solely as music — that is to say, by the ear alone, and the question of its value depends on whether it can stand up to this test.

Arthur Bliss, quoted in Manvell and Huntley, *The Technique of Film Music* (1957, rev. Arnell and Day, 1975)

18 The dreadful salads of sections of classic works, sentimental melodies, and popular songs which are generally confected to accompany films prove nothing but the inability of producers to conceive original cinematographic works with their own music.

Carlos Chavez, *Towards a New Music* (1937)

19 The composers who will make a true musical drama of the cinema will be those who know how to manage its various instrumentalities as perfectly as Chopin dominated the piano.

Carlos Chavez, *Towards a New Music* (1937)

20 I believe that film music is capable of becoming, and to a certain extent already is, a fine art.

Ralph Vaughan Williams, in *The Royal College of Music Magazine*, 1944

21 The truth is, that within limits, any music can be made to fit any situation.

Ralph Vaughan Williams, *Film Music Notes* (1944)

22 Film music is like a small lamp that you place below the screen to warm it.

Aaron Copland, attr.

23 In film the visual effect is of course predominant, and the music subserves the visual sequences, providing a subtle form of

punctuation — lines can seem to have been given the emphasis of italics, exclamation marks added to details of stage 'business', phases of the action broken into paragraphs, and the turning of the page at a crossfade or cut can be helped by music's power to summarise the immediate past or heighten expectation of what is to come.

William Walton, quoted in Manvell and Huntley, *The Technique of Film Music* (1957, rev. Arnell and Day, 1975)

1 A [film] musician is like a mortician. He can't bring a body to life, but he can make it look better.

Adolf Deutsch, quoted in Schafer, *British Composers in Interview* (1963)

2 Music [in film] . . . can become a short cut to emotion.

Roger Manvell and John Huntley, *The Technique of Film Music* (1957, rev. Arnell and Day, 1975)

3 A film which consisted entirely of a sound-track with nothing in the frame would still be a film as long as the rhythm of the splices was in harmony with the rhythm of the words or the music.

Alain Resnais, quoted in Manvell and Huntley, *The Technique of Film Music* (1957, rev. Arnell and Day, 1975)

4 The only way to accept music in films is for it to disappear as an autonomous expression in order to assume its role as one element in a general sensorial impression.

Michelangelo Antonioni, quoted in Manvell and Huntley, *The Technique of Film Music* (1957, rev. Arnell and Day, 1975)

5 I strongly resent the use of great and familiar music in the background of films. In nine cases out of ten it reduces the music to the level of the film, rather than raising the film to the level of the music, which is obviously the filmmaker's intention. There is nothing more disgusting than to find Mozart's B flat in G labelled as the Elvira Madigan Concerto.

Satyajit Ray, quoted in Manvell and Huntley, *The Technique of Film Music* (1957, rev. Arnell and Day, 1975)

THE FLUTE

6 The flute is not an instrument which has a good moral effect; it is too exciting.

Aristotle, *Politics*

7 The vile squeaking of the wry-necked fife. (Shylock)

William Shakespeare, *The Merchant of Venice*, II.v

8   The soft complaining flute
In dying notes discovers
The woes of hopeless lovers,

Whose dirge is whisper'd by the warbling lute.

John Dryden, 'A Song for St Cecilia's Day' (1687)

9 You cannot play the flute by merely blowing; you must use your fingers too.

Johann Wolfgang von Goethe, *Sprüche in Prosa* (1819)

10 I want to know a butcher paints,
A baker rhymes for his pursuit,
Candlestick-maker much acquaints
His soul with song, or, haply mute,
Blows out his brains upon the flute.

Robert Browning, 'Shop'

11 Flute, n. A variously perforated hollow stick intended for the punishment of sin, the minister of retribution being commonly a young man with straw-coloured eyes and lean hair.

Ambrose Bierce, *The Enlarged Devil's Dictionary* (pub. 1967)

FOLK MUSIC

12 I never heard the old song of Percy and Douglas, that I found not my heart moved more than with a trumpet; and yet it is sung but by some blind crowder, with no rougher voice than rude style.

Sir Philip Sidney, *Apology for Poesy* (1598)

13 Compared with these, Italian trills are tame;
The tickled ears no heartfelt raptures raise.

Robert Burns, 'The Cotter's Saturday Night'

14 Then came the merry masquers in,
And carols roared with blythesome din;
If unmelodious was the song,
It was a hearty note, and strong.

Sir Walter Scott, *Marmion* (1808)

15 It's extraordinary how much gipsy music is like modern counterpoint; every one plays what he likes, but it all comes out together and it sounds all right.

Antonín Dvořák, quoted in Robertson, *Dvořák* (1964)

16 The farmer's daughter hath soft brown hair;
    (Butter and eggs and a pound of cheese)
And I met with a ballad, I can't say where,
    Which wholly consisted of lines like these.

C.S. Calverley, 'Ballad'

17 What kind of music is most necessary to men — scholarly or folk music?

Leo Tolstoy, remark to Fyodor Chaliapin, quoted in Bertensson and Leyda, *Sergei Rachmaninoff* (1965)

18 The fashion for popular airs has spread quickly throughout the musical world. From east to west the tiniest villages have been ransacked, and simple tunes, plucked from the mouths of hoary peasants, find themselves, to their consternation, trimmed with harmonic frills.

Claude Debussy, quoted in Lockspeiser, *Debussy* (1963)

1 Folksongs must be dressed to be taken from the fields to the city. In urban attire, however, they are awkward and uncomfortable. Their apparel must be cut in a fashion that will not hinder their breathing. Whether for chorus or for piano, the accompaniment should always be of such a nature as to make up for the lost fields and village.

Zoltán Kodály, Foreward to *Hungarian Folksongs* (1906)

2 Folk music is the ungarbled and ingenuous expression of the human mind and on that account it must reflect the essential and basic qualities of the human mind.

Cecil Sharp, *English Folk Song* (1907)

3 Flood the streets ... with folk-tunes, and those who now vulgarize themselves and others by singing coarse music-hall songs will soon drop them in favour of equally attractive but far better tunes of the folk. This will make the streets a pleasanter place for those who have sensitive ears, and will do incalculable good in civilising the masses.

Cecil Sharp, *English Folk Song* (1907)

4 [Of folk music] It is the free, direct speech of the soul.

Zoltán Kodály, in *Nyugat*, 1918

5 It [folk music] is a natural phenomenon, just like the various forms of the animal or vegetable kingdom. As a result, its individual . organisms — the melodies themselves — are examples of the highest artistic perfection.

Béla Bartók, in 1921, quoted in Ujfalussy, *Béla Bartók* (1971)

6 A genuine peasant melody of our land is a musical example of perfected art. I consider it quite as much of a masterpiece — in miniature — as a Bach fugue or Mozart sonata is a masterpiece in the larger forms.

Béla Bartók, quoted in Machlis, *Introduction to Contemporary Music* (1963)

7 Each folk song contains an entire man; his body, his soul, his surroundings, everything, everything. He who grows up among folk songs, grows into a complete man.

Leoš Janáček, quoted in Štědroň (ed.), *Leoš Janáček: Letters and Reminiscences* (1955)

8 In form, this [Hungarian] peasant music is the most perfect and most varied. It has an amazing force of expression, and besides, it is completely devoid of any sentimentality or superfluous embellishment.

Béla Bartók, in 1931, quoted in Ujfalussy, *Béla Bartók* (1971)

9 To put it vulgarly, the whole trouble with a folk song is that once you have played it through there is nothing much you can do except play it over again and play it rather louder.

Constant Lambert, *Music Ho!* (1934)

10 [Of the folk song movement] Solemn wassailing around the village pump.

Ernest Newman, quoted in Burke, *Musical Landscapes* (1983)

11 [With reference to folk songs] The people has no wish to be folk.

Bertolt Brecht, quoted in Willett, *Brecht in Context* (1984)

12 One should try everything once, except incest and folk-dancing.

Sir Arnold Bax, *Farewell My Youth* (1943)

13 I guess all songs is folk songs. I never heard no horse sing 'em.

Big Bill Broonzy, quoted in C. Keil, *Urban Blues* (1966); also attr. Louis Armstrong.

14 'Primitive' music is really not so primitive. It is ancient and therefore sophisticated.

Carlos Chavez, quoted in Machlis, *Introduction to Contemporary Music* (1963)

15 A truly creative musician is capable of producing, from his own imagination, melodies that are more authentic than folk-lore itself.

Heitor Villa-Lobos, quoted in Machlis, *Introduction to Contemporary Music* (1963)

16 The folk song is rich in elements which may be the inspiration of new creations resembling the original as a desk resembles a tree — only in the nature of its material.

Nathaniel Dett, quoted in Ewen, *American Composers* (1982)

FRANCE

See also GUERRE DES BOUFFONS.

17 One must acknowledge that the accents of passion are very often lacking in French airs, because our songs are content to tickle the ear with ornamentation without concerning themselves with the excitation of passion in their listeners.

Marin Mersenne, *Harmonie universelle* (1636)

18 I believe that I have demonstrated that there is neither rhythm nor melody in French music ... that French singing is endless squawking, unbearable to the unbiased ear ... And so I deduce that the French have no music and cannot have any music — and if they ever have, more's the pity for them.

Jean-Jacques Rousseau, *Lettre sur la musique française* (1753)

19 If only the accursed French language were not so villainous with *musique*! — It is a misery —

even German is divine beside it. — And when it comes to the singers and songstresses — they ought never to be called that — for they do not sing, but shriek, howl, and that full-throatedly, through nose and gullet.

Wolfgang Amadeus Mozart, Letter, 1778

1 [Of the state of French music] Everything is dead, save the authority of fools.

Hector Berlioz, Letter to Auguste Morel, 1864

2 [Of the Paris Opéra]
A stranger would take it for a railway station and, once inside, would mistake it for a Turkish bath.
  They continue to produce curious noises which the people who pay call music, but there is no need to believe them implicitly.

Clause Debussy, *Monsieur Croche, antidilettante* (1921)

3 [To Debussy] We ought to have our own music — if possible, without sauerkraut.

Erik Satie, quoted in Machlis, *Introduction to Contemporary Music* (1963)

4 [Of Les Six] Their work was momentarily amusing; but as far as exploration and discovery are concerned, it had about as little to do with pioneering as an expensive and overheated journey in a 'Blue Train', and its ideal (if it had one) was a commonplace 'Madonna of the Sleeping-Cars'.

J.B. Trend, *Manuel de Falla* (1929)

5 The organization of musical life in Paris is more stupid than anywhere else. France has completely lost her importance. Nothing advances.

Pierre Boulez, in 1959, quoted in Jacobson, *Reverberations* (1975)

FRANCK

6 It is a matter of little importance whether the music is descriptive — that is to say, sets out to awaken ideas about a given external subject — or whether it limits its intentions to the expression of a state of mind that is purely internal and exclusively psychological. What is of the first importance is that a composition should be musical, and emotional as well.

César Franck, quoted in Vallas, *César Franck* (1951)

7 [Of the *Trois Trios Concertants*] The listener's imagination can jump at will from the austere invocation of a patriarch to the shrieks of the joy of cannibals surrounding their victim, from the tumultuous and bloodshot scenes of revolution to lugubrious processions of penitents under the deep shadows of their sombre veils. Here is unadulterated melodrama; it is like an English novel in the style of Ann Radcliffe.

Maurice Bourges, in *La Gazette musicale*, 1842

8 And now for the three Francks — father, son, and Holy — but no! We will only say 'the younger son' ... They are like those authors who after publishing a new book, not only think but loudly assert that the worst fate that can befall them is to be ignored; they would rather be attacked, made fun of, torn to pieces by the critics than not be noticed at all, and so die in obscurity. And, of course, the authors are perfectly right.

Henri Blanchard, in *La Gazette musicale*, 1845

9 M. César-Auguste Franck has made two mistakes. First, his Christian names are César-Auguste; second, he writes good music quite seriously.

Franz Liszt, Letter to Ary Scheffer, 1845

10 [Of Franck's Symphony in D minor] It is the negation of music.

Georges Bizet, quoted in *Le Figaro*, 1896

11 The Choral is not a choral and the Fugue is not a fugue.

Camille Saint-Saëns, of Franck's *Prélude, Choral et Fugue*, quoted in Demuth, *Vincent d'Indy* (1951)

12 [Of Franck's *Psyché*] Melody reigns supreme with the most exaggerated tyranny. Across an uninterrupted series of harmonic abracadabras, there wind in and out tunes formulated on no ordered plan, which, having no good reason for beginning, can find none for ending.

Barbedette, in *Le Ménestrel*, 1890

13 God in Heaven! It is possible that César Franck had a vision of Him in writing this work [*Les Béatitudes*], but never for one moment does he reveal that vision to us in his music.

Camille Bellaigue, in *La Revue des Deux-Mondes*, 1893

14 [Of César Franck's symphonies] Cathedrals in sound.

Alfred Bruneau, Speech, 1904

15 It was said of Franck that the discovery of one single new chord was sufficient to make him happy for a whole day.

Norman Demuth, *Vincent d'Indy* (1951)

FUNCTIONAL MUSIC

16 Without a song the bush-knife is dull.

West African proverb, quoted in Roberts, *Black Music of Two Worlds* (1973)

17 Among other things proper to recreate man and give him pleasure, music is either the first or one of the principal, and we must think it is a gift of God deputed to that purpose.

Jean Calvin, *The Geneva Psalter* (1543)

18 Preposterous ass, that never read so far
To know the cause why music was ordained.

Was it not to refresh the mind of man,
After his studies or his usual pain?
(Lucentio)

William Shakespeare, *The Taming of the Shrew*, III.i

1 'Tis a sure sign that work goes on merrily,
when folks sing at it.

Isaac Bickerstaffe, *The Maid of the Mill*, I.i (1765)

2 Music is the nearest at hand, the most orderly,
the most delicate, and the most perfect, of all
bodily pleasures; it is also the only one which is
equally helpful to all the ages of man.

John Ruskin, 'Music in Greek Education'

3 Music is the only one of the arts that can not be
prostituted to a base use.

Elbert Hubbard, *A Thousand and One Epigrams* (1900)

4 We must bring about a music which is like
furniture — a music, that is, which will be part
of the noises of the environment, will take them
into consideration.

Erik Satie, quoted in Cage, *Silence* (1961)

5 [Discussing Satie] Enough of clouds, waves,
aquariums, water-sprites and nocturnal scents;
what we need is a music of the earth, everyday
music . . . music one can live in like a house.

Jean Cocteau, *Le Coq et l'Arlequin* (1918)

6 [Introducing Milhaud and Satie's *musique
d'ameublement* — 'furniture music'] We
earnestly beg of you not to attach any
importance to it and to behave throughout . . .
as if it did not exist. This music . . . claims to
contribute to life in the same way as a private
conversation, as a picture in the gallery, or the
chair on which you may or may not be sitting.

Pierre Bertin, quoted in Harding, *Erik Satie* (1975)

7 Music is essentially useless, as life is: but both
lend utility to their conditions.

George Santayana, *Little Essays* (1920)

8 [Of Hindemith's *Gebrauchsmusik*] There is no
regular demand for musical material as there is
for writing material or boxes of matches; there
is only a demand for something which creates
its own demand — a good piece of music.

Constant Lambert, *Music Ho!* (1934)

9 Music should not decorate, it should be
truthful.

Arnold Schoenberg, quoted in Kolneder, *Anton Webern*
(1968)

10 Whistle While You Work.

Larry Morey, title of song in Walt Disney's *Snow White*
(1937)

11 The métier of a composer is . . . to produce a
product that no one wants to use. I would
compare it to the manufacture of Kronstadt
hats, shoes without buttons, or Mystère corset.

Arthur Honegger, *I am a Composer* (1951)

12 The use of music as a kind of ambrosia to
titillate the aural senses while one's conscious
mind is otherwise occupied is the abomination
of every composer who takes his work
seriously.

Aaron Copland, *The Pleasures of Music* (1959)

13 It is better to make a piece of music than to
perform one, better to perform one than to
listen to one, better to listen to one than to
misuse it as a means of distraction,
entertainment, or acquisition of 'culture'.

John Cage, *Silence* (1961)

14 Hindemith talked about music as an artifact; it
is surprising that he did not manufacture spare
parts to replace those that became worn out by
constant performance.

Colin Wilson, *Brandy of the Damned* (1964)

15 Music is art. Muzak the science.

Muzak Corporation, slogan

16 We are usually compared with music, but that
is not our purpose at all. It's easier to describe
what Muzak is not than what it is. It is not
background music and it is not piped music and
it is not entertainment music. Because it is used
specifically and entirely for commercial
purposes, we call it functional music.

Lee Valvoda of the Muzak Corporation, quoted in
Palmer, *All You Need Is Love* (1976)

17 [Muzak] Sound you inhale.

Quoted in Harding, *Erik Satie* (1975)

18 *Will Ogdon:* What of the recent environments in
Europe and Japan that immerse the visitor in a
continuous sound bath along with other
sensory stimuli . . . ?
Ernst Křenek: It sounds somehow familiar to me.
We have had it in this country for a long time.
We call it Muzak.

Will Ogdon, in *Perspectives of New Music*, 1972

19 In the brothels, music had the same function as
wine, spirits, and striptease; it helped prepare
clients for the main event upstairs.

Tony Palmer, *All You Need Is Love* (1976)

FUTURISM

20 We shall amuse ourselves by orchestrating in
our minds the noise of metal shutters of shop
windows, the slamming of doors, the bustle
and shuffle of crowds, the multitudinous
uproar of railway stations, forges, mills,
printing presses, power stations, and
underground railways.

Luigi Russolo, 'The Art of Noises' (1913)

GERMANY

21 Diverse nations have diverse fashions, and
differ in habits, diet, studies, speech and song.

Hence it is that the English do carol; the French sing; the Spaniards weep; the Italians, which dwell about the coasts of Ianua, caper with their voices; the others bark; but the Germans (which I am ashamed to utter) do howl like wolves.

John Dowland (trans.), *Andreas Ornithoparcus His Micrologus* (1609)

1   Our German musicians are left to take care of themselves, so that under the necessity of working for their bread many can never think of attaining proficiency, much less of distinguishing themselves.

Johann Sebastian Bach, 'A short, but indispensable sketch of what constitutes a well-appointed church music . . .' (1730)

2   Musical discussions are conducted in Berlin with more heat and animosity than elsewhere. Of course, as there are more theorists than practitioners in this city, there are more critics too.

Charles Burney, *Present State of Music in Germany* (1773)

3   Church music is less beautiful in Germany than in Italy, because instruments always predominate there. . . . violins and trumpets form part of the Dresden orchestra during divine service, and the music appears more martial than religious; the contrast between the vigorous impression it produces with the contemplativeness of a church is not agreeable.

Madame de Staël, *De l'Allemagne* (1813)

4   In order to succeed today you have to be either dead or German.

Georges Bizet, Letter to Louis Gallet

5   Germany, the country of music, is impossible for anyone who bears a French name and heart.

Georges Bizet, Letter, 1871

6   [Of German composers] *Ils ne sont pas de notre tempérament, ils sont si lourds, pas clairs.* They are not of our temperament, they are so heavy, and lack clarity.

Claude Debussy, quoted by Nadezhda von Meck, Letter to Tchaikovsky, 1880

7   There are only two kinds of music; German music and bad music.

H.L. Mencken, attr.

GERSHWIN

8   An entire composition written in jazz could not live.

George Gershwin, 'The Composer in the Machine Age' (1930)

9   I am a better melodist than Schubert.

George Gershwin, attr.

10   [Of Gershwin and jazz] He is the prince who has taken Cinderella by the hand and openly proclaimed her a princess to the astonished world.

Walter Damrosch, at the first performance of Gershwin's Concerto in F, quoted in Schwartz, *Gershwin* (1973)

11   George's music gets around so much before an opening that the first night audience think it's at a revival.

George S. Kaufman, quoted in Green, *The World of Musical Comedy* (1974)

12   An evening with Gershwin is a Gershwin evening.

Oscar Levant, quoted in Green, *The World of Musical Comedy* (1974)

13   [Of *Porgy and Bess*] A libretto that should never have been accepted on a subject that should never have been chosen [by] a man who should never have attempted it.

Virgil Thomson, in *Modern Music*, 1935

14   An occasional work of his on a programme is all very well, but an entire evening is too much. It is like a meal of chocolate eclairs.

Richard Drake Saunders, in *The Musical Courier*, 1937

15   George Gershwin died last week. I don't have to believe it if I don't want to.

John O'Hara, in 1937, attr.

16   The *Rhapsody* is not a composition at all. It's a string of separate paragraphs stuck together — with a thin paste of flour and water . . . I don't think there has been such an inspired melodist on this earth since Tchaikovsky . . . but if you want to speak of a *composer*, that's another matter.

Leonard Bernstein, in *The Atlantic Monthly*, 1955

GIBBONS

17   It is proportion that beautifies everything, this whole universe consists of it, and music is measured by it, which I have endeavoured to observe in the composition of these few airs.

Orlando Gibbons, Dedication to *The First Set of Madrigals and Motets* (1612)

18   They [his compositions] are like young scholars newly entered, that at first sing very fearfully; it requires your patience therefore to bear with their imperfections: they were taught to sing only to delight you, and if you shall take any pleasure in them, they have their end, and I my wish.

Orlando Gibbons, Dedication to *The First Set of Madrigals and Motets* (1612)

19   . . . this Orlando parallels di Lasso: Whose triple praise would tire a very Tasso.

Anon., *Parthenia, or the Maydenhead of the first musicke that ever was printed for the Virginalls* (1612)

1 *Inter musas et musicae nato.* Born among the
   Muses and Music.

   Anon., monument to Orlando Gibbons in Canterbury
   Cathedral; trans. William Boyce

GILBERT AND SULLIVAN

2 [On falling from a punt] I've always been a
   contrapuntalist.

   Sir Arthur Sullivan, quoted in Brahms, *Gilbert and
   Sullivan* (1975)

3 It has been our purpose to produce something
   that should be innocent but not imbecile.

   W.S. Gilbert, Speech after first American performance
   of *H.M.S. Pinafore*, 1879

4 I only know two tunes. One is 'God Save the
   Queen'. The other isn't.

   W.S. Gilbert, quoted in Lebrecht, *Discord* (1982)

5 You ought to write a *grand* opera, Sir Arthur,
   you would do it so well.

   Queen Victoria, remark to Sullivan, quoted in
   Lebrecht, *Discord* (1982)

6 A giant may play at times, but Mr Sullivan is
   always playing.

   The Figaro (London), 1878

7 I heard *Rosenkavalier* for the first time after the
   war (the First War) and I confess I prefer
   Gilbert and Sullivan ... Sullivan has a sense of
   timing and punctuation which I have never
   been able to find in Strauss.

   Igor Stravinsky, interview in *The New York Times*, 1968

THE GLASS HARMONICA

8 When Dr [Benjamin] Franklin invented the
   [glass] Harmonica, he concealed it from his wife
   till the instrument was fit to play; and then
   woke her with it one night, when she took it for
   the music of angels.

   Leigh Hunt, *Autobiography* (1850), 'Musical Memories'

GLINKA

9 It seems to me that I, too, should be able to give
   our theatre a work worthy of her ... I want
   everything to be national: above all, the subject
   — and the music likewise — so much so that
   my dear compatriots will feel they are at home,
   and so that abroad I shall not be considered a
   braggart or a crow who seeks to deck himself in
   borrowed plumes.

   Mikhail Glinka, Letter, 1832

10 I should like to unite in legitimate bonds the
   Russian popular song with the good old
   Western fugue. We are at the people's service
   to arrange such a marriage.

   Mikhail Glinka, speaking of *A Life for the Tsar*, quoted
   in Samuel, *Prokofiev* (trans. 1971)

11 If my muse should awaken unexpectedly, I shall
   write for orchestra without a text, renouncing
   Russian music like a Russian winter. I do not
   want a Russian play — I have had enough to do
   with that.

   Mikhail Glinka, Letter to Nestor Kukolnik, 1855

12 [Of *A Life for the Tsar*]
   Hearing the new creation
   Let envy, darkened with spiteful lust,
   Rail — but yet it cannot
   Trample our Glinka in the dust.

   Aleksander Pushkin, *Comic Canon*

13 How came Glinka, who had long been an
   insipid dilettante, suddenly in a single stride to
   stand alongside (yes! alongside!) Mozart,
   Beethoven, and whomsoever you will?

   Piotr Ilyich Tchaikovsky, Diary, 1888

GLUCK

14 There is no musical rule that I have not
   willingly sacrificed to dramatic effect.

   Christoph Willibald von Gluck, Preface to *Alceste*
   (1767)

15 I am searching, with a noble, sensitive and
   natural melody, and with a form of declamation
   exactly in accord with the prosody of each
   language and the character of each people, to
   establish the means of producing a music
   belonging to all nations, and to obliterate the
   ridiculous distinction of national musics.

   Christoph Willibald von Gluck, Letter to d'Auvergne,
   published in *Le Mercure de France*, 1773

16 If you wait a little I shall be able to tell you from
   personal experience.

   Christoph Willibald von Gluck, in *c.* 1783, when asked
   by Salieri whether a bass or a tenor should sing the
   part of Christ in *The Last Judgement*, quoted in Cooper,
   Gluck (1935)

17 My cook understands more about counterpoint
   than he does.

   George Frideric Handel, attr.

18 I don't know whether this passage conforms to
   the rules of art or not, but I can say this to you
   — that we should all be proud, myself included,
   had we conceived and written it.

   Francesco Durante, remark while perusing the score of
   Gluck's *La Clemenza di Tito*, *c.* 1752, quoted in Cooper,
   Gluck (1935)

19 Hearing *Iphigénie* I forget that I am in an opera
   house and think I am hearing a Greek tragedy.

   Baron Grimm, quoted in Graf, *Composer and Critic*
   (1947)

20 Between ourselves, your prosody was very bad;
   at least, you turn the French language into an

accentuated language when it is, on the contrary, a language of fine shades.

Claude Debussy, Open letter to Gluck, in *Gil Blas*, 1903

1   The melodies of Gluck are at times mediocre, and the beauty of his art is above all moral.

Romain Rolland, quoted in Cooper, *Gluck* (1935)

GOUNOD

2   Musical ideas sprang to my mind like a flight of butterflies, and all I had to do was to stretch out my hand to catch them.

Charles Gounod, of his period in Provence, 1863, quoted in Harding, *Gounod* (1973)

3   My humiliating profession of decomposer of music.

Charles Gounod, after demands for major changes to his opera *Mireille*, quoted in Harding, *Gounod* (1973)

4   The resources of sonority are still largely unexplored.

Charles Gounod, Letter to Saint-Saëns

5   I fight against the void, I think I've written something acceptable, and then, when I look at it again, I find it execrable.

Charles Gounod, in 1870, quoted in Harding, *Gounod* (1973)

6   *Female admirer:* How do you think of those lovely melodies?
Gounod: God, Madame, sends me down some of his angels and they whisper sweet melodies in my ear.

Quoted in Harding, *Gounod* (1973)

7   A man has only a certain number of virtues, and all of Gounod's are concentrated on his art.

Georges Bizet, Letter to his father, 1859

8   For him art is priesthood: he has said so himself ... he is the only man among our modern musicians who truly loves his art.

Georges Bizet, Letter to Gruyer

9   [Referring to Gounod] To be a great artist it is not necessary to be an honourable man.

Georges Bizet, quoted in Dean, *Bizet* (1975)

10 *Faust* was Gounod's Austerlitz. *La Reine de Saba* will be his Waterloo.

Unnamed critic, in 1862, quoted in Harding, *Gounod* (1973)

11 You were the beginning of my life as an artist. I spring from you. You are the cause and I am the consequence.

Georges Bizet, Letter to Gounod, 1872

12 [Of Gounod's *Faust*] *Musique de cocottes.* Hens' music *or* Tarts' music.

Richard Wagner, quoted in Dean, *Bizet* (1975)

13 [The church music] of Gounod and company seems to come from some kind of hysterical mysticism and has the effect of a sinister farce.

Claude Debussy, Letter to Vasnier, 1885

14 A base soul who poured a sort of bath-water melody down the back of every woman he met. Margaret or Madeleine, it was all the same.

George Moore, *Memoirs of my Dead Life* (1906)

15 [Of Gounod's *Faust*] How ironical that the world's profoundest expression of the denying spirit and of man's genius for creative life [Goethe's *Faust*] ... should have served as the basis of an opera which glorifies insincerity of mind and sentiment!

Neville Cardus, in *The Manchester Guardian*, 1938

GRAINGER

16 Salvation Army Booth objected to the devil having all the good tunes. I object to jazz and vaudeville having all the best instruments!

Percy Grainger, Preface to *Spoon River* (1930)

17 The big object of the modern composer is to bring music more and more into line with the irregularities and complexities of nature and away from the straight lines and simplifications imposed by man.

Percy Grainger, quoted in Ewen, *American Composers* (1982)

GRIEG

18 I've also done something about the Hall of the Old Man of Dovre [in *Peer Gynt*], and I literally can't bear to listen to it, it is so full of cow-turds, Norse-Norsehood, and Be-to-thyself-enoughness!

Edvard Grieg, Letter to Frants Beyer, 1874

19 Many a time I go and stare up at the clouds, as if I could find there the Norwegian drama in Norwegian music which I have dreamt of, which I have always believed I could create one day, but which I now begin to believe is fated to come from another.

Edvard Grieg, Letter to Frants Beyer, 1886

20 The more deeply the heart is moved, the more reticent, the more enigmatic is the expression.

Edvard Grieg, Letter to Henry T. Finck

21 I am sure my music has a taste of codfish in it.

Edvard Grieg, Speech, 1903

22 Persevere; I tell you, you have the gifts, and — do not let them intimidate you!

Franz Liszt, Letter to Grieg

1 What charm, what inimitable and rich musical imagery! ... What interest, novelty, and independence!

Pyotr Ilyich Tchaikovsky, quoted in Finck, *Grieg and his Music* (1929)

2 Orpheus with his wondrous tones
Roused souls in beasts, struck fire from stones.
Of stones has Norway not a few,
And beasts she has in plenty too.
Play then, that sparks from rocks may leap!
Play then, and pierce the brutes' hides deep!

Henrik Ibsen, verse written in Grieg's album; trans. Horton.

3 Grieg's Peer Gynt music ... consists of two or three catchpenny phrases served up with plenty of orchestral sugar.

George Bernard Shaw, in *The World*, 1892

4 He walked here beside me,
the great tone-poet;
I heard the waters flow
with a lovelier cadence.
And never in the world before,
no matter how often I had trod the same path,
had I understood completely
how dear Nature had become to me in this place.

Bjørnsterne Bjørnsen, verses, 1899; trans. Horton.

5 [Of Grieg's music] *L'on a dans la bouche le goût bizarre et charmant d'un bonbon rose qui serait fourré de neige.* One has in one's mouth the bizarre and charming taste of a pink sweet stuffed with snow.

Claude Debussy, in *Gil Blas*, 1903

6 In these days when much music suggests nervous maladies and the mad house, when there seems to be a fetid atmosphere hanging over the concert room and opera house, Grieg comes to this disgusted and stifling musician like a whiff of pure air.

Louis C. Elson, quoted in Finck, *Grieg and his Music* (1929)

GUERRE DES BOUFFONS

See also FRANCE, ITALY.

7 I find the musical schism, which our Italian actors have caused in Paris, highly amusing. To tell the truth the Italians have for the most part so concentrated on vocal display ... that they have not only forgotten this same Nature, but often go so far as completely to suppress her.

Pietro Antonio Domenico Bonaventura Metastasio, Letter to Raniero de Calzabigi, 1752

8 The best way of playing the clavier or any other instrument is that which succeeds in skilfully combining what is neat and brilliant in the French taste with what is ingratiating in the Italian way of singing. For this the Germans are particularly well adapted as long as they remain unprejudiced.

Carl Philipp Emanuel Bach, *Essay* (1753)

9 Any voice is good in Italian music, because the beauties of Italian singing are in the music itself, whereas those of French singing, if there are any, are all in the art of the singer.

Jean-Jacques Rousseau, *Letter on French Music* (1753)

10 Italian music is deficient in that of which it has an excess; French music in that which it lacks.

Jean d'Alembert, Letter to Rameau

11 To embrace one national taste rather than another is to prove that one is very much a novice in the art.

Jean-Philippe Rameau, *Code de musique pratique* (1760)

THE GUITAR

12 To use a woman or a guitar, one must know how to tune them.

Spanish proverb

13 The harmonic effects which our guitarists produce unconsciously represent one of the marvels of natural art.

Manuel de Falla, 'Cante Jondo' (1922)

14 I smash a guitar because I like them. I usually smash a guitar when it's at its best.

Pete Townshend, in 1965, quoted in Green, *The Book of Rock Quotes* (1982)

HANDEL

15 [Asked why he borrowed material composed by Bononcini] It's much too good for him; he did not know what to do with it.

George Frideric Handel, attr. in Lang, *George Frideric Handel* (1967)

16 [To a singer who had threatened to jump on Handel's harpischord] Let me know when you will do that and I will advertise it. For I am sure more people will come to see you jump than to hear you sing.

George Frideric Handel, quoted in Lebrecht, *Discord* (1982)

17 *Madame, je sais que vous êtes une veritable diablesse, mais je vous ferai savoir, moi, que je suis Béelzebub, le chef de diables.* Madam, I know you are a veritable devil, but I would have you know that I am Beelzebub, the head devil.

George Frideric Handel, remark to the singer Francesca Cuzzoni, 1723, quoted in Young, *Handel* (1947)

18 My Lord, I should be sorry if I only entertained them; I wished to make them better.

George Frideric Handel, remark to Lord Kinnoul after a performance of *Messiah*, quoted in Young, *Handel* (1947)

1 [On composing the Hallelujah Chorus] Whether
I was in my body or out of my body as I wrote
it I know not. God knows.

George Frideric Handel, quoted in Rolland, *Essays on
Music* (1948), 'Handel'

2 [On composing *Messiah*] I did think I did see all
Heaven before me and the great God Himself.

George Frideric Handel, attr., quoted in Lang, *Georg
Frideric Handel* (1967)

3 Handel asked the King [George III], then a
young child, and listening very earnestly while
he played, if he liked the music, and the Prince
warmly expressed his pleasure. 'A good boy, a
good boy,' he cried, 'you shall protect my fame
when I am dead.'

Quoted in Southey, *Commonplace Book* (1849-51)

4 [Of Handel's playing] I found . . . nothing
worthy to remark but the elasticity of his
fingers.

Sir Isaac Newton, quoted in Hawkins, *Life of Johnson*
(1787)

5 [Of Burlington House]
There *Handel* strikes the strings, the melting
     strain
Transports the soul, and thrills through ev'ry
     vein.

John Gay, *Trivia* (1716)

6 Conceive the highest you can of his abilities,
and they are far beyond anything you can
conceive.

Dr John Arbuthnot, quoted in Young, *Handel* (1947)

7 Yet as thy volant touch pursues
Through all proportions low and high
The wondrous fugue, it peace renews
Serene as the unsullied sky.

Daniel Prat, 'Ode to Mr Handel, on his Playing the
Organ, 1722'

8 The inspired master of our art.

Christoph Willibald von Gluck, quoted in Kelly,
Reminiscences (1826)

9 [Awaiting a visit from Handel] O pray let me
see a German genius before I die!

Jonathan Swift, quoted in Hughes, *Haydn* (1970)

10 [Handel's] oratorios thrive abundantly. For my
part, they give me an idea of heaven, where
everybody is to sing whether they have voices
or not.

Horace Walpole, Letter, 1743

11 [Of Handel's playing] Silence, the truest
applause, succeeded, the instant that he
addressed himself to the instrument; and that
was so profound, that it checked respiration,
and seemed to control the functions of nature.

John Hawkins, *A General History of the Science and
Practice of Music* (1776)

12 [On hearing the Hallelujah Chorus] He is the
master of us all.

Joseph Haydn, quoted in Headington, *The Bodley Head
History of Western Music* (1974)

13 Remember Handel? Who, that was not born
Deaf as the dead to harmony, forgets,
Or can, the more than Homer of his age?

William Cowper, *The Task*, VI (1785)

14 Commemoration-mad; content to hear
(Oh wonderful effect of music's pow'r!)
Messiah's eulogy, for Handel's sake.

William Cowper, *The Task*, VI (1785)

15 Handel's general look was somewhat heavy
and sour; but when he did smile, it was his sire
the sun, bursting out of a black cloud.

Charles Burney, *An Account of the Musical Performances
. . . in Commemoration of Handel* (1785)

16 Handel understands effect better than any of us
— when he chooses, he strikes like a
thunderbolt.

Wolfgang Amadeus Mozart, quoted in Young, *Handel*
(1947)

17 Handel, to him I bow the knee.

Ludwig van Beethoven, when asked who was the
greatest ever composer, quoted in Scott, *Beethoven*
(1934)

18 [Of an edition of Handel's works] There is the
truth.

Ludwig van Beethoven, remark on his deathbed,
quoted in Young, *Handel* (1947)

19 A good old pagan at heart.

Edward Fitzgerald, quoted in Young, *Handel* (1947)

20 I think Handel never gets out of his wig, that is,
out of his age: his Hallelujah Chorus is a
chorus, not of angels, but of well-fed earthly
choristers, ranged tier above tier in a Gothic
cathedral, with princes for audience, and their
military trumpets flourishing over the full
volume of the organ. Handel's gods are like
Homer's, and his sublime never reached
beyond the region of the clouds.

Edward Fitzgerald, Letter, 1842

21 Handel was the Jupiter of music . . . his
hallelujahs open the heavens. He utters the
word 'Wonderful' as if all their trumpets spoke
together. And then, when he comes to earth, to
make love amidst nymphs and shepherds (for
the beauties of all religions find room in his
breast), his strains drop milk and honey, and
his love is the youthfulness of the Golden Age.

Leigh Hunt, *Table Talk* (1851)

22 A tub of pork and beer.

Hector Berlioz, quoted in Elliot, *Berlioz* (1967)

1 We have all had our Handelian training in church, and the perfect church-going mood is one of pure abstract reverence. A mood of active intelligence would be scandalous. Thus we get broken into the custom of singing Handel as if he meant nothing; and as it happens that he meant a great deal, and was tremendously in earnest about it, we know rather less about him in England than they do in the Andaman Islands, since the Andamans are only unconscious of him, whereas we are misconscious.

George Bernard Shaw, *Music in London 1890-94* (1931)

2 Handel is so great and so simple that no one but a professional musician is unable to understand him.

Samuel Butler, *Note-Books* (pub. 1912)

3 If Handel ... were confronted with the gigantic crowds of singers that now strive to interpret his music, he would at once cut them down to a quarter of their bloated dimensions or rewrite the orchestral portions of his scores for the largest combination of instruments he could lay his hands upon.

Sir Thomas Beecham, *A Mingled Chime* (1944)

4 I've never been moved by *Messiah* in my life. The importance of *Messiah* is that it is a work in the *grand* manner. It is one of the *grand* scores.

Sir Thomas Beecham, quoted in Reid, *Thomas Beecham* (1961)

5 If Income Tax collectors ever indulge in community singing, I have no doubt that they sing the choruses from the *Messiah*, for the *Messiah* is the first great anthem of man's enslavement by materialism.

Compton Mackenzie, quoted in Hughes and Van Thal, *The Music Lover's Companion* (1971)

6 He worked in a style which had, so far as music can ever have, utilitarian significance ... wherein both God and man were served in the same homely, well-bred idiom.

Percy M. Young, *Handel* (1947)

7 Bach invaded the *Himmelreich*; Handel founded *Lebensraum* on earth.

Percy M. Young, *Handel* (1947)

HARMONY

See also DISSONANCE.

8 *Armonia est amenitas quaedam ex convenienti sono causata.* Harmony is a certain pleasantness caused by an agreeable sound.

Johannes Tinctoris, *Dictionary of Musical Terms* (c. 1475)

9 Do you know that our soul is composed of harmony?

Leonardo da Vinci, *Notebooks*

10 Just accord all music makes.

Sir Philip Sidney, 'To the Tune of a Spanish Song'

11 All concord's born of contraries.

Ben Jonson, *Cynthia's Revels*, V.ii (1601)

12 How doth music amaze us when of sound discords she maketh the sweetest harmony? And who can show us the reason why two basins, bowls, brass pots, or the like, of the same bigness, the one being full, the other empty, shall stricken be a just diapason in sound one to the other?

Henry Peacham, *The Compleat Gentleman* (1622)

13 The melting voice through mazes running,
Untwisting all the chains that tie
The hidden soul of harmony.

John Milton, 'L'Allegro' (1632)

14 From harmony, from heav'nly harmony
　　This universal frame began:
　　From harmony to harmony
Through all the compass of the notes it ran,
The diapason closing full in man.

John Dryden, 'A Song for St Cecilia's Day' (1687)

15 Many have held the soul to be
Nearly allied to harmony.

Matthew Green, *The Spleen* (1737)

16 Melody is the main thing; harmony is useful only to charm the ear.

Joseph Haydn, quoted in Landowska, *Landowska on Music* (1969)

17 CONSONANCE is derived from a coincidence of two or more sounds, which being heard together, by their agreement and union, afford to ears capable of judging and feeling, a delight of a most grateful kind.

Charles Burney, *A General History of Music* (1776-89)

18 Dust as we are, the immortal spirit grows
Like harmony in music; there is a dark
Inscrutable workmanship that reconciles
Discordant elements, makes them cling
　　together
In one society.

William Wordsworth, *The Prelude*, I

19 I struck one chord of music
Like the sound of a great Amen.

Adelaide Ann Proctor, 'A Lost Chord' (1858); see Samuel Butler below

20 Give me the keys. I feel for the common chord
　　again,
Sliding by semitones, till I sink to the minor, —
　　yes,
And I blunt it into a ninth, and I stand on alien
　　ground,
Surveying awhile the heights I rolled from into
　　the deep;
Which, hark, I have dared and done, for my
　　resting-place is found,

The C Major of this life: so, now I will try to
   sleep.

Robert Browning, 'Abt Vogler'

1 The realm of harmonies was always my dream-
world.

Edvard Grieg, Letter to Henry T. Finck

2 'Getting into the key of C sharp', he said, 'is
like an unprotected female travelling on the
Metropolitan Railway, and finding herself at
Shepherd's Bush, without quite knowing where
she wants to go to. How is she ever to get safe
back to Clapham Junction?'

Samuel Butler, *The Way of All Flesh* (1903)

3 It should be 'The Lost Progression', for the
young lady was mistaken in supposing she had
ever heard any single chord 'like the sound of a
great Amen' ... Fancy being in the room with
her while she was strumming about and
hunting after her chord! Fancy being in heaven
with her when she had found it!

Samuel Butler, *Note-Books* (pub. 1912)

4 It is quite evident that there is no further
revolution possible in the harmonic sphere,
none, at any rate, so long as we confine
ourselves to the tempered scale and normal
division by half tones.

Aaron Copland, *Music and Imagination* (1952)

5 Nowadays *harmony* comes almost as a shock.

Kathleen Raine, Letter to Arthur Bliss

THE HARP

6 Then will I go unto the altar of God, unto God
my exceeding joy: yea, upon the harp will I
praise thee, O God my God.

Psalms 43:4

7 Wherefore my bowels shall sound like a harp
for Moab, and mine inward parts for Kirharesh.

Isaiah 16:11

8 Harp not on that string, madam.
(Richard)

William Shakespeare, *Richard III*, IV.iv

9 If the pulse of the patriot, soldier, or lover,
Have throbb'd at our lay, 'tis thy glory alone;
I was but as the wind, passing heedlessly over,
And all the wild sweetness I wak'd was thy
   own.

Thomas Moore, 'Dear Harp of My Country'

10 Hearken, my minstrels! which of ye all
Touched his harp with that dying fall,
   So sweet, so soft, so faint,
It seemed an angel's whispered call
   To an expiring saint?

Sir Walter Scott, *The Bridal of Triermain* (1813)

THE HARPSICHORD

11 The harpsichord is perfect as to its compass,
and brilliant in itself, but as it is impossible to
swell out or diminish the volume of its sound, I
shall always feel grateful to any who, by the
exercise of infinite art supported by fine taste,
contrive to render this instrument capable of
expression.

François Couperin, Preface to *Pièces de Clavecin*, Book 1
(1713)

12 Sounds like two skeletons copulating on a
corrugated tin roof.

Sir Thomas Beecham, quoted in Atkins and Newman
Beecham Stories (1978)

HAYDN

13 [Of his period as *Kapellmeister* at the Esterházy
court] I was cut off from the world. There was
no one to confuse or torment me, and I was
forced to become original.

Joseph Haydn, quoted in Hadden, *Haydn* (1934)

14 I get up early, and as soon as I have dressed I
go down on my knees and pray God and the
Blessed Virgin that I may have another
successful day. Then when I've had some
breakfast I sit down at the clavier and begin my
search. If I hit on an idea quickly, it goes ahead
easily and without much trouble. But if I can't
get on, I know that I must have forfeited God's
grace by some fault of mine, and then I pray
once more for grace till I feel I'm forgiven.

Joseph Haydn, quoted in Hughes, *Haydn* (1970)

15 I was never a quick writer.

Joseph Haydn, quoted in Hughes, *Haydn* (1970)

16 [On being asked for an opera] I should ... be
taking a great risk, since it is hardly possible for
anyone to stand beside the great Mozart.

Joseph Haydn, Letter to Roth, 1787 (two months after
the première of *Don Giovanni*)

17 Friends often flatter me that I have some
genius, but he [Mozart] stands far above me.

Joseph Haydn, quoted in Hughes, *Haydn* (1970)

18 That will make the ladies scream.

Joseph Haydn, of the 'surprise' in the 'Surprise'
Symphony, No. 94, quoted in Gyrowetz, *Memoirs*
(1848)

19 [To a child violinist] No need to be scared of *me*,
my boy, I'm a bad player myself.

Joseph Haydn, quoted in Hughes, *Haydn* (1970)

20 [At a performance of *The Creation*] Not from me
— it came from above.

Joseph Haydn, quoted in Headington, *The Bodley Head
History of Western Music* (1974)

1 I was never so devout as when I was at work on
   The Creation.

   Joseph Haydn, quoted in Hughes, *Haydn* (1970)

2 Oh God, how much is still to be done in this
   splendid art, even by such a man as I have
   been!

   Joseph Haydn, Letter to George August Griesinger,
   1799

3 I really am a living keyboard.

   Joseph Haydn, quoted in Dies, *Biographische
   Nachrichten über Joseph Haydn* (1810)

4 Don't be frightened, children, where Haydn is
   no harm can come to you.

   Joseph Haydn, to his terrified servants during the
   French bombardment of Vienna, 1809, quoted in
   Hughes, *Haydn* (1970)

5 Anyone can see that I'm a good-natured fellow.

   Joseph Haydn, attr.

6 I cannot compose anything without it [a 'glad
   ring']: for I translate into music the state of my
   heart. When I think of the Grace of God in
   Jesus Christ, my heart is so full of joy that the
   notes fairly dance and leap from my pen.

   Josef Haydn, attr.

7 [Of the young Haydn] That boy doesn't sing, he
   crows.

   Empress Maria Theresa, quoted in Hughes, *Haydn*
   (1970)

8 There are painted on his countenance all the
   genius, goodness, propriety, benevolence and
   rectitude which constantly characterise his
   writings.

   Charles Burney, *The Present State of Music in Germany*
   (1773)

9 I have had the great Haydn here, I think him as
   good a creature as great musician.

   Charles Burney, Letter to Arthur Young, 1791

10 Among other observations His Majesty [George
   III] said: 'Dr Haydn, you have written a good
   deal.' Haydn modestly replied: 'Yes, Sire, a
   great deal more than is good.' His Majesty
   neatly rejoined: 'Oh, no, the world contradicts
   that.'

   A. Gyrowetz, *Memoirs* (1848)

11 Though I had some instruction from Haydn, I
   never learned anything from him.

   Ludwig van Beethoven, quoted in Scott, *Beethoven*
   (1934)

12 Haydn, that genius of vulgar music who
   induces an inordinate thirst for beer.

   Mily Balakirev, Letter to Tchaikovsky, 1869

13 So far as genius can exist in a man who is
   merely virtuous, Haydn had it. He went as far
   as the limits that morality sets to intellect.

   Friedrich Nietzsche, *The Will to Power* (1888)

HEAVENLY MUSIC

See also SPHERES.

14 ... we shall all be changed,
   In a moment, in the twinkling of an eye, at the
   last trump; for the trumpet shall sound, and the
   dead shall be raised incorruptible ...

   1 Corinthians 15:51-2

15 And I heard a voice from heaven, as the voice
   of many waters, and as the voice of a great
   thunder: and I heard the voice of harpers
   harping with their harps:
   And they sung as it were a new song ... and no
   man could learn that song but the hundred and
   forty and four thousand, which were redeemed
   from the earth.

   Revelation 14:2-3

16 Proportionis fine with sound celestiall,
   Duplat, triplat, diatesserial,
   Sequi altera, and decupla resortis
   Diapason of mony sindrie sortis.

   Gavin Douglas, *The Palice of Honour* (c. 1501)

17 In that house they shall dwell, where there
   shall be ... no noise nor silence, but one equal
   music.

   John Donne, Sermon

18 Since I am coming to that holy room,
   Where, with thy Choir of Saints for evermore,
   I shall be made thy music; as I come
   I tune the instrument here at the door,
   And what I must do then, think now before.

   John Donne, 'Hymn to God my God, in my Sickness'

19 When I but hear her sing, I fare
   Like one that raised, holds his ear
       To some bright star in the supremest
       Round,
   Through which, besides the light that's seen,
   There may be heard, from Heaven within,
       The rests of Anthems, that the Angels
       sound.

   Owen Felltham, *Lusoria*, 'When, dearest, I but think of
   thee' (also attr. to John Suckling)

20 Where the bright seraphim in burning row
   Their loud up-lifted Angel trumpets blow.

   John Milton, 'At a Solemn Musick'

21 Then, crowned again, their golden harps they
       took,
   Harps ever tuned, that glittering by their side
   Like quivers hung; and with preamble sweet
   Of charming symphony they introduce
   Their sacred song, and waken raptures high;
   No voice exempt, no voice but well could join
   Melodious part; such concord is in heaven.

   John Milton, *Paradise Lost*, III

22 So he passed over, and all the trumpets
   sounded for him on the other side.

   John Bunyan, *Pilgrim's Progress* (1678)

1   The angels all were singing out of tune,
    And hoarse with having little else to do.
    Lord Byron, *The Vision of Judgement* (1822)

2   As I went under the new telegraph-wire, I
    heard it vibrating like a harp high overhead. It
    was as the sound of a far-off glorious life, a
    supernal life, which came down to us, and
    vibrated the lattice-work of this life of ours.
    Henry David Thoreau, Journal, 1851

HENZE

3   I detest politicking, the struggle for or against
    something in music; music reaches people of its
    own accord, when it wants to. It cannot be
    imposed, can hardly be explained, cannot be
    propagated.
    Hans Werner Henze, *Music and Politics* (1982),
    'Wavering and Positionless' (1957)

4   When I start a work I never have a plan, a
    preconceived opinion or theory to direct me. I
    do not think so little of music that I fancy I
    know more than it does.
    Hans Werner Henze, *Music and Politics* (1982)
    'Wavering and Positionless' (1957)

5   My own music keeps its distance, and will
    continue to do so, as long as it is possible for
    people with authorized murderous intentions or
    an unpunished murderous past to listen to it,
    talk about it and judge it.
    Hans Werner Henze, *Music and Politics* (1982), 'Music
    as a Means of Resistance' (1963)

6   Old forms seem to me, as it were, like classical
    ideals of beauty, no longer attainable but still
    visible in the far distance, stirring memory like
    dreams; but the path towards them is filled
    with the age's greatest darkness and is the most
    difficult and the most impossible. To me it
    seems the only folly worth living for.
    Hans Werner Henze, *Music and Politics* (1982)
    'Instrumental Composition' (1963)

7   I have taken the decision that in my work I will
    embody all the difficulties and all the problems
    of contemporary bourgeois music, and that I
    will, however, try to transform these into
    something usable, into something that the
    masses can understand.
    Hans Werner Henze, *Music and Politics* (1982) 'Art and
    the Revolution' (1971)

8   My profession ... consists of bringing truths
    nearer to the point where they explode.
    Hans Werner Henze, *Music and Politics* (1982),
    'German music in the 1940s and 1950s'

HINDEMITH

9   *Richard Strauss:* Why do you compose atonal
    music? You have plenty of talent.
    Hindemith: Herr Professor, you make your
    music, and I'll make mine.
    Quoted in Skelton, *Paul Hindemith* (1975)

10 In whatever we begin we must keep our
    integrity, directing our acts to both centres. Let
    us thank the earth. Let us praise heaven.
    Paul Hindemith, *Mathis der Maler* (1935)

11 The key and its body of chords is not the
    natural basis of tonal activity. What Nature
    provides is the intervals. The juxtaposition of
    intervals, as of chords, which are the extensions
    of intervals, *gives rise to the key*. We are no
    longer the prisoners of the key.
    Paul Hindemith, *The Craft of Musical Composition* (1937)

12 Tonality is a natural force, like gravity.
    Paul Hindemith, *The Craft of Musical Composition* (1937)

13 A true musician believes only what he hears.
    Paul Hindemith, *The Craft of Musical Composition* (1937)

14 There are only two things worth aiming for;
    good music and a clean conscience.
    Paul Hindemith, Letter to Willy Strecker, 1938

15 I don't ever begin at the beginning.
    Paul Hindemith, quoted in Skelton, *Paul Hindemith*
    (1975)

16 I am gradually beginning to feel like a
    cornerstone on which every passerby can pass
    the water of his artistic opinion.
    Paul Hindemith, Letter to Willy Strecker, 1946

17 Tell Hindemith that *I am extremely pleased with
    him.*
    Arnold Schoenberg, Letter to Hermann Scherchen,
    1924

18 [Hindemith's Viola Concerto] A toy Tower
    Bridge made from a Meccano set.
    Unnamed English critic, in 1930, quoted in Skelton,
    Paul Hindemith (1975)

HOLST

19 Mildness is the very devil.
    Gustav Holst, Letter to Vaughan Williams, 1903

20 Every artist ought to pray that he may not be 'a
    success'. If he's a failure he stands a good
    chance of concentrating upon the best work of
    which he's capable.
    Gustav Holst, remark to Clifford Bax, quoted in Holst,
    Holst (1974)

21 Never compose anything unless the not
    composing of it becomes a positive nuisance to
    you.
    Gustav Holst, Letter, 1921

22 A sympathetic critic's disapproval is the most
    interesting and stimulating experience I know.
    Gustav Holst, quoted in Holst, *Holst* (1974)

1   'Personality' no longer counts for anything, and
    when that happens, music begins.
    Gustav Holst, quoted in Holst, *Holst* (1974)

2   Always ask for advice but never take it.
    Gustav Holst, quoted in Holst, *Holst* (1974)

3   Four chief reasons for gratitude ... Music, the
    Cotswolds, RVW [Vaughan Williams], and
    having known the impersonality of orchestral
    playing.
    Gustav Holst, quoted in Holst, *Holst* (1974)

HONEGGER

4   I have sought above all a melodic line, which
    should be ample, generous, free-flowing, and
    not the laboured juxtaposition of little
    fragments which jar on one another.
    Arthur Honegger, *I am a Composer* (1951)

5   To write music is to raise a ladder without a
    wall to lean it against. There is no scaffolding:
    the building under construction is held in
    balance only by the miracle of a kind of internal
    logic, an innate sense of proportion.
    Arthur Honegger, *I am a Composer* (1951)

6   I am like a steam engine: I need to be stoked up,
    it takes me a long time to get ready for genuine
    work.
    Arthur Honegger, *I am a Composer* (1951)

7   My inclination and my effort have always been
    to write music which would be comprehensible
    to the great mass of listeners and at the same
    time sufficiently free of banality to interest
    genuine music lovers.
    Arthur Honegger, *I am a Composer* (1951)

8   We must be the new player in the same old
    game, because to change the rules is to destroy
    the game and to throw it back to its starting
    point. Economy of means seems to me more
    difficult, but also more useful, than a too
    headstrong audacity. There is no profit in
    smashing the door which you might open.
    Arthur Honegger, *I am a Composer* (1951)

9   [In reference to Honegger] The European boys
    have small ideas but they sure know how to
    dress 'em up.
    George Gershwin, quoted in *The Musical Quarterly*,
    1947

THE HORN

10 Triton blowing loud his wreathed horn.
    Edmund Spenser, *Colin Clout's Come Home Again* (1595)

11 The horn, the horn, the lusty horn
    Is not a thing to laugh to scorn.
    (Lord)
    William Shakespeare, *As You Like It*, IV,ii

12 *Dieu! que le son du cor est triste au fond des bois!*
    God, how sad is the sound of the horn in the
    depths of the wood!
    Alfred de Vigny, 'Le Cor'

13 I blow through here;
    The music goes 'round and around ...
    And it comes up here.
    'Red' Hodgson, 'The Music Goes 'Round and Around'
    (1935)

IMPROVISATION

14 I thought this art was dead, but I see it still lives
    in you.
    Jan Adam Reinken, on hearing Bach improvise in
    extended fantasia style in 1720, quoted in Geiringer,
    The Bach Family (1954)

15 [To a violinist who had wandered through
    complex modulations in an improvised cadenza
    and at last landed back in the tonic] You are
    welcome home, Mr Dubourg.
    George Frideric Handel, quoted in Young, *Handel*
    (1947)

16 I would sit down and begin to improvise,
    whether my spirits were sad or happy, serious
    or playful. Once I had captured an idea, I strove
    with all my might to develop and sustain it in
    conformity with the rules of art.
    Joseph Haydn, quoted in Hopkins, *Music all around me*
    (1967)

17 Written music is like the handcuffs; and so is
    the pendulum in white-tie-and-tails up in the
    conductor's stand. Symphony means slavery in
    any jazzman's dictionary.
    Mezz Mezzrow and Bernard Wolfe, *Really the Blues*
    (1946)

18 A jam session is a polite endeavour — an
    exchange of compliments. In the old days, they
    had cutting contests where you defended your
    honour with your instrument.
    Duke Ellington, in 1968, quoted in Jewell, *Duke* (1977)

19 Improvisation? Anyone who plays anything
    worth hearing knows what he's going to play,
    no matter whether he prepares a day ahead or a
    beat ahead. It has to be with intent.
    Duke Ellington, quoted in Jewell, *Duke* (1977)

20 My playing is spontaneous, not a style. A style
    happens when your phrasing hardens.
    Ornette Coleman, quoted in Wilmer, *As Serious as Your
    Life* (1977)

21 Improvisation is not the expression of accident
    but rather of the accumulated yearnings,
    dreams and wisdom of our very soul.
    Yehudi Menuhin, *Theme and Variations* (1972)

INSPIRATION

22 The divine inspirations of music, poetry, and

painting do not arrive at perfection by degrees, like the other sciences, but by starts, and like flashes of lightning, one here, another there, appear in various lands, then suddenly vanish.

Pierre de Ronsard, Dedication to *Livre des mélanges* (1560)

1   Like as the lute delights, or else dislikes,
    As is his art that plays upon the same,
    So sounds my Muse according as she strikes
    On my heart strings, high tuned unto her fame.

Samuel Danyel, Song (1606)

2   Whether on Ida's shady brow,
    Or in the chambers of the East,
    The chambers of the sun, that now
    From ancient melody have ceas'd . . .
    How have you left the ancient love
    That bards of old enjoy'd in you!
    The languid strings do scarcely move!
    The sound is forc'd, the notes are few!

William Blake, 'To the Muses'

3   Musical ideas pursue me to the point of torture. I cannot get rid of them, they stand before me like a wall. If it is an *allegro* that pursues me, my pulse beats faster, I cannot sleep; if an *adagio*, I find my pulse beating slowly. My imagination plays upon me as if I were a keyboard.

Joseph Haydn, in old age, quoted in Dies, *Biographische Nachrichten über Joseph Haydn* (1810)

4   You will ask where my ideas come from. I cannot say for certain. They come uncalled, sometimes independently, sometimes in association with other things. It seems to me that I could wrest them from Nature herself with my own hands, as I go walking in the woods. They come to me in the silence of the night or in the early morning, stirred into being by moods which the poet would translate into words, but which I put into sounds; and these go through my head ringing and singing and storming until at last I have them before me as notes.

Ludwig van Beethoven, Letter to Louis Schlösser, 1823

5   But God has a few of us whom he whispers in the ear;
    The rest may reason and welcome: 'tis we musicians know.

Robert Browning, 'Abt Vogler'

6   [On composer's block] When the biscuits arrived, I realized what had been lacking; the biscuits I had here were much too salty, so they could not give me any sensible ideas; but when I took the sweet ones I had always been accustomed to, and dipped them in milk, everything suddenly fell into place. And so I threw aside the revision and went back to composing.

Richard Wagner, Letter, 1859

7   There is no real creating without hard work. That which you would call invention — that is to say, a thought, an idea — is simply an inspiration for which I am not responsible, which is no merit of mine. It is a present, a gift, which I ought even to despise until I have made it my own by dint of hard work.

Johannes Brahms, quoted in Gall, *Johannes Brahms* (1961)

8   Without craftsmanship, inspiration is a mere reed shaken in the wind.

Johannes Brahms, quoted in Hopkins, *Music all around me* (1967)

9   The sound of the sea, the curve of the horizon, the wind in the leaves, the cry of a bird register complex impressions within us. Then, suddenly, without any deliberate consent on our part, one of these memories issues forth to express itself in the language of music. It bears its own harmony within it. By no effort of ours can we achieve anything more truthful or accurate. In this way only does a soul destined for music discover its own most beautiful ideas.

Claude Debussy, quoted in Vallas, *Debussy* (1926)

10 Works of art are not created; they are there, waiting to be discovered.

Edward Elgar, quoted in Walker, *Anatomy of Musical Criticism* (1966)

11 If you can get the words, the Almighty sends you a tune.

Charles Pottipher, a Suffolk labourer, quoted by Vaughan Williams, Lecture, 1912

12 I frequently hear music in the heart of noise.

George Gershwin, quoted in Goldberg, *George Gershwin* (1931)

13 Genius is one per cent inspiration and ninety-nine per cent perspiration.

Thomas Alva Edison, *Life* (1932)

14 [The] unexpected element strikes me. I make a note of it. At the proper time I put it to profitable use . . . An accident is perhaps the only thing that really inspires us. A composer improvises aimlessly the way an animal grubs about.

Igor Stravinsky, *Poetics of Music* (1947)

15 Take Beethoven's notebooks. There is no thematic conception there as God gave it. He remoulds it and adds 'Meilleur'. Scant confidence in God's prompting, scant respect for it is expressed in that 'Meilleur' — itself not very enthusiastic either. A genuine inspiration, immediate, absolute, unquestioned, ravishing, where there is no choice, no tinkering, no possible improvement; where all is as a sacred mandate, a visitation received by the possessed one with faltering and stumbling step, with shudders of awe from head to foot, with tears

of joy blinding his eyes: no, that is not possible with God, who leaves the understanding too much to do. It comes but from the divel, the true master and giver of such rapture. (Leverkühn's 'Document')

Thomas Mann, *Doctor Faustus* (1947); trans. Lowe-Porter

1 A rational composer finds the golden mean between prose and poetry, between work and what you like to call inspiration.

Arthur Honegger, *I am a Composer* (1951)

2 All the inspiration I ever needed was a phonecall from a producer.

Cole Porter, in 1955, quoted in Green, *Dictionary of Contemporary Quotations* (1982)

3 A composer knows about as little as anyone else about where the substance of his work comes from.

Edgar Varèse, Lecture, 1959

4 I didn't know composers had to take to the hills or the beach and talk with the muses for a few months to get a show.

Duke Ellington, quoted in Jewell, *Duke* (1977)

5 About a third of our songs are pure slog.

Paul McCartney, quoted in Doney, *Lennon and McCartney* (1981)

INTELLECT AND FEELING

See also EXPRESSION.

6 Music, in truth, is the mediator between intellectual and sensuous life.

Ludwig van Beethoven, quoted by Bettina von Arnim, Letter to Goethe, 1810

7 For music is an intellectual or a sensual pleasure, according to the temperament of him who hears it.

Thomas de Quincey, *Confessions of an English Opium Eater* (1822)

8 People often complain that music is too ambiguous; that what they should think when they hear it is so unclear ...

Felix Mendelssohn, Letter to Souchay

9 The first concept is always the best and most natural. The intellect can err, the sentiment — never.

Robert Schumann, quoted in Shapiro, *An Encyclopedia of Quotations about Music* (1978)

10 The other arts persuade us, but music takes us by surprise.

Eduard Hanslick, *The Beautiful in Music* (1854)

11 To the devil with all those who have seen in our sublime art nothing but an innocent tickling of the ear.

Georges Bizet, Letter to Marmontel, 1857

12 Cleverness in art is almost indispensable, but it only ceases to be dangerous the moment the man and the artist find themselves.

Georges Bizet, Letter to Gounod, 1858

13 *Il faut méditerraniser la musique.* Music must be Mediterraneanised.

Friedrich Nietzsche, quoted in Schafer, *British Composers in Interview* (1963)

14 In a long talk I had with him [Beecham], I caught him thinking. By GAWD, a musician *thinking, straight off his own bat!*

Ezra Pound, quoted in Reid, *Thomas Beecham* (1961)

15 The function of music is to release us from the tyranny of conscious thought.

Sir Thomas Beecham, quoted in Atkins and Newman, *Beecham Stories* (1978)

16 The art of music is so deep and profound that to approach it very seriously *only*, is not enough. One must approach music with a serious vigour and, at the same time, with a great, affectionate joy.

Nadia Boulanger, quoted in Kendall, *The Tender Tyrant: Nadia Boulanger* (1976)

17 God guard me from the thoughts men think
In the mind alone;
He that sings a lasting song
Thinks in the marrow-bone.

William Butler Yeats, 'A Prayer for Old Age' (1935)

18 'Satanic' music is rare; the art scarcely lends itself to the expression of irony, which is an intellectual matter.

Neville Cardus, in *The Manchester Guardian*, 1939

19 Music always does penance in advance for her retreat into the sensual. (Leverkühn)

Thomas Mann, *Doctor Faustus* (1947); trans. Lowe-Porter

20 [Of music] Her strictness, or whatever you like to call the moralism of her form, must stand for an excuse for the ravishments of her actual sounds. (Leverkühn)

Thomas Mann, *Doctor Faustus* (1947); trans. Lowe-Porter

21 One piece of music is superior to another essentially only in the quality of its feeling.

Igor Stravinsky, quoted in Ewen, *American Composers* (1982)

22 The sound of music — as opposed to rustling leaves or words of love — is sensual only secondarily. First it must make sense.

Ned Rorem, *Music from Inside Out* (1967)

INTERNATIONALISM

See also NATIONALISM.

1   All the disorders, all the wars which we see in the world, only occur because of the neglect to learn music ... Were all men to learn music, would not this be the means of agreeing together, and of seeing universal peace reign throughout the world?

    Molière, *Le Bourgeois Gentilhomme* (1670)

2   But all the world understands my language.

    Joseph Haydn, reply to Mozart, who had tried to dissuade him from visiting England, citing his ignorance of the language

3   The language of music is common to all generations and nations; it is understood by everybody, since it is understood with the heart.

    Gioacchino Rossini, quoted in Zanolini, *Biografia di Gioacchino Rossini* (1875)

4   Music is the universal language of mankind.

    Christopher North, *Noctes Ambrosianae* (1822-35)

5   [Music] The only universal tongue.

    Samuel Rogers, *Italy* (1822-8)

6   The language of tones belongs equally to all mankind, and melody is the absolute language in which the musician speaks to every heart.

    Richard Wagner, *Beethoven* (1870)

7   Folk songs bind the nation, bind all nations and all people with one spirit, one happiness, one paradise.

    Leoš Janáček, quoted in Štědroň (ed.), *Leoš Janáček: Letters and Reminiscences* (1955)

8   We must, of course, be careful to avoid the fallacy that music is a 'universal language'. There are many music-communities in the world, though not, probably, as many as there are speech communities. Many of them are mutually unintelligible.

    Charles Seeger, 'Music and Culture' (1941)

9   There is no such thing as nationality in music. Music is universal. We have northern and southern music if you like. Greig was northern, not Norwegian. The melody of Strauss is not German at all. It is Italian.

    Sir Thomas Beecham, quoted in Reid, *Thomas Beecham* (1961)

10 If humanity was stripped of all support systems but one, I am convinced the one choice would be in the area of communications. And if one had to choose the universal communicators, music would be the adaptable language.

    Thomas Anderson, quoted in Ewen, *American Composers* (1982)

11 The closest Western civilisation has come to unity since the Congress of Vienna in 1815 was the week that the *Sgt Pepper* album was released.

    Langdon Winner, quoted in Green, *The Book of Rock Quotes* (1982)

INTERPRETATION

See also CONDUCTING, PERFORMANCE, TEMPO.

12 Those who make cuts know only how to cut out the good things; in castrating, it is precisely the noblest parts that are removed.

    Hector Berlioz, review of Rossini's *William Tell*, 1834

13 [Refusing to give metronome guidance] Idiot! do you think I want to hear my music always played at the same speed?

    Johannes Brahms, quoted in Walker (ed.), *Robert Schumann: the Man and his Music* (1972)

14 Notation, the writing out of compositions, is primarily an ingenious expedient for catching an inspiration, with the purpose of exploiting it later. But notation is to improvisation as the portrait to the living model. It is for the interpreter to resolve the rigidity of the signs into the primitive emotion.

    Ferruccio Busoni, *Sketch of a New Aesthetic of Music* (trans. 1911)

15 Never be carried away by temperament, for that dissipates strength.

    Ferruccio Busoni, 'Advice to pianists'

16 [On emending Ravel's Concerto for Left Hand] *Paul Wittgenstein:* Performers must not be slaves.
    Ravel: Performers *are* slaves.

    Quoted in Long, *At the Piano with Ravel* (1973)

17 Beethoven, like many other composers, made changements in his scores, even after publication, and then he also vos deaf. So vy no the conductor also, who often knows better than the composer?

    Willem Mengelberg, quoted in Shore, *The Orchestra Speaks* (1938)

18 The greater the works of art confronting the interpreter, the wider becomes the range of possible great performances.

    Eric Blom, *Beethoven's Pianoforte Sonatas Discussed* (1938)

19 During actual performance, emotion may be safely given the head. Having been controlled by the mind during preparation, it will be in no danger of mocking the composer by letting the interpreter interpose his own personality too obtrusively.

    Eric Blom, *Beethoven's Pianoforte Sonatas Discussed* (1938)

20 Unfortunately, his [Balakirev's] First Symphony was not 'thoroughly composed', as the

Germans say; at each performance of it the conductor needs to be a sort of obstetrician.

Neville Cardus, in *The Manchester Guardian*, 1938

1   We are becoming the slaves of little marks on a piece of white paper which we call music.

Leopold Stokowski, quoted in Jacobson, *Reverberations* (1975)

2   We can never exhaust the multiplicity of nuances and subtleties which make the charm of music . . . How can we expect to produce a vital performance if we don't recreate the work every time? Every year the leaves of the trees reappear with the Spring, but they are different every time.

Pablo Casals, *Conversations with Casals* (1956)

3   I can't stand to sing the same song the same way two nights in succession. If you can, then it ain't music, it's close order drill or exercise or yodelling or something, not music.

Billie Holliday, *Lady Sings the Blues* (1956)

4   The greatest thing for us [performers] is to make a phrase sound like you never heard it before.

Janet Baker, in 1971, quoted Jacobson, *Reverberations* (1975)

INTONATION

5   I cannot sing. I'll weep, and word it with thee, For notes of sorrow out of tune are worse Than priests and fanes that lie. (Guiderius)

William Shakespeare, *Cymbeline*, IV.ii

6   [On an off-key hymn singer] Old John is a supreme musician. Look into his face and hear the music of the ages. Don't pay too much attention to the sounds. If you do, you may miss the music.

George Ives, quoted in Nyman, *Experimental Music* (1974)

7   [On a wavering 'A' proffered by the principal oboe] Gentlemen, take your pick!

Sir Thomas Beecham, quoted in Atkins and Newman, *Beecham Stories* (1978)

8   You can play sharp in tune and you can play flat in tune.

Ornette Coleman, quoted in Williams, *The Jazz Tradition* (1970)

9   Ladies and Gentlemen, I want you to know that during my stay in London your orchestras have been most generous to me. When tuning, all I asked for was one pitch. You have invariably given me two or three at least!

George Szell, quoted in Brymer, *From Where I Sit* (1979)

10   It's often said that there are four rigidly forbidden topics of conversation in polite society. Religion, Women, Politics — and Intonation! Wrong notes we may admit, poor phrasing possibly, bad ensemble, yes (it's *his* fault, of course); but out of tune — never! So the word is rarely uttered.

Jack Brymer, *From Where I Sit* (1979)

IRELAND

11   Where clerics sing like birds.

St Adamnan, *Life of St Columba*

12   Hang the harpers wherever found.

Elizabeth I, Proclamation of 1603, quoted in O Boyle, *The Irish Song Tradition* (1976)

13   Know, that I would accounted be True brother of a company That sang, to sweeten Ireland's wrong, Ballad and story, rann and song.

W.B. Yeats, 'To Ireland in the Coming Times' (1893)

14   For the great Gaels of Ireland Are the men that God made mad, For all their wars are merry, And all their songs are sad.

G.K. Chesterton, 'Ballad of the White Horse'

15   It is next to impossible, I believe, to toss a brick in the air anywhere in County Galway without it landing on the head of some musician.

James Galway, *An Autobiography* (1978)

ITALY

See also GUERRE DES BOUFFONS.

16   The Italians . . . represent as much as they can the passions and the affections of the soul and of the spirit, for example, anger, fury, vexation, rage, the weaknesses of the heart, and many other passions, with a violence so extraordinary that one would judge that they are touched with the same affections as they represent in their singing.

Marin Mersenne, *Harmonie universelle* (1636)

17   There was an age, (its memory will last!) Before Italian airs debauched our taste.

Elijah Fenton, 'An Epistle to Mr Southerne, from Kent, January 28, 1710-11'

18   Curse on this damn'd Italian pathic mode, To Sodom and to Hell the ready road.

Henry Carey, 'A Satire on the Luxury and Effeminacy of the Age'

19   [Of Italian opera] It is all very fine, but it doesn't draw blood.

Christoph Willibald von Gluck, quoted in Lebrecht, *Discord* (1982)

20   This gloomy, anti-musical country.

Hector Berlioz, Letter to Ferdinand Hiller, 1831

1   There are no pianists in Italy, and if you can
    only play the scale of C with both hands you
    pass for a great artist.
    Georges Bizet, Letter, 1858

2   I sometimes get lost in artistic houses of ill
    fame. And I confess to you under my breath, I
    find infinite pleasure there. I love Italian music
    as one loves a courtesan.
    Georges Bizet, Letter to Paul Lacombe, 1867

3   Our music differs from German music. Their
    symphonies can live in halls; their chamber
    music can live in the home. Our music, I say,
    resides principally in the theatre.
    Giuseppe Verdi, Letter to Piroli, 1883

IVES

4   Please don't try to make things nice! All the
    wrong notes are *right*. Just copy as I have — I
    want it that way.
    Charles Ives, MS note to his copyist on score of *The
    Fourth of July*

5   Beauty in music is too often confused with
    something that lets the ears lie back in an easy
    chair.
    Charles Ives, quoted in Machlis, *Introduction to
    Contemporary Music* (1963)

6   I'm the only one, with the exception of Mrs Ives
    and one or two others perhaps ... who likes
    any of my music ... Why do I like these things?
    ... Are my ears on wrong?
    Charles Ives, quoted in Wooldridge, *Charles Ives* (1974)

7   I began to feel more and more, after seances
    with nice musicians, that if I wanted to write
    music that, to me, seemed worth while, I must
    keep away from musicians.
    Charles Ives, quoted in Wooldridge, *Charles Ives* (1974)

8   You'll not get a wild, heroic ride to heaven on
    pretty little sounds ... If you listen to the
    sound, you may miss the music.
    George Ives (the composer's father), quoted in
    Wooldridge, *Charles Ives* (1974)

9   When you get awfully indigestible food in your
    stomach that distresses you, you can get rid of
    it, but I cannot get those horrible sounds out of
    my ears by a dose of oil.
    Franz Milcke, after attempting to play Ives' Violin
    Sonata No. 3, quoted in Woodridge, *Charles Ives* (1974)

10 A composer who has not the slightest idea of
    self-ridicule and who dares to jump with feet
    and hands and a reckless somersault or two on
    his way to his destination.
    Olin Downes, in *The New York Times*, 1927

11 There is a great Man living in this Country — a
    composer.
    He has solved the problem how to preserve
    one's self and to learn.

He responds to negligence by contempt.
He is not forced to accept praise or blame.
His name is Ives.
Arnold Schoenberg, MS note, *c.* 1945, quoted in
Cowell, *Charles Ives* (1955)

12 This fascinating composer ... was exploring the
    1960s during the heyday of Strauss and
    Debussy.
    Igor Stravinsky, *Dialogues and a Diary* (1968)

13 An Old Testament prophet crying a New
    Mythology in the American wilderness.
    David Woodridge, *Charles Ives* (1974)

JANÁČEK

14 The worse the time, the quicker the avalanche
    of ideas for composition.
    Leoš Janáček, in *Lidové Noviny*, 1917

15 I do not play about with empty melodies. I dip
    them in life and nature. I find work very
    difficult and serious — perhaps for this reason.
    Leoš Janáček, Letter to K.E. Sokol, 1924

16 Grow out of your innermost selves
    Never renounce your beliefs
    Do not toil for recognition
    But always do all you can
    So that the field alloted to you
    May prosper.
    Leoš Janáček, Letter to the members of the Ostrava
    musical societies, 1925

17 I proclaimed freedom in harmonic progressions
    long before Debussy, and really do not need
    French impressionism.
    Leoš Janáček, Letter to Jan Mikota, 1926

18 I want to be in direct contact with the clouds,
    I want to feast my eyes on the blue of the sky,
    I want to gather the sun's rays into my hands,
    I want to plunge myself in shadow, I want to
    pour out my longings to the full: all directly.
    Leoš Janáček, in *Lidové Noviny*, 1927

19 [Of his *Glagolitic Mass*] I wanted to portray the
    faith in the certainty of the nation, not on a
    religious basis but on a basis of moral strength
    which takes God for witness.
    Leoš Janáček, interview in *Literární svět*, 1928

JAZZ

20 In the matter of jass [sic], New Orleans is
    particularly interested since it has been widely
    suggested that this particular form of musical
    vice had its birth in this city, that it came, in
    fact, from doubtful surroundings in our slums.
    We do not recognise the honour of parenthood.
    The New Orleans Times Picayune, 1918

21 [Jazz] gives a sensual delight more intense than
    the Viennese waltz or the refined sentiment and

respectful emotion of the eighteenth-century minuet.

The New Orleans Times Picayune, 1918

1 Drum on your drums, batter on your banjos, sob on the long cool winding saxophones. Go to it, O jazzmen.

Carl Sandburg, *Smoke and Steel* (1920)

2 [Referring to *Rhapsody in Blue*] Mr Gershwin ... may yet bring jazz out of the kitchen.

Deems Taylor, in *The World* (New York), 1924

3 Jazz came to America three hundred years ago in chains.

Paul Whiteman, *Jazz* (1926)

4 If it ain't got swing, it ain't worth playin'; if it ain't got gutbucket, it ain't worth doin'.

Bubber Miley, quoted by Duke Ellington

5 It [jazz] is a word of sarcasm. It signifies everything that is old-fashioned.

The Melody Maker, 1931

6 The more grotesque orchestral timbres, the brute complaints of the saxophone, the vicious spurts from the muted brass ... are only thorns protecting a fleshy cactus — a sauce piquante poured over a nice juicy steak.

Constant Lambert, *Music Ho!* (1934)

7 Jazz opposes to our classical conception of music a strange and subversive chaos of sounds ... it is a fashion and, as such, destined some day to disappear.

Igor Stravinsky, quoted in Gammond and Clayton, *Fourteen Miles on a Clear Night* (1966)

8 [Reply to question 'What is jazz?'] Madam, if you don't know by now, DON'T MESS WITH IT!

Fats Waller, quoted in Stearns, *The Story of Jazz* (1956)

9 I play piano, but God is in the house.

Fats Waller, when Art Tatum entered the club where he was playing, quoted in Palmer, *All You Need Is Love* (1976)

10 [Fats Waller] The black Horowitz.

Oscar Levant, quoted in Palmer, *All You Need Is Love* (1976)

11 The jazz band can be used for artificial excitement and aphrodisiac purposes, but not for spreading eternal truths.

Arthur Bliss, 'Music Policy' (1941)

12 Jazz? Bah — nothing but the debasement of noble brass instruments by blowing them into mutes, hats, caps, nooks, crannies, holes and corners!

Sir Thomas Beecham, quoted in Brymer, *From Where I Sit* (1979)

13 Jazz is to be played, sweet, soft, plenty rhythm.

Jelly Roll Morton, *Mister Jelly Roll* (1950)

14 Bop is mad, wild, frantic, crazy — and not to be dug unless you've seen dark days, too.

Langston Hughes, *Simple Takes a Wife* (1953)

15 I was always in a panic.

Charlie Parker, quoted in Williams, *The Jazz Tradition* (1970)

16 Bop is the shorthand of jazz, an epigram made by defying the platitude of conventional harmony; it performs a post-mortem on the dissected melody. The chastity of this music is significant. It shuns climaxes of feeling, and affirms nothing but disintegration.

Kenneth Tynan, in *The Observer*, 1955

17 *Leopold Stokowski:* You and I should go to Africa and hear that music.
Duke Ellington: The only thing I could get in Africa that I haven't got now is fever.

Quoted in Jewell, *Duke* (1977)

18 Jazz is about the only form of art existing today in which there is freedom of the individual without the loss of group contact.

Dave Brubeck, quoted in Berendt, *The Jazz Book* (1976)

19 Jazz has always been a man telling the truth about himself.

Quincy Jones, quoted in Horricks, *These Jazzmen of Our Times*, (1959)

20 If you see me up there on the stand smiling, I'm lost!

Earl Hines, quoted in Palmer, *All You Need Is Love* (1976)

21 [Jazz] The sound of surprise.

Whitney Balliett, *The Sound of Surprise* (1960)

22 A jazz musician is a juggler who uses harmonies instead of oranges.

Benny Green, *The Reluctant Art* (1962)

23 You don't need to think to play weird. That ain't no freedom. You need controlled freedom.

Miles Davis, quoted in Berendt, *The Jazz Book* (1976)

24 [Of Bop] It was a kind of desire to avoid meeting the customers half-way ... the complex response of over-sensitive men to a world they are afraid would reject the natural expression of their emotions.

Colin Wilson, *Brandy of the Damned* (1964)

25 Jazz is the only music in which the same note can be played night after night but differently each time.

Ornette Coleman, quoted in Mellers, *Music in a New Found Land* (1964)

26 The basic difference between classical music and jazz is that in the former the music is always greater than its performance — whereas the way jazz is performed is always more important than what is being played.

André Previn, in *The Times*, 1967

1　We've all worked and fought under the banner of jazz for many years, but the word itself has no meaning. There's a form of condescension in it.

Duke Ellington, Radio interview, 1968

2　One jazzer's jazz is another jazzer's junk.

Ian Whitcomb, *After the Ball* (1972)

3　Free is not a style. It's a personal ability. Playing free is not having to have a style.

Ornette Coleman, quoted in *Down Beat*, 1973

4　Jazz became corrupted by the Western idea of what art is all about — that the audience is an accidental eavesdropper on a great performance.

Ian Carr, quoted in Palmer, *All You Need Is Love* (1976)

5　Jazz is a symbol of the triumph of the human spirit, not of its degradation. It is a lily in spite of the swamp.

Archie Shepp, quoted in Wilmer, *Jazz People* (1977)

6　I don't think any music should be called jazz . . . if it sounds good, that's all you need.

Duke Ellington, quoted in Jewell, *Duke* (1977)

7　If it hadn't been for him, there wouldn't have been none of us. I want to thank Mr Louis Armstrong for my livelihood.

Dizzy Gillespie, at Armstrong's 70th birthday celebration, quoted in Hentoff, *Jazz is* (1978)

8　It's taken me all my life to learn what not to play.

Dizzy Gillespie, quoted in Hentoff, *Jazz is* (1978)

9　Nobody is as serious about music as a jazz musician is serious about music.

Duke Ellington, quoted in Hentoff, *Jazz is* (1978)

JOSQUIN DES PRÈS

10　Josquin is master of the notes; others are mastered by them.

Martin Luther, quoted in Headington, *The Bodley Head History of Western Music* (1974)

11　[Of Josquin's music] Frightful mechanical ingenuities.

Cecil Forsyth, *A History of Music* (1916)

KEYBOARD INSTRUMENTS

See also individual instruments.

12　[On fingering] Let a player run up and down with either first, middle, or third finger, aye even with his nose if that could help him, provided everything is done clearly, correctly, and gracefully.

Michael Praetorius, *Syntagma Musicum* (1619)

13　Lose no opportunity to hear artistic singing. In so doing, the keyboard player will learn to think in terms of song. Indeed, it is a good practice to sing instrumental melodies in order to reach an understanding of their correct performance.

Carl Philipp Emanuel Bach, *Essay on the True Art of Playing Keyboard Instruments* (1753-62)

KODÁLY

14　Some day the ringing tower of Hungarian music is going to stand. And if in its pedestal some of these stones [his works] will be lying intact and the rest destroyed I shall . . . regard without concern the night of my deep grave.

Zoltán Kodály, Lecture, 1932

15　There is no better stimulus for artistic work than suffering.

Zoltán Kodály, Lecture, 1946

16　The laws of morals and the laws of art are the same.

Zoltán Kodály, Address to the Budapest Academy of Music, 1953

17　The music of the people . . . can be lifted out from beneath the rubbish heaped on top of it, and a higher art can be built upon it.

Zoltán Kodály, Speech, 1955

KŘENEK

18　The unmeasured stands in need of number, in the numbered we miss measure.

Ernst Křenek, *Sestina* (1957)

19　My own private turnabout from modernism became, eventually, somewhat different from everybody else's reactionary spree, of which I could be proud if I cared to. I did not visualise returning to the seventeenth century but to the early romanticism of Franz Schubert.

Ernst Křenek, *Horizons Circled* (1974)

20　To my knowledge I am the only composer of my generation who has thoroughly and consistently practiced what is called 'serialism', and I have been blamed (a) for doing it at all, (b) for doing it too late, and (c) for still being at it.

Ernst Křenek, *Horizons Circled* (1974)

21　My apparently aimless meandering through the styles was explained handsomely by some of my critics as unscrupulous opportunism. Plausible as it seems, this interpretation takes in no account the small detail that I seemed to embrace almost each of these styles just when it was utterly impractical to do so, as seen from worldly viewpoints.

Ernst Křenek, quoted in Ewen, *American Composers* (1982)

LAWES

1 Harry, whose tuneful and well measured song
  First taught our English music how to span
  Words with just note and accent, not to scan
  With Midas ears, committing short and long.
  John Milton, 'To Mr H. Lawes on the Publishing his Airs'

2 Thou'rt all so fit, that some have pass'd their votes
  Thy notes beget the words, not words thy notes.
  T.Norton, Commendatory verses on Henry Lawes (1653)

3 But you alone may truly boast
  That not a syllable is lost;
  The writer's, and the setter's skill
  At once the ravished ears do fill.
  Edmund Waller, 'To Mr Henry Lawes'

4 You by the help of tune and time,
  Can make that song that was but rhyme.
  Edmund Waller, 'To Mr Henry Lawes'

LIBRETTI

See also WORDS AND MUSIC.

5 [On translated libretti] I have known the word *And* pursued through the whole gamut, have been entertained with many a melodious *The*, and have heard the most beautiful graces, quavers, and divisions bestowed upon *Then*, *For*, and *From*; to the eternal honour of our English particles.
  Joseph Addison, *The Spectator*, 1711

6 [Instructions to librettists] If the modern poet discovers that the singer enunciates badly, he must not correct him, because if the singer should remedy his fault and speak distinctly, it might hurt the sale of the libretto.
  Benedetto Marcello, *Il teatro alla moda* (1720)

7 *Handel* [to librettist]: Damn your iambics!
  Morell: Don't put yourself in a passion, they are easily trochees.
  Handel: Trochees, what are trochees?
  Morell: Why, the very reverse of iambics, by leaving out a syllable in every line.
  Rev. Thomas Morell, quoted in Blom, *The Music Lover's Miscellany* (1935)

8 Music must be considered the true language of opera.
  Christoph Martin Wieland, 'Essay concerning German Opera' (1775)

9 Verse is no doubt indispensable to music, but rhyme, for the sake of rhyme — is a curse.
  Wolfgang Amadeus Mozart, Letter to his father, 1781

10 Carve in your head in letters of brass: An opera must draw tears, cause horror, bring death, by means of song.
  Vincenzo Bellini, Letter to his librettist, 1834

11 In the end it all depends on a libretto. A libretto, a libretto and the opera is made!
  Giuseppe Verdi, Letter, 1865

12 If the action demanded it, I would immediately abandon rhythm, rhyme, and stanza. I would use blank verse in order to say clearly and forthrightly all that the action demands.
  Giuseppe Verdi, Letter to his librettist, 1870

13 It is much harder to write a good libretto than a beautiful play.
  Richard Strauss, Letter to Hugo von Hofmannsthal, 1908

14 The writer must be convinced that opera offers possibilities that are excluded from drama, and that these very possibilities are worth more than everything of which drama is capable.
  W.H. Auden, quoted in Henze, *Music and Politics* (1982)

LIGETI

15 It is precisely a dread of deep significance and ideology that makes any kind of engaged art out of the question for me.
  György Ligeti, quoted in Henze, *Music and Politics* (1982)

LISZT

16 Devil of a fellow — such a young rascal!
  Ludwig van Beethoven, quoted in Hamburger, *Beethoven: Letters, Journals and Conversations* (1952)

17 [Of Liszt's concerts] Terrified pianos flee into every corner ... gutted instruments strew the stage, and the audience sits mute with fear and amazement.
  Unnamed contemporary, quoted in Hedley, *Chopin* (1947)

18 When I think of Liszt as a creative artist, he appears before my eyes rouged, on stilts, and blowing into Jericho trumpets *fortissimo* and *pianissimo*.
  Fryderyk Chopin, Letter, quoted in Beckett, *Liszt* (1963)

19 Liszt, the Polyphemus of the pianoforte — the Aurora Borealis of musical effulgence — the Niagara of thundering harmonies!
  The Musical World, 1841

20 He performed works by Beethoven, Bach, Handel and Weber in such a pitiably imperfect style, so uncleanly, so ignorantly, that I could

have listened to many a middling pianist with more pleasure.

Felix Mendelssohn, quoted in Newman, *The Man Liszt* (1934)

1   I have not seen any musician in whom musical feeling ran, as in Liszt, into the very tips of the fingers and there streamed out immediately.

Felix Mendelssohn, quoted in *The Musical Times*, 1886

2   When he sits at the piano and, having repeatedly pushed his hair back over his brow, begins to improvise, then he often rages all too madly upon the ivory keys and lets loose a deluge of heaven-storming ideas, with here and there a few sweet flowers to shed fragrance upon the whole. One feels both blessedness and anxiety, but rather more anxiety . . .

Heinrich Heine, in 1837, quoted in Beckett, *Liszt* (1963)

3   *Chez Liszt on ne pense plus a la difficulté vaincue; l'instrument disparaît et la musique se révèle!* With Liszt, one no longer thinks of difficulty overcome; the instrument disappears and the music reveals itself.

Heinrich Heine, quoted in Beckett, *Liszt* (1963)

4   He must be heard — and also seen; for if he played behind the scenes a great deal of the poetry of his playing would be lost.

Robert Schumann, in *Neue Zeitschrift*

5   A smasher of pianos.

Clara Schumann, quoted in Walker (ed.), *Robert Schumann: the Man and his Music* (1972)

6   I will no longer conceal from you what your manly spirit has a right to demand: I am quite impervious to your music; it contradicts everything in the works of our great masters.

Joseph Joachim, Letter to Liszt, 1857

7   Liszt knows only too well how to arouse enthusiasm and how to exploit it for his own ends; consequently an honest fight with these bacchantes and sycophants is not possible. And it is really not necessary. Their uncouth fanaticism and their false harmonies will dig their own graves for them.

Joseph Joachim, Letter to Brahms

8   An inspired charlatan.

Hermann Levi, Letter to Clara Schumann

9   I expect that he [Liszt] will bring forth still another symphonic poem before this winter is over. The disease spreads more and more, and in any event lengthens and ruins the ass's ears of audience and young composers alike.

Johannes Brahms, Letter to Clara Schumann, 1860

10   Whoever has not heard Liszt cannot even speak of piano playing.

Johannes Brahms, quoted in Gall, *Johannes Brahms* (1961)

11   The prodigy, the itinerant virtuoso, and the man of fashion ruined the composer before he had even started.

Johannes Brahms, comment to Eusebius Mandyczewski, quoted in Gall, *Johannes Brahms* (1961)

12   Mephistopheles disguised as an Abbé.

Anon., quoted in Beckett, *Liszt* (1963)

13   My dear old, white-haired Venus.

Alexander Borodin, Letter to Alexander and Evgeny Dianin, 1881

14   Franz Liszt also came to Albion Street, but he frightened us. His hair was so long, and he had such a wild appearance, that when he played the pianoforte we were always glad to leave the room.

Willert Beale, recalling his childhood, quoted in Beckett, *Liszt* (1963)

15   He collected princesses and countesses as other men collect rare butterflies, or Japanese prints, or first editions.

Ernest Newman, quoted in Beckett, *Liszt* (1963)

16   [Of Liszt's Piano Concerto No. 2] Sawdust and spangles.

Neville Cardus, in *The Manchester Guardian*, 1938

17   It is men like the taciturn and thin-skinned Wagner, or the modest bourgeois Richard Strauss, who produced the music that is the true counterpart of Liszt's extraordinary life.

Colin Wilson, *Brandy of the Damned* (1964)

18   It is a question whether Liszt should ever be deprived of the tawdry and the swaggering. He needs to be presented behind the foot-lights of the old fustian theatres and country booths.

Neville Cardus, *The Delights of Music* (1966)

19   That Hungarian boy with warts. (Beethoven)

Peter Ustinov, *Beethoven's Tenth* (1983)

LOVE AND SEX

20   Cicala to cicala is dear, and ant to ant, and hawk to hawk, but to me the muse and song.

Theocritus, *Idylls*, IX; trans. Lang

21   Some sang ring-sangs, dancis, ledis and roundis,
With vocis schil, quil all the dale resoundis;
Quhareto thay walk into thare karoling,
For amourus layis dois all the rochis ring.

Gavin Douglas, *Aeneid* (early 16th century)

22   So in their ear I sing them a song
And make them so long to muse

That some of them runneth straight to the
        stews.
(Folly)

John Skelton, *Magnyfycence* (1529-32) (*stews* =
brothels)

1   Love me little, love me long,
    Is the burden of my song.

Anon., 'Love me Little, Love me Long' (*c.* 1570)

2   Harping always upon love, till you be as blind
    as a harper.

John Lyly, *Sapho and Phao* (*c.* 1584), IV.iii

3   There exists a vast mass of love songs of the
    poets, written in a fashion entirely foreign to
    the profession and name of Christian. They are
    the songs of men ruled by passion, and a great
    number of musicians, corrupters of youth,
    make them the concern of their art and their
    industry; in proportion as they flourish through
    praise of their skill, so do they offend good and
    serious-minded men by the depraved taste of
    their work. I blush and grieve to think that once
    I was of their number.

Giovanni Pierluigi da Palestrina, Dedication to *Fourth
Book of Motets* (1584)

4   Doubt you to whom my Muse these notes
        intendeth,
    Which now my breast o'ercharged to music
        lendeth?
    To you, to you, all song of praise is due;
        Only in you my song begins and endeth.

Sir Philip Sidney, *Astrophel and Stella* (1591)

5   Visit by night your lady's chamber window
    With some sweet consort; to their instruments
    Tune a deploring dump — the night's dead
        silence
    Will well become such sweet-complaining
        grievance.
    This, or nothing else, will inherit her.
(Proteus)

William Shakespeare, *The Two Gentlemen of Verona*,
III.ii

6   And when love speaks, the voice of all the gods
    Makes heaven drowsy with the harmony.
(Berowne)

William Shakespeare, *Love's Labour's Lost*, IV.iii

7   How silver-sweet sound lovers' tongues by
        night,
    Like softest music to attending ears.
(Romeo)

William Shakespeare, *Romeo and Juliet*, II.ii

8   Haply I think on thee — and then my state,
    Like to the lark at break of day arising
    From sullen earth, sings at heaven's gate.

William Shakespeare, Sonnet 29

9   Come sing me a bawdy song, make me merry.
(Falstaff)

William Shakespeare, *Henry IV, Part One*, III.iii

10   If music be the food of love, play on,
     Give me excess of it, that, surfeiting,
     The appetite may sicken and so die.
     That strain again — it had a dying fall.
(Duke Orsino)

William Shakespeare, *Twelfth Night*, I.i

11   ... thy small pipe
     Is as the maiden's organ, shrill and sound,
     And all is semblative a woman's part.
(Duke Orsino to the disguised Viola)

William Shakespeare, *Twelfth Night*, I.iv

12   *Duke Orsino*: ... How dost thou like this tune?
     Viola: It gives a very echo to the seat
     Where love is enthroned.

William Shakespeare, *Twelfth Night*, II.iv

13   The barge she sat in, like a burnished throne,
     Burned on the water ...
                        ... the oars were silver,
     Which to the tune of flutes kept stroke, and
         made
     The water which they beat to follow faster,
     As amorous of their strokes.
(Enobarbus's description of Cleopatra's barge)

William Shakespeare, *Antony and Cleopatra*, II.ii

14   Give me some music — music, moody food
     Of us that trade in love.
(Cleopatra)

William Shakespeare, *Antony and Cleopatra*, II.v

15   I am advised to give her music a mornings; they
     say it will penetrate.
(Cloten)

William Shakespeare, *Cymbeline*, II.iii

16   The sly whoresons
     Have got a speeding trick to lay down ladies —
     A French song and a fiddle has no fellow.
(Lovell)

William Shakespeare, *Henry VIII*, I.iii

17   Lewis the Eleventh, when he invited Edward
     the Fourth to come to Paris, told him, that, as a
     principal part of his entertainment, he should
     hear sweet voices of children, Ionic and Lydian
     tunes, exquisite music, he should have a
     ———, and the Cardinal of Burbon to be his
     confessor; which he used as a most plausible
     argument, as to a sensual man indeed it is.

Robert Burton, *Anatomy of Melancholy* (1621)

18   I would have all lovers begin and end their
     pricksong with *Lachrimae*, till they have wept
     themselves dry as I have.

Thomas Nabbes, *Microcosmus* (1637), referring to
Dowland's collection of consort music

19   Sure there is music even in the beauty, and the
     silent note which Cupid strikes, far sweeter
     than the sound of an instrument. For there is
     music wherever there is a harmony, order or
     proportion.

Sir Thomas Browne, *Religio Medici* (1643)

1   Music and women I cannot but give way to,
    whatever my business is.
    Samuel Pepys, Diary, 1666

2   As the custom prevails at present there is scarce
    a young man of any fashion ... who does not
    make love with the town music.
    The Tatler, 1710

3   O, my Luve's like a red red rose
        That's newly sprung in June:
    O my Luve's like the melodie
        That's sweetly play'd in tune.
    Robert Burns, 'My Love is like a Red Red Rose'

4   Music arose with its voluptuous swell,
    Soft eyes look'd love to eyes which spake again,
    And all went merry as a marriage bell.
    Lord Byron, Childe Harold's Pilgrimage, III (1816)

5   Who of men can tell
    ... that fish would have bright mail ...
    The seed its harvest, or the lute its tones,
    Tones ravishment, or ravishment its sweet
    If human souls did never kiss and greet?
    John Keats, Endymion (1818)

6   We — are we not formed, as notes of music are,
    For one another, though dissimilar?
    Percy Bysshe Shelley, Epipsychidion (1821)

7   No, Music thou art not the 'food of love',
    Unless love feeds upon its own sweet self,
    Till it becomes all Music murmurs of.
    Percy Bysshe Shelley, 'Fragment: To Music'

8   Here with a Loaf of Bread beneath the bough,
    A flask of Wine, a Book of Verse — and Thou
        Beside me singing in the Wilderness —
    And Wilderness is Paradise enow.
    Edward Fitzgerald, The Rubáiyát of Omar Khayyám
    (1859)

9   Which of the two powers, Love or Music can
    elevate man to the sublimest heights? It is a
    great problem, and yet it seems to me that this
    is the answer: 'Love can give no idea of music;
    music can give an idea of love.' Why separate
    them? They are the two wings of the soul.
    Hector Berlioz, Memoirs (1865)

10 I conclude that musical notes and rhythms were
    first acquired by the male or female progenitors
    of mankind for the sake of charming the
    opposite sex.
    Charles Darwin, The Descent of Man (1871)

11 Take that Kreutzer Sonata, for instance, how
    can that first presto be played in a drawing-
    room among ladies in low-necked dresses? ...
    An awakening of energy and feeling unsuited
    both to the time and the place, to which no
    outlet is given, cannot but act harmfully.
    Leo Tolstoy, 'The Kreutzer Sonata' (1890); trans.
    Maude

12 For a day and a night Love sang to us, played
        with us,
        Folded us round from the dark and the
            light;
    And our hearts were fulfilled with the music he
        made with us,
    Made with our hands and our lips while he
        stayed with us,
        Stayed in mid passage his pinions from
            flight
                For a day and a night.
    Algernon Charles Swinburne, 'At Parting'

13 [The kind of music] a pederast might hum
    when raping a choirboy.
    Marcel Proust, quoted in Musical Quarterly, 1924,
    referring to Fauré's Romances sans paroles

14 The red-eyed elders watching, felt
    The basses of their beings throb
    In witching chords, and their thin blood
    Pulse pizzicati of Hosanna.
    Wallace Stevens, 'Peter Quince at the Clavier' (1924)

15 A breath upon her hand
    Muted the night.
    She turned —
    A cymbal crashed,
    And roaring horns.
    Wallace Stevens, 'Peter Quince at the Clavier' (1924)

16 Through this dress I feel your body as music.
    These ankles: a Grazioso;
    This enticing swelling: a Cantabile;
    These knees; a Misterioso;
    And the powerful Andante of voluptuousness.
    Alban Berg, Lulu, adapting Wedekind in order to
    allude to the first four movements of his Lyric Suite

17 You and the Night and the Music.
    Howard Dietz, title of song, 1934

18 Alone and alone nine nights I lay
    Between two bushes under the rain;
    I thought to have whistled her down that way,
    I whistled and whistled and whistled in vain.
                                    Oro, oro!
    To-morrow night I will break down the door.
    W.B. Yeats, 'Two Songs rewritten for the Tune's Sake'
    (1935)

19 Down from the mountain walls
    From where Pan's cavern is
    Intolerable music falls.
    Foul goat-head, brutal arm appear,
    Belly, shoulder, bum,
    Flash fishlike, nymphs and satyrs
    Copulate in the foam.
    W.B. Yeats, 'News for the Delphic Oracle' (1936-39)

20 Let a florid music praise,
        The flute and the trumpet,
    Beauty's conquest of your face.
    W.H. Auden, 'Twelve Songs'

1   'Bed,' as the Italian proverb succinctly puts it,
    'is the poor man's opera.'

    Aldous Huxley, *Heaven and Hell* (1956)

2   [Dissonance functions] from the very outset as
    the disguised representation of everything that
    has to be sacrificed to the taboo of order. It
    substitutes for the censored instinctual drive,
    and includes, as tension, a libidinal moment as
    well, in its lament over enforced renunciation.

    T.W. Adorno, *Philosophie der neuen Musik* (1958)

3   If music be the breakfast food of love, kindly do
    not disturb until lunch time.

    James Agee, *Agee on Film, 1958-60* (1963)

4   It might not be a bad idea for some teenagers,
    when they are being 'sent' by a piece of jazz, to
    ask themselves where the music stopped and
    the sex began and vice-versa.

    Beverley Nichols, in the 1960s, quoted in Lee, *Music of
    the People* (1970)

5   I have a mistress. Lovers have come and gone,
    but only my mistress stays. She is beautiful and
    gentle ... She is a swinger. She has grace. To
    hear her speak, you can't believe your ears. She
    is ten thousand years old. She is as modern as
    tomorrow, a brand-new woman every day, and
    as endless as time mathematics. Living with her
    is a labyrinth of ramifications. I look forward to
    her every gesture.
        Music is my mistress, and she plays second
    fiddle to none.

    Duke Ellington, *Music Is My Mistress* (1973)

6   All my life I was having trouble with women ...
    I've done a lot of writing about women. Then,
    after I quit having trouble with them, I could
    feel in my heart that somebody would always
    have trouble with them, so I kept writing those
    blues.

    Muddy Waters, quoted in Palmer, *All You Need Is Love*
    (1976)

LULLY

7   The king is the master; he can wait as long as
    he pleases.

    Jean-Baptiste Lully, on being told that Louis XIV was
    becoming impatient about the long-delayed start of a
    ballet, quoted in Scott, *Jean-Baptiste Lully* (1973)

8   It remains that I give my advice in general for
    all comedies where any singing is used; and
    that is to leave to the poet's discretion the
    management of the piece. The musician is to
    follow the poet's direction, only in my opinion,
    Lully is to be exempted, who knows the
    passions and enters further into the heart of
    man than the authors themselves.

    Sieur de Saint-Evremond, quoted in Mellers, *François
    Couperin* (1950)

9   He merits with good reason the title of Prince
    of French Musicians, being regarded as the
    inventor of this beautiful and great French
    music.

    Titon du Tillet, quoted in Mellers, *François Couperin*
    (1950)

10 [Of Lully's *Alceste*] It's awful! it's frightful! it's
    not music, it's iron!

    Jean Auguste Dominique Ingres, quoted in Harding,
    Gounod (1973)

THE LUTE

11 My lute, awake! perform the last
    Labour that thou and I shall waste,
        An end that I have now begun;
    For when this song is done and past,
        My lute, be still, for I have done.

    Sir Thomas Wyatt, 'To his Lute'

12 He capers nimbly in a lady's chamber*
    To the lascivious pleasing of a lute.
    (Richard)

    William Shakespeare, *Richard III*, I.i

13 When to her lute Corinna sings,
    Her voice revives the leaden strings,
    And both in highest notes appear,
    As any challeng'd echo clear.

    But when she doth of mourning speak,
    Ev'n with her sighs the strings do break.

    Thomas Campion, *A Book of Airs* (1610-12)

14 In a sadly pleasing strain
    Let the warbling lute complain.

    Alexander Pope, 'Ode for Musick, on St Cecilia's Day'
    (*c.* 1708)

THE LYRE

15   *Dapibus supremi*
    Grata testudo Jovis.
    The lyre is welcome at the feasts of
    supreme Jupiter.

    Horace, *Odes*, I, 32

16 If she with ivory fingers drive a tune through
        the lyre,
    We look at the process.

    Ezra Pound, 'Homage to Sextus Propertius'

MAHLER

17 Only when I experience intensely do I compose.
    Only when I compose do I experience intensely.

    Gustav Mahler, quoted in Machlis, *Introduction to
    Contemporary Music* (1963)

18 To write a symphony is, for me, to construct a
    world.

    Gustav Mahler, quoted in Machlis, *Introduction to
    Contemporary Music* (1963)

1 My time will come.

Gustav Mahler, quoted in Blaukopf, *Gustav Mahler* (1973)

2 What is best in music is not to be found in the notes.

Gustav Mahler, attr.

3 We do not compose — we are composed.

Gustav Mahler, attr.

4 I am three times homeless: a native of Bohemia in Austria; an Austrian among Germans; a Jew throughout the whole world.

Gustav Mahler, quoted in Yates, *Twentieth Century Music* (1968)

5 [Of his 'Symphony of a Thousand'] Imagine the whole universe beginning to sing and resound.

Gustav Mahler, Letter, 1906

6 [On seeing Niagara Falls] Fortissimo at last!

Gustav Mahler, quoted in Blaukopf, *Gustav Mahler* (1973)

7 [Of the Symphony No.2] If that was music, I no longer understand anything about the subject.

Hans von Bülow, quoted in Lebrecht, *Discord* (1982)

8 [Of the Symphony No.9] The expression of exceptional love for this earth, the longing to live at peace in it, to enjoy nature to its depths before death comes, for he comes irresistibly.

Alban Berg, quoted in Headington, *Britten* (1981)

9 [Of the Symphony No.3] It's all very well, but you can't call *that* a symphony.

Sir William Walton, quoted in *The Observer*, 1983

10 [Of the Symphony No.4] It seemed to be an impertinence to want all those people to make that particular music, as if *size* had become a morbid obsession with him.

Sir John Barbirolli, Letter to Charles Parker, 1930

11 In Mahler's symphonies there are many highlights, but only one real climax.

Sir John Barbirolli, interview in *Die Welt*

12 For the first time in musical history, music is interrogating itself about the reasons for its existence and about its nature ... it is a knowing music, with the same tragic consciousness as Freud, Kafka, Musil.

Hans Werner Henze, *Music and Politics* (1982), 'Gustav Mahler' (1975)

THE MANDOLIN

13 The pleasant whining of a mandoline.

T.S. Eliot, *The Waste Land* (1922)

MARTIAL MUSIC

14 If ye go to war ... ye shall blow an alarm with the trumpets.

Numbers 10:9

15 He saith among the trumpets, Ha, ha.

Job 39:24

16 If the trumpet give an uncertain sound, who shall prepare himself to the battle?

1 Corinthians 14:8

17 ... my Muse, to some ears not unsweet,
Tempers her words to trampling horses' feet
    More oft than to a chamber melody.

Sir Philip Sidney, Sonnet 74

18 Sound all the lofty instruments of war
And by that music let us all embrace,
For, heaven to earth, some of us never shall
A second time do such a courtesy.
(Hotspur)

William Shakespeare, *Henry IV, Part One*, V.ii

19 Make all our trumpets speak; give them all
        breath,
Those clamorous harbingers of blood and
        death.
(Macduff)

William Shakespeare, *Macbeth*, V.v

20   Trumpeters,
With brazen din blast you the city's ear,
Make mingle with our rattling tabourines,
That heaven and earth may strike their sounds
    together,
Applauding our approach.
(Antony)

William Shakespeare, *Antony and Cleopatra*, IV.viii

21 Where Drums speak out, Laws hold their tongues.

Thomas Fuller, attr.

22 The double double beat
    Of the thundring drum
    Cries, hark the foes come;
Charge, charge, 'tis too late to retreat.

John Dryden, 'A Song for St Cecilia's Day' (1687)

23 The Trumpet's loud clangor
    Excites us to arms
With shrill notes of anger
    And mortal alarms.

John Dryden, 'A Song for St Cecilia's Day' (1687)

24 I am devilishly afraid, that's certain; but ... I'll sing, that I may seem valiant.

John Dryden, *Amphytrion*, II.i (1690)

25 But when our Country's cause provokes to
        arms,
How martial music every bosom warms!

Alexander Pope, 'Ode for Musick, on St Cecilia's Day' (c. 1708)

26 See, the conquering hero comes!
Sound the trumpets, beat the drums!

Thomas Morell, libretto for Handel's oratorio *Joshua* (1748)

1 All the delusive seduction of martial music.
Fanny Burney, *Diary*, 1802

2 Where, where was Roderick then?
One blast upon his bugle-horn
Were worth a thousand men!
Sir Walter Scott, *The Lady of the Lake* (1810)

3 The best sort of music is what it should be —
sacred; the next best, the military, has fallen to
the lot of the devil.
Samuel Taylor Coleridge, *Table Talk* (1833)

4 Oh, the brave music of a *distant* Drum!
Edward Fitzgerald, *The Rubáiyát of Omar Khayyám*
(1859)

5 ... And with the clashing of their sword-blades
make
A rapturous music, till the morning break.
W.B. Yeats, 'To Some I have Talked with by the Fire'
(1893)

6 When I was young,
I had not given a penny for a song
Did not the poet sing it with such airs
That one believed he had a sword upstairs.
W.B. Yeats, 'All Things can Tempt me' (1910)

MARTINŮ

7 I do not perform any miracles. I am merely
exact.
Bohuslav Martinů, quoted in Šafránek, *Bohuslav
Martinů* (1946)

MASCAGNI

8 It was a pity I wrote *Cavalleria* first.
I was crowned before I was king.
Pietro Mascagni, quoted in Carner, *Puccini* (1974)

MASSENET

9 We must pay attention to this little chap, he's
going to leave us standing.
Georges Bizet, quoted in Dean, *Bizet* (1975)

10 The vulgar, impassioned whinings of Massenet.
Gabriel Fauré, Letter to his wife, 1909

11 I would give the whole of Bach's Brandenburg
Concertos for Massenet's Manon and would
think I had vastly profited by the exchange.
Sir Thomas Beecham, quoted in Harding, *Massenet*
(1970)

MELANCHOLY

12 *Minuentur atrae*
Carmine curae.
Dark worries will be lessened by song.
Horace, *Odes*, IV, 11

13 When gripping grief the heart doth wound,
And doleful dumps the mind oppress,
Then music with her silver sound
With speedy help doth lend redress.
Richard Edwards, 'In Commendation of Music', in *The
Paradise of Dainty Devices* (1576), quoted in
Shakespeare, *Romeo and Juliet*, IV.v

14 A lamentable tune is the sweetest music to a
woeful mind.
Sir Philip Sidney, *Arcadia*, II (1590)

15 Music to hear, why hear'st thou music sadly?
Sweets with sweets war not, joy delights in joy:
Why lov'st thou that which thou receiv'st not
gladly,
Or else receiv'st with pleasure thine annoy?
If the true concord of well-tuned sounds,
By unions married, do offend thine ear,
They do but sweetly chide thee.
William Shakespeare, Sonnet 8

16 I am never merry when I hear sweet music.
(Jessica)
William Shakespeare, *The Merchant of Venice*, V.i

17 I can suck melancholy out of a song as a weasel
sucks eggs.
(Jaques)
William Shakespeare, *As You Like It*, II.v

18 *Clown*: By my troth, I take my young lord to be
a very melancholy man.
Countess: By what observance, I pray you?
Clown: Why, he will look upon his boot and
sing, mend the ruff and sing, ask questions and
sing, pick his teeth and sing. I know a man that
had his trick of melancholy sold a goodly manor
for a song.
William Shakespeare, *All's Well that Ends Well*, III.ii

19 *Quien canta sus males espanta.* He who sings
scares away his woes.
Miguel de Cervantes, *Don Quixote*, I (1605)

20 Many men are melancholy by hearing music,
but it is a pleasing melancholy that it causeth;
and therefore, to such as are discontent, in woe,
fear, sorrow, or dejected, it is a most present
remedy.
Robert Burton, *Anatomy of Melancholy* (1621)

21 Music is a roaring-meg against melancholy, to
rear and revive the languishing soul; affecting
not only the ears, but the very arteries, the vital
and animal spirits, it erects the mind and makes
it nimble.
Robert Burton, *Anatomy of Melancholy* (1621)

22 The mellow touch of music most doth wound
The soul, when it doth rather sigh than sound.
Robert Herrick, 'Soft Music'

23 The sweetness and delightfulness of music has
a natural power to lessify melancholy passions.
Increase Mather, *Remarkable Providences* (1684)

1 With eyes up-rais'd, as one inspir'd
   Pale Melancholy sate retir'd
   And from her wild sequester'd seat,
   In notes by distance made more sweet,
   Pour'd thro' the mellow horn her pensive soul.
   William Collins, 'The Passions, an Ode for Music'

2   Music's golden tongue
   Flatter'd to tears this aged man and poor.
   John Keats, 'The Eve of St Agnes' (1819)

3 Our sweetest songs are those that tell of
      saddest thought.
   Percy Bysshe Shelley, 'To a Skylark' (1819)

4 I'm Saddest when I Sing
   Thomas Haynes Bayly, title of poem

5 When people hear good music, it makes them
   homesick for something they never had and
   never will have.
   Ed Howe, *Country Town Sayings* (1911)

MELODY

6 You must recognise before all that music is a
   very limited art, especially in that part of it
   which is called melody. You would seek in vain,
   in the combination of notes which compose the
   air, a character proper to certain passions; it
   does not exist.
   Christoph Willibald von Gluck, quoted in Cooper,
   Gluck (1935)

7 It is the melody which is the charm of music,
   and it is that which is most difficult to produce.
   Joseph Haydn, quoted in Machlis, *Introduction to
   Contemporary Music* (1963)

8 By MELODY is implied a series of sounds more
   fixed, and generally more lengthened, than
   those of common speech; arranged with grace,
   and, with respect to TIME, of proportional
   lengths, such as the mind can easily measure,
   and the voice express.
   Charles Burney, *A General History of Music* (1776—89)

9 Melody is the very essence of music. When I
   think of a good melodist I think of a fine race-
   horse. A contrapuntist is only a post-horse.
   Wolfgang Amadeus Mozart, Letter to Michael Kelly,
   1786

10 Melody! The battle-cry of dilettanti!
    Robert Schumann, quoted in *La Revue musicale* (1921)

11 Melody, always melody ... that is the sole, the
    unique secret of our art.
    Charles Gounod, quoted in Harding, *Gounod* (1973)

12 Rhapsodies ... are not a very difficult formula,
    if one can think up enough tunes.
    Virgil Thomson, in *Modern Music*, 1935

13 What survives every change of system is
    melody.
    Igor Stravinsky, *Poetics of Music* (1947)

14 Composers should write tunes the chauffeurs
    and errand boys can whistle.
    Sir Thomas Beecham, quoted in *The New York Times*,
    1961

15 If an opera cannot be played by an organ-
    grinder, as Puccini's and Verdi's melodies were
    played, than that opera is not going to achieve
    immortality.
    Sir Thomas Beecham, quoted in Ayre, *The Wit of Music*
    (1966)

16 The grand tune is the only thing in music that
    the great public really understands.
    Sir Thomas Beecham, quoted in Atkins and Newman,
    Beecham Stories (1978)

17 A melody is not merely something you can
    hum.
    Aaron Copland, in *The New York Times*, 1949

18 I conceive the highest of melodic forms to be
    like the rainbow, which mounts and re-
    descends without one's being able to say at any
    one moment: 'Here, you see, it has returned to
    fragment B, and there to fragment A.'
    Arthur Honegger, *I am a Composer* (1951)

MENDELSSOHN

19 I have grown accustomed to composing in our
    garden ... today or tomorrow I am going to
    dream there the *Midsummer Night's Dream*.
    Felix Mendelssohn, Letter to Fanny Mendelssohn,
    1826

20 The thoughts which are expressed to me by
    music that I love are not too indefinite to be put
    into words, but on the contrary, too definite.
    Felix Mendelssohn, Letter to Souchay

21 Art and life are not two different things.
    Felix Mendelssohn, Letter

22 Joking apart, Prince Albert asked me to go to
    him on Saturday at two o'clock so that I may
    try his organ.
    Felix Mendelssohn, quoted in Bonavia, *Musicians on
    Music* (1956)

23 Ever since I began to compose, I have remained
    true to my starting principle: not to write a page
    because no matter what public, or what pretty
    girl wanted it to be thus or thus; but to write
    solely as I myself thought best, and as it gave
    me pleasure.
    Felix Mendelssohn, Letter, 1843

24 Mendelssohn is a generous high-minded
    creature, but, to descend from these heights, he
    was dressed very badly, and looked in sad want

of a piece of soap and the nail brush which I
have so often threatened to offer him.

Fanny Horsley, Letter, 1833

1   The Mozart of the nineteenth century.

Robert Schumann, in *Neue Zeitschrift*, 1840

2   Bach reborn.

Franz Liszt, quoted in Marek, *Gentle Genius* (1972)

3   A romantic who felt at ease within the mould of
classicism.

Pablo Casals, quoted in Corredor, *Conversations with
Casals* (1954)

MESSIAEN

4   [Of *Vingt regards sur l'enfant-Jésus*] It is possible
to make sounds on a piano that are more
orchestral than those of an orchestra.

Olivier Messiaen, quoted in Nichols, *Messiaen* (1975)

5   [On his inspiration by birdsong] When my
uselessness is brutally revealed to me and all
the musical languages of the world seem to be
merely an effort of patient research.

Olivier Messiaen, quoted in Nichols, *Messiaen* (1975)

6   [On his transcriptions of bird songs]
Involuntarily, I introduce something of my own
style, my own way of listening, when
interpreting the birdsongs.

Olivier Messiaen, quoted in Johnson, *Messiaen* (1975)

7   In Messiaen I see very clearly the musical
reflection of stalactites: a succession of fourths,
perfect or augmented, tumbling down or
mounting again in pyramids, from low to high,
in a ladder of sound.

Arthur Honegger, *I am a Composer* (1951)

8   [Of Messiaen's *Turangalîla-symphonie*] Little
more can be required to write such things than
a plentiful supply of ink.

Igor Stravinsky, *Themes and Conclusions* (1972)

9   [Of Messiaen's music] Fantastic music of the
stars.

Karlheinz Stockhausen, quoted in Wörner,
Stockhausen: Life and Work (1973)

MEYERBEER

10   Let me tell you that I — *who am but a humble
worm* — am sometimes ill for a whole month
after a first night.

Giacomo Meyerbeer, remark to Gounod, quoted in
Harding, *Gounod* (1973)

11   What genius, what loftiness — *such music hits
the ceiling.*

Charles Gounod, on listening to Meyerbeer's *Le
Prophète*, quoted in Harding, *Gounod* (1973)

12   Meyerbeer feels as Michelangelo felt.

Georges Bizet, Letter to Hector Gruyer, 1858

13   [To the composer of music for Meyerbeer's
funeral] Would it not have been better if you
had died and Meyerbeer had written your
funeral march!

Gioacchino Rossini, quoted in Tovey, *Essays In Musical
Analysis* (1935)

14   [Meyerbeer] had the luck to be talented, but,
above all, the talent to be lucky.

Hector Berlioz, quoted in Elliot, *Berlioz* (1967)

15   That's music for you.

Antonín Dvořák, quoted in Mařák, *Reminiscences of
Antonín Dvořák* (1910-11)

MILHAUD

16   [Of *Le Boeuf sur le toit*] I thought that the
character of the music would make it suitable as
an accompaniment for one of Charlie Chaplin's
films.

Darius Milhaud, quoted in Harding, *The Ox on the Roof*
(1972)

17   The indifference of the public is what's
depressing. Enthusiasm, or vehement protest,
shows that your work really lives.

Darius Milhaud, after public outrage expressed at his
music for *Protée* (1920), quoted in Harding, *The Ox on
the Roof* (1972)

18   I have no aesthetic rules, or philosophy, or
theories. I love to write music. I always do it
with pleasure, otherwise I just do not write it.

Darius Milhaud, quoted by Copland, *Darius Milhaud*
(1947)

19   [Of Milhaud's dissonances] The worst of it is
that you get used to them!

Charles-Marie Widor, quoted in Machlis, *Introduction
to Contemporary Music* (1963)

20   [Of *Le Boeuf sur le toit*] It ain't that it makes you
laugh; but it's different, see, so it makes you
laugh.

Anon. working man, hearing the piece in a Paris
music-hall, quoted by Milhaud, *Notes without Music*
(trans. 1952)

21   Darius Milhaud is the most gifted of us all.

Arthur Honegger, quoted in Harding, *The Ox on the
Roof* (1972)

MONARCHS

See also PATRONAGE.

22   If the king loves music, there is little wrong in
the land.

Mencius, *Discourses*

23   *Cedant carminibus reges regumque triumphi.* Let
kings and the triumphs of kings yield before
songs.

Ovid, *Amores*, I, 15

1   [Cleopatra's] barge ... kept stroke in rowing
    after the sound of the music of flutes, hautboys,
    citterns, viols, and such other instruments as
    they played upon.

    Plutarch, *Life of Mark Antony*; trans. North (1579)

2   Old King Cole was a merry old soul,
    And a merry old soul was he;
    He called for his pipe and he called for his
         bowl,
    And he called for his fiddlers three.

    Anon. nursery rhyme

3   It were therefore better that no music were
    taught to a noble man, than by exact knowledge
    thereof he should have therein inordinate
    delight, and by that be illicited to wantonness,
    avandoning gravity and the necessary cure and
    office in the public weal in him committed.

    Sir Thomas Elyot, *The Boke of the Governour* (1531)

4   [Of Anne Boleyn] Besides singing like a siren,
    accompanying herself on the lute, she harped
    better than Kind David and handled cleverly
    both flute and rebec.

    Viscount Chateaubriant, quoted in Strickland, *Lives of
    the Queens of England* (1840)

5   I maintain at least sixty musicians, and in my
    youth I danced very well, composed ballets and
    music, and played and danced them myself.

    Queen Elizabeth I, quoted in Chamberlin, *The Sayings
    of Queen Elizabeth* (1923)

6   [Of Elizabeth I]
    *Nec contenta graves aliorum audire labores
    Ipsa etiam egregie voce manuque canit.*
    Not content with listening to the serious
    performances of others, she sings quite
    exceptionally both with voice and hand.

    Richard Mulcaster, 'In Musicam Thomae Tallisii, et
    Guilielmi Birdi'

7   Organs and Regals thair did carpe
    With thair gay goldin gilttering strings,
    Thair was the Hautbois and the Harpe
    Playing maist sweit and pleasant springs;
    And some on Lutis did play and sing,
    Of instruments the onely king.

    Viols and Virginals were heir
    With Githornis maist jucundious,
    Trumpets and Timbrels maid gret beir,
    With instruments melodious;
    The Seister and the Sumphion,
    With Clarche Pipe and Clarion.

    John Burel, *The Queenis ... Entry* (1590)

8   The eagle suffers little birds to sing,
    And is not careful what they mean thereby.
    (Tamora)

    William Shakespeare, *Titus Andronicus*, IV.iv

9   Music do I hear?
    Ha — ha. Keep time. How sour sweet music is

When time is broke, and no proportion kept;
So is it in the music of men's lives.
And here have I the daintiness of ear
To check time broke in a disordered string,
But for the concord of my state and time,
Had not an ear to hear my true time broke.
(Richard)

William Shakespeare, *Richard II*, V.v

10 This will prove a brave kingdom to me, where I
    shall have my music for nothing.
    (Stephano)

    William Shakespeare, *The Tempest*, III.ii

11 King Henry the Eighth could not only sing his
    part sure, but of himself composed a service of
    four, five, and six parts.

    Henry Peacham, *The Compleat Gentleman* (1622)

12 I dedicate my work to Your Majesty, whose
    hand is more skilful in carving victory in war
    than in playing the guitar.

    Robert de Visée, Dedication to Louis XIV in a book of
    guitar music

13 Whilst thus I sing, I am a King,
         Altho' a poor blind boy.

    Colley Cibber, 'The Blind Boy'

14 A careless song, with a little nonsense in it now
    and then, does not misbecome a monarch.

    Horace Walpole, Letter to Horace Mann, 1774

15 Art, true art, catches chill in splendid
    apartments hung with red damask, and swoons
    away completely in *salons* of pale yellow or
    shimmering blue ... When at court, keep it
    short: what you actually say matters little,
    provided that the rhythm gets into their toes
    and makes them think of yesterday's or
    tomorrow's waltz!

    Franz Liszt, quoted in Hedley, *Chopin* (1947)

16 Music herself should be silent when Nicholas
    speaks.

    Franz Liszt, sarcastically explaining why he stopped
    playing when Tsar Nicholas I was talking, quoted in
    Beckett, *Liszt* (1963)

MONEY

See also PATRONAGE.

17 He who pays the piper calls the tune.

    English proverb

18 What? All this for a song?

    William Cecil, Lord Burleigh, remark to Elizabeth I
    when she told him to give £100 to Edmund Spenser

19 It is 'music with her silver sound', because
    musicians have no gold for sounding.
    (Peter)

    William Shakespeare, *Romeo and Juliet*, IV.v; see
    Richard Edwards, 'In Commendation of Music'

1   *Duke Orsino*: There's for thy pains.
    Clown: No pains, sir, I take pleasure in singing,
    sir.
    Duke Orsino: I'll pay thy pleasure then.
    Clown: Truly, sir, and pleasure will be paid one
    time or another.
    William Shakespeare, *Twelfth Night*, II.iv

2   The singing man keeps a shop in his throat.
    George Herbert, *Jacula Prudentum* (1640)

3   I bought it for a song.
    John Crowne, *Regulus*, II.i (1694)

4   Men of our profession hang between the church
    and the playhouse, as Mahomet's tomb does
    between the two load-stones, and must equally
    incline to both, because by both we are equally
    supported.
    Tom Brown, *Letters from the Dead to the Living* (1704),
    'John Blow'

5   The theatre composer should be satisfied with
    less pay than the least of them [the singers],
    though he should not tolerate the injustice of
    receiving less than the theatre bear or the
    extras.
    Benedetto Marcello, *Il teatro alla moda* (1720)

6   *Amphion Thebas, ego domum.* Amphion built
    Thebes, I only a house.
    Caffarelli, Inscription over the door of his house,
    quoted in Burney, *The Present State of Music in France
    and Italy* (1773)

7   Feed the musician, and he's out of tune.
    George Crabbe, *The Newspaper* (1785)

8   Do the sounds
    Which slumber in the lute, belong alone
    To him who buys the chords?
    Johann Christoph Friedrich von Schiller, *Don Carlos*,
    IV (1787)

9   There should be a single Art Exchange in the
    world, to which the artist would simply send
    his works and be given in return as much as he
    needs. As it is, one has to be half a merchant on
    top of everything else, and how badly one goes
    about it!
    Ludwig van Beethoven, Letter, 1801

10 I know nothing about music. My music is this
    [striking his change pocket]. They hearken to it
    on the Exchange.
    Baron de Rothschild, quoted by Spohr, *Autobiography*
    (1861)

11 Music is the only noise for which one is obliged
    to pay.
    Alexandre Dumas, attr.

12 I have always held the opinion that when the
    abandoned composer is faced with poor
    receipts, there is nothing for him to say.
    Charles Gounod, quoted in Harding, *Gounod* (1973)

13 I've bested you. *Faust* has made 20,000 francs
    this week and your *Le Cid* only 16,000 . . .
    suicide's the only thing left for you now.
    Charles Gounod, remark to Massenet, quoted in
    Harding, *Gounod* (1973)

14 A wandering minstrel I —
    A thing of shreds and patches,
    Of ballads, songs and snatches,
    And dreamy lullaby!
    W.S. Gilbert, *The Mikado*, I (1885)

15 It cannot be emphasised too strongly that art,
    as such does not 'pay' . . . and that the art that
    has to pay its own way is apt to become vitiated
    and cheap.
    Antonín Dvořák, 'Music in America' (1895)

16 Art . . . is deaf to the demands of supply and
    demand.
    Ernst Bloch, 'Man and Music' (1917)

17 Don't ever dream of becoming a 'professional'
    composer unless you have private means.
    Frederick Delius, quoted in Reid, *Thomas Beecham*
    (1961)

18 Music-making as a means of getting money is
    hell.
    Gustav Holst, quoted in Holst, *Holst* (1974)

19 [Asked why he charged high fees] I do it on
    behalf of my brother composers, Schubert and
    Mozart, who died in poverty.
    Igor Stravinsky, quoted in Ayre, *The Wit of Music*
    (1966)

20 Music is something that people can get on
    without, and if it costs too much they will.
    Sir Thomas Beecham, *A Mingled Chime* (1944)

21 Grand opera will never pay.
    Sir Thomas Beecham, quoted in Reid, *Thomas Beecham*
    (1961)

22 The composer expends an enormous amount of
    time and energy — and, usually considerable
    money — on the creation of a commodity which
    has little, none or negative commodity value.
    He is, in essence, a 'vanity' composer.
    Milton Babbitt, quoted in Ewen, *American Composers*
    (1982)

23 I shall consider it my patriotic duty to keep
    Elvis in the ninety per cent tax bracket.
    Colonel Tom Parker, Presley's manager, quoted in
    Palmer, *All You Need Is Love* (1976)

24 [On his reaction to adverse criticism] I cried all
    the way to the bank.
    Liberace, *Autobiography* (1973)

25 I long ago decided there wasn't any sense in
    making money. The US government simply
    takes it away to build more things to drop

bombs out of ... So the only thing to do is to sing for free.

Pete Seeger, quoted in Palmer, *All You Need Is Love* (1976)

1   Most of the blues singers didn't know what 'royalty' meant. I didn't know until Roosevelt Sykes told me I wasn't getting any.

Memphis Slim, quoted in Palmer, *All You Need Is Love* (1976)

2   When you get in the record business, someone gonna rip you anyway so that don't bother me. If you don't rip me, she gonna rip me, and if she don't rip me, he gonna rip me, so I'm gonna get ripped, so you don't be bothered by that, because people round you gonna rip you if they can.

Muddy Waters, quoted in Green, *The Book of Rock Quotes* (1982)

MONTEVERDI

3   [Of his *seconda prattica*] The modern composer builds his works on the basis of truth.

Claudio Monteverdi, Preface to *Fifth Book of Madrigals* (1605)

4   [In defence of his style] I do not write things by accident.

Claudio Monteverdi, Preface to *Fifth Book of Madrigals* (1605)

5   [Introducing his *stile agitato*] I consider the principal passions or emotions of the soul to be three, namely, anger, serenity, and humility. The best philosophers affirm this; the very nature of our voice, with its high, low and middle ranges, shows it; and the art of music clearly manifests it in these three terms: agitated, soft and moderate.

Claudio Monteverdi, Preface to *Eighth Book of Madrigals* (1638)

6   Claudio Monteverdi, in moving the affections ... becomes the most pleasant tyrant of human minds.

Aquilino Coppini, in 1608, quoted in Stravinsky, *Themes and Conclusions* (1972)

7   [Of Monteverdi] Amazingly modern and, if one can say such a thing, near to me in spirit.

Igor Stravinsky, quoted in Druskin, *Igor Stravinsky* (1983)

MOZART

8   Mamma said to me: 'I bet that you have let one off.' 'I don't think so, Mamma,' I replied. 'Well, I am certain that you have,' she insisted. Well, I thought, 'Let's see,' put my finger to my arse and then to my nose and — *Ecce, provatum est!* Mamma was right after all.

Wolfgang Amadeus Mozart, Letter to Maria Anna Thekla Mozart, 1777

9   I like an aria to fit a singer as perfectly as a well-tailored suit of clothes.

Wolfgang Amadeus Mozart, Letter, 1778

10   I pay no attention whatever to anybody's praise or blame ... I simply follow my own feelings.

Wolfgang Amadeus Mozart, Letter to his father, 1781

11   Opera to me comes before everything else.

Wolfgang Amadeus Mozart, Letter, 1782

12   As death ... is the true goal of our existence, I have formed, during the last few years, such close relations with this best and truest friend of mankind, that his image is not only no longer terrifying to me, but is indeed very soothing and consoling.

Wolfgang Amadeus Mozart, Letter to his father, 1787

13   [Of the 15-year-old Mozart] This boy will cause us all to be forgotten.

Johann Adolf Hasse, quoted in Headington, *The Bodley Head History of Western Music* (1974)

14   I tell you before God, as an honest man, that your son is the greatest composer I know, either personally or by repute.

Joseph Haydn, Letter to Leopold Mozart, 1785

15   I love the man too much.

Joseph Haydn, Letter to Roth, 1787

16   O Mozart, immortal Mozart, how many, how infinitely many inspiring suggestions of a finer, better life have you left in our souls!

Franz Schubert, Diary, 1816

17   Mozart should have composed *Faust*.

Johann Wolfgang von Goethe, *Conversations with Eckermann* (1827)

18   Beethoven is the greatest composer — but Mozart is the only one.

Gioacchino Rossini, attr.

19   I am in love with Mozart like a young girl. Immortal Mozart! I owe you everything ... I have you to thank that I did not die without having loved.

Sören Kierkegaard, *Either/Or* (1843)

20   Mozart is to Palestrina and Bach what the New Testament is to the Old in the spirit of the Bible, one and indivisible.

Charles Gounod, quoted in Harding, *Gounod* (1973)

21   Raphael is the same man as Mozart.

Georges Bizet, Letter to Hector Gruyer, 1858

22   [Of a Madonna by Raphael] That is Mozart.

Antonín Dvořák, quoted in Zubatý, 'With Dvořák in London'

23   Mozart is sunshine.

Antonín Dvořák, quoted in Šourek (ed.), *Antonín Dvořák: Letters and Reminiscences* (1954)

1 [Of the beginning of Mozart's Piano Concerto No.23 in A major] If any of us were to die and then wake hearing it we should know at once that (after all) we had got to the right place.

Neville Cardus, in *The Manchester Guardian*, 1938

2 In *Così fan tutte* the dying eighteenth century casts a backward glance over a period outstanding in European life for grace and charm and, averting its eyes from a new age suckled in a creed of iconoclasm, sings its swan-song in praise of a civilisation that has passed away for ever.

Sir Thomas Beecham, *A Mingled Chime* (1944)

3 He emancipated music from the bonds of a formal age, while remaining the true voice of the eighteenth century.

Sir Thomas Beecham, quoted in Brymer, *From Where I Sit* (1979)

4 The piece was recognisable to Dixon as some skein of untiring facetiousness by filthy Mozart.

Kingsley Amis, *Lucky Jim* (1954)

5 [Of *The Magic Flute*] The opera . . . is the only one in existence that might conceivably have been composed by God.

Neville Cardus, in *The Manchester Guardian*, 1961

6 Whether the angels play only Bach in praising God I am not quite sure: I am sure, however, that *en famille* they play Mozart.

Karl Barth, quoted in *The New York Times*, 1968

THE MUSICAL

7 The question of how simple-minded the book of a musical comedy can be was debated last night, and the verdict arrived at was 'no end'.

Richard Watts, Jr., reviewing *The Desert Song* in *The New York Herald Tribune*, 1926

8 [Of *Oklahoma!*] This was the first musical I ever saw on the stage where the people were not complete idiots.

Ernst Lubitsch, quoted in Palmer, *All You Need Is Love* (1976)

9 [Of Richard Rodgers] His work tended to make people think of him as an unsophisticated, platitudinous hick, whereas he was a highly intelligent, strongly principled, very firm-minded, and philosophic man. Which is just what his work seemed not to be.

Stephen Sondheim, quoted in Palmer, *All You Need Is Love* (1976)

MUSSORGSKY

10 My music must be an artistic reproduction of human speech in all its finest shades.

Modest Mussorgsky, Letter, 1868

11 I regard the people as one great being, inspired by one idea. This is my problem. I strove to solve it in this opera.

Modest Mussorgsky, unused MS dedication to *Boris Godunov* (1874)

12 Life, wherever it is shown; truth, however bitter; speaking out boldly, frankly, point-blank to men — that is my aim . . . I am a realist in the highest sense — that is, my business is to portray the soul of man in all its profundity.

Modest Mussorgsky, quoted in Shapiro, *An Encyclopedia of Quotations about Music* (1978)

13 [Of Mussorgsky] His nature is not of the finest quality; he likes what is coarse, unpolished, and ugly.

Piotr Ilyich Tchaikovsky, Letter to Nadezhda von Meck, 1878

14 It seems easy enough to correct Mussorgsky's defects; but when this is done, it is impossible not to feel that the result is no longer Mussorgsky.

Anatol Liadov, quoted in Morgenstern, *Composers on Music* (1958)

15 Mussorgsky was an amateur with moments of genius.

Ernest Newman, in *The Nation*, 1914

16 Mussorgsky's operas completely overthrow Wagner's system and show what extraordinarily dramatic and deeply human music can be written if Wagnerian verbosity be replaced by a strict limitation to the barest essentials and by setting down music as it flows from the heart instead of building it up laboriously from so many bricks that have been carefully trimmed beforehand.

Eric Blom, in *The Musical Quarterly*, 1923

17 Mussorgsky's greatest misfortune was that he came into the world half a century too early. The technique he would have required in order to achieve his ends had not yet come into being.

Igor Gliebof, *Boris Godunov: articles and studies* (1930)

NATIONALISM

See also INTERNATIONALISM, and individual countries.

18 It is easier to understand a nation by listening to its music than by learning its language.

Anon., quoted in Mencken, *Dictionary of Quotations* (1942)

19 A composer should fit his music to the genius of the people, and consider that the delicacy of hearing, and taste of harmony, has been formed upon those sounds which every country abounds with. In short, that music is of a relative nature, and what is harmony to one ear, may be dissonance to another.

Joseph Addison, in *The Spectator*, 1710

1 It is the accent of languages that determines the melody of each nation.

Jean-Jacques Rousseau, *Dictionnaire de musique* (1768)

2 *La distinction ridicule de musiques nationales.*
The ridiculous distinction of national musics.

Christoph Willibald von Gluck, Letter to d'Auvergne, published in *Le Mercure de France*, 1773

3 Music is the melody whose text is the world.

Arthur Schopenhauer, attr.

4 The North is most assuredly entitled to a language of its own.

Robert Schumann, quoted in Finck, *Grieg and his Music* (1929)

5 Tell me where you live, and I will tell you how you compose.

Robert Schumann, quoted in Walker (ed.), *Robert Schumann: the Man and his Music* (1972)

6 The song that nerves a nation's heart
Is in itself a deed.

Alfred, Lord Tennyson, 'The Charge of the Heavy Brigade', Epilogue

7 An artist also has his country in which he must have firm faith and to which his heart must always warm.

Antonín Dvořák, Letter to Simrock, 1885

8 Racial consciousness is absolutely necessary in music, even though nationalism is not.

Ernest Bloch, in *c.* 1912, quoted in Ewen, *American Composers* (1982)

9 Art must be parochial in the beginning to be cosmopolitan in the end.

George Moore, *Hail and Farewell* (1911-14)

10 Not long ago I asked a distinguished Austrian musician, 'When are they going to understand and take to Elgar's music in Vienna?' His reply was very much to the point: 'As soon as you in England take to and understand Mahler.'

Neville Cardus, in *The Radio Times*, 1931

11 The business of finding a nation's soul is a long and slow one at the best, and a great many prophets must be slain in the course of it. Perhaps when we have slain enough prophets, future generations will begin to build their tombs.

Ralph Vaughan Williams, *National Music* (1934)

12 Art, like charity, should begin at home ... The greatest artist belongs inevitably to his country as much as the humblest singer in a remote village.

Ralph Vaughan Williams, quoted in Machlis, *Introduction to Contemporary Music* (1963)

13 The art of music above all other arts is the expression of the soul of a nation.

Ralph Vaughan Williams, quoted in Headington, *The Bodley Head History of Western Music* (1974)

14 Though musical folklore owed a great deal to nationalism, today it is so harmed by ultra-nationalism that the damage now exceeds the former benefits.

Béla Bartók, 'Folk Song Research and Nationalism' (1937)

15 [On nationalism in music] One has to have a passport.

Igor Stravinsky, quoted in Myers, *Modern French Music* (1971)

16 According to Schumann, the world's music is like a great fugue in which the various nations sound alternately.

Zoltán Kodály, Address, 1956

17 The first response to any really strange music is laughter — the Javanese conceal well-bred smiles on hearing Beethoven, and we grin shamelessly at their love songs accompanied by nose-blown flutes.

Jacques Barzun, *Pleasures of Music* (1977)

18 There is ... a nationalism ... where a composer's musical roots are in his native soil, and he does not have to use folk tunes to prove it.

Alan Kendall, *The Tender Tyrant: Nadia Boulanger* (1976)

NATURE

See also BIRDSONG.

19 The pastures are clothed with flocks; the valleys also are covered over with corn; they shout for joy, they also sing.

Psalms 65:13

20 The dolphin, a creature fond not only of man but of the musical art, is charmed by harmonious melody, and especially the sound of the hydraulus [hydraulic organ].

Pliny, *Natural History*

21 The Dolphins — the sweet conceipters of Music.

Robert Greene, *Menaphon* (1587)

22 Be not afeard: the isle is full of noises,
Sounds and sweet airs, that give delight, and
       hurt not.
(Caliban)

William Shakespeare, *The Tempest*, III.ii

23   The thunder,
That deep and dreadful organ pipe.
(Alonso)

William Shakespeare, *The Tempest*, III.iii

24 [Of Bach's music] One admires the onerous labour and uncommon effort — which, however, are vainly employed, since they conflict with Nature.

Johann Adolf Scheiber, in *Der critische Musicus*, 1737

1 A melody . . . imitates either physical noises or the accents of passion.

Denis Diderot, *Rameau's Nephew* (1762)

2 I might perhaps have written something more beautiful from a musical point of view, and varied it so as to please your ears; but in that case I should have only been a musician and should have been untrue to nature, which I must never abandon.

Christoph Willibald von Gluck, referring to passage in his opera *Iphigénie en Aulide*, quoted in Cooper, *Gluck* (1935)

3 All the sounds that nature utters are delightful, — at least in this country. I should not perhaps find the roaring of lions in Africa, or of bears in Russia, very pleasing; but I know no beast in England whose voice I do not account musical, save and except always the braying of an ass.

William Cowper, Letter, 1784

4 No sound is uttered, — but a deep
And solemn harmony pervades
The hollow vale from steep to steep,
And penetrates the glades.

William Wordsworth, 'Composed Upon an Evening of Extraordinary Splendour and Beauty'

5 There is society, where none intrudes,
By the deep sea and music in its roar.

Lord Byron, *Childe Harold's Pilgrimage*, IV (1818)

6 Give me books, fruit, french wine and fine weather and a little music out of doors, played by somebody I do not know.

John Keats, Letter to Fanny Keats, 1819

7 'Tis not through envy of thy happy lot,
But being too happy in thine happiness, —
     That thou, light-winged Dryad of the trees,
          In some melodious plot
Of beechen green, and shadows numberless,
     Singest of summer in full-throated ease.

John Keats, 'Ode to a Nightingale' (1819)

8 Where are the songs of Spring? Ay, where are
          they?
     Think not of them, thou hast thy music too.

John Keats, 'Ode to Autumn' (1819)

9 He is made one with Nature: there is heard
His voice in all her music, from the moan
Of thunder, to the song of night's sweet bird.

Percy Bysshe Shelley, *Adonais* (1821)

10 See deep enough, and you see musically; the heart of nature being everywhere music, if you can only reach it.

Thomas Carlyle, *On Heroes, Hero-Worship and the Heroic in History* (1841)

11 'Tis not in the high stars alone,
Nor in the cups of budding flowers,
Nor in the redbreast's mellow tone,
Nor in the bow that smiles in showers,

But in the mud and scum of things
There alway, alway something sings.

Ralph Waldo Emerson, 'The Poet'

12 I hear the wind among the trees
Playing the celestial symphonies;
I see the branches downward bent,
Like keys of some great instrument.

Henry Wadsworth Longfellow, 'A Day of Sunshine'

13 The formation of scales and of the web of harmony is a product of artistic invention, and is in no way given by the natural structure or by the natural behaviour of our hearing, as used to be generally maintained hitherto.

Hermann von Helmholtz, *Theory of Sound* (1862)

14 Singing mice have often been mentioned and exhibited but imposture has commonly been suspected.

Charles Darwin, quoted in Ayre, *The Wit of Music* (1966)

15 There is no music in nature, neither melody or harmony. Music is the creation of man.

H.R. Haweis, *Music and Morals* (1871)

16 The God of Music dwelleth out of doors.

Edith M. Thomas, 'Music'

17 My music is, throughout and always, but a sound of nature.

Gustav Mahler, quoted in Machlis, *Introduction to Contemporary Music* (1963)

18 We probably derive all our basic rhythms and themes from Nature, which offers them to us, pregnant with meaning, in every animal noise.

Gustav Mahler, quoted in Bauer-Lechner, *Recollections of Gustav Mahler* (1980)

19 We cannot doubt that animals both love and practice music. That is evident. But it seems their musical system differs from ours. It is another school . . . We are not familiar with their didactic works. Perhaps they don't have any.

Erik Satie, quoted in Cage, *Silence* (1961)

20 What music is and is to be may lie somewhere in the belief of an unknown philosopher of half a century ago who said: 'How can there be any bad music? All music is from heaven. If there is anything bad in it, I put it there — by my implications and limitations. Nature builds the mountains and meadows and man puts in the fences and labels.' He may have been nearer right than we think.

Charles Ives, quoted in Ewen, *American Composers* (1982)

21 I have seen dawn and sunset on moors and
          windy hills
Coming in solemn beauty like slow old tunes of
          Spain.

John Masefield, 'Beauty'

1 An artist ... has to create something that will
have a life of its own, with the vitality of
Nature's own creations.
Benjamin Britten (with Imogen Holst), *The Wonderful
World of Music* (1958)

2 The hills are alive with the sound of music.
Oscar Hammerstein II, song from *The Sound of Music*
(1959)

NEOCLASSICISM

3 Now, once we agree that Hindemith's music is
a lamentable error, we must go on to dismiss
neoclassicism as a whole and, with it, nearly all
of American music. For Piston, Thomson, and
Copland have all been schooled in a tradition of
decadent Stravinskyism.
André Hodeir, quoted in Kendall, *The Tender Tyrant:
Nadia Boulanger* (1976)

4 Stravinsky's 'neoclassism' was no new
classicism at all, but a primitivism-romanticism,
if for no other reason than that Stravinsky so
violently opposed all limiting rules except those
which he made and destroyed daily for himself.
George Antheil, *Bad Boy of Music* (1945)

5 The folklorists and neo-classic asylists whose
modernness consists of their forbidding
themselves a musical outbreak and in wearing
with more or less dignity the style-garment of a
pre-individualistic period. Persuade themselves
and others that the tedious has become
interesting, because the interesting has begun
to grow tedious.
(Leverkühn's 'Document')
Thomas Mann, *Doctor Faustus* (1947); trans. Lowe-
Porter

6 [On Stravinsky as 'neo-classicist'] A music-
restorer.
T.W. Adorno, quoted in Druskin, *Igor Stravinsky*
(1983)

7 Neoclassicism is at best a chromium-plated
brownstone, a snappy resurfacing job that fools
no real modern who has perceived the
soundness of organised architecture, and the
form which flows from grace within, and from
the nature of materials without.
Peggy Glanville-Hicks, quoted in Ewen, *American
Composers* (1982)

8 The twelve-tone school tried to revive the spirit
of the old forms, while neo-classicism
presented replicas of their façades with
interesting cracks added.
Ernst Křenek, *Horizons Circled* (1974)

NIELSEN

9 Music is life, and, like it, inextinguishable.
Carl Nielsen, motto of his Symphony No. 4 (1916)

10 [Of his *Sinfonia semplice*] Each instrument is like
a person who sleeps, whom I have to wake to
life.
Carl Nielsen, quoted in Simpson, *Carl Nielsen* (1952)

11 I think through the instruments themselves,
almost as if I had crept inside them.
Carl Nielsen, in *Politiken*, 1925

12 If my music has any value at all, then it is in
one thing, that it has a certain current, a certain
motion, and if that is broken it's no good any
more.
Carl Nielsen, quoted in Simpson, *Carl Nielsen* (1952)

THE OBOE

13 The oboe — an ill wind that nobody blows any
good.
Oral tradition

14 Now the bass oboe. . . is to be endured only if
manipulated with supreme cunning and
control; otherwise its presence in the orchestra
is a strain upon the nervous system of
conductor and players alike, a danger to the
seemly rendering of the piece, and a cause of
astonishment and risibility in the audience. A
perfect breath control is the essential requisite
for keeping it well in order, and this alone can
obviate the eruption of sounds that would
arouse attention in a circus.
Sir Thomas Beecham, *A Mingled Chime* (1944)

15 All first oboists are gangsters. They are tough,
irascible, double-reed roosters, feared by
colleagues and conductors.
Harry Ellis Dickson, *Gentlemen, more Dolce Please*
(1969)

OFFENBACH

16 The Mozart of the Champs-Elysées.
Gioacchino Rossini, quoted in Faris, *Jacques Offenbach*
(1980)

17 He will be, indeed he already is, the Liszt of the
violoncello.
L'Artiste, 1841

18 The opéra-bouffe [*La Belle Hélène*] is simply the
sexual instinct expressed in melody.
The New York Times, 1876

19 Offenbach possesses the warmth that Daniel
Auber lacks — but it is the warmth of the
dungheap. All Europe is wallowing in it.
Richard Wagner, quoted in Lebrecht, *Discord* (1982)

20 Offenbach could have been like Mozart.
Richard Wagner, Letter to Mottl, 1882

1 Offenbach's music is wicked. It is abandoned stuff; every accent is a snap of the fingers in the face of moral responsibility.

George Bernard Shaw, quoted in Faris, *Jacques Offenbach* (1980)

OPERA

See also LIBRETTI, THE OVERTURE.

2 Opera is the delight of Princes.

Marco da Gagliano, quoted in Raynor, *Social History of Music* (1972)

3 Recitative . . . is noble and elevated, neither mangling, torturing, nor destroying the life and sense of the words, but rather enforcing their energy and spirit.

Angelo Grillo, Letter to Giulio Caccini, 1600

4 One of the most magnificient and expenseful diversions the wit of man can invent.

John Evelyn, Diary, 1645

5 I have seen to it that nothing is sung that is necessary for the comprehension of the play, because usually the words that are sung are only poorly understood by the audience.

Pierre Corneille, Preface to *Andromède* (1650)

6 Opera is a bizarre mixture of poetry and music where the writer and the composer, equally embarrassed by each other, go to a lot of trouble to create an execrable work.

Sieur de Saint-Evremond, 'Letter to the Duke of Buckingham' (1677)

7 A fatuity laden with music, with dances, with machinery and scenery, is a magnificent fatuity, but fatuous none the less.

Sieur de Saint-Evremond, Letter, 1678

8 No good opera will ever be written. Music does not know how to narrate.

Nicolas Boileau-Despréaux, quoted by Beaumarchais, Preface to *Tarare* (1790)

9 There is no question but our grand-children will be very curious to know the reason why their forefathers used to sit together like an audience of foreigners in their own country, and to hear whole plays acted before them in a tongue which they did not understand.

Joseph Addison, in *The Spectator*, 1710

10 An opera may be allowed to be extravagantly lavish in its decorations, as its only design is to gratify the senses, and keep up an indolent attention in the audience.

Joseph Addison, in *The Spectator*, 1711

11 If some aria should fail to please the virtuosi or their protectors, the composer will say that it needs to be heard in the theatre with the costumes, the lights, the supernumeraries, etc.

Benedetto Marcello, *Il teatro alla moda* (1720)

12 [On semi-operas] Some that would come to the play hated the music, and others that were very desirous of the music, would not bear the interruption that so much rehearsal [i.e., dialogue] gave.

Roger North, *Memoirs of Musick* (pub. 1846)

13 I hope I may be forgiven, that I have not made my opera unnatural, like those in vogue, for I have no recitative.

John Gay, Preface to *The Beggar's Opera* (1728)

14 Leave your reason at home and take only your ears with you when you go to an opera house.

J.C. Gotsched, *Kritische Dichtkunst* (1729)

15 Ballad opera pelted Italian opera off the stage with Lumps of Pudding [a tune in *The Beggar's Opera*].

George Frideric Handel, quoted in Lee, *Music of the People* (1970)

16 The Opéra is nothing but a public gathering place, where we assemble on certain days without precisely knowing why.

Voltaire, Letter to Cideville, 1732

17 One goes to see a tragedy to be moved; to the Opéra one goes either for want of any other interest or to facilitate digestion.

Voltaire, quoted in Wechsberg, *The Opera* (1972)

18 You see actresses virtually in convulsions as they rend from their lungs the most violent ululations; both fists clenched against the breast, the head thrown back, cheeks aflame, veins bursting, and diaphragm heaving. It is impossible to say which is the more unpleasantly assailed, the eye or the ear; these motions cause as much pain to those who look as the singing to those who listen, but what is still more astonishing is that the howls and cries are almost the only thing applauded by the audience.

Jean-Jacques Rousseau, quoted in Barzun, *Pleasures of Music* (1977)

19 As for operas, they are essentially too absurd and extravagant to mention; I look upon them as a magic scene contrived to please the eyes and the ears at the expense of the understanding.

Lord Chesterfield, Letter to his son, 1752

20 Opera: An exotic and irrational entertainment.

Samuel Johnson, *Dictionary* (1755)

21 Operas are not calculated to please the judgment, but to tickle the ear; so that propriety of characters is as little to be expected in these places, as sublime and poetical language.

John George Keysler, *Travels* (1756)

22 I have thought it necessary to reduce music to its true function, which is that of seconding

poetry in the expression of sentiments and dramatic situations of a story, neither interrupting the action nor detracting from its vividness by useless and superfluous ornament.

Christoph Willibald von Gluck, Preface to *Alceste* (1767)

1   Music should give to poetry what the brightness of colour and the happy combination of light and shade give to a well-executed and finely composed drawing — it should fill its characters with life without destroying their outline.

Christoph Willibald von Gluck, Preface to *Alceste* (1767)

2   It is surely in the nature of things that good theatrical music should frequently be unsuccessful in a concert-room.

Christoph Willibald von Gluck, quoted in Cooper, *Gluck* (1935)

3   [A maxim for opera] To the best orchestra in the world I addressed only the words: PLAY MORE SOFTLY!

Pierre Augustin Caron de Beaumarchais, Preface to *Tarare* (1790)

4   Music is in the opera what the verses are in the drama — a more stately expression, a stronger means of presenting thoughts and emotions.

Pierre Augustin Caron de Beaumarchais, Preface to *Tarare* (1790)

5   There is too much music in our music for the theatre.

Pierre Augustin Caron de Beaumarchais, Preface to *Tarare* (1790)

6   Opera is free from any servile imitation of nature. By the power of music it attunes the soul to a beautiful receptiveness.

Friedrich von Schiller, Letter to Goethe

7   [In *The Marriage of Figaro*] Music, dominated as it is by sensibility, has changed into true passions the lightish tastes which in Beaumarchais keep the amiable inhabitants of the palace of Aguas Frescas amused.

Stendhal, Letter, 1814

8   The Opera ... does not subsist as an imitation of nature, but in contempt of it ... At the theatre, we see and hear what has been said, thought and done by various people elsewhere; at the Opera we see and hear what was never said, thought or done anywhere but at the Opera.

William Hazlitt, 'The Opera'

9   [Declining an invitation to the opera] It would be rather out of etiquette for a Canon of St Paul's to go to an opera, and where etiquette prevents me from doing things disagreeable to myself, I am a perfect martinet.

Sydney Smith, Letter to Lady Holland, 1842

10   What else is *opéra comique*, in fact, but sung vaudeville?

Jacques Offenbach, in *Le Ménestrel*, 1856

11   The success of our operas rests most of the time in the hands of the conductor. This person is as necessary as a tenor or a prima donna.

Giuseppe Verdi, Letter, 1869

12   Superfluous detail has no place in opera. Everything should be drawn in bold strokes, as clearly and vividly as is practically possible for voice and orchestra. The voices should take first place, and the orchestra second.

Alexander Borodin, quoted in Dianin, *Borodin* (1963)

13   Operetta is the daughter of the *opéra comique* — a daughter who went to the bad. Not that daughters who go to the bad are always lacking in charm.

Camille Saint-Saëns, quoted in Cooper, *Opéra Comique* (1949)

14   One cannot do a greater disservice to Wagner than by bringing his music into a concert hall. It is created solely for the theatrical stage, and that is where it belongs.

Johannes Brahms, quoted in Gall, *Johannes Brahms* (1961)

15   This particularly rapid, unintelligible patter, Isn't generally heard, and if it is it doesn't matter!

W.S. Gilbert, *Ruddigore*, II (1887)

16   I have never encountered anything more false and foolish than the effort to get truth into opera. In opera everything is based upon the not-true.

Pyotr Ilyich Tchaikovsky, Diary, 1888

17   In opera there is always too much singing.

Claude Debussy, quoted in Myers, *Modern French Music* (1971)

18   There is no need for the orchestra to grimace when a character comes on stage. Do the trees in the scenery grimace? What we have to do is to create a musical scenery, a musical atmosphere in which the characters move and talk.

Erik Satie, quoted in Nyman, *Experimental Music* (1974)

19   The art of dramatic writing is to compose a melodic curve which will, as if by magic, reveal immediately a human being in one definite phase of his existence.

Leoš Janáček, 'Last Year, This Year' (1905)

20   [Stopping singing during a rehearsal of Ethel Smyth's *The Wreckers*] Is this the place where I'm supposed to be drowned by the waves or by the orchestra?

John Coates, quoted in Reid, *Thomas Beecham* (1961)

1 [Immediately before the London premiere of Richard Strauss's *Elektra*] The singers think they're going to be heard, and I'm going to make jolly well certain that they are not!

Sir Thomas Beecham, quoted in Reid, *Thomas Beecham* (1961)

2 Opera, n. A play representing life in another world, whose inhabitants have no speech but song, no motions but gestures and no postures but attitudes. All acting is simulation, and the word *simulation* is from *simia*, an ape; but in opera the actor takes for his model *Simia audibilis* (or *Pithecanthropos stentor*) — the ape that howls.

Ambrose Bierce, *The Devil's Dictionary* (1911)

3 She [the opera singer] must bear in mind that the world of opera is one of illusion, of fantasy, of exaggeration — and that it is hard to nurse poetic and fantastic illusions, no matter how fine the voice, when the eye is oppressed by the sight of some three hundred pounds of human avoirdupois.

Geraldine Farrar, quoted in Martens, *The Art of the Prima Donna* (1923)

4 On the stage, it is not always the best word for vocalising that we require; we need the everyday word, its melodic turn, torn from life, misery congealed, despair in sharp relief. Real life is needed in opera.

Leoš Janáček, quoted in *The Slavonic Review*, 1922-23

5 The opera . . . is to music what a bawdy house is to a cathedral.

H.L. Mencken, Letter to Isaac Goldberg, 1925

6 I want the classical operas produced as if they were modern, and vice versa.

Alban Berg, in 1928, quoted in Barzun, *Pleasures of Music* (1977)

7 It is evident that an art form which employs the human voice will not renounce any of the possibilities which are open to the latter. Accordingly, the spoken word — either without accompaniment or as melodrama — is just as appropriate in opera as are the various modes of singing.

Alban Berg, 'The Voice in Opera' (1929)

8 A modern opera needs just as nice singing as *Trovatore*!

Alban Berg, quoted in Reich, *The Life and Work of Alban Berg* (1963)

9 Opera today is a culinary opera.

Bertolt Brecht, Notes to *The Rise and Fall of the City of Mahagonny* (1929)

10 [Of opera] A concert in fancy dress.

Paul Claudel, 'Modern Drama and Music', in *Yale Review*, 1930

11 [Of *Tristan and Isolde*] The actor who takes the lover's part can only do two things with the prima donna: either hold her at arm's length in order to view his good fortune the better — all the while vigorously shaking his head — or passionately clasp her in his arms.

Paul Claudel, 'Modern Drama and Music', in *Yale Review*, 1930

12 People are wrong when they say that the opera isn't what it used to be. It is what it used to be. That's what wrong with it.

Noel Coward, *Design for Living* (1933)

13 I sometimes wonder which would be nicer — an opera without an interval, or an interval without an opera.

Ernest Newman, *Berlioz, Romantic and Classic* (1972, ed. Heyworth)

14 The opera and operetta have not finished dying, and the sound film has not finished being born.

Carlos Chavez, *Towards a New Music* (1937)

15 The conventional prima donna's gestures: (a) both hands outstretched as though pushing open a door with a heavily laden tea-tray; (b) one hand suddenly raised straight on high, like Frank Chester giving Bradman out leg-before-wicket; and (c) a kick of the train of her dress outwards — to suggest imperiousness, presumably.

Neville Cardus, in *The Manchester Guardian*, 1938

16 Music in the theatre is a powerful, an almost immorally potent weapon.

Marc Blitzstein, quoted in Ewen, *American Composers* (1982)

17 [Of Grand Opera] I have often wondered whether its creator would not have paused after the first experimental effort if he could have foreseen the incredible amount of trouble he was bringing into the world.

Sir Thomas Beecham, *A Mingled Chime* (1944)

18 I admit freely that it is good to be roused now and then by the cheering spectacle of a gentleman vigorously chasing a lady round the room in spite of the unoriginality of the motive, or a father towing behind him the mangled remains of his child in a sack: but such excitements are not the necessary Alpha and Omega of every stage work.

Sir Thomas Beecham, *A Mingled Chime* (1944)

19 [Modern opera] Eternally the same old sauce, just stirred round a bit differently.

Paul Hindemith, quoted in Skelton, *Paul Hindemith* (1975)

20 Only music can measure up to tragedy, as she is both its mother and its daughter.

Wieland Wagner, 'Thoughts on the Mythical Element in Wagner's *Tristan und Isolde*'

1 [Opera] *La forme fatale.*

Aaron Copland, quoted in Jacobson, *Reverberations* (1975)

2 I do not mind what language an opera is sung in so long as it is a language I don't understand.

Sir Edward Appleton, quoted in *The Observer*, 'Sayings of the Week', 1955

3 In order to ensure the success of an art-luxury such as Grand Opera, it was absolutely necessary to be able to rely upon a regular attendance by numskulls, nitwits and morons addicted to the mode, even if they did not care in the least for music.

Osbert Sitwell, quoted in Reid, *Thomas Beecham* (1961)

4 Theatre music must make its point and communicate its emotion at the same moment the action develops. It cannot wait to be understood until after the curtain comes down.

Gian Carlo Menotti, quoted in Ewen, *American Composers* (1982)

5 No good opera plot can be sensible, for people do not sing when they are feeling sensible.

W.H. Auden, quoted in *Time*, 1961

6 The most expensive solution would be to blow up the opera houses.

Pierre Boulez, quoted in Wechsberg, *The Opera* (1972)

7 I came to the conclusion that perhaps the theatre of the absurd did not have to be invented, for opera as such seemed absurd enough.

Ernst Křenek, *Horizons Circled* (1974)

8 In my productions the principals are of the least importance.

Franco Zeffirelli, quoted in Jacobson, *Reverberations* (1975)

9 Critics attacked Wagner for his excessive use of chromatic harmony ... failing to appreciate that (practical man of the theatre that he was) he knew the singers would be lost for much of the time, and that therefore it was only fair that the orchestra shouldn't know which key they were in either.

Antony Hopkins, *Downbeat Music Guide* (1977)

10 Opera is where a guy gets stabbed in the back, and instead of dying, he sings.

Richard Benchley, attr.

THE OPHICLEIDE

11 A chromatic bullock.

Hector Berlioz, quoted by George Bernard Shaw, Letter to Arthur Bliss, 1944

ORATORIO

12 [Of an oratorio of Porpora] To have words of piety made use of *only* to introduce good music, is *reversing* what it ought to be.

Mary Pendarves, Letter to Anne Grenville, 1734

13 Oratorio (that profanation of the purposes of the cheerful playhouse).

Charles Lamb, *Essays of Elia* (1820-3), 'A Chapter on Ears'

14 [Oratorios] Unstaged operettas on scriptural themes, written in a style in which solemnity and triviality are blended in the right proportion for boring an atheist out of his senses.

George Bernard Shaw, quoted in Graf, *Composer and Critic* (1947)

THE ORCHESTRA

See also CONDUCTING, CONDUCTORS.

15 Take a psalm, and bring hither the timbrel, the pleasant harp with the psaltery.
Blow up the trumpet in the new moon, in the time appointed, on our solemn feast day.

Psalms 81:2-3

16 That noise or sound which musicians make while they are tuning their instruments, is nothing pleasant to hear, but yet is a cause why the music is sweeter afterwards.

Francis Bacon, *The Advancement of Learning* (1605)

17 See to their desks Apollo's sons repair, —
Swift rides the rosin o'er the horse's hair!
In unison their various tones to tune,
Murmurs the hautboy, growls the hoarse
        bassoon;
In soft vibration sighs the whispering lute,
Tang goes the harpsichord, too-too the flute,
Brays the loud trumpet, squeaks the fiddle
        sharp,
Winds the French horn, and twangs the tingling
        harp;
Till, like great Jove, the leader, figuring in,
Attunes to order the chaotic din.

Horace and James Smith, *Rejected Addresses* (1812), 'The Theatre'

18 Gentlemen of the first fiddles, this isn't a bees' wedding; it's something elemental.

Unnamed English conductor, quoted by Arnold Bennett, *Things that have interested me* (1906)

19 You must sing every note you play, sing, even through your rests.

Arturo Toscanini, quoted in Gattey, *Peacocks on the Podium* (1982)

20 'The fiddlers are all thumbs,
Or the fiddle-string accursed,
The drums and the kettledrums

And the trumpets all are burst,
And the trombone,' cried he,
'The trumpet and trombone.'

W.B. Yeats, 'I am of Ireland' (1933)

1 A conductor should reconcile himself to the realisation that regardless of his approach or temperament the eventual result is the same — the orchestra will hate him.

Oscar Levant, *A Smattering of Ignorance* (1940)

2 I would in nineteen cases out of twenty abide by the verdict or accept the opinion of a great orchestra far more confidently than I would that of either the Press or the public.

Sir Thomas Beecham, *A Mingled Chime* (1944)

3 There are two golden rules for an orchestra: start together and finish together. The public doesn't give a damn what goes on in between.

Sir Thomas Beecham, quoted in Atkins and Newman, *Beecham Stories* (1978)

4 [When Rodzinski asked the New York Philharmonic if they had any suggestions for improving the performance of a Mahler symphony] Yep. Send for Bruno Walter.

Harry Glantz, quoted in Kennedy, *Barbirolli, Conductor Laureate* (1971)

5 [Of Bruno Walter] It took us five years to have him realise there was nothing he could teach us.

Unnamed player of the New York Philharmonic, quoted in Kennedy, *Barbirolli, Conductor Laureate* (1971)

6 Murder Incorporated. [Nickname of the New York Philharmonic]

Oral tradition

7 [When asked about the pension prospects at the Hallé] My dear, if you're worrying about retiring or dying you run along to the BBC. If you want to live and enjoy it, come to my orchestra.

Sir John Barbirolli, quoted in Kennedy, *Barbirolli, Conductor Laureate* (1971)

8 I look for ... a working atmosphere where men play beyond the call of duty.

Sir John Barbirolli, quoted in Kennedy, *Barbirolli, Conductor Laureate* (1971)

9 [When working with English orchestras] Personally I look on a group of rehearsals as a cumulative series, and only rarely do I ask for full concert pressure. I like to feel that each rehearsal is a step forward, with a further step still to be made from the last rehearsal to the concert itself. We are a sporting people and I cannot see why our artistic processes should not be managed in a way similar to the main rules of sports training.

Sir Adrian Boult, *My Own Trumpet* (1973)

10 *Bar:* Where to find orchestral musicians whenever they are not actually playing ... In America the term 'measure' is used instead, probably because during Prohibition conductors didn't wish to make the players break down at the mention of the word 'bar'.

Antony Hopkins, *Downbeat Music Guide* (1977)

11 [Of playing in an orchestra] It's like being one of the rather jagged bits of a jigsaw puzzle, except that you are looking at it the wrong way up.

Jack Brymer, *From Where I Sit* (1979)

12 [Of playing in an orchestra] I learned with surprise that what happens on a tennis court also happens in music — if a real expert slaps the ball at you, you usually slap it back with surprising accuracy.

Jack Brymer, *From Where I Sit* (1979)

13 [Of orchestral players] Only when you go wrong do you seem to be important.

Jack Brymer, *From Where I Sit* (1979)

ORCHESTRATION AND INSTRUMENTATION

See also TRANSCRIPTION.

14 [Told by Emperor Joseph II that *Die Entführung* had 'very many notes'] Exactly the necessary number, your majesty.

Wolfgang Amadeus Mozart, quoted in Sadie, *The New Grove Mozart* (1982)

15 Tone is light in another shape ... In music instruments perform the functions of the colours employed in painting.

Honoré de Balzac, *Gambara* (1839)

16 Instrumentation is, in music, the exact equivalent of colour in painting.

Hector Berlioz, *A travers chants* (1862)

17 In the orchestra you must have air.

Georges Bizet, quoted in Dean, *Bizet* (1975)

18 Let in air to your score.

Charles Villiers Stanford, advice to students, quoted in Bliss, *As I Remember* (1970)

19 If you want to learn how to orchestrate, don't study Wagner's scores, study the score of *Carmen*.

Richard Strauss, quoted in *The Gramophone*, 1971

20 I cannot stand Parry's orchestration: it's dead and is never more than an organ part arranged.

Edward Elgar, quoted in *The Elgar Society Newsletter*, 1978

21 Not many composers have ideas. Far more of them know how to use strange instruments which do not require ideas.

George Gershwin, 'The Composer in the Machine Age' (1930)

1 We have had enough of this orchestral dappling and these thick sonorities. One is tired of being saturated with timbres and wants no more of all this overfeeding.

Igor Stravinsky, quoted in Machlis, *Introduction to Contemporary Music* (1963)

2 *Craft:* What is good instrumentation?
Stravinsky: When you are unaware that it *is* instrumentation.

Igor Stravinsky and Robert Craft, *Conversations with Stravinsky* (1959)

ORFF

3 [Describing his own music] *Urgrund Musik.* Basic music.

Carl Orff, quoted in Liess, *Carl Orff* (1968)

4 In all my work, my final concern is not with musical but with spiritual exposition.

Carl Orff, quoted in Liess, *Carl Orff* (1968)

5 Melody and speech belong together. I reject the idea of a pure music.

Carl Orff, attr.

THE ORGAN

6 *Dryfat:* The organs of the body, as some term them.
Mrs Purge: Organs! fie, fie, they have a most abominable sound in mine ears; they edify not a whit, I detest 'em. I hope my body has no organs.

Thomas Middleton, *The Family of Love*, III.ii (1608)

7 [Ordinance of 1644] for the speedy demolishing of all organs, images and all matters of superstitious monuments in all Cathedrals, and Collegiate or Parish-churches and Chapels, throughout the Kingdom of England and the Dominion of Wales, the better to accomplish the blessed reformation so happily begun and to remove offences and things illegal in the worship of God.

Quoted in Sumner, *The Organ* (1973)

8 [Of the organ for St Paul's] A confounded box of whistles.

Sir Christopher Wren, quoted in Phillips, *The Singing Church* (1968)

9 But oh! what art can teach,
What human voice can reach
The sacred organ's praise?
Notes inspiring holy love,
Notes that wing their heav'nly ways
To mend the choirs above.

John Dryden, 'A Song for St Cecilia's Day' (1687)

10 When the full organ joins the tuneful choir,
Th'Immortal Pow'rs incline their ear.

Alexander Pope, 'Ode for Musick, on St Cecilia's Day' (c. 1708)

11 The instrument of instruments.

Johann Mathias Gesner, Commentary on Quintilian's *De Institutio Oratoria* (c. 1730)

12 There is nothing to it. You only have to hit the right notes at the right time and the instrument plays itself.

Johann Sebastian Bach, on playing the organ, quoted in Geiringer, *The Bach Family* (1954)

13 If it were to be asked what instrument is capable of affording the GREATEST EFFECTS? I should answer, the Organ ... It is, however, very remote from perfection, as it wants expression, and a more perfect intonation.

Charles Burney, *A General History of Music* (1776–89)

14 In my eyes and ears the organ will ever be the King of Instruments.

Wolfgang Amadeus Mozart, Letter, 1777

15 The use of organs in the public worship of God is contrary to the law of the land, and to the law and constitution of our Established Church.

Presbytery of Glasgow, Proceedings (1807)

16 I, too, played the organ frequently in my youth, but my nerves could not withstand the power of the gigantic instrument. I should place an organist who is master of his instrument at the very head of all virtuosi.

Ludwig van Beethoven, quoted in Hamburger (ed.), *Beethoven: Letters, Journals and Conversations* (1951)

17 Neglect no opportunity of practising on the organ. There is no other instrument which inflicts such prompt chastisement on offensive and defective composition or execution.

Robert Schumann, 'Advice to Young Musicians' (1848)

18 An organist an accomplished man! ... Well, I suppose it is possible, but it rather upsets one's notions, does it not?
(Lady Gosstre)

George Meredith, *Sandra Belloni* (1886)

19 To play the organ properly one should have a vision of Eternity.

Charles-Marie Widor, quoted in Sumner, *The Organ* (1973)

20 Nor will anyone guess the delicious touch when George Thalben Ball walked in and promptly pushed his organ round till he got it in the right place.

The Church Times, quoted in Hopkins, *Music all around me* (1967)

21 The cinema organ exploits with skill its red plush quality. The Germans prohibit what they know is a depressant and not a stimulant. It is a dope as insidious as opium.

Arthur Bliss, 'Music Policy' (1941)

1 It's organ organ organ all the time with him.
(Mrs Organ Morgan)

Dylan Thomas, *Under Milk Wood* (1954)

2 It is a fact that the Inland Revenue allow
organists more pairs of trousers per annum
than any other profession, on account of all the
sliding about they have to do.

Antony Hopkins, *Downbeat Music Guide* (1977)

ORIGINS OF MUSIC

3 [Jubal] He was the father of all such as handle
the harp and organ.

Genesis 4:21

4 The Greeks say that Pythagoras found [music's]
beginnings in the sound of hammers and the
striking of stretched strings.

Isidore of Seville, *Etymologiarum*, III

5 What passion cannot music raise and quell!
    When Jubal struck the corded shell,
His list'ning brethren stood around
And wond'ring, on their faces fell
To worship that celestial sound.

John Dryden, 'A Song for St Cecilia's Day' (1687)

6 Music! soft charm of heav'n and earth,
Whence didst thou borrow thy auspicious
        birth?
Or art thou of eternal date,
Sire to thyself, thyself as old as fate?

Edmund Smith, 'Ode in Praise of Music'

7 When Music, Heav'nly Maid, was young,
While yet in early Greece she sung,
The Passions oft, to hear her shell,
Throng'd around her magic cell.

William Collins, 'The Passions, an Ode for Music'

8 [I] know no more of Stave or Crotchet,
Than did the primitive Peruvians,
Or those old ante-queer-Diluvians
That lived in the unwash'd world with Tubal,
Before that dirty Blacksmith Jubal,
By stroke on anvil, or by summ'at,
Found out, to his great surprise, the gamut.

Charles Lamb, 'To William Ayrton'

9 Human song is generally admitted to be the
basis or origin of instrumental music. As
neither the enjoyment nor the capacity of
producing musical notes are faculties of the
least use to man in reference to his daily habits
of life, they must be ranked among the most
mysterious with which he is endowed.

Charles Darwin, *The Descent of Man* (1871)

ORNAMENTATION

10 A, Godys dere dominus, what was that sang?
It was wonder curiose, with small notes emang.

Towneley First Shepherd's Play (early 15th century)

11 That deluge of unbounded *Extravaganzi*, which
the unskillful call invention, and which are
merely calculated to shew an execution,
without either propriety or grace.

Charles Avison, *An Essay on Musical Expression* (1752)

12 No one disputes the need for embellishments
... They improve mediocre compositions.
Without them the best melody is empty and
ineffective, the clearest content clouded.

Carl Philipp Emanuel Bach, *Essay on the True Art of
Playing Keyboard Instruments* (1753-62)

ORPHEUS

13 Bifor the king he sat adoun
And tok his harpe so miri of soun,
And trempreth his harp as he wele can,
And blisseful notes he ther gan.

Anon., *Orfeo and Heurodis* (14th century)

14 For Orpheus' lute was strung with poets'
        sinews,
Whose golden touch could soften steel and
        stones,
Make tigers tame and huge leviathans
Forsake unbounded deeps to dance on sands.
(Proteus)

William Shakespeare, *The Two Gentlemen of Verona*,
III.ii

15 Orpheus with his lute made trees
And the mountain tops that freeze
        Bow themselves when he did sing.
To his music plants and flowers
Ever sprung, as sun and showers
        There had made a lasting spring.

Every thing that heard him play,
Even the billows of the sea,
        Hung their heads and then lay by.
In such music is such art,
Killing care and grief of heart
        Fall asleep, or hearing, die.

William Shakespeare, *Henry VIII*, III.i

16 Or bid the soul of Orpheus sing
Such notes as, warbled to the string,
Drew iron tears down Pluto's cheek.

John Milton, 'Il Penseroso' (1632)

17 When Orpheus strikes the trembling lyre,
The streams stand still, the stones admire;
        The list'ning savages advance,
The wolf and lamb around him trip,
The bears in awkward measures leap,
        And tigers mingle in the dance:
The moving woods attended as he play'd,
And Rhodope was left without a shade.

Joseph Addison, 'A Song for St Cecilia's Day'

18 But when through all th'infernal bounds
Which flaming Phlegeton surrounds,
Love, strong as death, the poet led
To the pale nations of the dead,

What sounds were heard,
What scenes appeared,
   O'er all the dreary coasts!
      Dreadful gleams,
      Dismal screams,
      Fires that glow,
      Shrieks of woe,
      Sullen moans,
      Hollow groans,
   And cries of tortur'd ghosts
But hark! he strikes the golden lyre;
And see! the tortur'd ghosts respire.

Alexander Pope, 'Ode for Musick, on St Cecilia's Day'
(c. 1708)

1 Wi sang aa birds and beasts could I owrecome,
   Aa men and wemen o' the mapamound subdue,
      The flours o' the fields,
   Rocks and trees, boued doun to hear my leid,
   Gurlie waters rase upon the land to mak
      A throwgang for my feet.

Sydney Goodsir Smith, 'Elegy XII: Orpheus'
(mapamound = map of the world; boued = bowed;
leid = song; gurlie = angry; throwgang =
thoroughfare)

2 Ye ken the tale, hou, wi my lute
      I doungaed amang the Shades
   (Gray mauchie Hades, lichtless airt)
   And Pluto and the damned stude round
      And grat, hearan my sang;
   I lou, haean wan her manumissioun
   Frae the Profund magnifico,
   I, cryan her name, socht and fand my luve
      Amang thae wearie shadaws,
      Yet tint her in the end.

Sydney Goodsir Smith, 'Elegy XII: Orpheus'
(doungaed = went down; mauchie = dark; airt =
place; grat = wept; tint = lost)

THE OVERTURE

3 The overture ought to apprise the spectators of
the nature of the action that is to be represented
and to form, so to speak, its argument.

Christoph Willibald von Gluck, Dedication to *Alceste*
(1769)

4 [On composing overtures] Wait until the
evening before opening night. Nothing primes
inspiration more than necessity, whether it be
the presence of a copyist waiting for your work
or the prodding of an impresario tearing his
hair. In my time, all the impresarios in Italy
were bald at thirty.

Gioacchino Rossini, undated letter, quoted in
Morgenstern (ed.), *Composers on Music* (1958)

5 I am no friend of overtures. On first hearing,
when they are entirely unfamiliar, the audience
cannot even understand them.

Bedřich Smetana, quoted in Morgenstern (ed.),
Composers on Music (1958)

PAGANINI

6 No one ever asks if you have heard Paganini,
but if you have seen him.

Niccolò Paganini, Letter to Germi, 1832

7 [On seeing the first movement of Berlioz's
Harold in Italy] That's no good. There's not
enough for me to do here. I should be playing
all the time.

Niccolò Paganini, quoted in Berlioz, *Memoirs* (1865)

8 The demonic is that which cannot be explained
in a cerebral and a rational manner . . .
Napoleon possessed the quality to the highest
degree . . . Paganini is imbued with it to a
remarkable degree and it is through this that he
produces such a great effect.

Johann Wilhelm von Goethe, *Conversations with
Eckermann* (1827)

9 Everybody is talking of Paganini and his violin.
The man seems to be a miracle. The
newspapers say that long streamy flakes of
music fall from his string, interspersed with
luminous points of sound which ascend the air
and appear like stars. This eloquence is quite
beyond me.

Thomas Babington Macaulay, Letter, 1831

10 Paganini, the first time I saw and heard him,
and the first moment he struck a note, seemed
literally to strike it; to give it a blow.

Leigh Hunt, *Autobiography* (1850)

11 From this did Paganini comb the fierce
Electric sparks, or to tenuity
Pull forth the inmost wailing of the wire —
No cat-gut could swoon out so much of soul!

Robert Browning, *Red Cotton Night-Cap Country* (1873)

PALESTRINA

12 If men take such pains to compose beautiful
music for profane songs, one should devote as
much thought to sacred song, nay, even more
than to mere worldly matters.

Giovanni Pierluigi da Palestrina, Preface to *First Book
of Motets* (1563)

13 Worldly cares of any kind . . . are adverse to the
Muses, and particularly those which arise from
a lack of private means.

Giovanni Pierluigi da Palestrina, Dedication to
Lamentations (1588)

14 [Of Palestrina's madrigals] The most frivolous
and gallant words are set to exactly the same
music as those of the Bible . . . the truth is that
he could not write any other kind of music.

Hector Berlioz, *Memoirs* (1865)

1   This severe ascetic music, calm and horizontal as the line of the ocean, monotonous by virtue of its serenity, anti-sensuous, and yet so intense in its contemplativeness that it verges sometimes on ecstasy.

    Charles Gounod, quoted in Harding, *Gounod* (1973)

2   He is the real king of sacred music, and the Eternal Father of Italian music.

    Giuseppe Verdi, Letter to Giuseppe Gallignani, 1891

3   At the time of its composition, this music represented the last word in luxurious art; it only appears to us today to be a simple art because of all that has happened to music in the meantime.

    Gabriel Fauré, in *Le Monde musicale*, 1904, following Pope Pius X's instructions that Palestrina should be regarded as the model of simplicity in the composition of liturgical music

PATRONAGE

4   Music must be supported by the king and the princes, for the maintenance of the arts is their duty no less than the maintenance of the laws.

    Martin Luther, *Table Talk* (pub. 1566)

5   Is not a Patron, my Lord, one who looks with unconcern on a man struggling for life in the water, and, when he has reached the ground, encumbers him with help?

    Samuel Johnson, Letter to Lord Chesterfield, 1755

6   The master of music, Mr Haydn, is reminded to apply himself more assiduously to composition than he has done so far, especially with respect to pieces for the gamba [the Prince's favourite instrument], of which we have seen very little up to now; and, to show his zeal, he will hand in the first piece of every composition in a clean, tidy copy.

    Prince Esterházy, quoted in Gal (ed.), *The Musician's World* (1965)

7   Having been obliged to compose most of my works for particular individuals . . . I have been placed under more restraint in these works than in the few pieces I have written for my own pleasure. Indeed, sometimes I have been compelled to follow very ludicrous instructions; still, it is possible that these far from agreeable suggestions may have inspired my creative imagination with a variety of ideas which probably would never otherwise have occurred to me.

    Carl Philipp Emanuel Bach, *Autobiography* (1773)

8   If I could impress Mozart's inimitable works as deeply, and with that musical understanding and keen feeling with which I myself grasp and feel them, upon the soul of every music-lover, especially those in high places, the nations would compete for the possession of such a jewel within their borders.

    Joseph Haydn, Letter to Roth, 1787

9   It is a sad thing always to be a slave, but Providence will have it so, poor wretch that I am!

    Joseph Haydn, Letter to Marianne von Genzinger, 1790

10 Not one of the many millionaires in Paris thinks of doing anything for serious music.

    Hector Berlioz, in 1854, quoted in Orledge, *Gabriel Fauré* (1979)

11 The severest test that an orchestral conductor must face in this town [New York] . . . is neither the critics nor the musicians but the society ladies who pay the bills.

    Anon. journalist, *c.* 1936, quoted in Kennedy, *Barbirolli, Conductor Laureate* (1971)

12 Modern history, alas, has not yet furnished the refreshing phenomenon of a multi-millionaire who has taken a really serious interest in music, probably for the reason that his concrete soul is shocked by the intangible and unsatisfactory nature of the art itself.

    Sir Thomas Beecham, *A Mingled Chime* (1944)

13 *Bernard Gavoty:* How does one subsist as a composer?
    Honegger: Society women, industrialists, bankers, agree that it is a prosaic problem, unworthy of creative artists: a musician lives by talent, nay, by genius. Having set this up as an axiom, they prefer not to look more deeply into the question.

    Arthur Honegger, *I am a Composer* (1951)

PERFORMANCE

See also INTERPRETATION, VIRTUOSITY.

14 Sing unto him a new song; play skilfully with a loud noise.

    Psalms 33:3 (King James version); the Book of Common Prayer has: 'Sing unto the Lord a new song: sing praises lustily unto him with a good courage.'

15 Instruments sound sweetest when they be touched softest.

    John Lyly, *Euphues* (1580)

16 One should have an easy manner at the harpsichord and avoid either staring fixedly at any object, or looking too vague; in short, one should look at the audience, if there is any, as if one were occupied with nothing else.

    François Couperin, *L'Art de toucher le clavecin* (1716)

17 It is much easier to play a thing quickly than to play it slowly.

    Wolfgang Amadeus Mozart, Letter, 1778

1 [The aim of sight-reading] To play the piece . . . so as to make believe that it had been composed by the one who plays it.

Wolfgang Amadeus Mozart, Letter, 1778

2 Performance is a crucifixion.

Charles Gounod, quoted in Harding, *Gounod* (1973)

3 [Beethoven] was a declared opponent of miniature painting in all musical performance, and accordingly demanded strength of expression throughout.

Anton Schindler, *Life of Beethoven* (1840)

4 Musical performance is born in those same sublime regions from which music itself has descended. Whenever the music is in danger of becoming earthbound, the performance must elevate it and help it to regain its original ethereal quality . . . It is the duty of the performer to liberate it from the deadness of the printed page and bring it to life again.

Ferruccio Busoni, *Entwurf einer neuen Aesthetik der Tonkunst* (1907)

5 A musical work, which is still only a piece of writing, is a cheque drawn on the fund of talent of an eventual performer.

Paul Valéry, quoted in Bernac, *Francis Poulenc* (1977)

6 To me the greatest objective is when the composer disappears, the performer disappears, and there remains only the work.

Nadia Boulanger, quoted in Kendall, *The Tender Tyrant: Nadia Boulanger* (1976)

7 As far as the execution is concerned . . . one might say that the most frequent and most serious mistake is to follow the music instead of preceding it.

Nadia Boulanger, quoted in Kendall, *The Tender Tyrant: Nadia Boulanger* (1976)

8 Great music is better than it can be performed.

Artur Schnabel, quoted in Stravinsky, *Themes and Conclusions* (1972)

9 [Asked the secret of piano-playing] I always make sure that the lid over the keyboard is open before I start to play.

Artur Schnabel, attr.

10 A composer is usually right — when his music seems to be written badly for an instrument we can safely ascribe the fault to the instrumentalist.

Neville Cardus, in *The Manchester Guardian*, 1939

11 When you are playing, do not be concerned about who is listening to you. Always play as though a master were listening to you.

Zoltán Kodály, Address to the Budapest Academy of Music, 1953

12 A sin against the spirit of a work always begins with a sin against the letter.

Igor Stravinsky, quoted in Bernac, *Francis Poulenc* (1977)

13 You can't write music right unless you know how the man that'll play it plays poker.

Duke Ellington, quoted in Jewell, *Duke* (1977)

14 In music, abandonment is fine, but indiscipline is death.

George Shearing, quoted in Palmer, *All You Need Is Love* (1976)

15 It's all right letting yourself go, as long as you can let yourself back.

Mick Jagger, quoted in Green, *The Book of Rock Quotes* (1982)

THE PERFORMER

See also CONDUCTORS, STARS

16 These three take crooked ways: carts, boats, and musicians.

Hindu proverb, quoted in Mencken, *Dictionary of Quotations* (1942)

17 If a man lacks the virtues proper to humanity, what has he to do with music?

Confucius, *Analects*

18 We shall never become musicians unless we understand the ideals of temperance, fortitude, liberality and magnificence.

Plato, *Republic*

19 *Musicorum et cantorum magna est differentia.*
Illi sciunt ipsi dicunt quae componit musica.
Et qui dicit quod non sapit reputatur bestia.
There is a big difference between musicians and singers. The latter know, the former talk about, what music is. And he who doesn't know what he talks about is considered an animal.

Guido d'Arezzo, attr., quoted in Tinctoris, *Dictionary of Musical Terms* (c. 1475)

20 *Hotspur:* Now I understand the Devil
        understands Welsh,
And 'tis no marvel he is so humorous,
By'r Lady, he is a good musician.
Lady Percy: Then should you be nothing but
        musical,
For you are altogether governed by humours.

William Shakespeare, *Henry IV, Part One*, III.i

21 'Tis the common disease of all your musicians, that they know no mean, to be entreated either to begin or end.
(Julia)

Ben Jonson, *The Poetaster*, II.i

22 Thus sang the uncouth swain to th' oaks and rills,
While the still morn went out with sandals gray;

He touch'd the tender stops of various quills,
With eager thought warbling his Doric lay.

John Milton, *Lycidas* (1637)

1 When a musician hath forgot his note,
He makes as though a crumb stuck in his
throat.

John Clarke, *Paroemiologia* (1639)

2 The tenor's voice is spoilt by affectation
And for the bass, the beast can only bellow;
In fact, he had no singing education,
An ignorant, noteless, timeless, tuneless fellow.

Lord Byron, *Don Juan* (1818-22)

3 I loathe Divas, they are the curse of true music
and musicians.

Hector Berlioz, Letter, 1839

4 It is now possible for composers to make music
directly, without the assistance of intermediary
performers.

John Cage, *Silence* (1961), 'The Future of Music: Credo'
(1937)

5 Even if performers of any kind . . . were actually
demi-gods that many of them want us to think
they are and some of them believe themselves
to be, in reality they are, in respect to the
current that flows from the composer's brain to
the listener's mind, nothing but an intermediate
station, a roadside stop, a transformer house,
and their duty is to pass along what they
received from the generating mind . . . The ideal
performer will never try to express his own
feelings.

Paul Hindemith, *A Composer's World* (1952)

6 In how many famous artists' playing lurks
invisible disease!

Zoltán Kodály, Foreword to the Hungarian edition of
J.M. Corredor, *My Talks with Pablo Casals* (1960)

7 I am a man. I love very much the human being.
Playing music is the love approach.

Carlo Maria Giulini, quoted in Jacobson,
Reverberations (1975)

8 Music is a wonderful thing, a fine profession.
Write it, arrange it, conduct it, record
performances of it, be a contractor or 'fixer', an
impresario or a publisher; but for God's sake, if
you ever want to get anywhere, don't *play* it!

Philip Green, quoted in Brymer, *From Where I Sit*
(1979)

9 [Of musicians] Our business is emotion and
sensitivity — to be the sensors of the human
race.

Janet Baker, interview in *The Observer*, 1982

THE PIANO
See also KEYBOARD INSTRUMENTS.

10 A harp in a box.

Leigh Hunt, *The Seer* (1840)

11 This predominance of piano playing, not to
speak of the triumphal processions of the piano
virtuosi, are characteristic of our time and bear
witness to the victory of mechanism upon
spirit.

Heinrich Heine, *Lutetia* (1843)

12 A piano-forte is a fine resource,
All Balzac's novels occupy one shelf,
The new edition fifty volumes long.

Robert Browning, 'Bishop Blougram's Apology'

13 'Tis wonderful how soon a piano gets into a
log-hut on the frontier.

Ralph Waldo Emerson, 'Civilization' (1870)

14 Her ivory hands on the ivory keys
Strayed in a fitful fantasy,
Like the silver gleam when the poplar trees
Rustle their pale leaves listlessly.

Oscar Wilde, 'In the Gold Room: A Harmony'

15 The pianoforte is the most important of all
musical instruments: its invention was to music
what the invention of printing was to poetry.

George Bernard Shaw, in *The Fortnightly Review*, 1894

16 The pedal has a bad name. The senseless
liberties people have taken with it are entirely
to blame. Let them try taking significant
liberties with it.

Ferruccio Busoni, quoted in Stuckenschmidt, *Ferruccio
Busoni* (1967)

17 Bach is the foundation of piano playing, Liszt
the summit. The two make Beethoven possible.

Ferruccio Busoni, Letter to Woltersdorf, 1898

18 Take it for granted from the beginning that
everthing is possible on the piano, even when it
seems impossible to you, or really is so.

Ferruccio Busoni, Letter to Woltersdorf, 1898

19 Piano, n. A parlor utensil for subduing the
impenitent visitor. It is operated by depressing
the keys of the machine and the spirits of the
audience.

Ambrose Bierce, *The Devil's Dictionary* (1911)

20 So now it is vain for the singer to burst into
clamour
With the great black piano appassionato.

D.H. Lawrence, 'Piano'

21 [Of Chopin] He had an instinct amounting to
genius for inventing melodies that would be
actually ineffective if sung or played on an
instrument capable of sustaining tone but
which, picked out in percussive points of sound
each beginning to die as soon as born, are
enchanting and give an illusion of singing that
is often lovelier than singing itself.

Gerald Abraham, *A Hundred Years of Music* (1938)

1   I wish the Government would put a tax on
    pianos for the incompetent.
    Edith Sitwell, *Selected Letters 1916-1964* (1970)

2   The piano is the social instrument par
    excellence. It is drawing-room furniture, a sign
    of bourgeois prosperity, the most massive of
    the devices by which the young are tortured in
    the name of education and the grown-up in the
    name of entertainment.
    Jacques Barzun, Preface to Loesser, *Men, Women and
    Pianos* (1954)

POLITICS

See also CLASS, RACISM.

3   By the rivers of Babylon, there we sat down,
    yea, we wept, when we remembered Zion.
    We hanged our harps upon the willows in the
    midst thereof.
    For there they that carried us away captive
    required of us a song; and they that wasted us
    required of us mirth, saying, Sing us one of the
    songs of Zion.
    How shall we sing the Lord's song in a strange
    land?
    Psalms 137:1-4

4   If you would know if a people are well
    governed, and if its laws are good or bad,
    examine the music it practises.
    Confucius, *Analects*

5   Musical innovation is full of danger to the state,
    for when modes of music change, the laws of
    the state always change with them.
    Plato, *The Republic*

6   We may compare the best form of government
    to the most harmonious piece of music; the
    oligarchic and despotic to the more violent
    tunes; and the democratic to the soft and gentle
    airs.
    Aristotle, *Politics*

7   It is of great importance for the morals of the
    citizens of a town that the music current in a
    country should be retained under certain laws
    ... for where music is disordered, there morals
    are also depraved, and where it is well ordered,
    there men are well tutored.
    Charles IX of France, Letters Patent confirming the
    opening of the Académie de Poésie et de Musique,
    1570

8   Take but degree away, untune that string,
    And hark what discord follows; each thing
                                            melts
    In mere oppugnancy.
    (Ulysses)
    William Shakespeare, *Troilus and Cressida*, I.iii

9   *Donde hay Musica no puede haber cosa mala.*
    Where's there's music there can't be mischief.
    Miguel Cervantes, *Don Quixote*, II (1615)

10 Who shall silence all the airs and madrigals that
    whisper softness in chambers?
    John Milton, *Areopagitica* (1644)

11 Music is almost as dangerous as gunpowder;
    and it maybe requires looking after no less than
    the press, or the mint. 'Tis possible a public
    regulation might not be amiss.
    Jeremy Collier, *A Short View of the Immorality and
    Profaneness of the English Stage* (1698)

12 If a man were permitted to make all the ballads,
    he need not care who should make the laws of a
    nation.
    Andrew Fletcher of Saltoun, *Political Works*, 'Letter to
    the Marquis of Montrose, and Others' (1703)

13 'Music hath charms to soothe the savage beast,'
    And therefore proper at a sheriff's feast.
    James Bramston, *Man of Taste* (1729)

14 ['Lilliburlero'] whistled King James [II] out of
    three kingdoms.
    Thomas Warton, quoted in Westrup, *Purcell* (1937)

15 The still sad music of humanity.
    William Wordsworth, 'Lines composed a few miles
    above Tintern Abbey'

16 The Ritter Gluck confessed that the groundtone
    of the noblest passage, in one of his noblest
    operas, was the voice of the populace he had
    heard in Vienna, crying to the Kaiser: Bread!
    Bread!
    Thomas Carlyle, *The French Revolution* (1837)

17 [Of musicians] The crickets in the grass chirp
    their national song at all hours, quite heedless
    who conquers, Federals or rebels, in the war,
    and so do these.
    Ralph Waldo Emerson, Journal, 1862

18 Let me write the songs of a nashun and I don't
    care a cuss who goes to the legislater.
    Artemus Ward, *In Washington* (1863)

19 We are the music-makers,
        And we are the dreamers of dreams,
    Wandering by lone sea-breakers,
        And sitting by desolate streams;
    World-losers and world-forsakers,
        On whom the pale moon gleams:
    Yet we are the movers and shakers
        Of the world for ever, it seems.
    Arthur O'Shaugnessy, 'Ode'

20 The most profound truths, the most
    blasphemous things, the most terrible ideas,
    may be incorporated within the walls of a
    symphony, and the police be none the wiser. It
    is its freedom from the meddlesome hand of the
    censor that makes of music a playground for
    great brave souls.
    James Huneker, *Mezzotints in Modern Music* (1898)

1 For me Wagner's music is as rascally as the Dreyfus affair.

Mily Balakirev, quoted in Garden, *Balakirev* (1967)

2 The masses need to be shaken. In this way they can be rendered perceptive of finer vibrations than usual. How deeply mistaken it is to view war merely as discord between nations.

Alexander Skryabin, in 1914, quoted in Macdonald, *Skryabin* (1978)

3 I'd like to see a Tank come down the stalls, Lurching to rag-time tunes, or 'Home, sweet Home,' — And there'd be no more jokes in Music-halls To mock the riddled corpses round Bapaume.

Siegfried Sassoon, 'Blighters'

4 Music, as a final incitement to the spirit of men, is invaluable — as a force which draws onward and upward the spirit she finds prepared for her ministrations. But literature must precede her ... Music quickens time, she quickens us to the finest enjoyment of time; she quickens — and in so far she has moral value. Art has moral value, in so far as it quickens. But what if it does the opposite? What if it dulls us, sends us to sleep, works against action and progress? Music can do that too; she is an old hand at using opiates. But the opiate, my dear sirs, is a gift of the devil; it makes for lethargy, inertia, slavish inaction, stagnation. There is something suspicious about music, gentlemen. I insist that she is, by her nature, equivocal. I shall not be going too far in saying at once that she is politically suspect. (Settembrini)

Thomas Mann, *The Magic Mountain* (1924)

5 One thing is certain: you cannot persuade anyone with art. It is like beating an eiderdown with your fist, it merely bulges somewhere else.

Leoš Janáček, Letter to Kamila Stössel, 1925

6 Slavedrivers know well enough that when the slave is singing a hymn to liberty he is consoling himself for his slavery and not thinking about breaking his chain.

Miguel de Unamuno, *Essays and Soliloquies* (trans. 1925)

7 We must cultivate a sense of musical citizenship: why should not the musician be the servant of the State and build national monuments like the painter, the writer or the architect?

Ralph Vaughan Williams, quoted in Machlis, *Introduction to Contemporary Music* (1963)

8 Jazz was borrowed from Central Africa by a gang of wealthy international Bolshevists from America, their aim being to strike at Christian civilisation throughout the world.

Monseigneur Conefrey, in *The New York Times*, 1934

9 In the rejection of Hindemith by the Kulturgemeinde the value or lack of value of his creative work is beside the point. National Socialism puts the personality of a creative artist before his work. The fact that before the new regime Hindemith showed signs of an un-German attitude disqualifies him from taking part in the movement's cultural reclamation work.

Bernhard Rust, spokesman of the Nazi Kulturgemeinde, in 1934, quoted in Skelton, *Paul Hindemith* (1975)

10 It is lucky that Handel and Bach were born in 1685 and not two hundred years later. Else the citizenship of the one might have been questioned, just as the music of the other might have been found 'bolshevistic'. Prepared to prove which is the undersigned,
Alban Berg

Alban Berg, in *Eine Wiener Musikzeitschrift*, 1935

11 Supposing times were normal — normal as they were before 1914 — then the music of our time would be in a different situation.

Arnold Schoenberg, in 1936, quoted in Rosen, *Schoenberg* (1976)

12 The composer must learn to master all musical resources for the complete musical expression of the ideas and passions motivating Soviet heroes.

Josef Stalin, quoted in Cooper, *Russian Opera* (1951)

13 If Hitler likes Wagner's music, it is all the more reason why every non-Nazi should shun and loathe it.

Carl Engel, in *Musical Quarterly* (New York), 1941

14 Party allegiance cannot be expressed in music.

Zoltán Kodály, Lecture, 1946

15 No matter where music is heard today, it sketches in the clearest possible lines the contradictions and flaws which cut through present-day society. At the same time, music is separated from this same society by the deepest of all flaws produced by this society itself.

T.W. Adorno, 'On the Social Situation of Music' (pub. 1978)

16 It is not for music to stare in helpless horror at society. It fulfils its social function more precisely when it presents social problems through its own material and according to its own formal laws — problems which music contains within itself in the innermost cells of its technique.

T.W. Adorno, 'On the Social Situation of Music' (pub. 1978)

17 It's all right for some cat on a soapbox to go making speeches and such, but in the theatre you've got to find some way of saying it without saying it, you dig?

Duke Ellington, quoted in Jewell, *Duke* (1977)

1 The building of Socialism proceeds more lightly
and more rhythmically to the accompaniment
of jazz.
   Polish Government announcement, 1955, quoted in
   Stearns, *The Story of Jazz* (1956)

2 We shall not permit one of the most significant
works of our great German poet Goethe to be
formalistically violated.
   Walter Ulbricht, referring to Hanns Eisler's libretto for
   a Faust opera, quoted in Willett, *Brecht in Context*
   (1984)

3 [Of Elvis Presley] A weapon of the American
psychological war aimed at infecting a part of
the population with a new philosophical
outlook of inhumanity . . . to destroy anything
that is beautiful, in order to prepare for war.
   East German newspaper, *c.* 1958, quoted in Palmer,
   All You Need Is Love (1976)

4 I don't think there was ever a piece of music
that changed a man's decision on how to vote.
   Artur Schnabel, *My Life and Music* (1961)

5 Music in our time is granted little opportunity
for glorification and flooding people with
illumination. The flames of Hiroshima have
gone beyond all that.
   Hans Werner Henze, *Music and Politics* (1982) 'Music
   as a Means of Resistance' (1963)

6 These Beatles are completely anti-Christ. They
are preparing our teenagers for riot and
ultimate revolution against our Christian
Republic.
   Rev. David Noebel, Sermon to his congregation in
   Claremont, California, quoted in Palmer, *All You Need
   Is Love* (1976)

7 Erotic politicians, that's what we are. We're
interested in everything about revolt, disorder,
and *all* activity that appears to have no
meaning.
   Jim Morrison, quoted in Palmer, *All You Need Is Love*
   (1976)

8 Today I consider it more important that music
should take up and mirror the contradictions
that a musician encounters in his society. But
the problem of how such a dialectical musical
thinking can be socially mediated is a class
problem which cannot be resolved outside the
revolutionary process.
   Hans Werner Henze, *Music and Politics* (1982), 'Art and
   the Revolution' (1971)

9 All I ever had is songs of freedom . . .
Won't you help me to sing these songs of
         freedom
'Cause all I ever had redemption songs.
   Bob Marley, 'Redemption Song'

10 Don't just move to the music, listen to what I'm
saying.
   Bob Marley, quoted in Johnson and Pines, *Reggae*
   (1982)

11 Well, there are some stupid bastards who can't
understand how the commandant of a Nazi
concentration camp could go home after
torturing Jews all day and then weep tears of
joy at a Schubert symphony on the radio. They
say: here's a man dedicated to evil capable of
enjoying the good. But what the imbecilic sods
don't realise is that there are two kinds of good
— one is neutral, outside ethics, purely
aesthetic. You get it in music . . .
(Enderby)
   Anthony Burgess, *The Clockwork Testament* (1974)

12 The powers-that-be, regardless of their politics,
invariably prefer the thoroughly conformist
traditional music that suggests the image of an
unshakeable, perfect universe . . . because they
have to entertain the illusion that the order they
have established is perfect and immutable.
They distrust any progressive type of music and
prosecute its practitioners because such music
reflects a higher and more alert status of
consciousness and therefore might induce
doubt and dissent.
   Ernst Křenek, *Horizons Circled* (1974)

13 Revolutions have no chance of success unless
they are joined or inaugurated by the armed
forces, and the top brass do not usually belong
to the opera-going minority nor are they likely
to be swayed in their philosophy by hearing
atonal music.
   Ernst Křenek, *Horizons Circled* (1974)

14 A real musical culture should not be a museum
culture based mainly on music of past ages; nor
should it be, like most commercial music, a
drug. It should be the active embodiment in
sound of the life of a community — of the
everyday demands of people's work and play
and of their deepest spiritual needs.
   Wilfrid Mellers, quoted in Kendall, *The Tender Tyrant:
   Nadia Boulanger* (1976)

POLYPHONY
See COUNTERPOINT.

POPULAR MUSIC
See also THE BLUES, COUNTRY AND WESTERN,
JAZZ, THE MUSICAL, RAGTIME, REGGAE, ROCK
MUSIC.

15 I have a reasonable ear in music. Let's have the
tongs and the bones.
(Bottom)
   William Shakespeare, *A Midsummer Night's Dream*, IV.i

16 [Of Autolycus] He sings several tunes faster
than you'll tell money. He utters them as he
had eaten ballads, and all men's ears grow to
his tunes.
(Servant)
   William Shakespeare, *The Winter's Tale*, IV.iv

1 For even that vulgar and tavern music, which
makes one merry, another mad, strikes in me a
deep fit of devotion, and a profound
contemplation of the first Composer, there is
something in it of divinity more than the ear
discovers.

Sir Thomas Browne, *Religio Medici* (1643)

2 Let not the ballad-singer's shrilling strain
Amid the swarm thy list'ning ear detain:
Guard well thy pocket; for these sirens stand
To aid the labours of the diving hand;
Confed'rate in the cheat, they draw the throng,
And cambric handkerchiefs reward the song.

John Gay, *Trivia* (1727)

3 He who writes for the many does better work
than he who writes only for the few.

Georg Phillipp Telemann, quoted in Headington, *The
Bodley Head History of Western Music* (1974)

4 [Of Neapolitan street singing] I sent for the
whole band upstairs, but, like other street
music, it was best at a distance; in the room it
was coarse, out of tune, and out of harmony;
whereas, in the street, it seemed the contrary of
all this.

Charles Burney, *The Present State of Music in France and
Italy* (1773)

5 Music must be made popular, not by debasing
the art, but by elevating the people.

Henry Cleveland, *National Music* (1840)

6 I would rather hear Annie Laurie sung with
feeling than the greatest singer in the world
declaiming a scene from *Tristan und Isolde*.

W.S. Gilbert, quoted in Pearson, *Gilbert and Sullivan*
(1935)

7 And the tunes that mean so much to you
        alone —
Common tunes that make you choke and blow
        your nose,
Vulgar tunes that bring the laugh that brings
        the groan —
I can rip your very heartstrings out with those.

Rudyard Kipling, 'The Song of the Banjo'

8 The modern popular song reminds one of the
outer circumference of our terrible overgrown
towns ... It is for the people who live in those
unhealthy regions, people who have the most
false ideals, who are always scrambling for
subsistence, who think that the commonest
rowdyism is the highest expression of human
emotion; for them this popular music is made,
and it is made, with a commercial object, of
snippets of slang.

Hubert Parry, in 1899, quoted in Lee, *Music of the
People* (1970)

9 There's a barrel-organ carolling across a golden
        street
    In the city as the sun sinks low;

And the music's not immortal; but the world
        has made it sweet
And fulfilled it with the sunset glow.

Alfred Noyes, 'The Barrel-Organ'

10 Leave strumming at the doors of inns
    To vagabonds and sharpers.
Where men seek minstrels for their sins
    They shall not lack for harpers.

Laurence Housman, 'Farewell to Town'

11 What is the Ninth Symphony compared to a
pop tune played by a hurdy-gurdy and a
memory!

Karl Kraus, quoted in Zohn, *Karl Kraus* (1971)

12 If it is art it is not for all, and if it is for all it is
not art.

Arnold Schoenberg, attr.

13 It is a pleasure to live at a time when light
amusement is at last losing its brutally cretin
aspect, and such delicacies as your jingles prove
that songs can be both popular and intelligent.

Lorenz Hart, Letter to Ira Gershwin

14 The Tin Pantithesis of melody.

Cole Porter, 'It's De-Lovely'

15 The song of today is machine-made, machine-
played, machine-heard.

Isaac Goldberg, *Tin Pan Alley* (1930)

16 Extraordinary how potent cheap music is.

Noël Coward, *Private Lives*, I (1930)

17 I have never acknowledged the difference
between 'serious' music and 'light' music.
There is only good music and bad music.

Kurt Weill, quoted in Sanders, *The Days Grow Short*
(1980)

18 *Crush the Girlish Male Crooner*
This is obviously a case for the application of
'peine forte et dure'.

Arthur Bliss, 'Music Policy' (1941)

19 The people do not need music which they
cannot understand.

Andrei A. Zhdanov, Speech, 1947

20 The more vulgar it is, the better they like it.

Liberace, quoted in Palmer, *All You Need Is Love* (1976)

21 Trinidad is probably the only place in the
Western world where a teen-ager's position in
his gang is determined by his musical skills. As
a result, well over half the urban Trinidadian
young men can play the steel drums skilfully
enough not to be criticised by their peers.

Daniel Crowley, 'Song and Dance in St Lucia,' in
Ethnomusicology Newsletter, 1957

22 Life would be awful if we were trapped in
genius all the time. But pop music is the
hamburger of every day. It is everday-life music

— you can't brush your teeth to *Erwartung*. If you go for a quick lunch, you don't have pheasant and wine of 1935.

Pierre Boulez, in 1969, quoted in Jacobson, *Reverberations* (1975)

1 Sir Arthur Bliss, Master of the Queen's Music, once described the BBC's pop programme as 'aural hashish', but it's not *that* good.

Richard Neville, *Playpower* (1970)

2 The essential misapprehension about popular music is that it is anything other than a totally capitalistic enterprise.

Lester Bangs, quoted in Palmer, *All You Need Is Love* (1976)

3 What pop does is make me very rich.

Donovan, quoted in Palmer, *All You Need Is Love* (1976)

4 Pop music *is* the classical music of now.

Paul McCartney, quoted in Palmer, *All You Need Is Love* (1976)

5 The popular music industry has tried, repeatedly, to do with music what Ford attempts with cars. It works better with cars.

Tony Palmer, *All You Need Is Love* (1976)

6 Popular music is not even what most people like. Janis Joplin sang popular music and most people . . . did not like Janis Joplin. Van Cliburn's version of Tchaikovsky's First Piano Concerto . . . has outsold most pop music. But Tchaikovsky is classical music. So why is Janis Joplin's music not classical music? Because it is popular music. And so on.

Tony Palmer, *All You Need Is Love* (1976)

7 I've always said that pop music is disposable . . . If it wasn't disposable, it'd be a pain in the fuckin' arse.

Elton John, quoted in Green, *The Book of Rock Quotes* (1982)

PORTER

8 [On Rodgers and Hammerstein's 'Some Enchanted Evening'] Imagine it taking two men to write one song.

Cole Porter, quoted in Eells, *The Life that Late He Led* (1967)

9 The Adlai Stevenson of songwriters . . . He was an aristocrat in everything he did and everything he wrote. Everything had class . . .

Larry Adler, quoted in Eells, *The Life that Late He Led* (1967)

POSTERITY

10 *Carmina morte carent.* Song is untouched by death.

Ovid, *Amores*, I, 15

11 Often when I was wrestling with obstacles of every kind, when my physical and mental strength alike were running low and it was hard for me to persevere in the path on which I had set my feet, a secret feeling within me whispered: 'There are so few happy and contented people here below, sorrow and anxiety pursue them everywhere; perhaps your work may, some day, become a spring from which the careworn may draw a few moments' rest and refreshment.' And that was a powerful motive for pressing onward.

Joseph Haydn, Letter to a group of music-lovers in Bergen

12 [Of the Leipzig critics] As for the oxen from Leipzig, they may say what they will. They will make nobody immortal with their talking, and, likewise, they will not take immortality from that man whom Apollo has destined for immortality.

Ludwig van Beethoven, quoted in Graf, *Composer and Critic* (1947)

13 [Of the Rasumovsky Quartets] I said to him that he surely did not consider these works to be music? Beethoven replied: 'Oh, they are not for you but for a later age!'

Felice Radicati, quoted in Scott, *Beethoven* (1934)

14 Fair the fall of songs
　　When the singer sings them.
Still they are carolled and said —
　　On wings they are carried —
After the singer is dead
　　And the maker buried.

Robert Louis Stevenson, *Songs of Travel* (1896)

15 If there is in my music anything of lasting value it will live; if not, it will perish. That is my belief, for I am convinced that truth will prevail *ultimately*.

Edvard Grieg, Letter to Henry T. Finck, 1905

16 When I am no longer here you will hear it said of my works: 'After all, that was nothing much to write home about!' You must not let that hurt or depress you. It is the way of the world . . . There is always a moment of oblivion. But all that is of no importance. I did what I could . . . now . . . let God judge!

Gabriel Fauré, last words to his sons, 1924, quoted in Fauré-Fremiet, *Gabriel Fauré* (1957)

17 The good composer is slowly discovered; the bad composer is slowly found out.

Ernest Newman, attr.

18 So far we have respected the artist largely only after his death. We have left him to die and then by means of a splendid funeral we have sought to set right what we had done against him during his life.

Zoltán Kodály, Lecture, 1946

1 It takes approximately twenty years to make an artistic curiosity out of a modernistic monstrosity, and another twenty years to elevate it to a masterpiece.

Nicolas Slonimsky, *The Lexicon of Musical Invective* (1953)

2 I do not write for posterity ... I write music, now, in Aldeburgh ... for anyone who cares to play or listen to it.

Benjamin Britten, quoted in Headington, *Britten* (1981)

3 We're not interested in writing for posterity. We just want it to sound good right now!

Duke Ellington, quoted in Jewell, *Duke* (1977)

POULENC

4 My music is my portrait.

Francis Poulenc, quoted in Bernac, *Francis Poulenc* (1977)

5 Above all do not analyse my music — love it!

Francis Poulenc, quoted in Bernac, *Francis Poulenc* (1977)

PRACTICE

6 First, rehearse your song by rote,
To each word a warbling note.
Hand in hand, with fairy grace,
Will we sing and bless this place.
(Titania)

William Shakespeare, *A Midsummer Night's Dream*, V.i

7 One can correct facial grimaces by placing a mirror on the reading desk of the spinet or harpsichord.

François Couperin, *L'Art de toucher le clavecin* (1716)

8 I find piano practising a great effort, yet one dare not ignore it. It's like an animal whose heads are continually growing again, however many one cuts off.

Ferruccio Busoni, Letter to Gerda Busoni, 1907

9 If I don't practise for one day, I know it; if I don't practise for two days, the critics know it; if I don't practise for three days, the audience knows it.

Ignacy Jan Paderewski, quoted in Shapiro, *An Encyclopedia of Quotations about Music* (1978)

PRESLEY

10 I can't sing very well, but I'd like to try.

Elvis Presley, on first entering a recording studio, quoted in Palmer, *All You Need Is Love* (1976)

11 God gave me a voice. If I turned against God, I'd be finished.

Elvis Presley, quoted in Palmer, *All You Need Is Love* (1976)

12 I was very lucky. The people were looking for something different and I came along just in time.

Elvis Presley, quoted in Farren, *Elvis in His Own Words* (1977)

13 Is it a sausage? It is certainly smooth and damp-looking, but whoever heard of a 172 lb sausage 6 ft. tall?

Time magazine, 1956, reviewing Presley in the film *Love Me Tender*

14 We never sold no sex or sideburns. If we wanted to sell sex or sideburns, we'd have dressed differently.

Bill Haley, quoted in Palmer, *All You Need Is Love* (1976)

15 Nothing really affected me until Elvis.

John Lennon, quoted in Davies, *The Beatles* (1968)

PRODIGIES

16 [On hearing a young chorister urged to perform certain embellishments] Oh, let him alone, he will grace it more naturally than you or I can teach him.

Henry Purcell, quoted in Holst (ed.), *Henry Purcell* (1959)

17 What will a child learn sooner than a song?

Alexander Pope, *Imitations of Horace*, Epistle II.i

18 [Of his boyhood] I used to write like the devil in those days.

George Frideric Handel, quoted in Burney, *An Account of the Musical Performances ... in Commemoration of Handel* (1785)

19 Almighty God ... gave me such facility in music that in my sixth year I could already sing several masses in the choir without hesitation.

Joseph Haydn, quoted in Hughes, *Haydn* (1970)

20 You cannot imagine how it spoils one to have been a child prodigy.

Franz Liszt, attr.

21 One thing I can say, from my own experiences as an infant prodigy, is, that it was a great help having it impressed upon me from the beginning, that I could and should become a great man; however, no one ever appeared satisfied with my actual achievements.

Ferruccio Busoni, Letter to Henri Petri, 1890

22 When he [Bartók] was four years old, he could beat out with one finger on the piano the melodies of all the folk songs he knew; he knew forty in all ...

Paula Bartók (the composer's mother), quoted in Ujfalussy, *Béla Bartók* (1971)

23 When I was eight it was said of me: 'The boy will outdo his father ... I simply had it in me from the cradle.

Leoš Janáček, interview in *Literární svět*, 1928

1   [Of musical biographies] We are always invited
    to believe that the hero of the tale performed
    fabulous feats while hardly out of the cradle. In
    one instance we may read how the mighty atom
    of virtuosity committed to memory the entire
    well-tempered clavichord of Bach before
    mastering his alphabet. In another there is a
    beautiful account of an oratorio for double
    chorus and orchestra, all composed at the age
    of five and informed with the deepest religious
    feeling ... None of this god-like dispensation
    was my lot.
    Sir Thomas Beecham, *A Mingled Chime* (1944)

2   I sang before I could speak, and I sang more
    than I spoke.
    Zoltán Kodály, in *Család és Iskola*, 1950

3   You know, the critics never change; I'm still
    getting the same notices I used to get as a child.
    They tell me I play very well for my age.
    Mischa Elman, in his seventies, quoted in Hopkins,
    Music all around me (1967)

PROGRAMME MUSIC

See also EXPRESSION.

4   The painter turns a poem into a painting; the
    musician sets a picture to music.
    Robert Schumann, Aphorisms (c. 1833)

5   [Of his *Spring Symphony*] The music is not
    intended to describe or paint anything definite,
    but I believe the season did much to shape the
    particular form it took.
    Robert Schumann, Letter to Ludwig Spohr

6   I always say, 'First of all let me hear that you
    have made beautiful music; after that I will like
    your programme too.'
    Robert Schumann, in *Neue Zeitschrift*, 1843

7   [Programme music] This ... always seems to
    me rather like a joke, somewhat like the
    paintings in juvenile spelling-books, where the
    roofs are coloured bright red to make the
    children aware that they are indeed supposed
    to be roofs.
    Felix Mendelssohn, Letter

8   [Of Tchaikovsky's *Romeo and Juliet*] You have
    unfortunately omitted all reference to Juliet's
    nurse, that inspired Shakespearean creation,
    and also the picture of dawn, on which the love
    scene is built up.
    Vladimir Stassov, Letter to Tchaikovsky, 1873

9   If descriptive music is a mistake, let it be: the
    mistake usually lies in the description only, not
    in the music.
    Sidney Lanier, *The Physics of Music* (1875)

10 I despise all music that has to follow some
    literary text that one happens to have got hold
    of.
    Claude Debussy, Letter to Émile Baron, 1887. This was
    five years before he started the composition of *Prélude
    à l'après-midi d'un faune.*

11 The creative urge for a musical organism
    certainly springs from an experience of its
    author, that is, from a fact which after all
    should be positive enough to be expressible in
    words ... there need be no objections to a
    programme.
    Gustav Mahler, quoted in Headington, *The Bodley
    Head History of Western Music* (1974)

12 The music [the scherzo of Beethoven's
    Symphony No.5] started with a goblin walking
    quietly over the universe, from end to end.
    Others followed him. They were not aggressive
    creatures; it was that that made them so terrible
    to Helen. They merely observed in passing that
    there was no such thing as splendour or
    heroism in the world. After the interlude of the
    elephants dancing, they returned and made the
    observation for the second time. Helen could
    not contradict them ...
    E.M. Forster, *Howard's End* (1910)

13 I do not say that programme music should not
    be written ... But I do maintain that it is a
    lower form of art than absolute music.
    Edward Elgar, quoted in Cumberland, *Set Down in
    Malice* (1919)

14 There is no such thing as Abstract music; there
    is good music and bad music. If it is good, it
    means something; and then it is Programme
    Music.
    Richard Strauss, quoted in Shapiro, *An Encyclopedia of
    Quotations about Music* (1978)

15 Good music resembles something. It resembles
    the composer.
    Jean Cocteau, *Le Coq et l'arlequin* (1918)

16 The programme or title must in itself contain a
    germ of feeling or movement, but never a crude
    description of concrete events.
    Carl Nielsen, quoted in Simpson, *Carl Nielsen* (1952)

17 The less musical portrayal continues to be a
    portrayal of something, the more the essence of
    the means comes to agree with the essence of
    that which is portrayed.
    T.W. Adorno, 'Music and Technique' (pub. 1977)

18 Almost the only thing music can represent
    unambiguously is the cuckoo — and that it
    can't differentiate from a cuckoo-clock.
    Brigid Brophy, *A Literary Person's Guide to Opera* (1965)

19 Even if it [music] seems emotionally loaded to
    the brim, its movement can only be felt or
    understood as an image of the intensity of the

emotion that may have generated it, but never as a likeness of the object of that emotion.

Ernst Křenek, *Horizons Circled* (1974)

PROKOFIEV

1 Formalism is music that people don't understand at first hearing.

Sergey Prokofiev, quoted in Lebrecht, *Discord* (1982). Prokofiev, Shostakovich and others had been castigated by the Soviet press for 'formalism'.

2 Asked to give a piano recital] No, it would cost me half a sonata.

Sergey Prokofiev, quoted in Samuel, *Prokofiev* (trans. 1971)

3 It is the duty of the composer, like the poet, the sculptor or the painter, to serve his fellow men, to beautify human life and point the way to a radiant future. Such is the immutable code of art as I see it.

Sergey Prokofiev, *Autobiography* (1946)

4 The chief merit of my life (or, if you prefer it, its chief inconvenience) has always been the search for originality in my own musical language. I abhor imitation and I abhor the familiar.

Sergey Prokofiev, quoted in Samuel, *Prokofiev* (trans. 1971)

5 Of Prokofiev's Symphony No.5] It is obviously a work of major importance, but I was rather alarmed to find how easy and agreeable it seemed to me at first hearing.

Sir Adrian Boult, *My Own Trumpet* (1973)

PRO-MUSIC

See also ANTI-MUSIC.

6 Music produces a kind of pleasure which human nature cannot do without.

Confucius, *Book of Rites*

7 The life of man in every part has need of harmony and rhythm.

Plato, *Laws*

8 The man who has music in his soul will be most in love with the loveliest.

Plato, *The Republic*

9 Melody is the mirthful maistrace.

Anon., *Cockelbie's Sow* (15th century)

10 Eftsoons they heard a most melodious sound, Of all that mote delight a dainty ear.

Edmund Spenser, *The Faerie Queene*, II (1589)

11 The ingenious profession of music.

John Dowland, *The First Booke of Songes* (1597)

12 Whom God loveth not, they love not music.

Thomas Morley, *Madrigals to five voyces* (1598)

13 Music sits solitary among her sister Sciences, and ... often wants the fortune to be esteemed (for so she is worthy) even among the worthiest.

John Wilbye, Dedication to his second book of madrigals (1609)

14 Music ... is made particularly and principally to charm the spirit and the ear, and to enable us to pass our lives with a little sweetness amidst all the bitterness that we encounter there.

Marin Mersenne, *Harmonie universelle* (1636)

15 Then music, the mosaic of the air,
Did of all these a solemn noise prepare:
With which she gained the empire of the ear,
Including all between the earth and sphere.

Andrew Marvell, 'Music's Empire'

16 The best company for music I ever was in, in my life. I wish I could live and die by it ... I spent the night in ecstasy almost.

Samuel Pepys, Diary, 1665

17 Music is the thing of the world that I love most.

Samuel Pepys, Diary, 1666

18 Music is a science peculiarly productive of a pleasure that no state of life, public or private, secular or sacred; no difference of age or season; no temper of mind or condition of health exempt from present anguish; nor, lastly, distinction of quality, renders either improper, untimely, or unentertaining.

Samuel Pepys, Letter to the Master of University College, Oxford (1700)

19 Music, the greatest good that mortals know, And all of heaven we have below.

Joseph Addison, 'Song for St Cecilia's Day'

20 O Music, sphere-descended maid, Friend of pleasure, wisdom's aid.

William Collins, 'The Passions, an Ode for Music'

21 Now the rich stream of music winds along, Deep, majestic, smooth, and strong.

Thomas Gray, 'The Progress of Poesy' (1757)

22 An ear for music is a very different from a taste for music. I have no ear whatever; I could not sing an air to save my life; but I have the intensest delight in music, and can detect good from bad.

Samuel Taylor Coleridge, *Table Talk* (1830)

23 And music pours on mortals Her magnificent disdain.

Ralph Waldo Emerson, 'The Sphinx'

24 Music hath caught a higher pace than any virtue that I know. It is the arch-reformer; it hastens the sun to its setting; it invites him to his rising; it is the sweetest reproach, a measured satire.

Henry David Thoreau, Journal, 1842

1 If I were to begin life again, I would devote it to music. It is the only cheap and unpunished rapture upon earth.

Sydney Smith, Letter to the Countess of Carlisle, 1844

2 There is no truer truth obtainable
By Man than comes of music.

Robert Browning, *Parleyings with Certain People*, 'Charles Avison'

3 All art constantly aspires towards the condition of music.

Walter Pater, *Studies in the History of the Renaissance* (1873), 'The School of Giorgione'

4 Without music, life would be an error.

Friedrich Nietzsche, *Twilight of the Idols* (1888)

5 When I seek for a word to replace that of music, I can think only of Venice.

Friedrich Nietzsche, quoted in Kendall, *Vivaldi* (1978)

6 Music has been one of the greatest passions in my life. I say *has been*, because now I have scarcely any opportunity of hearing any except in my memories. It has brought me ineffable joys and certitudes — the proof that there exists something other than the void I have encountered on all sides; it runs like a guide-line throughout all my work.

Marcel Proust, quoted in Myers, *Modern French Music* (1971)

7 Nothing is better than music; when it takes us out of time, it has done more for us than we have the right to hope for.

Nadia Boulanger, in *Le Monde musical*, 1919

8 All the worst things happen in the best works, and the worst music appears to be streaked all through with the most luscious bits.

Bernard Van Dieren, *Down Among the Dead Men* (1935)

9 Pour out your presence, a delight cascading
The falls of the knee and the weirs of the spine,
Our climate of silence and doubt invading;

You alone, alone, imaginary song,
Are unable to say an existence is wrong,
And pour out your forgiveness like a wine.

W.H. Auden, 'The Composer'

10 I like most music unless it's wrong.

Coleman Hawkins, quoted in Dance, *The World of Swing* (1974)

PUCCINI

11 God touched me with His little finger and said, 'Write for the theatre, only for the theatre'.

Giacomo Puccini, quoted in Wechsberg, *The Opera* (1972)

12 The difficulty is, how to begin an opera, that is, how to find its musical atmosphere. Once the opening is fixed and composed, there is no more to fear.

Giacomo Puccini, quoted in Adami, *Puccini* (1935)

13 [On the story of *Manon Lescaut*] Massenet feels it as a Frenchman, with powder and minuets. I shall feel it as an Italian, with desperate passion.

Giacomo Puccini, quoted in Carner, *Puccini* (1974)

14 [At the first night rejection of *Madame Butterfly*] It is I who am right, I! You shall see!

Giacomo Puccini, quoted in Specht, *Giacomo Puccini* (1931)

15 [After the first performance of *Manon Lescaut* in London] Puccini looks to me more like the heir of Verdi than any of his rivals.

George Bernard Shaw, in *The World*, 1894

16 While *La Bohème* is all poetry and no plot, *Tosca* is all plot and no poetry.

Giuseppe Giacosa, Letter to Ricordi, 1896

17 [Of *Tosca*] A shabby little shocker.

Anon.

18 He made 12 operas, lacking in personality, and not concealing any of the faults of the 'verist' school. However, his style is perhaps less abominably commonplace than that of Leoncavallo.

Vincent d'Indy, *Cours de composition musicale*, III (pub. 1950)

19 *Shostakovich*: What do you think of Puccini?
Britten: I think his operas are dreadful.
Shostakovich: No, Ben, you are wrong. He wrote marvellous operas, but dreadful music.

Quoted in Harewood, *The Tongs and the Bones* (1981)

PURCELL

20 Instead of an elaborate harangue on the beauty and the charms of music (which after all the learned encomiums that words can contrive commends itself best by the performance of a skilful hand, and an angelical voice), I shall say but a very few things by way of Preface . . .

Henry Purcell, Preface to *Sonatas of III Parts* (1683); probably written by John Playford

21 Mr Purcell; in whose person we have at length found an Englishman equal with the best abroad.

John Dryden, Dedication to *Amphitryon* (1690)

22 [Purcell] One of the most celebrated masters of the service of music in the kingdom, and scarce inferior to any in Europe.

Obituary in *The Flying-Post*, 1695

1 Here lies Henry Purcell Esquire, who left life
   and is gone to that blessed place where only his
   harmony can be exceeded.
   Epitaph, 1695

2 The divine Purcell.
   Roger North, *Memoirs of Musick* (pub. 1846)

3 All the other solo songs [in *King Arthur*] of
   Purcell are infamously bad; so very bad that
   they are the objects of sneer and ridicule to the
   musicians.
   Thomas Arne, Letter to David Garrick

4 The ear will patiently bear very rough usage
   from an artist [Purcell] who in general makes it
   such ample amends.
   Charles Burney, *A General History of Music* (1776—89)

5 In one way Purcell is a finer stage composer
   than Wagner: his music is full of movement, of
   dance. His is the easiest music in all the world
   to act.
   Gustav Holst, *The Heritage of Music* (1928)

6 [Of *Dido and Aeneas*] The only perfect English
   opera ever written.
   Gustav Holst, *The Heritage of Music* (1928)

RACISM

7 In music, the blacks are more generally gifted
   than the whites, with accurate ears for tune and
   time, and they have been found capable of
   imagining a small catch. Whether they will be
   capable of the composition of a more extensive
   melody or of complicated harmony, is yet to be
   proved.
   Thomas Jefferson, *Notes on the State of Virginia* (1781)

8 A singing Negro is a good Negro.
   François Postif, quoted in Berendt, *The Jazz Book* (1976)

9 To think that it was ... a Jew who gave back to
   the German people their greatest Christian
   work.
   Felix Mendelssohn, commenting on his performance
   of the St Matthew Passion (1829); quoted in Marek,
   Gentle Genius (1972)

10 Mendelssohn has demonstrated that the Jew
   may be highly talented, greatly cultured, and be
   possessed of the finest sense of honour, but
   that these qualities do not enable him ever to
   imbue us with that deep and heart-piercing
   effect which we demand of art.
   Richard Wagner, in *Neue Zeitschrift*, 1850

11 Purely German his [Hindemith's] blood may be,
   but this only provides drastic confirmation of
   how deeply the Jewish intellectual infection has
   eaten into the body of our own people.
   Joseph Goebbels, Speech, 1934

12 [On Mendelssohn's statue in Leipzig] Without
   wishing to discuss the merits of the composer,
   it is certainly true that it goes against the
   healthy instincts of our nation when —
   prompted by false piety and consideration —
   we let stand a monument to a Jew, while we
   consistently endeavour to expunge the damage
   done to our cultural heritage by Judaism.
   Anon., in *Leipziger Tageszeitung*, 1936

13 Rock 'n' roll is a means of pulling down the
   white man to the level of the 'Negro'. It is part
   of a plot to undermine the morals of the youth
   of our nation. It is sexualistic, unmoralistic, and
   the best way to bring people of both races
   together.
   Asa Carter, member of the North Alabama White
   Citizen's Council, quoted in *The Melody Maker*, 1956

RAGTIME

14 I got a ragtime dog and a ragtime cat
   A ragtime piano in my ragtime flat.
   I'm wearing ragtime clothes from hat to shoes
   I read a paper called the ragtime news.
   I got ragtime habits and I talk that way
   I sleep in ragtime and rag all day.
   Got ragtime troubles with my ragtime wife
   I'm certainly leading a ragtime life!
   Jefferson and Roberts, Rag (1899)

15 A wave of vulgar, filthy and suggestive music
   has inundated the land. The pabulum of theatre
   and summer hotel orchestras is coon music.
   Nothing but ragtime prevails and the cake-walk
   with its obscene posturings, its lewd gestures.
   It is artistically and morally depressing and
   should be suppressed by press and pulpit.
   The Musical Courier, 1899

16 Syncopations are no indication of light or
   trashy music, and to shy bricks at 'hateful
   ragtime' no longer passes for musical culture.
   Scott Joplin, *The School of Ragtime* (1908)

17 Ragtime is the American Creation and the
   Marvel of Musicians in all Civilized Countries.
   John Stark, Scott Joplin's publisher, quoted in
   Whitcomb, *After the Ball* (1972)

18 Here is the genius whose spirit — though
   diluted — was filtered through thousands of
   cheap songs and vain imitations.
   John Stark, Obituary on Scott Joplin, quoted in
   Palmer, *All You Need Is Love* (1976)

19 You know, I never did find out what ragtime
   was.
   Irving Berlin, composer of *Alexander's Ragtime Band*,
   quoted in Palmer, *All You Need Is Love* (1976)

1   O O O O that Shakespeherian Rag —
    It's so elegant
    So intelligent.

    T.S. Eliot, *The Waste Land* (1922), misquoting from
    Gene Buck, Herman Ruby and David Stamper, 'That
    Shakespearian Rag' (1912): 'That Shakespearian Rag,
    most intelligent, very elegant ...'

2   Though she [Lady Macbeth] was a lady of noble
    birth, we suspect there was a little ragtime in
    her soul.

    Duke Ellington, quoted in Jewell, *Duke* (1977)

3   [Ragtime] White music — played black.

    Joachim Berendt, *The Jazz Book* (1976)

RAKHMANINOV

4   [Asked why he was not composing] How can I
    compose without melody?

    Sergey Rakhmaninov, in 1924, quoted in Bertensson
    and Leyda, *Sergei Rachmaninoff* (1965)

5   When I conduct, I experience much the same
    feeling as when I drive my car — an inner calm
    that gives me complete mastery of myself and
    of the forces, musical or mechanical, at my
    disposal.

    Sergey Rakhmaninov, quoted in Bertensson and
    Leyda, *Sergei Rachmaninoff* (1965)

6   I feel like a ghost wandering in a world grown
    alien. I cannot cast out the old way of writing,
    and I cannot acquire the new. I have made
    intense efforts to feel the musical manner of
    today, but it will not come to me.

    Sergey Rakhmaninov, quoted in Ewen, *American
    Composers* (1982)

7   Mr Rachmaninoff, who is perhaps the tallest
    known pianist ...

    Richard Aldrich, in *The New York Times*, 1909

8   Rakhmaninov's music is ruined if it is made to
    sound deliberate.

    Neville Cardus, in *The Manchester Guardian*, 1936

9   [Of Rakhmaninov's playing] Even an ordinary
    broken chord is made to disclose rare beauties;
    we are reminded of the fairies' hazel-nuts in
    which diamonds were concealed but you could
    break the shell only if your hands were blessed.

    Neville Cardus, in *The Manchester Guardian*, 1939

10 The prospect of having to sit through one of his
    extended symphonies or piano concertos tends,
    quite frankly, to depress me. All those notes,
    think I, and to what end?

    Aaron Copland, quoted in Kendall, *The Tender Tyrant:
    Nadia Boulanger* (1976)

11 The only pianist I have ever seen who did not
    grimace.

    Igor Stravinsky, quoted in Craft, *Conversations with
    Igor Stravinsky* (1958)

RAMEAU

12 We must have recourse to the rules [of music]
    only when our genius and our ear seem to deny
    what we are seeking.

    Jean-Philippe Rameau, *Le Nouveau Système de musique
    théorique* (1726)

13 In music the ear obeys only nature. It takes
    account of neither measure nor range. Instinct
    alone leads it.

    Jean-Philippe Rameau, *Observations sur notre instinct
    pour la musique* (1734)

14 [Of a persistently barking dog] *Madame, de grâce
    faites taire cet animal; il a la voix on ne peut plus
    désagréable.* Madame, I beg you to silence that
    animal; it couldn't have a more disagreeable
    voice.

    Jean-Philippe Rameau, quoted in Girdlestone, *Jean-
    Philippe Rameau* (1957)

15 The expression of thought, of sentiment, of the
    passions, must be the true aim of music.

    Jean-Philippe Rameau, quoted in Mellers, *François
    Couperin* (1950)

RAVEL

16 Music, I feel, must be emotional first and
    intellectual second.

    Maurice Ravel, attr.

17 I am artificial by nature.

    Maurice Ravel, quoted in Machlis, *Introduction to
    Contemporary Music* (1963)

18 I make logarithms — it is for you to understand
    them.

    Maurice Ravel, quoted in Machlis, *Introduction to
    Contemporary Music* (1963)

19 [Of *Gaspard de la nuit*] I wanted to make a
    caricature of romanticism — perhaps it got the
    better of me.

    Maurice Ravel, quoted in Jourdan-Morhange and
    Perlemuter, *Ravel d'après Ravel* (1957)

20 [Of *Le Tombeau de Couperin*] The tribute is not so
    much to the individual figure of Couperin as to
    the whole of French music of the eighteenth
    century.

    Maurice Ravel, in his autobiographical sketch (1928)

21 [Of *Boléro*] A piece for orchestra without music.

    Maurice Ravel, quoted in Nichols, *Ravel* (1977)

22 [After a performance of *Daphnis et Chloé*] *Tout
    de même, il avait du talent, ce Ravel.* All the same,
    he had talent, that Ravel.

    Maurice Ravel, quoted in Nichols, *Ravel* (1977)

23 [Nearing his death] I still have so much music
    in my head. I have said nothing. I have so much
    more to say.

    Maurice Ravel, quoted in Jourdan-Morhange, *Ravel et
    nous* (1945)

1   [Of Ravel's Quartet in F] In the name of God, I
    implore you not to change a note of your
    quartet.

    Claude Debussy, attr., quoted in Nichols, *Ravel* (1977)

2   M. Ravel refuses the Legion of Honour, but all
    his music accepts it.

    Erik Satie, quoted in Machlis, *Introduction to
    Contemporary Music* (1963)

3   There is a definite limit to the length of time a
    composer can go on writing in one dance
    rhythm. This limit is obviously reached by
    Ravel toward the end of *La Valse* and toward the
    beginning of *Boléro.*

    Constant Lambert, *Music Ho!* (1934)

4   The most perfect of Swiss clockmakers.

    Igor Stravinsky, quoted in Nichols, *Ravel* (1977)

5   Another time someone was screaming for a
    rumba when I put on Ravel's *Daphnis and Chloé.*
    'Hey, *that's* a rumba,' Duke [Ellington] said.

    Edmund Anderson, quoted in Jewell, *Duke* (1977)

RECORDED AND BROADCAST MUSIC

6   We represent and imitate all articulate sounds
    and letters, and the voices and notes of beasts
    and birds. We have certain helps, which set to
    the ear do further the hearing greatly. We have
    also strange and artificial echoes, reflecting the
    voice many times, and as it were tossing it; and
    some that give back the voice louder than it
    came, some shriller and some deeper; yea, some
    rendering the voice, differing in the letters or
    articulate sound from that they receive. We
    have also means to convey sounds in trunks
    and pipes, in strange lines and distances.

    Francis Bacon, *New Atlantis* (1627)

7   I am . . . terrified at the thought that so much
    hideous and bad music will be put on records
    forever.

    Arthur Sullivan, recorded on a 'phonogram' for
    Thomas Edison, 1888

8   The gramophone seems to me a marvellous
    instrument. Moreover, it assures music of a
    complete and meticulous immortality.

    Claude Debussy, in 1904, quoted in Orenstein, *Ravel:
    Man and Musician* (1975)

9   [Of the gramophone] Should we not fear this
    domestication of sound, this magic that anyone
    can bring from a disk at will? Will it not bring to
    waste the mysterious force of an art which one
    might have thought indestructible?

    Claude Debussy, in *La Revue S.I.M.,* 1913

10 When lovely woman stoops to folly and
    Paces about her room again, alone,
    She smoothes her hair with automatic hand,
    And puts a record on the gramophone.

    T.S. Eliot, *The Waste Land* (1922)

11 [Of music on the radio] I believe one shouldn't
    be too comfortable when listening to really
    great music . . . You can't enjoy and
    understand it merely by sitting still and letting
    it soak into your ears.

    Sergey Rakhmaninov, interview in 1925, quoted in
    Bertensson and Leyda, *Sergei Rachmaninoff* (1965)

12 [The gramophone] I have music here in a box,
    shut up, like one of those bottled djinns in the
    Arabian Nights, and ready at a touch to break
    out of its prison.

    Aldous Huxley, *Music at Night* (1931)

13 Since the advent of the gramophone, and more
    particularly the wireless, music of a sort is
    everywhere and at every time; in the heavens,
    the lower parts of the earth, the mountains, the
    forest and every tree therein. It is a Psalmist's
    nightmare.

    Constant Lambert, *Music Ho!* (1934)

14 *Threefold Function of Broadcast Music*
    1. Inexorably to continue and expand the
    principle of great music as an ultimate value,
    indeed a justification of life.
    2. Faithfully to enrich leisure hours with
    entertainment.
    3. Physically and mentally to stimulate tired
    bodies and worn nerves.
    N.B. It betrays its trust if it debases spiritual
    value of music, acts as a narcotic or drug, or
    bores by sheer inanity.

    Arthur Bliss, 'Music Policy' (1941)

15 [Of musical boxes] To have them back again I
    would cheerfully throw into the sea or on to the
    dust-heap most of those triumphs of modern
    invention which claim to be trustworthier
    instruments of reproduction.

    Sir Thomas Beecham, *A Mingled Chime* (1944)

16 [Of music on the radio] The most abominable
    row that ever stunned and cursed the human
    ear, a horrible gibbering, chortling and
    shrieking of devils and goblins.

    Sir Thomas Beecham, quoted in Reid, *Thomas Beecham*
    (1961)

17 Put another nickel in,
    In the nickelodeon,
    All I want is loving you
    And music, music, music!

    Stephen Weiss and Bernie Baum, 'Music, Music,
    Music' (1950)

18 It's what's in the grooves that counts.

    Tamla Motown Records, corporate slogan

19 The Recording Angel I am concerned with is
    not CBS, in any case, but the One with the Big
    Book.

    Igor Stravinsky, *Themes and Conclusions* (1972)

THE RECORDER

1   [Of playing the recorder] It is as easy as lying.
    Govern these vantages with your fingers and
    thumb, give it breath with your mouth, and it
    will discourse most eloquent music.
    (Hamlet to Guildenstern)
    William Shakespeare, *Hamlet,* III.ii

2   Anon they move
    In perfect phalanx to the Dorian mood
    Of flutes and soft recorders.
    John Milton, *Paradise Lost,* I

3   To Drumbleby's and did there talk a great deal
    about pipes, and did buy a recorder which I do
    intend to learn to play on, the sound of it being
    of all sounds in the world most pleasing to me.
    Samuel Pepys, Diary, 1668

REGER

4   Creation must be completely free. Every fetter
    one imposes on oneself by taking into account
    playability or public taste leads to disaster.
    Max Reger, Letter to Ella Kerndl, 1900

5   Every piece of organ music which is not at
    bottom related to Bach is impossible.
    Max Reger, Letter to Renner, 1900

REGGAE

6   Reggae music is one of them stones that was
    refused by the builders.
    Charlie Ace, quoted in Johnson and Pines, *Reggae*
    (1982)

7   Reggae means comin' from the people, y'know?
    Like a everyday thing. Like from the ghetto.
    From *majority*. Everyday thing that people use
    like food, we just put music to it and make a
    dance out of it. Reggae mean *regular* people
    who are suffering, and don't have what they
    want.
    Toots Hibbert, quoted in Davis and Simon, *Reggae
    Bloodlines* (1979)

8   Reggae is a gift from Jah to the Jamaican
    people.
    Harry J., quoted in Johnson and Pines, *Reggae* (1982)

9   Some call it reggae explosion. But I call it Deep
    Roots Music . . . As seventy-two nations must
    bow to reggae music, rock steady music, ska
    music, meringue music, calypso music, jazz
    music — don't care what the music might be,
    but music is the only comforter, I'm telling you
    the truth, man.
    Lee 'Scratch' Perry, quoted in Johnson and Pines,
    Reggae (1982)

RELIGION

See also CHURCH MUSIC, HEAVENLY MUSIC.

10 O sing unto God with the voice of melody.
    Psalms 47:1 (version in the Book of Common Prayer)

11 God is gone up with a merry noise: and the
    Lord with the sound of the trump.
    Psalms 47:5 (version in the Book of Common Prayer)

12 Serve the Lord with gladness, and come before
    his presence with a song.
    Psalms 100:1 (version in the Book of Common Prayer)

13 To you it is commanded, O peoples, nations,
    and languages,
    That at that time ye hear the sound of the
    cornet, flute, harp, sackbut, psaltery, dulcimer,
    and all kinds of musick, ye fall down and
    worship the golden image that Nebuchadnezzar
    the king hath set up:
    And whoso falleth not down and worshippeth
    shall the same hour be cast into the middle of a
    burning fiery furnace.
    Daniel 3:4–6

14 Zeus does not sing and harp to the poets
    himself.
    Aristotle, *Politics*

15 *Carmine di superi placantur carmine Manes.* Both
    the gods above and in the underworld are
    placated by song.
    Horace, *Epistles,* II, 1

16 Be not drunk with wine, wherein is excess; but
    be filled with the Spirit;
    Speaking to yourselves in psalms and hymns
    and spiritual songs, singing and making melody
    in your heart to the Lord.
    Ephesians 5:18–19

17 The musician's fingers . . . may often make
    mistakes on the small strings, but in the
    congregation that great Musician, the [Holy]
    Spirit, cannot err.
    St Ambrose, quoted in Routley, *The Church and Music*
    (1950)

18 Music defiles the service of religion.
    John of Salisbury, *c.* 1160, quoted in *The Oxford
    History of Music* (1929)

19 I am not of the opinion that all the arts shall be
    crushed to earth and perish through the
    Gospel, as some bigoted persons pretend, but
    would willingly see them all, and especially
    music, servants of Him who gave and created
    them.
    Martin Luther, Foreword to the *Wittemberg Gesangbuch*
    (1524)

20 Music is one of the greatest gifts that God has
    given us: it is divine and therefore Satan is its

enemy. For with its aid many dire temptations are overcome; the devil does not stay where music is.

Martin Luther, 'In Praise of Music'

1 The better the voice is, the meeter it is to honour and serve God therewith: and the voice of man is chiefly to be employed to that end.

William Byrd, *Psalmes, Sonets and Songs* (1588)

2 Even on my jolie Lute, by night,
And trimling trible string,
I shall with all my minde and might,
Thy glorie gladlie sing.

Alexander Hume, *Hymnes or Sacred Songs* (1599)

3 That music itself is lawful, useful, and commendable, no man, no Christian dares deny, since the Scriptures, Fathers, and generally all Christians, all pagan authors extant, do with one consent aver it.

William Prynne, *Histriomastix* (1632)

4 Those things that act through the ears are said to make a noise, discord, or harmony, and this last has caused men to lose their heads to such a degree that they have believed God himself is delighted with it.

Baruch Spinoza, *Ethics* (1677)

5 The end and goal of thorough bass is nothing but the honour of God.

Johann Sebastian Bach, note on MS rules for accompaniment, quoted in Graf, *Composer and Critic* (1947)

6 Glorious the song, when God's the theme.

Christopher Smart, *Song to David* (1763)

7 The Most High has a decided taste for vocal music, provided it be lugubrious and gloomy enough.

Voltaire, *Dictionnaire philosophique* (1764)

8 Among all the arts, music alone can be purely religious.

Madame de Staël, *Corinne* (1807)

9 When I open my eyes I must sigh, for what I see is contrary to my religion, and I must despise the world which does not know that music is a higher revelation than all wisdom and philosophy.

Ludwig van Beethoven, quoted by Bettina von Arnim, Letter to Goethe, 1810

10 I pant for music which is divine;
My heart in its thirst is a dying flower;
Pour forth the sound like enchanted wine,
Loosen the notes in a silver shower;
Like a herbless plain, for the gentle rain,
I gasp, I faint, till they wake again.

Percy Bysshe Shelley, 'Music'

11 Song is the daughter of prayer, and prayer is the companion of religion.

François René de Chateaubriand, *Genius of Christianity* (1856)

12 The societies most deeply tainted with superstition have been the greatest promoters of art.

Georges Bizet, Letter, 1866

13 My objective . . . is to . . . wish for the religion of music before and above the religion of the career.

Nadia Boulanger, in *Le Monde musical,* 1920

14 Music is one of the ways God has of beating in on man.

Charles Ives, 'Epitaph for David Twichell' (1924)

15 I always said God was against art and I still believe it.

Edward Elgar, quoted in Moore, *Edward Elgar: A Creative Life* (1984)

16 Given a young composer of genius, the surest way to ruin him is to make a Christian of him.

Frederick Delius, quoted in Fenby, *Delius as I knew him* (1936)

17 Poetry
Exceeding music must take the place
Of empty heaven and its hymns.

Wallace Stevens, *The Man with the Blue Guitar* (1937)

18 A strange theory [arising in the First World War] . . . that while the pantheist Beethoven represents a spirit completely in accordance with that of the struggle to preserve the religious ideal of the past nineteen hundred years, the Christian Wagner is as much of an opposing element to him as Beelzebub was to Jehovah.

Sir Thomas Beecham, *A Mingled Chime* (1944)

19 Every high C accurately struck demolishes the theory that we are the irresponsible puppets of fate or chance.

W.H. Auden, 'Some Reflections on Music and Opera', in *Partisan Review* (1952)

20 All music is praise of the Lord, which some people cannot or will not understand, the real jazz form of a spiritual soil, is truly the musical psalms of the twentieth-century man's torment in the tigerish growl of the trumpet. God's wrath and mercy are in the demonic drumbeat and the milk-smooth sound of the saxophone . . .

The Indian Express, 1963

21 'What is this big thing? God, if you like. What's it, shehit, like? I would say,' Enderby said thoughtfully, 'like a big symphony, the page of the score of infinite length, the number of instruments infinite but all bound into one big unity. This big symphony plays itself for ever

and ever. And who listens to it? It listens to itself. Enjoys itself for ever and ever and ever. It doesn't give a bugger whether you hear it or not.'

Anthony Burgess, *The Clockwork Testament* (1974)

1 Them have reggae music as a little dance music. But there's a form of reggae music called Jah music. Seen. That is the music that inspire black people. The music is philosophical, so much so that it brings people out of darkness. Jah music tells people about themselves.

Big Youth, quoted in Johnson and Pines, *Reggae* (1982)

RHYTHM

2 In the beginning was rhythm.

Hans von Bülow, quoted in Machlis, *Introduction to Contemporary Music* (1963)

3 Rhythm, the primitive and predominating element of all Art.

Vincent d'Indy, *Cours de composition musicale,* I (1903)

4 I got rhythm,
I got music.

Ira Gershwin, song from *Girl Crazy* (1930)

5 It don't mean a thing
If it ain't got that swing.

Duke Ellington and Irving Mills, Song (1932)

6 All God's Chillun Got Rhythm.

Gus Kahn, title of song (1937)

7 Rhythm and motion, not the element of feeling, are the foundations of musical art.

Igor Stravinsky, quoted in Machlis, *Introduction to Contemporary Music* (1963)

8 Perhaps in our joy in musical rhythm, there is expressed something of the primal joy of procreation . . . The domain of rhythm extends from the spiritual to the carnal.

Bruno Walter, *Of Music and Music-Making* (1957)

RIMSKY-KORSAKOV

9 [Of Rimsky-Korsakov's *Scheherazade*] It reminds one more of a bazaar than of the Orient.

Claude Debussy, Letter to Raoul Bardac, 1906

10 A cultured aromatist.

Neville Cardus, in *The Manchester Guardian,* 1935

11 Swinburne revising Burns might sound as quaint an idea, before the event, as Rimsky-Korsakov revising Mussorgsky.

Neville Cardus, in *The Manchester Guardian,* 1935

ROCK MUSIC

12 Make battery to our ears with the loud music. (Enobarbus)

William Shakespeare, *Antony and Cleopatra,* II.vii

13 Our airways have been flooded in recent years with whining guitarists, musical riots put to a switchblade beat, obscure lyrics about hugging, squeezing, and rocking all night long . . . The constant aim of the broadcasters is to obtain music in bulk cheaply. They are so relentless in this resolve that they would be willing, I am convinced, to drive us all back to the dark ages of music, if necessary, in order to achieve their goal.

Vance Packard, evidence before the Anti-Trust Subcommittee of the House Judiciary Committee, 1956

14 You know my temperature's risin',
The jukebox's blowin' a fuse,
My heart's beatin' rhythm,
My soul keeps a singin' the blues —
Roll over Beethoven,
Tell Tchaikovsky the news.

Chuck Berry, 'Roll over Beethoven'

15 I came from a family where people didn't like rhythm and blues. Bing Crosby, 'Pennies From Heaven', Ella Fitzgerald was all I heard. And I knew there was something that could be louder than that, but I didn't know where to find it. And I found it was me.

Little Richard, quoted in Rogers, *Rock 'n' Roll* (1982)

16 I picked songs . . . that could be understood not just by some old spade in the cotton-fields sixty years ago, but also by the tram-driver in East Ham High Street.

Lonnie Donegan, quoted in *The Melody Maker,* 1978

17 [Of Rhythm and Blues] It's not a music. It's a disease.

Mitch Miller of Columbia Records, c. 1960, quoted in Palmer, *All You Need Is Love* (1976)

18 [Of Rhythm and Blues] The music was not particularly rhythmic, and it was almost never true blues.

Jerry Wexler of Atlantic Records, who coined the term, quoted in Palmer, *All You Need Is Love* (1976)

19 I've just got to get out. Maybe to Venus or somewhere. Some place *you* won't be able to find me.

Jimi Hendrix, quoted in Palmer, *All You Need Is Love* (1976)

20 If it screams for truth rather than help, if it commits itself with a courage that it can't be sure it really has, if it stands up and admits something is wrong but doesn't insist on blood, then it is rock 'n' roll.

Pete Townshend, quoted in Green, *The Book of Rock Quotes* (1982)

21 Good rock stars take drugs, put their penises in plaster of paris, collectivise their sex, molest policemen, promote self-curiosity, unlock myriad spirits, epitomise fun, freedom and

bullshit. Can the busiest anarchist on your block match THAT?

Richard Neville, *Playpower* (1970)

1   Rock music must give birth to orgasm and revolution.

Jerry Rubin, *Do It!* (1970)

2   In modern rock . . . loudness becomes paradoxically more silent than silence, since one is no longer aware of gradation!

Wilfrid Mellers, *The Music of the Beatles* (1973)

3   It's only rock 'n' roll, but I like it.

The Rolling Stones, 'It's Only Rock 'n' Roll'

4   Rock groups . . . are more concerned with doing things to an audience in a particular way than with creating a form which might puzzle the audience at first but ultimately yield a much greater satisfaction.

Chick Corea, quoted in Palmer, *All You Need Is Love* (1976)

5   Gene Vincent . . . sounded like a Southern razor boy who could slit a man from ear to ear without flinching an eyelid or missing a beat of 'Beebopalula'.

Tony Palmer, *All You Need Is love* (1976)

6   Sex 'n' Drugs 'n' Rock 'n' Roll.

Ian Dury, title of song

7   Rock 'n' roll is instant coffee.

Bob Geldof of The Boomtown Rats, quoted in Green, *The Book of Rock Quotes* (1982)

8   Rock 'n' roll isn't even music. It's a mistreating of instruments to get feelings over.

Mark Smith of The Fall, quoted in Green, *The Book of Rock Quotes* (1982)

9   A generation that believed it was saving the world by wallowing in mud at rock festivals for days on end, dressed in some of the silliest clothes ever seen, stuffed to the eyebrows with hallucinogenics, listening to distant millionaires droning on about togetherness, should feel thoroughly ashamed of itself.

Robert Elms, in *The Observer,* 1984

THE ROLLING STONES

10 [When asked whether he was satisfied] Financially, yes; sexually,no; philosophically, trying.

Mick Jagger, in the film *Gimme Shelter*

11 I believe there can be no evolution without revolution. Why *should* we try to fit in?

Mick Jagger, quoted in Palmer, *All You Need Is Love* (1976)

12 ⁄I knew what I was looking at. It was sex. And I was just ahead of the pack.

Andrew Oldham, manager of the Rolling Stones, quoted in Norman, *The Stones* (1984)

13 The singer'll have to go, the BBC won't like him.

Eric Easton, quoted in Green, *The Book of Rock Quotes* (1982)

14 They look like boys whom any self-respecting mum would lock in the bathroom.

The Daily Express, 1964

15 [Of Mick Jagger] He took my music. But he gave me my name.

Muddy Waters, quoted in Palmer, *All You Need Is Love* (1976)

ROMANTICISM

16 Every real creation of art is independent, more powerful than the artist himself and returns to the divine through its manifestation. It is one with man only in this, that it bears testimony to the mediation of the divine in him.

Ludwig van Beethoven, quoted by Bettina von Arnim, Letter to Goethe, 1810

17 Haydn's music reminds us of a blissful, eternally youthful life before the Fall . . . while Beethoven's music sets in motion the lever of fear, of awe, of horror, of suffering, and awakens just that infinite longing which is the essence of romanticism.

E.T.A. Hoffmann, in 1813, quoted in Headington, *The Bodley Head History of Western Music* (1974)

18 Sounds overflow the listener's brain, So sweet, that joy is almost pain.

Percy Bysshe Shelley, *Prometheus Unbound,* II.ii (1820)

19 Sing again, with your dear voice revealing
      A tone
        Of some world far from ours,
    Where music and moonlight and feeling
      Are one.

Percy Bysshe Shelley, 'To Jane: The Keen Stars were Twinkling'

20 It is scarcely credible that a distinct romantic school could be formed in music, which is in itself romantic.

Robert Schumann, quoted in Strunk, *Source Readings in Musical History* (1952)

21 It is in music, perhaps, that the soul most nearly attains the great end for which, when inspired by the poetic sentiment, it struggles — the creation of supernal beauty.

Edgar Allen Poe, 'The Poetic Principle' (1850)

22 At no time has any art been so mistreated as is now our beloved music. Let us hope that somewhere in obscurity something better is emerging, for otherwise our epoch would go down in the annals of art as a pit for trash.

Johannes Brahms, Letter to Berta Porubszky, 1859

1 [Of Bruckner] His music has the fragrance of heavenly roses, but it is poisonous with the sulphurs of hell.
   Unnamed critic, in 1884, quoted in Watson, *Bruckner* (1975)

2 Wagner is a neurotic . . . And just because there is nothing more modern than this collective illness, this sluggishness and oversensitivity of the nervous machinery, Wagner is a modern artist *par excellence*, the Cagliostro of modernity.
   Friedrich Nietzsche, *Der Fall Wagner* (1888)

3 The old romanticism is dead; long live the new!
   Arnold Schoenberg, quoted in Machlis, *Introduction to Contemporary Music* (1963)

4 As Beethoven is the morning and Wagner the high noon, so Delius is the sunset of that great period of music which is called Romantic.
   Peter Warlock, quoted in Machlis, *Introduction to Contemporary Music* (1963)

5 All the successors of Beethoven who aspired to his position of authority . . . quite consciously imbued their music with the 'masterpiece' tone. This tone is lugubrious, portentous, world-shaking; and length, as well as heavy instrumentation, is essential to it . . . It tends to substitute an impressive manner for specific expression, just as oratory does.
   Virgil Thomson, in *The New York Herald Tribune,* 1944

6 [Of Romanticism] It emancipated her [i.e. music] from the sphere of small-town specialism and piping and brought her into contact with the great world of the mind, the general artistic and intellectual movement of the time.
   (Leverkühn)
   Thomas Mann, *Doctor Faustus* (1947); trans. Lowe-Porter

7 [To Arnold Bax, after listening to a 'modern' work] You know, Arnold, there's no room in this world for a couple of romantic old sods like us.
   John Ireland, attr.

8 The romanticists have done in music.
   Roy Ellsworth Harris, quoted in Ewen, *American Composers* (1982)

9 There is something enfeebling about the vapours of the nineteenth century. And yet it remains fascinating, for all that striving came to so little: Berlioz, Wagner, Brahms, and Mahler, all that torment and effort; and when we ask to see their heirs, the spotlight switches on to Stravinsky, Schoenberg, Hindemith, Boulez — all looking a little blinded and more than a little embarrassed.
   Colin Wilson, *Brandy of the Damned* (1964)

10 The romantic aims at expressing himself in such a way that, if possible, his own voice shall be strange to him.
    Colin Wilson, *Brandy of the Damned* (1964)

11 [Of Romanticism] All that doodle, doodle.
    Rudolf Serkin, quoted in Jacobson, *Reverberations* (1975)

12 It seems now that many of the great Romantics managed to say little superbly well, and at great length.
    Alan Kendall, *The Tender Tyrant: Nadia Boulanger* (1976)

13 I should imagine that the tensions and releases of Beethoven have as much to do with visceral problems as with the fight towards the ecstatic vision.
    Anthony Burgess, in *The Observer,* 1983

ROSSINI

14 Give me a laundry list and I will set it to music.
    Gioacchino Rossini, attr.

15 Thou knowest, O Lord, as well as I, that really I am only a composer of *opera buffa.*
    Gioacchino Rossini, Dedication to *Petite Messe solennelle* (1864)

16 Delight must be the basis and aim of this art. Simple melody — clear rhythm!
    Gioacchino Rossini, Letter, 1868

17 Who would not gladly listen to Rossini's lively flights of fancy, to the piquant titillation of his melodies? But who could be so blind as to attribute to him dramatic truth?
    Carl Maria von Weber, in 1820, quoted in Morgenstern (ed.), *Composers on Music* (1958)

18 Rossini, in music, is the genius of sheer animal spirits. It is a species as inferior to that of Mozart, as the cleverness of a smart boy is to that of a man of sentiment; but it is genius nevertheless.
    Leigh Hunt, 'Going to the Play Again' (1828)

19 Rossini . . . directed his letters to his mother as 'mother of the famous composer'.
    Robert Browning, Letter, 1846

20 The point is . . . a person feels *good* listening to Rossini. All you feel like listening to Beethoven is going out and invading Poland. Ode to Joy indeed. The man didn't even have a sense of humour. I tell you . . . there is more of the Sublime in the snare-drum part of *La Gazza Ladra* than in the whole Ninth Symphony.
    (Säure)
    Thomas Pynchon, *Gravity's Rainbow* (1973)

ROUSSEL

1 What I should like to achieve is music which is
self-contained . . . divorced from any
illustrative or descriptive elements . . . I want
my music to be nothing but music.

   Albert Roussel, quoted in Deane, *Albert Roussel* (1961)

2 *Roussel est quelque chose comme un Debussy formé à
l'école du contrepoint.* Roussel is a sort of
Debussy trained in counterpoint.

   Paul Landormy, quoted in Myers, *Modern French Music*
(1971)

RUGGLES

3 Music that does not surge is not great music.

   Carl Ruggles, quoted in Wilson, *Brandy of the Damned*
(1964)

4 You goddam sissy! — when you hear strong
masculine music like this, get up and USE YOUR
EARS LIKE A MAN!

   Charles Ives, to a noisy member of the audience
during the 1931 performance of Ruggles' *Men and
Mountains,* quoted in Wooldridge, *Charles Ives* (1974)

5 If the materials of the art of music are ever
assembled into a new style comparable to that
of the great styles of the past . . . Ruggles will
be among the men who will have contributed to
its making.

   Charles Seeger, in 1932, quoted in Yates, *Twentieth
Century Music* (1968)

RUSSIA

6 [Of Glinka's *A Life for the Tsar*] What an opera
you can make out of our national tunes! Show
me a people who have more songs! . . .
Glinka's opera is only a beautiful beginning.

   Nikolai Gogol, in *The Contemporary,* 1836

7 The new Russian school has undertaken to
bring to light certain principles of the highest
importance . . . Dramatic music must always
have an intrinsic worth, as absolute music,
independent of the text . . . Vocal music must
be in perfect agreement with the sense of the
words . . . The structure of the scenes
composing an opera must depend entirely on
the relation of the characters, and on the
general movement of the play.

   César Cui, in *La Revue et gazette musicale,* 1878–9

8 [Of Stravinsky's *The Firebird*] Lord, how much
more than genius this is – it is real Russia!

   Sergey Rakhmaninov, quoted in Bertensson and
Leyda, *Sergey Rachmaninoff* (1965)

9 [Of Russia] I would describe the music needed
here as 'light serious' or 'serious light' music; it
is by no means easy to find the term which
suits it. Above all, it must be tuneful, simply

and comprehensibly tuneful, and must not be
repetitious or stamped with triviality.

   Sergey Prokofiev, in *Izvestia,* 1934

10 But oh, these Russians! — as Busoni once
remarked, these chemists, admirals, and
amateurs, with their fur collars and the flavour
of dandruff.

   Neville Cardus, in *The Manchester Guardian,* 1938

11 The Russian contribution to the repertoire of
the lyric theatre, although less vigorous and
revolutionary than the German, and inferior in
architectonic skill to the French or in lyrical
facility to the Italian, is perhaps the most
noteworthy of the nineteenth century. Of a
consistently higher musical level than the first
and of a more dignified order of utterance than
the others, its two principal attributes are
nobility of conception and the absence of
cheapness and vulgarity, both evidences of a
culture rooted soundly in simplicity and good
taste.

   Sir Thomas Beecham, *A Mingled Chime* (1944)

12 The greatest crisis in my life as a composer was
the loss of Russia, and its language not only of
music but of words.

   Igor Stravinsky, *Themes and Conclusions* (1972)

13 [Of Rackmaninov's Vespers] I have heard some
people call it extreme. They fail to understand
there are no extremes in Russia.

   Michael Moorcock, *Byzantium Endures* (1981)

SAINT-SAËNS

14 There is nothing more difficult than talking
about music.

   Camille Saint-Saëns, quoted in Harding, *Saint-Saëns*
(1965)

15 We pursued a different ideal, he [Bizet] seeking
passion and life above all things, I running after
the chimera of purity of style and perfection of
form.

   Camille Saint-Saëns, quoted in Dean, *Bizet* (1975)

16 [Returning unsolicited compositions] Do *I* send
you *my* works to look at?

   Camille Saint-Saëns, quoted in Harding, *Saint-Saëns*
(1965)

17 He who does not prefer a folk tune of a lovely
character, or a Gregorian chant without any
accompaniment, to a series of dissonant and
pretentious chords does not love music.

   Camille Saint-Saëns, *Ecole buissonnière* (1913)

18 It's very odd! When I hear Massenet's operas I
always long for Saint-Saëns'. I should add that
hearing Saint-Saëns' operas makes me long for
Massenet's.

   Henri Gauthier-Villars, quoted in Harding, *Massenet*
(1970)

1   Saint-Saëns has informed a delighted public
    that since the war began he has composed
    music for the stage, melodies, an elegy, and a
    piece for the trombone. If he'd been making
    shell-cases instead it might have been all the
    better for music.

    Maurice Ravel, Letter, 1916

SATIE

2   Two or three hundred years ago, very few of
    today's musicians of the Butte were alive: their
    names were unknown to the public at large, or
    at small. All that has changed, especially — it
    seems — during the last ten years.

    Erik Satie, 'Montmartre Musicians' (1900)

3   Before I compose a piece, I walk round it
    several times, accompanied by myself.

    Erik Satie, quoted in *Bulletin des editions musicales*, 1913

4   An artist must organize his life. Here is the
    exact timetable of my daily activities. Get up:
    7.18 am; be inspired: 10.23 to 11.47 am. I take
    lunch at 12.11 pm and leave the table at 12.14
    pm.

    Erik Satie, *Memoirs of an Amnesiac* (1914), 'A
    Musician's Day'

5   When I was young, people used to say to me:
    Wait until you're fifty, you'll see. I am fifty. I
    haven't seen anything.

    Erik Satie, *Le Coq* (1920)

6   I have never written a note I didn't mean.

    Erik Satie, quoted in Harding, *Erik Satie* (1975)

7   For Erik Satie, the sweet medieval musician
    who has strayed into this century for the joy of
    his very friendly Claude Debussy.

    Claude Debussy, dedication on a copy of his *Cinq
    poèmes de Baudelaire* made in 1892

8   [Of Satie's *Parade*] One does not know which to
    admire most, the pretentiousness or the
    poverty.

    André Gide, Diary, 1921

9   Satie gave comic titles to his music in order to
    protect his works from persons obsessed with
    the sublime.

    Jean Cocteau, quoted in Myers, *Modern French Music*
    (1971)

10 My brother was always difficult to understand.
    He doesn't seem to have been quite normal.

    Olga Satie, quoted in Harding, *Erik Satie* (1975)

11 *Parade* confirmed me still further in my
    conviction of Satie's merit in the part he had
    played in French music by opposing to the
    vagueness of a decrepit impressionism a precise
    and firm language stripped of all pictorial
    embellishments.

    Igor Stravinsky, quoted in Kendall, *The Tender Tyrant:
    Nadia Boulanger* (1976)

THE SAXOPHONE

12 Posterity will never forgive you, Adolphe Sax!

    Saturday Review of Literature, caption to cartoon of
    Sax in his saxophone workshop, quoted in Horwood,
    Adolphe Sax (1980)

13 The saxophone is the embodied spirit of beer.

    Arnold Bennett, attr.

ALESSANDRO AND DOMENICO SCARLATTI

14 [Of Alessandro Scarlatti's cantatas] He makes
    use of all sorts of dissonance to express the
    force of the words and afterwards resolves
    them so well that indeed the most beautiful
    concords are hardly so sweet and harmonious
    as his discords.

    François Raguenet, *Parallèle des italiens et des français*
    (trans. 1709)

15 [Domenico] Scarlatti frequently told M.
    L'Augier that he was sensible he had broke
    through all the rules of composition in his
    lessons [i.e. *Essercizi*]; but asked if his
    deviations offended the ear? and, upon being
    answered in the negative, he said, that he
    thought there was scarce any other rule, worth
    the attention of a man of genius, than that of
    not displeasing the only sense of which music
    is the object.

    Charles Burney, *A General History of Music* (1776-89)

16 It is time to consider how Domenico Scarlatti
    condensed so much music into so few bars
    with never a crabbed turn or congested
                        cadence,
    never a boast or a see-here.

    Basil Bunting, *Briggflatts* (1966)

SCHOENBERG

See also TWELVE-NOTE MUSIC.

17 I believe art is born, not of 'I can', but of 'I
    must'!

    Arnold Schoenberg, 'Problems in Teaching Art', in
    Musikalisches Taschenbuch, II, 1910

18 [Of Richard Strauss] He is no longer of the
    slightest artistic interest to me, and whatever I
    may once have learned from him, I am thankful
    to say I misunderstood.

    Arnold Schoenberg, in 1914, quoted in Rosen,
    Schoenberg (1976)

19 *Pierrot lunaire is not to be sung!* Song melodies
    must be balanced and shaped in quite a
    different way from spoken melodies.

    Arnold Schoenberg, Letter, 1931

20 [Of his Violin Concerto] I am delighted to add
    another unplayable work to the repertoire. I
    want the Concerto to be difficult and I want the
    little finger to become longer. I can wait.

    Arnold Schoenberg, quoted in Machlis, *Introduction to
    Contemporary Music* (1963)

1 I have made many friends here [in Barcelona] who have never heard my works but who play tennis with me. What will they think of me when they hear my horrible dissonances?

Arnold Schoenberg, quoted in Rosen, *Schoenberg* (1976)

2 My music is not modern, it is only badly played.

Arnold Schoenberg, quoted in Rosen, *Schoenberg* (1976)

3 There is still much good music to be written in C major.

Arnold Schoenberg, quoted in Machlis, *Introduction to Contemporary Music* (1963)

4 [Asked if he was Schoenberg the controversial composer] I have to admit that I am: but it's like this — somebody had to be, and nobody else wanted to, so I took it on myself.

Arnold Schoenberg, quoted in Reich, *Schoenberg* (1971)

5 I am a conservative who was forced to become a revolutionary.

Arnold Schoenberg, quoted in Reich, *Schoenberg* (1971)

6 That you should regard all I have tried to do in the last fifty years as an achievement strikes me as in some respects an overestimate. My own feeling was that I had fallen into an ocean of boiling water; and, as I couldn't swim and knew no other way out, I struggled with my arms and legs as best I could. I don't know what saved me, or why I wasn't drowned or boiled alive — perhaps my only merit was that I never gave in.

Arnold Schoenberg, quoted in Stuckenschmidt, *Arnold Schoenberg* (1957)

7 [Of Schoenberg's *Verklärte Nacht*] It sounds as if someone had smeared the score of *Tristan* while it was still wet.

Unnamed contemporary, quoted in Rosen, *Schoenberg* (1976)

8 His day will come.

Alban Berg, Letter to Frida Semler Seabury, 1907

9 Not the lunatic he is generally taken for.

Ernest Newman, in *The Birmingham Post*, 1912

10 Only a psychiatrist can help poor Schoenberg now ... He would do better to shovel snow instead of scribbling on music paper ... Better give him the grant [from the Mahler Memorial Foundation] anyway ... You can never tell what posterity will say.

Richard Strauss, Letter to Alma Mahler, 1913

11 Why is Schoenberg's Music so Hard to Understand?

Alban Berg, title of article in Schoenberg *Festschrift* (1924)

12 [Of Schoenberg's twelve-note system] From now on music will no longer be what it was, but has become what it will be. This change can be likened to the change from the Euclidean geometry to the higher mathematics of a Minkowski, an Einstein.

Louis Danz, 'Schoenberg the Inevitable', in Armitage (ed.), *Schoenberg* (1937)

13 These works [of Schoenberg] are magnificent in their failure. It is not the composer who fails in the work; history, rather, denies the work in itself.

T.W. Adorno, *The Philosophy of Modern Music* (1949)

14 Emotionally Schoenberg was still a part of the nineteenth century.

Aaron Copland, in 1970, quoted in Jacobson, *Reverberations* (1975)

15 [Of *Gurrelieder*] A proof if you want it — and I often do — that Schoenberg could, as they used to say about Picasso, draw when he wanted to.

Lord Harewood, *The Tongs and the Bones* (1981)

SCHUBERT

16 It sometimes seems to me as if I did not belong to this world at all.

Franz Schubert, attr., quoted in Einstein, *Schubert* (trans. 1951)

17 'My peace is gone, my heart is sore, I shall find it never and nevermore,' I may well sing every day now, for each night, on retiring to bed, I hope I may not wake again, and each morning but recalls yesterday's grief.

Franz Schubert, Letter to Kupelwiesser, 1824

18 [Of his *Ave Maria*] I never force myself into a devout mood, and never compose such hymns or prayers except when I am unconsciously inspired by Her. Then, however, it is generally real, true devotion.

Franz Schubert, Letter, 1825

19 Here lie rich treasure and still fairer hopes.

Franz Grillparzer, Epitaph for Schubert

20 [On Schubert's premature death] A man is not taken away before he has said all he has to say.

Hugo Wolf, quoted in Rolland, *Essays on Music* (1948), 'Hugo Wolf'

21 I wish I had written that.

Paul Hindemith, on playing Schubert's marches for piano duet, quoted in Skelton, *Paul Hindemith* (1975)

22 [Of Schubert's Symphony No. 5] This is charming music to hear in a beer garden, with the right company.

Neville Cardus, in *The Manchester Guardian*, 1938

23 Words for Schubert were like a sort of preliminary scaffolding — which could be dispensed with once the tonal edifice was up.

Neville Cardus, in *The Manchester Guardian*, 1960

1 Schubert was a miracle — he did not even need brains.

Neville Cardus, *The Delights of Music* (1966)

SCHUMANN

2 I still consider that music is the ideal music of the soul: but some think it is only meant to tickle the ear, others treat it like a sum in arithmetic and act accordingly.

Robert Schumann, Letter to Johanna Schumann, 1832

3 I have been composing so much that it really seems quite uncanny at times. I cannot help it, and should like to sing myself to death, like a nightingale.

Robert Schumann, Letter to Clara Wieck, 1840

4 Only when the form grows clear to you, will the spirit become so too.

Robert Schumann, 'Advice to Young Musicians' (1848)

5 The laws of morality are also those of art.

Robert Schumann, 'Advice to Young Musicians' (1848)

6 Everything beautiful is difficult, the short the most difficult.

Robert Schumann, quoted in Walker (ed.), *Robert Schumann: the Man and his Music* (1972)

7 I should not like to be understood by everybody.

Robert Schumann, quoted in Headington, *The Bodley Head History of Western Music* (1974)

8 It is impossible to communicate with Schumann. The man is hopeless; he does not talk at all.

Richard Wagner, quoted in Gall, *Johannes Brahms* (1961)

9 Schumann's our music-maker now.

Robert Browning, 'Dis aliter visum'

10 To me, Schumann's memory is holy. The noble, pure artist forever remains my ideal. I will hardly be privileged ever to love a better person.

Johannes Brahms, Letter to J.O. Grimm

11 [Of *Manfred*] What a masterpiece, but what despair! It's enough to make you long for death.

Georges Bizet, quoted in Dean, *Bizet* (1975)

12 My ideal!

Edward Elgar, Letter, 1883

13 I disagree with this idea of re-orchestrating Schumann but I do think he can be *helped*.

Sir John Barbirolli, Letter to Evelyn Rothwell, 1939

14 [Schumann's] intimate approach ... salutes us, not so much as an audience to be conquered by rhetorical argument as a friend to be talked over by gentle persuasion.

Sir Thomas Beecham, *A Mingled Chime* (1944)

15 Schumann ... has accomplished the miraculous feat of clothing exquisite and delicate fancies in subtle and secret phrases that each one of us feels to have been devised for his own particular understanding.

Sir Thomas Beecham, *A Mingled Chime* (1944)

16 Schumann is *the* composer of childhood ... both because he created a children's imaginative world and because children learn some of their first music in his marvellous piano albums.

Igor Stravinsky, *Themes and Conclusions* (1972)

SCHÜTZ

17 If one or the other tune displeases you, then use, instead, the old, familiar melodies which you will find listed in the index to this book, or else try to help others compose better melodies and publish them to the greater Glory of God.

Heinrich Schütz, Preface to *The Psalms of David* (1628)

18 The most spiritual musician the world has ever seen.

Alfred Einstein, *Heinrich Schütz* (1928)

SCOTLAND

19 In the opinion of many, Scotland not only equalled Ireland her teacher in music, but has prevailed over and surpassed her, so that they look to Scotland as the fountain of this art.

Giraldus Cambrensis, *Topographia Hibernica* (c. 1185)

20 I cannot understand bot musike sall perish in this land alutterlye.

Thomas Wood, *Psalter* (1562-6)

21 And show that music may have as good a fate
In Albion's Glen as Umbria's green retreat,
And with Corelli's soft Italian song,
Mix 'Cowdenknowes' and 'Winter nights are long'.

Allan Ramsay, 'To the Music Club' (1721). (In this context, 'Albion' is Scotland.)

22 The Scots are all musicians. Every man you meet plays on the flute, the violin or the violoncello, and there is one nobleman whose compositions are universally admired.

Tobias Smollett, Letter, 1756

23 For nought can cheer the heart sae weel
As can a canty Highland reel.

Robert Fergusson, 'An Elegy on Scotch Music'

24 That I for puir auld Scotland's sake
Some usefu' plan or buik could make
Or sing a sang at least.

Robert Burns, 'To the Guidwife of Wauchope House'

25 Contented wi' little and cantie wi' mair,
Whene'er I forgather wi' Sorrow and Care,

I gie them a skelp, as they're creeping alang,
Wi' a cog o' gude swats and an auld Scottish
sang.

Robert Burns, 'Contented wi' Little'

1 The Chinese scale, take it which way we will, is
certainly very Scottish.

Charles Burney, in 1789, quoted in Headington, *The
Bodley Head History of Western Music* (1974)

2 Of all districts of the inhabited world, pre-
eminently the singing country.

John Ruskin, quoted in Farmer, *A History of Music in
Scotland* (1947)

3 Let me play to you tunes without measure or
end,
Tunes that are born to die without a herald,
As a flight of storks rises from a marsh, circles,
And alights on the spot from which it rose.

Hugh MacDiarmid, 'Bagpipe Music' (1943)

SHOSTAKOVICH

4 Creative reply of a Soviet artist to just criticism.

Dmitri Shostakovich, note on score of his Symphony
No. 5 (1937)

5 I always try to make myself as widely
understood as possible; and if I don't succeed, I
consider it my own fault.

Dmitri Shostakovich, quoted in Machlis, *Introduction
to Contemporary Music* (1963)

6 [Of *Lady Macbeth of Mtsensk*] It is a leftist
bedlam instead of human music. The inspiring
quality of good music is sacrificed in favour of
petty-bourgeois clowning. This game may end
badly.

Pravda, 1936

7 [Of *Lady Macbeth of Mtsensk*] The composer
apparently does not set himself the task of
listening to the desires and expectations of the
Soviet public. He scrambles sounds to make
them interesting to formalist elements who
have lost all taste.

Pravda, 1936

8 [Of *Lady Macbeth of Mtsensk*] Pornophony.

Unnamed American critic, quoted in Lebrecht, *Discord*
(1982)

9 [On Shostakovich's Symphony No. 11] This
symphony is supposed to be concerned with
the events of the 1905 revolution. I was quite
sure when I heard it that the use of 1905 was a
kind of political alibi, since this was a matter of
known revolutionary history. The music to me
was self-evidently about Shostakovich's own
experiences in the catastrophe of his life.

Michael Tippett, quoted in Bowen, *Michael Tippett*
(1982)

SIBELIUS

10 I believe that music alone — that is to say,
absolute music — cannot by itself satisfy.

Jean Sibelius, Letter to J.H. Erkko, 1893

11 Give me the loneliness either of the Finnish
forest or of a big city.

Jean Sibelius, quoted in Layton, *Sibelius* (1965)

12 Now, it's Sibelius, and when they're tired of
him, they'll boost up Mahler and Bruckner.

Frederick Delius, quoted in Fenby, *Delius as I knew him*
(1936)

13 Ah, Sibelius! Poor, poor Sibelius! A tragic case!

Nadia Boulanger, quoted in Johnson, *Sibelius* (1960)

14 In his work a means of escape has been found
from outmoded romanticism on the one hand
and from a barren objectivity on the other.

Neville Cardus, in *The Manchester Guardian*, 1935

15 Sibelius justified the austerity of his old age by
saying that while other composers were
engaged in manufacturing cocktails he offered
the public pure cold water.

Neville Cardus, in *The Manchester Guardian*, 1938

16 [Of a passage in Sibelius's Symphony No. 6] I
think he must have been drunk when he wrote
that.

Benjamin Britten, quoted in Headington, *Britten* (1981)

SILENCE

17 Thus with violence shall that great city Babylon
be thrown down, and shall be found no more at
all.
And the voice of harpers, and musicians, and of
pipers, and trumpeters, shall be heard no more
at all in thee.

Revelation 18:21-22

18 *Portia:* . . . Music — hark.
Nerissa: It is your music, madam, of the house.
Portia: Nothing is good, I see, without respect
— Methinks it sounds much sweeter than by
day.
Nerissa: Silence bestows that virtue on it,
madam.

William Shakespeare, *The Merchant of Venice*, V.i

19 Rose-cheeked Laura, come;
Sing thou smoothly with thy beauty's
Silent music, either other
    Sweetly gracing.

Thomas Campion, *Observations in the Art of English
Poesie* (1602), 'Laura'

20 No voice; but oh! the silence sank
Like music on my heart.

Samuel Taylor Coleridge, 'The Rime of the Ancient
Mariner' (1798)

1 Heard melodies are sweet, but those unheard
   Are sweeter; therefore, ye soft pipes, play
   on;
   Not to the sensual ear, but, more endear'd,
   Pipe to the spirit ditties of no tone.

John Keats, 'Ode on a Grecian Urn' (1819)

2 [Of the grave]
   Silence more musical than any song.

Christina Rossetti, 'Rest' (1849)

3 To drop some golden orb of perfect song
   Into our deep, dear silence.

Elizabeth Barrett Browning, *Sonnets from the Portuguese*
(1850)

4 It is the little rift within the lute,
   That by and by will make the music mute,
   And ever widening slowly silence all.

Alfred, Lord Tennyson, *Idylls of the King*, 'Merlin and
Vivien'

5 There's no music in a 'rest', Katie, that I know
   of: but there's the making of music in it. And
   people are always missing that part of the life-
   melody.

John Ruskin, *Ethics of the Dust* (1886)

6 [In *Pelléas et Mélisande*] Quite spontaneously I
   have used silence as a means of expression
   (don't laugh). It is perhaps the only means of
   bringing into relief the emotional value of a
   phrase.

Claude Debussy, Letter to Chausson, 1893

7 Elected Silence, sing to me
   And beat upon my whorlèd ear,
   Pipe me to pastures still and be
   The music that I care to hear.

Gerald Manley Hopkins, 'The Habit of Perfection'

8 The tense silence between two movements — in
   itself music, in this environment — leaves
   wider scope for divination than the more
   determinate, but therefore less elastic, sound.

Ferruccio Busoni, *Entwurf einer neuen Aesthetik der
Tonkunst* (1907)

9 Rests always sound well!

Arnold Schoenberg, quoted in Reich, *Schoenberg* (1971)

10 The song is ended
   But the melody lingers on.

Irving Berlin, song from *Ziegfeld Follies* (1927)

11 After silence that which comes nearest to
   expressing the inexpressible is music.

Aldous Huxley, 'Music at Night' (1931)

12 Perhaps, said Kretschmar, it was music's
   deepest wish not to be heard at all, nor even
   seen, nor yet felt: but only — if that were
   possible — in some Beyond, the other side of
   sense and sentiment, to be perceived and
   contemplated as pure mind, pure spirit.

Thomas Mann, *Doctor Faustus* (1947); trans. Lowe-Porter

13 If one takes composing with deadly
   seriousness, one ultimately has to ask whether,
   today, it is not becoming totally ideological.
   Therefore, without the consolation that it can't
   go on like this, one must unmetaphorically
   come face to face with the possibility of falling
   silent.

T.W. Adorno, quoted in Henze, *Music and Politics*
(1982)

14 Try as we may to make a silence, we cannot.

John Cage, *Silence* (1961), 'Experimental Music' (1957)

15 The notes I handle no better than many
   pianists. But the pauses between the notes —
   ah, that is where the art resides.

Artur Schnabel, quoted in *Chicago Daily News*, 1958

16 Night and silence — these are two of the things
   I cherish most.

Benjamin Britten, quoted in Headington, *Britten* (1981)

17 All my concerts had no sounds in them: they
   were completely silent ... people had to make
   their own music in their minds.

Yoko Ono, interview in *Rolling Stone*, 1968

18 Remember silence is curious about its opposite
   Element which you shall learn to represent.

W.S. Graham, 'Johann Joachim Quantz's Five
Lessons'

SINGING

See also SONG.

19 O come let us sing unto the Lord.

Psalms 95:1

20 [Hostile definition of 'hocketting'] Sometimes
   thou mayest see a man with open mouth, not to
   sing, but as it were to breath out his last gasp,
   by shutting in his breath and by a certain
   ridiculous interception of his voice to threaten
   silence, and now again to imitate the agonies of
   a dying man, or the ecstasies of such as suffer.

Aelred of Rievaulx, quoted in Reese, *Music in the
Middle Ages* (1941)

21 *Bouche qui mord a la chanson ne mord pas a la
   grappe.* The mouth which is busy with song is
   not busy with the grape.

Proverb, quoted in About, *Les Mariages de Paris* (1856)

22 Since singing is so good a thing
   I wish all men would learn to sing.

William Byrd, *Psalmes, Sonets & Songs* (1588)

23 The exercise of singing is delightful to nature
   and good to preserve the health of man.
   It doth strengthen all the parts of the breast,
   and doth open the pipes.
   It is a singular good remedy for a stutting and
   stammering in the speech.

William Byrd, *Psalmes, Sonets & Songs* (1588)

1   There is not any music of instruments
    whatsoever comparable to that which is made
    of the voices of men, where the voices are good,
    and the same well sorted and ordered.
    William Byrd, *Psalmes, Sonets & Songs* (1588)

2   Can you sing? . . . Basely . . . And you? . . .
    Meanly . . . And what can you do? . . . If they
    double it I will treble it.
    John Lyly, *Gallathea* (1588), V.iii. (The *meane* was the
    voice between treble and tenor.)

3   Warble, child, make passionate my sense of
    hearing.
    (Armado)
    William Shakespeare, *Love's Labour's Lost*, III.i

4   . . . thy tongue
    Makes Welsh as sweet as ditties highly penned,
    Sung by a fair queen in a summer's bower
    With ravishing division to her lute.
    (Mortimer)
    William Shakespeare, *Henry IV, Part One*, III.i

5   *Sir Andrew Aguecheek:* A mellifluous voice, as I
    am a true knight.
    Sir Toby Belch: A contagious breath.
    Sir Andrew Aguecheek: Very sweet and
    contagious, i' faith.
    Sir Toby Belch: To hear by the nose, it is dulcet
    in contagion.
    William Shakespeare, *Twelfth Night*, II.iii

6   List to the heavy part the music bears,
    Woe weeps out her division, when she sings.
    Ben Jonson, *Cynthia's Revels*, I.i (1600)

7   I see ye have a singing face.
    John Fletcher, *The Wild-Goose Chase*, II.ii (1621)

8   Let but thy voice engender with the string
    And angels will be born, while thou dost sing.
    Robert Herrick, 'Upon Her Voice'

9   So smooth, so sweet, so sil'vry is thy voice,
    As, could they hear, the damn'd would make
                                        no noise,
    But listen to thee (walking in thy chamber)
    Melting melodious words, to lutes of amber.
    Robert Herrick, 'Upon Julia's Voice'

10 So just, so small, yet in so sweet a note,
    It seem'd the music melted in the throat.
    John Dryden, 'The Flower and the Leaf'

11 [Of one of Handel's singers]
    When *Anastasia's* voice commands the strain,
    The melting warble thrills through every vein;
    Thought stands suspense, and silence pleas'd
                                        attends,
    While in her notes the heav'nly Choir descends.
    John Gay, *Epistles on Several Occasions* (1720)

12 Whoever plays an instrument must be
    conversant with singing.
    Georg Phillipp Telemann, quoted in Young, *Handel*
    (1947)

13 Let the singing singers
    With vocal voices, most vociferous,
    In sweet vociferation, out-vociferise
    Ev'n sound itself.
    Henry Carey, *Chrononhotonthologos* (1734)

14 Man was never meant to sing:
    And all his mimic organs e'er expressed
    Was but an imitative howl at best.
    John Langhorne, *The Country Justice* (c. 1766)

15 Singing is no more than a form of declamation.
    Christoph Willibald von Gluck, Preface to *Paride ed
    Elena* (1770)

16 Of MUSICAL TONES the most grateful to the ear
    are such as are produced by the vocal organ.
    And, next to singing, the most pleasing kinds
    are those which approach nearest to the vocal;
    such as can be sustained, swelled, and
    diminished, at pleasure. Of these, the first in
    rank are such as the most excellent performers
    produce from the violin, flute, and hautbois.
    Charles Burney, *A General History of Music* (1776-89)

17 Piping songs of pleasant glee.
    William Blake, Introduction to *Songs of Innocence*
    (1789)

18 The first and most sacred duty in singing is the
    utmost fidelity to diction. None the less, cases
    occur — in songs less than in extended pieces
    — where the altogether correct stress of single
    syllables must perhaps be sacrificed to the
    complete inner truth of the melody.
    Carl Maria von Weber, Letter, 1817

19   None knew whether
    The voice or lute was most divine,
    So wondrously they went together.
    Thomas Moore, *Lalla Rookh*, Prologue (1817)

20 My soul is an enchanted boat,
    Which, like a sleeping swan, doth float
    Upon the silver waves of thy sweet singing.
    Percy Bysshe Shelley, *Prometheus Unbound*, II.v (1820)

21 No instrument is satisfactory except in so far as
    it approximates to the sound of the human
    voice.
    Stendhal, *Life of Rossini* (1824)

22 Her fingers witched the chords they passed
                                        along,
    And her lips seemed to kiss the soul in song.
    Thomas Campbell, 'Theodric' (1824)

23 I do but sing because I must,
    And pipe but as the linnets sing.
    Alfred, Lord Tennyson, *In Memoriam A.H.H.* (1850)

24 I cannot sing the old songs
    I sang long years ago,
    For heart and voice would fail me,
    And foolish tears would flow.
    Claribel, 'Fireside Thoughts'

1   I cannot sing the old songs now!
        It is not that I deem them low;
    'Tis that I can't remember how
        They go.

    C.S. Calverley, 'Changed'

2   A singer able to sing so much as sixteen bars of
    good music in a natural, well-poised and
    sympathetic voice, without effort, without
    affectation, without tricks, without
    exaggeration, without hiatuses, without
    hiccupping, without barking, without baa-ing
    — such a singer is a rare, a very rare, an
    excessively rare bird.

    Hector Berlioz, *A travers chant* (1862)

3   *Et, Ô ces voix d'enfants chantants dans la coupole!*
    And, O those voices of children singing under
    the dome!

    Paul Verlaine, 'Parsifal, A Jules Tellier'

4   A tenor is not a man but a disease.

    Hans von Bülow, attr.

5   [To a tenor whose singing Massenet disliked]
    You sang like a composer.

    Jules Massenet, quoted in Harding, *Massenet* (1970)

6   The singer's frock is very valuable in helping
    her to make clear the meaning of her songs.

    Ursula Greville, quoted in Martens, *The Art of the
    Prima Donna* (1923)

7   Tenors get women by the score.

    James Joyce, *Ulysses* (1922)

8   A base barreltone voice.

    James Joyce, *Ulysses* (1922)

9   Concerted singing does have one clear
    advantage over other kinds, inasmuch as it
    enables a man to let off all the emotional steam
    with which he may be seething, without
    hearing in the glorious welter of noise around
    him either the sound of his neighbour's voice or
    that of his own.

    Sir Thomas Beecham, *A Mingled Chime* (1944)

10 Abstract it may be, the human voice ... But that
    is a kind of abstraction more like that of the
    naked body — it is after all more a pudendum.
    (Leverkühn)

    Thomas Mann, *Doctor Faustus* (1947); trans. Lowe-
    Porter

11 There must be a strenuous attempt to replace
    music that comes from the fingers and the
    mechanical playing of instruments with music
    from the soul and based on singing.

    Zoltán Kodály, Preface to *Fifty-five Two-part Exercises*
    (1954)

12 Singing lieder is like putting a piece of music
    under a microscope.

    Janet Baker, quoted in *Opera News*, 1977

13 It was my idea to make my voice work in the
    same way as a trombone or violin — not
    sounding like them, but 'playing' the voice like
    those instruments.

    Frank Sinatra, quoted in Shepherd, *Tin Pan Alley*
    (1982)

SIRENS

14 Since once I sat upon a promontory,
    And heard a mermaid on a dolphin's back
    Uttering such dulcet and harmonious breath,
    That the rude sea grew civil at her song,
    And certain stars shot madly from their
        spheres,
    To hear the sea-maid's music.
    (Oberon)

    William Shakespeare, *A Midsummer Night's Dream*, II.i

15 What song the Sirens sang, or what name
    Achilles assumed when he hid himself among
    women, though puzzling questions, are not
    beyond all conjecture.

    Sir Thomas Browne, *Urn Burial* (1658)

16 Fair Melody! kind Siren! I've no choice;
    I must be thy sad servant evermore;
    I cannot choose but kneel here and adore.

    John Keats, *Endymion*, IV (1818)

17 'The name of those fabulous animals (pagan, I
    regret to say) who used to sing in the water,
    has quite escaped me.' Mr George Chuzzlewit
    suggested 'Swans.' 'No,' said Mr Pecksniff.
    'Not swans. Very like swans, too. Thank you.'
    The nephew ... propounded 'Oysters.' 'No,'
    said Mr Pecksniff ... 'nor oysters. But by no
    means unlike oysters; a very excellent idea;
    thank you my dear sir, very much. Wait. Sirens!
    Dear me! Sirens, of course.'

    Charles Dickens, *Martin Chuzzlewit* (1843-4)

18 I have heard the mermaids singing, each to
        each;
    I do not think that they will sing to me.

    T.S. Eliot, 'The Love Song of J. Alfred Prufrock'

SKRYABIN

19 I wish I could possess the world as I possess a
    woman.

    Alexander Skryabin, quoted in Macdonald, *Skryabin*
    (1978)

20 I was once a Chopinist, then a Wagnerist, now I
    am only a Scriabinist.

    Alexander Skryabin, in 1903, quoted in Bowers,
    Scriabin (1969)

21 [Skryabin's *Poem of Esctasy*] The obscenest piece
    of music ever written.

    Anon., quoted in Macdonald, *Skryabin* (1978)

22 The voluptuous dentist.

    Aldous Huxley, *Essays Old and New* (1926)

1   Scriabin's music sounds like I think —
    sometimes. Has that faroff cosmic itch. Divinely
    fouled up. All fire and air ... It was like a bath
    of ice; cocaine and rainbows.

    Henry Miller, *Nexus* (1945)

2   One morning I woke up with the realisation
    that Scriabin's eroticism was good only for
    high-strung adolescents, that his orgasms were
    fake, and that his musical craft was singularly
    old-fashioned, dusty, and academic.

    Nicolas Nabokov, *Old Friends and New Music* (1951)

3   When he had pulled out all the stops he looked
    for more stops to pull out instead of
    recognizing the need for a new discipline.

    Colin Wilson, *Brandy of the Damned* (1964)

4   Skryabin is near to us because he embraces in
    his work that fascination of revolution.

    Anatol Lunacharsky, *Revolutionary Silhouettes* (1968)

SLEEP

5   She bids you on the wanton rushes lay you
                                            down
    And rest your gentle head upon her lap,
    And she will sing the song that pleaseth you
    And on your eyelids crown the god of sleep.
    (Glendower)

    William Shakespeare, *Henry IV, Part One*, III.i

6   Why rather, sleep, liest thou in the smoky cribs
    Upon uneasy pallets stretching thee
    And hushed with buzzing night-flies to thy
                                            slumber,
    Than in the perfumed chambers of the great
    Under the canopies of costly state
    And lulled with sound of sweetest melody?
    (King Henry)

    William Shakespeare, *Henry IV, Part Two*, III.i

7   The isle of full of noises,
    Sounds and sweet airs, that give delight and
                                            hurt not.
    Sometimes a thousand twangling instruments
    Will hum about mine ears, and sometime voices
    That, if I then had waked after long sleep,
    Will make me sleep again.
    (Caliban)

    William Shakespeare, *The Tempest*, III.ii

8   While the bee with honied thigh,
    That at her flowery work doth sing,
    And the waters murmuring
    And such consort as they keep,
    Entice the dewy-feather'd sleep.

    John Milton, 'Il Penseroso' (1632)

9   Music, to a nice ear, is a hazardous amusement,
    as long attention to it is very fatiguing.

    William Cullen, *First Lines of the Practice of Physic*,
    (1778-84)

10 There is sweet music here that softer falls
    Than petals from blown roses on the grass ...
    Music that gentlier on the spirit lies,
    Than tired eyelids upon tire eyes;
    Music that brings sweet sleep down from the
                                            blissful skies.

    Alfred, Lord Tennyson, 'The Lotos-Eaters' (1833)

11   ... stupor, such as music makes
    For sleepers halfway waking.

    Wallace Stevens, 'The Comedian as the Letter C'
    (1924)

SMETANA

12 By the grace of God and with his help I shall
    one day be a Liszt in technique and a Mozart in
    composition.

    Bedřich Smetana, Diary, 1845

13 [On his deafness] If my illness is incurable,
    then I should prefer to be delivered from this
    miserable existence.

    Bedřich Smetana, Diary, 1875

14 My quartet, *From My Life*, does not consist
    merely of a formal game of tones and motives,
    by means of which the composer exhibits his
    skill. On the contrary, my aim was to present to
    the listener scenes from my life.

    Bedřich Smetana, quoted in Morgenstern, *Composers
    on Music* (1958)

15 [Of his quartet, *From My Life*] A work which in
    a sense is private, and therefore written for four
    instruments which should converse together in
    an intimate circle about the things which so
    deeply trouble me. Nothing more.

    Bedřich Smetana, quoted in Cardus, *The Delights of
    Music* (1966)

16 [Of his opera *Libuše*] I am not counterfeiting an
    esteemed composer ... but others ... think I
    introduce Wagnerism!!! I am sufficiently
    occupied with Smetanism, since that is the only
    honest style!

    Bedřich Smetana, Letter to Adolf Čech, 1882

17 With me, the form of each composition is the
    outcome of the subject.

    Bedřich Smetana, quoted in Cardus, *The Delights of
    Music* (1966)

18 Here is a composer with a genuine Czech heart,
    an artist by the Grace of God!

    Franz Liszt, in 1857, quoted in Clapham, *Smetana*
    (1972)

19 My memories of Bedřich Smetana are like a
    picture of how children imagine God: in the
    clouds.

    Leoš Janáček, in *Dalibor*, 1909

THE SONATA

1 I see you have a singing face — a heavy, dull, sonata face.

George Farquhar, *The Inconstant*, II.i (1702)

2 *Sonate, que me veux-tu?*

Bernard Fontenelle, quoted in d'Alembert, *De la liberté de la musique* (1758)

3 How rich in content and full of significance the language of music is, we see from the repetitions, as well as the *Da capo*, the like of which would be unbearable in works composed in a language of words, but in music are very appropriate and beneficial, for, in order to comprehend it fully, we must hear it twice.

Arthur Schopenhauer, *The World as Will and Idea* (1818)

4 The sonata was said by a German critic to be intended by the earliest writers to show in the first movement what they could do, in the second what they could feel, and in the last how glad they were to have finished.

Philip H. Goepp, *Symphonies and their Meaning* (1897)

5 Back to 1st Theme — all nice Sonatas must have 1st Theme . . . made mostly as a joke to knock the mollycoddles out of their boxes and to kick out the softy ears!

Charles Ives, marginalia on the MS of his *Three-Page Sonata* (1905)

6 One yearns unspeakably for a composer who gives out his pair of honest themes, and then develops them unashamed, and then hangs a brisk coda to them, and then shuts up.

H.L. Mencken, 'Huneker in Motley' (1914)

7 [Of Beethoven's Sonata in C Minor, Op 111] The sonata had come, in the second, enormous movement, to an end, an end without any return. And when he [Kretschmar] said 'the sonata', he meant not only this one in C minor, but the sonata in general, as a species, as traditional art-form; it itself was here at an end, brought to its end, it had fulfilled its destiny.

Thomas Mann, *Doctor Faustus* (1947); trans. Lowe-Porter

8 I frequently compare a symphony or a sonata with a novel in which the themes are the characters. After we have made their acquaintance, we follow their evolution, the unfolding of their psychology. Their individual features linger with us as if present. Some of these characters arouse feelings of sympathy, others repel us. They are set off against one another or they join hands; they make love, they marry or they fight.

Arthur Honegger, *I am a Composer* (1951)

9 I believe the sonata/fugue problem will keep coming back at us, again and again, and will demand to be answered.

Hans Werner Henze, *Music and Politics* (1982), 'Experiments and the Avant-Garde' (1967)

10 The source . . . of the sonata . . . lies in concrete and vivid auditory imagery, an imagery necessarily conditioned by the cultural history of specific human societies, rather than in schematic abstractions.

Norman Cazden, quoted in Ewen, *American Composers* (1982)

SONG

See also SINGING, WORDS AND MUSIC.

11 The song of songs, which is Solomon's.

Song of Solomon 1:1

12 An I have not ballads made on you all and sung to filthy tunes, let a cup of sack be my poison. (Falstaff)

William Shakespeare, *Henry IV, Part One*, II.ii

13 And ever against eating cares,
Lap me in soft Lydian airs,
Married to immortal verse
Such as the meeting soul may pierce
In notes, with many a winding bout
Of linkèd sweetness, long drawn out.

John Milton, 'L'Allegro' (1632)

14 Soft words, with nothing in them, make a song.

Edmund Waller, 'To Mr Creech' (c. 1635)

15 *Tout finit par des chansons*. Everything ends in songs.

Pierre-Augustin Caron de Beaumarchais, *Le Mariage de Figaro*, last line (1784)

16 Our sweetest songs are those that tell of saddest thought.

Percy Bysshe Shelley, 'To a Skylark'

17 And deep things are song. It seems somehow the very central essence of us, song; as if all the rest were but wrappings and hulls.

Thomas Carlyle, *On Heroes, Hero-Worship, and the Heroic in History* (1841)

18 When I compose a song, my concern is not to make music but, first and foremost, to do justice to the poet's intentions. I have tried to let the poem reveal itself, and indeed to raise it to a higher power.

Edvard Grieg, Letter to Henry T. Finck

19 The setting to music of a poem must be an act of love, never a marriage of convenience.

Francis Poulenc, quoted in Bernac, *Francis Poulenc* (1977)

THE SPHERES

1 The morning stars sang together, and all the
   sons of God shouted for joy.

   Job 38:7

2 There is geometry in the humming of the
   strings. There is music in the spacings of the
   spheres.

   Pythagoras, quoted in Aristotle, *Metaphysics*

3 The single harmony produced by all the
   heavenly bodies singing and dancing together
   springs from one source and ends by achieving
   one purpose, and rightly bestowed the name
   not of 'disordered' but of 'ordered universe'
   upon the whole.

   Aristotle, *Metaphysics*

4 And after shewede he hym the nyne speres,
   And after that the melodye herde he
   That cometh of thilke speres thryes thre,
   That welle is of musik and melodye
   In this world here, and cause of armonye.

   Geoffrey Chaucer, *The Parlement of Foules*

5 And ther he saugh, with ful avysement,
   The erratik sterres, herkenyng armonye
   With sownes ful of hevenyssh melodie.

   Geoffrey Chaucer, *Troilus and Criseyde*

6 This mery musik and mellifluate
   Complete and full with novmeris od and evyn
   It causit be the moving of the hevin.

   Orpheus and Erudices (Asloan version)

7 The bodies of its circles, being solid smooth,
   and in their rolling motion, touching and
   rubbing against another, must of necessity
   produce a wonderful harmony: by the changes
   and entercaprings of which, the revolutions,
   motions, cadences, and carols of the asters and
   planets, are caused and transported. But that
   universally the hearing senses of these low
   world's creatures, dizzied and lulled asleep . . .
   by the continuation of that sound, how loud
   and great soever it be, cannot sensibly perceive
   or distinguish the same.

   Michel de Montaigne, *Essais* (1580); trans. Florio
   (1603)

8 How sweet the moonlight sleeps upon this
   bank.
   Here will we sit and let the sounds of music
   Creep in our ears; soft stillness and the night
   Become the touches of sweet harmony.
   Sit, Jessica. Look how the floor of heaven
   Is thick inlaid with patines of bright gold;
   There's not the smallest orb which thou
   behold'st
   But in his motion like an angel sings,
   Still quiring to the young-eyed cherubins;
   Such harmony is in immortal souls,

But whilst this muddy vesture of decay
Doth grossly close it in, we cannot hear it.
(Lorenzo)

   William Shakespeare, *The Merchant of Venice*, V.i

9   But hark, what music? . . .
   The music of the spheres . . .
                        Most heavenly music!
   It nips me unto listening, and thick slumber
   Hangs upon mine eyes.
   (Pericles)

   William Shakespeare, *Pericles*, V.i

10 Hark! hear you not a heavenly harmony?
    Is't Jove, think you, that plays upon the
         spheres?
    Heavens! is not this a heavenly melody,
    Where Jove himself a part in music bears?

    Thomas Bateson, Madrigal

11 Ring out ye crystal spheres,
    Once bless our human ears
       (If ye have power to touch our senses so)
    And let your silver chime
    Move in melodious time;
       And let the base of heav'n's deep organ
          blow,
    And with your ninefold harmony
    Make up full consort to th' angelic symphony.

    John Milton, 'On the Morning of Christ's Nativity'

12 Thus far we may maintain the music of the
    spheres; for those well ordered motions, and
    regular paces, though they give no sound unto
    the ear, yet to the understanding they strike a
    note most full of harmony.

    Sir Thomas Browne, *Religio Medici* (1643)

13 Pythagoras (saith Censorinus) asserted, that
    this whole world is made according to musical
    proportion, and that the seven planets . . . have
    a harmonious motion . . . and render various
    sounds, according to their several heights, so
    consonant, that they make most sweet melody;
    but to us inaudible, by reason of the greatness
    of the noise, which the narrow passage of our
    ears is not capable to receive.

    Thomas Stanley, *History of Philosophy* (1655-62)

14 Her voice, the music of the spheres,
    So loud, it deafens mortals' ears;
    As wise philosophers have thought,
    And that's the cause we hear it not.

    Samuel Butler, *Hudibras* (1664)

15 That day, as other solemn days, they spent
    In song and dance about the sacred hill —
    Mystical dance, which yonder starry sphere
    Of planets, and of fixed, in all her wheels
    Resembles nearest . . .
    And in their motions harmony divine
    So smoothes her charming tones that God's
         own ear
    Listens delighted.

    John Milton, *Paradise Lost*, V

1 ... from the pow'r of sacred Lays
   The spheres began to move.

John Dryden, 'A Song for St Cecilia's Day' (1687)

2 So when the last and dreadful hour
   This crumbling pageant shall devour,
   The trumpet shall be heard on high,
   The dead shall live, the living die,
   And music shall untune the sky.

John Dryden, 'A Song for St Cecilia's Day' (1687)

3 'This *must* be the music,' said he, 'of the *spears*,
   For I'm curst if each note of it doesn't run
        through one!'

Thomas Moore, *The Fudge Family* (1818)

4 There's music in the sighing of a reed;
   There's music in the gushing of a rill;
   There's music in all things, if men had ears:
   Their earth is but an echo of the spheres.

Lord Byron, *Don Juan*, XV (1819-24)

5 He that but once too nearly hears
   The music of forfended spheres
   Is thenceforth lonely, and for all
   His days as one who treads the Wall
   Of China, and, on this hand, sees
   Cities and their civilities,
   And, on the other, lions.

Coventry Patmore, *The Victories of Love*, I (1862)

6 ... thine own sadness, whereof stars, grown
        old
   In dancing silver-sandalled on the sea,
   Sing in their high and lonely melody.

W.B. Yeats, 'To the Rose upon the Rood of Time'
(1893)

7 He doubted; but God said 'Even so;
   Nothing is lost that's wrought with tears:
   The music that you made below
   Is now the music of the spheres.'

John Davidson, 'A Ballad of Heaven'

SPOHR

8 An academic pedant of the first rank.

Edvard Grieg, quoted in Finck, *Grieg and his Music*
(1929)

STARS

See also CONDUCTORS, LISZT, PAGANINI, THE
PERFORMER.

9 *Qualis artifex pereo!* What an artist dies with me!

Nero, attr.

10 [Francesca Cuzzoni had] a nest of nightingales
   in her belly.

Member of audience at Cuzzoni's London debut, 1723,
quoted in Young, *Handel* (1947)

11 [Francesca Cuzzoni]
   Little *Siren* of the stage,
   Charmer of an idle age,
   Empty warbler, breathing lyre,
   Wanton gale of fond desire,
   Bane of every manly art,
   Sweet enfeebler of the heart,
   O, too pleasing in thy strain,
   Hence to southern climes again;
   Tuneful mischief, vocal spell,
   To this island bid farewell;
   Leave us as we ought to be,
   Leave the *Britons* rough and free.

Ambrose Philips, 'To Signora Cuzzoni, May 25, 1724'

12 There's Madam Faustina, Catso,
   And eek Madam Cuzzoni;
   Likewise Signor Senesino
   Are *tutti Abbandonni*:
   Ha, Ha, Ha, Ha, Do, Re, Mi, Fa,
   Are now but farce and folly;
   We're ravish'd all with Toll, Loll, Loll,
   And pretty, pretty Polly.

Henry Carey, 'Polly Peachum' (1728)

13 The umbrage given to Cuzzoni by her [Faustina
   Bordoni's] coming hither, proves that as
   Turkish monarchs can bear no brother near the
   throne, an aspiring sister is as obnoxious to a
   theatrical queen.

Charles Burney, *A General History of Music* (1776-89)

14 [Of Moscheles] Chopin says his playing is
   'frightfully baroque'.

Stanislas Kozmian, Letter to his family, 1837

15 [Of Clara Schumann, née Wieck] The only
   woman in Germany who can play my music.

Fryderyk Chopin, quoted in Hedley, *Chopin* (1947)

16 Totay vill I blay de Kraitzer Sonahda to mak all
   de fur fly!

Eduard Reményi, quoted in Gall, *Johannes Brahms*
(1961)

17 [Of Paderewski] While his competitors were
   counting his wrong notes, he was counting his
   dollars.

Harold Schonberg, *The Great Pianists* (1963)

18 [Of Dame Nelly Melba as Manon] Madame
   Melba has the voice of a lark and, so far as her
   acting is evidence, the soul of one also.

The New York Times, quoted in Wechsberg, *The Opera*
(1972)

19 [Of Dame Nelly Melba] A singer who had
   nearly all the attributes inseparable from great
   artistry.

Sir Thomas Beecham, quoted in Lebrecht, *Discord*
(1982)

20 Every performance of Marie Lloyd is a
   performance by command of the British Public.

Marie Lloyd, quoted in Palmer, *All You Need Is Love*
(1976)

1 Kreisler plays as the thrush sings in Thomas Hardy's poem, hardly conscious of his own lovely significances.

Neville Cardus, *The Delights of Music* (1966)

2 There is such a thing as a tyranny of fine art. If I were Kreisler I might at times wish to corrupt my own lyricism, disturb its song with sterner stuff.

Neville Cardus, *The Delights of Music* (1966)

3 [Of Schnabel as composer] It seemed as though Wordsworth had suddenly gone off at a tangent and written like Gertrude Stein.

Neville Cardus, in *The Manchester Guardian*, 1939

4 Al Jolson: he wasn't a singer, he was a stylist, a great salesman.

Mickey Addy, quoted in Palmer, *All You Need Is Love* (1976)

5 [Flagstad] Schubert's 'Forelle' meant nothing to her, apparently; the trout was laid out on the fishmonger's block.

Neville Cardus, in *The Manchester Guardian*, 1938

6 [Horowitz] He is so rare an aromatist of the piano ... that to hear him with an orchestra is like trying to get the best out of champagne while eating roast beef.

Neville Cardus, in *The Manchester Guardian*, 1936

7 I think that every man who ... listens to my records, or who hears me on the radio, believes firmly that he sings as well as I do, especially when he's in the bathroom.

Bing Crosby, quoted in Shepherd, *Tin Pan Alley* (1982)

8 [Frankie Laine] The virility of a hairy goat and the delicacy of a white flower petal.

Unnamed American DJ, quoted in Whitcomb, *After the Ball* (1972)

9 [Tito Gobbi] I don't know why it is, Tito. I don't particularly like your voice, but when you sing I forget to play.

Unnamed orchestral player, quoted in Gobbi, *My Life* (1979)

10 Sinatra's idea of Paradise is a place where there are plenty of women and no newspapermen. He doesn't know it, but he'd be better off if it were the other way round.

Humphrey Bogart, quoted in Shepherd, *Tin Pan Alley* (1982)

11 If I play Tchaikovsky I play his melodies and skip his spiritual struggles ... If there's any time left over I fill in with a lot of runs up and down the keyboard.

Liberace, quoted in Hall and Whannel (eds.), *The Popular Arts* (1964)

12 The Nabob of Sob.

Johnnie Ray, self-description, quoted in Palmer, *All You Need Is Love* (1976)

13 Rostropovich got his works by bullying me.

Benjamin Britten, quoted in Headington, *Britten* (1981)

14 The magnificent 'cellist Rostropovich, looking very much like a bank clerk but playing like an angel.

Jack Brymer, *From Where I Sit* (1979)

15 It's nice not to be a prima donna.

Janet Baker, in 1971, quoted in Jacobson, *Reverberations* (1975)

16 I'm a performer by birth, but not by nature. I go into the music of an opera naked and raw and defenceless, because no other way can I perform.

Janet Baker, interview in *The Observer* 1982

17 I think it's a duty for a singer while he is at his best to let everyone around the world hear him.

Placido Domingo, in 1972, quoted in Jacobson, *Reverberations* (1975)

STOCKHAUSEN

18 Look, down there you can see the ocean of light that is Vienna. In a few years' time I will have progressed so far that, with a single electronic bang, I'll be able to blow the whole city sky-high!

Karlheinz Stockhausen, in the early 1950s, quoted in Henze, *Music and Politics* (1982)

19 Man has qualities which can never be replaced by a robot ... They are there so that he shall have more time for the truly human tasks — those of creation.

Karlheinz Stockhausen, in 1958, quoted in Ernst, *The Evolution of Electronic Music* (1977)

20 It makes me feel so good to know that I am on the right track.

Karlheinz Stockhausen, quoted in Cage, *Silence* (1961)

21 Musical form is life-form, thought-form, made audible.

Karlheinz Stockhausen, quoted in Wörner, *Stockhausen: Life and Work* (1973)

22 Think NOTHING
Wait until it is absolutely still within you
When you have attained this
Begin to play
As soon as you start to think stop
And try to retain
The state of NON-THINKING
Then continue playing.

Karlheinz Stockhausen, instructions to performers of *Es*

23 [Of Stockhausen's works] More boring than the most boring of eighteenth-century music.

Igor Stravinsky, quoted in Druskin, *Igor Stravinsky* (1983)

24 In Stockhausen's good period I came to trust his music more than anything else. I felt he

could solve all the problems, that it was no longer necessary for me to address myself to them.

Pierre Boulez, quoted in Peyser, *Boulez* (1976)

JOHANN STRAUSS (ELDER AND YOUNGER)

1 [Of the Elder] Where he fiddles, all dance — dance they must ... He himself dances, body and soul, while he plays — not with his feet but with his violin, which keeps bobbing up and down while the whole man marks the accent of every bar.

Ignaz Moscheles, Journal (1838)

2 [Effect of the Younger's waltzes] A strongly pungent odour exuded by venison that smells of the past and by music that smells of the future.

Eduard Hanslick, in 1865, quoted in Gall, *Johannes Brahms* (1961)

3 [Of *Die Fledermaus*] Here at last we had nearly everything to present that was dear to the heart of the average English playgoer, including a large spice of that rowdy humour on the stage which he feels is out of place nowhere ... By general consent it was agreed that here were the goods.

Sir Thomas Beecham, *A Mingled Chime* (1944)

RICHARD STRAUSS

4 I employ cacophony to outrage people.

Richard Strauss, remark to Mahler

5 My wife's a bit rough, but that's what I need.

Richard Strauss, remark to Mahler, quoted in Lebrecht, *Discord* (1982)

6 [At a rehearsal of Salomé] Gentlemen, this is not a question of music, but of a menagerie. Make a noise! Blow into your instruments!

Richard Strauss, quoted by Puccini, letter to Ricordi, 1908

7 Direct *Salomé* and *Elektra* as if they had been written by Mendelssohn: Elfin music.

Richard Strauss, 'Ten Golden Rules Inscribed in the Album of a Young Conductor' (1927)

8 Such an astounding lack of talent was never before united to such pretentiousness.

Pyotr Ilyich Tchaikovsky, Letter to Modeste Tchaikovsky, 1888

9 In the cookery book, under 'Jugged Hare', will be seen this wise recommendation: 'Take a hare'. Richard Strauss proceeds otherwise. To write a symphonic poem he takes anything.

Claude Debussy, referring to Strauss's *Tod und Verklärung*, quoted in Lockspeiser, *Debussy* (1963)

10 [Of *Till Eulenspiegel*] This piece might be called 'An hour of original music in a lunatic asylum'.

Claude Debussy, quoted in Bonavia, *Musicians on Music* (1956)

11 His absurd cacophony will not be music even in the 30th century.

César Cui, Letter, 1904

12 [Of *Salomé*] From time to time the cruellest discords are succeeded by exquisite suavities that caress the ear with delight. While listening to it all I thought of those lovely princesses in Sacher Masoch who lavished upon young men the most voluptuous kisses while drawing red-hot irons over their lovers' ribs.

Camille Saint-Saëns, quoted in Harding, *Saint-Saëns* (1965)

13 4000 SURVIVE THE MOST APPALLING TRAGEDY EVER SHOWN ON THE MIMIC STAGE

Newspaper headline following the US premier of Strauss's *Salomé*, quoted in Lebrecht, *Discord* (1982)

14 [Of *Elektra*] Pornographic rubbish.

Charles Villiers Stanford, quoted in Reid, *Thomas Beecham* (1961)

15 [After the band of the Grenadier Guards had just played an *Elektra* potpourri] His Majesty does not know what the Band has just played, but it is *never* to be played again.

George V, quoted in Reid, *Thomas Beecham* (1961)

16 With all its genius *Elektra* contains more bad music, more futile music and more stupid music than any opera produced by a man of first-class reputation.

Ernest Newman, in *The Birmingham Post*, 1913

17 The first complete realist in music.

Ernest Newman, quoted in Graf, *Composer and Critic* (1947)

18 [Of *Der Rosenkavalier*] Cheap and poor.

Igor Stravinsky, quoted in Reid, *Thomas Beecham* (1961)

19 [Of the *Alpensymphonie*] That's a real piece of hocus-pocus ... better to hang oneself than ever to write music like that.

Paul Hindemith, Letter to Emmy Ronnefeldt, 1917

20 [Of *Elektra*] The almost entire absence of charm and romance makes it unique, and if it is reported truly that Gluck in his austerity thought more of the Muses than the Graces, then Strauss might here be fairly said to have shown a preference for the Furies.

Sir Thomas Beecham, *A Mingled Chime* (1944)

21 One eminent British composer on leaving the theatre was asked what he thought of it. 'Words fail me,' he replied, 'and I'm going home at once to play the chord of C major

twenty times over to satisfy myself that it still exists.' The curious thing about this little piece of criticism is that *Elektra* actually finishes with the chord in question, thundered out several times in repetition on the full orchestra.

Sir Thomas Beecham, *A Mingled Chime* (1944)

1 I once spent a couple of days in a train with a German friend of mine. We amused ourselves by discovering how many notes we could take out of *Heldenleben* and leave the music essentially intact. By the time we finished we had taken out 15,000.

Sir Thomas Beecham, quoted in Reid, *Thomas Beecham* (1961)

2 Something like a court composer to Kaiser Wilhelm II.

Hans Werner Henze, *Music and Politics* (1982), 'Does Music have to be Political?' (1969)

STRAVINSKY

3 If, as is nearly always the case, music appears to express something, this is only an illusion and not a reality.

Igor Stravinsky, *Chronicles of my Life* (1936)

4 Music is far closer to mathematics than to literature — not perhaps to mathematics itself, but certainly to something like mathematical thinking and mathematical relationships.

Igor Stravinsky, *Conversations* (1958)

5 [When a misprint was discovered in one of his scores] That's the worst of my reputation as a modern composer — everyone must have thought I meant it.

Igor Stravinsky, quoted in Kennedy, *Barbirolli, Conductor Laureate* (1971)

6 The composer must avoid symmetry, but he can construct in parallelisms.

Igor Stravinsky, quoted in Druskin, *Igor Stravinsky* (1983)

7 My music is best understood by children and animals.

Igor Stravinsky, quoted in *The Observer*, 1961

8 When I know how long a piece must take, then it excites me.

Igor Stravinsky, quoted in Machlis, *Introduction to Contemporary Music* (1963)

9 I was born out of due time in the sense that by temperament and talent I should have been more suited for the life of a small Bach, living in anonymity and composing regularly for an established service and for God.

Igor Stravinsky, *Dialogues and a Diary* (1963)

10 [On hearing a Japanese musical instrument] We cannot describe sound, but we cannot forget it either.

Igor Stravinsky, *Dialogues and a Diary* (1963)

11 This *Sacre du printemps,* or rather a *Massacre du printemps.*

H. Moreno, *Le Ménestrel,* 1914

12 [*The Rite of Spring*] The twentieth century's Ninth Symphony.

Serge Diaghilev, quoted in Headington, *Bodley Head History of Western Music* (1974)

13 Stravinsky is a good composer, but he does not know about life. His compositions have no purpose.

Vaslav Nijinsky, quoted in Wilson, *Brandy of the Damned* (1964)

14 You can rave about Stravinsky without the slightest risk of being classed as a lunatic by the next generation.

George Bernard Shaw, in *Music and Letters,* 1920

15 Stravinsky's symphony for wind instruments was written in memory of Debussy; if my own memories of a friend were as painful as Stravinsky's seem to be, I would try to forget him.

Ernest Newman, quoted in Hughes and Van Thal, *The Music Lover's Companion* (1971)

16 His music used to be original. Now it is aboriginal.

Ernest Newman, in *The Musical Times,* 1921

17 Stravinsky is a cave man of music.

W.J. Henderson, in *The New York Sun,* 1924

18 Who's that drumming away there?
Why, it's little Modernsky!
he's got himself a pig-tail,
suits him quite well!
like real false hair! —
like a wig,
just (as little Modernsky imagines)
just like old Bach.

Arnold Schoenberg, *Three Satires for Mixed Chorus* (1925)

19 [Stravinsky's music] Bach on the wrong notes.

Sergey Prokofiev, quoted in Seroff, *Sergei Prokofiev* (1968)

20 I did not like *Le Sacre* then. I have conducted it fifty times since. I do not like it now.

Pierre Monteux, quoted in Reid, *Thomas Beecham* (1961)

21 Stravinsky said that music does not 'say' anything, and tried to make his art as impersonal as a block of ice cream.

Colin Wilson, *Brandy of the Damned* (1964)

22 New music? Hell, there's been no new music since Stravinsky.

Duke Ellington, in 1970, quoted in Jewell, *Duke* (1977)

23 Stravinsky looks like a man who was potty-trained too early and that music proves it as far as I'm concerned.

Russell Hoban, *Turtle Diary* (1975)

STRINGS

See also individual instruments.

1　Of instruments of strenges in acord
　　Herde I so playe a ravyshyng swetnesse
　　That God, that makere is of al and lord
　　Ne herde nevere beter, as I gesse.

　　Geoffrey Chaucer, *The Parlement of Foules*

2　They should ha' stuck to strings. Your brass-
　　man is a rafting dog — well and good; your
　　reed-man is a dab at stirring ye — well and
　　good; your drum-man is a rare bowel-shaker —
　　good again. But I don't care who hears me say
　　it, nothing will spak to your heart wi' the
　　sweetness o' the man of strings!
　　(Dewy)

　　Thomas Hardy, *Under the Greenwood Tree* (1872)

3　I don't know how, with no vibrato, Bach could
　　have so many sons.

　　Paul Hindemith, quoted in Jacobson, *Reverberations*
　　(1975)

4　[When trying to coax string-players to use more
　　portamento] It's not immoral, anyway I'll pay
　　the fine for indecency.

　　Sir John Barbirolli, quoted in Kennedy, *Barbirolli,*
　　Conductor Laureate (1971)

5　In trying to categorize string players, it's vital to
　　remember that they fall sharply into two kinds;
　　leaders — and others.

　　Jack Brymer, *From Where I Sit* (1979)

THE SYMPHONY

6　Since Beethoven, the futility of the symphony
　　seems to me an established fact.

　　Claude Debussy, quoted in Blaukopf, *Gustav Mahler*
　　(1973)

7　A symphony must be like the world, it must
　　embrace everything.

　　Gustav Mahler, remark to Jean Sibelius in Helsinki,
　　Finland, 1907

8　How thankful we ought to feel that
　　Wordsworth was only a poet and not a
　　musician. Fancy a symphony by Wordsworth!
　　Fancy having to sit it out! And fancy what it
　　would have been if he had written fugues!

　　Samuel Butler, *Note Books* (1912)

9　All those who have written symphonies during
　　the last hundred years may have charmed us
　　but have not succeeded in surprising us.

　　Sir Thomas Beecham, *A Mingled Chime* (1944)

10　A great symphony is like a man-made
　　Mississippi down which we irresistibly flow
　　from the instant of our leave-taking to a long
　　foreseen destination.

　　Aaron Copland, quoted in Machlis, *Introduction to*
　　Contemporary Music (1963)

11　Between Stravinsky and Webern everything
　　that still passes itself off as a symphony seems
　　either a replica, an obituary, or an echo.

　　Hanz Werner Henze, *Music and Politics* (1982),
　　'Instrumental Composition' (1963)

12　A symphony is a stage play with the parts
　　written for instruments instead of for actors.

　　Colin Wilson, *Brandy of the Damned* (1964)

SYNAESTHESIA

13　Music is the eye of the ear.

　　Thomas Draxe, *Bibliotheca* (1616)

14　All night have the roses heard
　　The flute, violin, bassoon.

　　Alfred, Lord Tennyson, *Maud* (1855)

15　I found myself referring to the programme to
　　find out whether I ought to be seeing red or
　　looking blue at certain moments, and some of it
　　made many of the audience feel green.

　　The Times, reviewing Bliss's *A Colour Symphony*, 1922

TALLIS

16　As he did live, so also did he die,
　　In mild and quiet sort,
　　(O! happy man).

　　Epitaph for Thomas Tallis, St Alfege, Greenwich

TAVERNER

17　[On Taverner's possession of heretical books]
　　Cardinal Wolsey for his music excused him,
　　saying he was but a musician, and so he
　　escaped.

　　John Foxe, *Actes and Monuments* (1563)

TCHAIKOVSKY

18　Oh, how difficult it is to make anyone see and
　　feel in music what we see and feel ourselves!

　　Pyotr Ilyich Tchaikovsky, Letter to Nadezdha von
　　Meck, 1878

19　[Of his instrumentation] I never compose in the
　　abstract; that is to say, the musical thought
　　never appears otherwise than in a suitable
　　external form. In this way I invent the musical
　　idea and the instrumentation simultaneously.

　　Pyotr Ilyich Tchaikovsky, Letter to Nadezdha von
　　Meck, 1878

20　I bow before the greatness of some of his works
　　— but I do not *love* Beethoven. My attitude
　　toward him reminds me of what I experienced
　　in childhood toward the God Jehovah. I had
　　toward Him ... a feeling of wonder, but at the
　　same time also of fear.

　　Pyotr Ilyich Tchaikovsky, Diary, 1886

1 Since I began to compose I have made it my
   object to be, in my craft, what the most
   illustrious masters were in theirs; that is to say,
   I wanted to be, like them, an artisan, just as a
   shoemaker is.

   Pyotr Ilyich Tchaikovsky, quoted in Stravinsky,
   Chronicles of my Life (1936)

2 I sit down to the piano regularly at nine o'clock
   in the morning and *Mesdames les Muses* have
   learned to be on time for that rendezvous.

   Pyotr Ilyich Tchaikovsky, quoted in Schafer, *British
   Composers in Interview* (1963)

3 Music is not illusion, but revelation.

   Pyotr Ilyich Tchaikovsky, attr.

4 [Of the Symphony No. 4] I cannot play it
   without a fever penetrating all the fibres of my
   being and for a whole day I cannot recover from
   the impression.

   Nadezhda von Meck, Letter to Tchaikovsky, 1880

5 Tchaikovsky's Violin Concerto gives us for the
   first time the hideous notion that there can be
   music that stinks to the ear.

   Eduard Hanslick, in *Neue Freie Presse*, 1881

6 [Of the Piano Concerto No. 1] A hackneyed
   battle-scarred work that usually has been
   hammered by the pugilists of the keyboard into
   cast-iron vulgarity.

   Neville Cardus, in *The Manchester Guardian*, 1936

7 [Of Tchaikovsky's music] A thrilling case of
   nerves.

   Neville Cardus, in *The Manchester Guardian*, 1938

8 Solid and workmanlike.

   Paul Hindemith, quoted in Skelton, *Paul Hindemith*
   (1975)

9 I am not a fascist. I hate Tchaikovsky and I will
   not conduct him. But if the audience wants him,
   it can have him.

   Pierre Boulez, quoted in Peyser, *Boulez* (1976)

TELEMANN

10 If there is nothing new to be found in melody
   then we must seek novelty in harmony.

   Georg Phillipp Telemann, Letter, 1751

11 I have always aimed at facility. Music ought not
   to be an effort.

   Georg Phillipp Telemann, quoted in Headington, *The
   Bodley Head History of Western Music* (1974)

12 A good composer should be able to set public
   notices to music.

   Georg Phillipp Telemann, quoted in Wolff (ed.), *On
   Music and Musicians* (1946)

13 A Lully is renowned; Corelli one may praise;
   but Telemann alone has above mere fame been
   raised.

   Johann Mattheson (1740), quoted in Petzoldt, *Georg
   Phillipp Telemann* (1974)

14 [Telemann] could write a motet for eight voices
   more quickly than one could write a letter.

   George Frideric Handel, quoted in Young, *Handel*
   (1946)

TEMPO

See also INTERPRETATION.

15 *Touchstone:* Truly, young gentlemen, though
   there was no great matter in the ditty, yet the
   note was very untuneable.
   First Page: You are deceived sir, we kept time,
   we lost not our time.
   Touchstone: By my troth, yes. I count it but time
   lost to hear such a foolish song. God buy you,
   and God mend your voices.

   William Shakespeare, *As You Like It*, V.iii

16 *Malvolio: ...* Do ye make an alehouse of my
   lady's house, that ye squeak out your coziers'
   catches without any mitigation or remorse of
   voice? Is there no respect of place, persons, nor
   time in you?
   Sir Toby Belch: We did keep time, sir, in our
   catches. Sneck up.

   William Shakespeare, *Twelfth Night*, II.iii

17 The means I find most serviceable as a guide to
   establish the tempo, are more convenient and
   cost so little effort to possess, for everyone
   always has it with him. It is the pulse beat of
   the hand of a healthy person.

   Johann Joachim Quantz, *Versuch einer Anweisung die
   Flöte* (1752)

18 [Of rubato] Play a piece lasting so many
   minutes through in strict time: then repeat it
   with any number of variations in speed, but let
   its total duration remain the same.

   Fryderyk Chopin, quoted in Beecham, *A Mingled
   Chime* (1944)

19 If a man does not keep pace with his
   companions, perhaps it is because he hears a
   different drummer. Let him step to the music
   which he hears, however measured or far away.

   Henry David Thoreau, quoted in Wilmer, *As Serious as
   Your Life* (1977)

20 'I know I have to beat time when I learn music.'
   'Ah! that accounts for it,' said the Hatter. 'He
   won't stand beating.'

   Lewis Carroll, *Alice's Adventures in Wonderland* (1865)

21 The metronome has no value ... for I myself
   have never believed that my blood and a
   mechanical instrument go well together.

   Johannes Brahms, Letter to George Henschel, 1880

1 [Of conductors] There are two kinds: one takes the music too fast, and the other too slow. There is no third!

Camille Saint-Saëns, quoted in Beecham, *A Mingled Chime* (1944)

2 A tempo is correct when everything can be heard. When a figure can no longer be understood because the tones run into one another, then the tempo is too fast.

Gustav Mahler, quoted in Morgenstern, *Composers on Music* (1958)

3 Good morning, Dame Ethel, and what are your tempi for today?

Sir Adrian Boult, attr. (Ethel Smyth was notoriously difficult at rehearsals of her own work.)

4 Please make a recording so that people realise what counting means, what is the succession in time, the growing in time, the gaining on time.

Nadia Boulanger, to Stravinsky, quoted in Kendall, *The Tender Tyrant: Nadia Boulanger* (1976)

5 [Of bad rubato] Loose is not beautiful — loose is loose.

Nadia Boulanger, quoted in Kendall, *The Tender Tyrant: Nadia Boulanger* (1976)

6 [After conducting Borodin's ballet *Polovtsian Dances* rather fast] We made the b——s hop, what?

Sir Thomas Beecham, quoted in Atkins and Newman, *Beecham Stories* (1978)

7 Every composer has his own basic tempo which decrees that speed in his music is not the same as speed in any other composer.

Neville Cardus, in *The Manchester Guardian*, 1936

8 Chopin's prescription for rubato playing, which is almost word for word Mozart's prescription for playing an accompanied melody, is that the right hand should take liberties with the time values, while the left hand remains rhythmically unaltered. This is exactly the effect you get when a good blues singer is accompanied by a good swing band. It is known to the modern world as *le style hot*.

Virgil Thomson, in *The New York Herald Tribune*, 1940

9 [During a dispute over tempi] Yes, Klemperer is here, Schnabel is here, but where is Beethoven?

Artur Schnabel, quoted in Osborne and Thomson (eds.), *Klemperer Stories* (1980)

10 Any musical composition must necessarily possess its unique tempo ... A piece of mine can survive almost anything but wrong or uncertain tempo.

Igor Stravinsky, *Conversations* (1958)

11 Man, I can't *listen* that fast.

Unnamed jazz musician, on hearing Parker and Gillespie's 'Shaw Nuff', quoted in Palmer, *All You Need Is Love* (1976)

THOMSON

12 [Of the early music of himself, Copland and others] A façade of dissonance.

Virgil Thomson, quoted in Kendall, *The Tender Tyrant: Nadia Boulanger* (1976)

13 My previous instructors had usually managed to create the impression that composing music was a risky procedure because you were really in competition with Beethoven and Brahms, and you'd better look out. Well, she [Nadia Boulanger] had no such attitude. For her, writing music was like writing a letter, it's a function of the musical mind, and in that way she put me at ease in front of the music paper, so that I wasn't writing Beethoven's music, I was writing my own, and my own was perfectly modest and perfectly immodest, like anybody else's.

Virgil Thomson, quoted in Kendall, *The Tender Tyrant: Nadia Boulanger* (1976)

14 In Thomson ... it is at times hard to decide whether one is dealing with ironically masked significance or with kindergarten stuff.

Ernst Křenek, *Musik im goldenen Westen* (1949)

TIPPETT

15 I like to think of composing as a physical business. I compose at the piano and like to feel involved in my work with my hands.

Michael Tippett, quoted in Schafer, *British Composers in Interview* (1963)

16 The composition of oratorio and opera is a collective as well as a personal experience. While indeed all artistic creation may be seen in that way, I believe the collective experience, whether conscious or unconscious, is more fundamental to an oratorio or an opera than to a string quartet.

Michael Tippett, *Moving into Aquarius* (1974)

17 The music of a song destroys the verbal music of a poem utterly. I am inclined to think that a composer responds less to a poem's verbal sound, when he chooses that poem as a vehicle for his musical art, than to the poem's situation, lyrical or dramatic.

Michael Tippett, quoted in Matthews, *Michael Tippett* (1980)

18 My epistemology is an endless agnosticism.

Michael Tippett, quoted in Bowen, *Michael Tippett* (1982)

TRADITION AND ORIGINALITY

19 O sing unto the Lord a new song.

Psalms 98:1

20 A' [Shallow] came ever in the rearward of the fashion, and sung those tunes to the

overscutched huswives that he heard the
carmen whistle, and sware they were his
fancies or his goodnights.
(Falstaff)

William Shakespeare, *Henry IV, Part Two*, III.ii

1   Usually I have to wait for other people to tell
me when I have new ideas, because I never
know this myself.

Ludwig van Beethoven, in 1802, quoted in Scott,
Beethoven (1934)

2   [Of his String Quartet in C Sharp Minor, Op
131] Put together from pilferings from one thing
and another.

Ludwig van Beethoven, written on the MS score sent
to his publisher, Schott

3   We all have the same eight notes to play with.

Sir Arthur Sullivan, attr., on being accused of
plagiarism

4   When 'Omer smote 'is bloomin' lyre,
    'E'd 'eard men sing by land an' sea;
    An' what 'e thought 'e might require,
    'E went an' took — the same as me!

Rudyard Kipling, Introduction to *Barrack-Room Ballads*
(1892)

5   There are no more schools of music. The main
business of musicians today is to avoid any
kind of outside influence.

Claude Debussy, quoted in Lockspeiser, *Debussy*
(1963)

6   Tradition is really just complacency and
slackness.

Gustav Mahler, quoted in Gattey, *Peacocks on the
Podium* (1982)

7   Music remains the only art, the last sanctuary,
wherein originality may reveal itself in the face
of fools and not pierce their mental opacity.

James Huneker, *Iconoclasts* (1905)

8   In one way or another every master 'knows'
less than his predecessors, because in other
ways he knows more.

Zoltán Kodály, in *Nyugat*, 1918

9   In maintaining that the question of the origin of
a theme is completely unimportant from the
artist's point of view, Stravinsky is right. The
question of origins can only be interesting from
the point of view of musical documentation.

Béla Bartók, in *Melos*, 1920

10 No composer appears absolutely new out of the
welkin; indeed when, like Schönberg, he is said
to do so he is to my mind at once suspect.

Ralph Vaughan Williams, in *Music and Letters*, 1935

11 It is one of the laws of nature that we often feel
nearer to remote generations than to those
which immediately precede us.

Igor Stravinsky, *Chronicles of my Life* (1938)

12 A good composer does not imitate; he steals.

Igor Stravinsky, quoted in Yates, *Twentieth Century
Music* (1967)

13 Present-day works that live off the past are
abnormal; those which only know the present,
or fashion, are useless; whilst the only true
ones are those which lead us on further, since
they alone are creating life.

Nadia Boulanger, quoted in Kendall, *The Tender
Tyrant: Nadia Boulanger* (1976)

14 Others write as if music were like a fashion in
dressmaking — this year a certain colour or
fabric, next year another. I used to be like that.
I've gone through many things, but now I know
there is only one thing that counts: to continue
the great art of music. It must follow the grand
line.

George Antheil, quoted in Ewen, *American Composers*
(1982)

15 One doesn't write the music of one's choice but
of necessity ... My love of the music of Chopin
and Mozart is as strong as that of the next
fellow, but it does me little good when I sit
down to write my own, because their world is
not mine and their language not mine.

Aaron Copland, in *The New York Times*, 1949

16 What I am composing is, at root, a single work,
which was started fifteen years ago, and which
one day will end; the beginnings and endings of
individual pieces are only apparent. Or perhaps
I should say, with somewhat more modesty,
that the beginning lies five or six hundred years
in the past.

Hans Werner Henze, *Music and Politics* (1982) 'Music
as a Means of Resistance' (1963)

17 Composition is notation of distortion of what
composers think they've heard before.
Masterpieces are marvellous misquotations.

Ned Rorem, *Paris Diary* (1966)

18 I feel it is perfectly legitimate for a composer to
look for something new and different just
because it is new and different, and he should
stop apologising for being curious.

Ernst Křenek, *Horizons Circled* (1974)

19 You cannot ignore the historical landmarks of
music because if you ignore them, then history
will ignore you. The fight is a bigger one than
getting the audience to cheer. The dilemma of
music is the dilemma of our civilization. We
have to fight the past to survive.

Pierre Boulez, quoted in Peyser, *Boulez* (1976)

20 If you are going to have a big foot in the future,
you've got to have a big foot in the past.

Lukas Foss, quoted in Ewen, *American Composers*
(1982)

1 They don't write songs like that any more.
   Anon.

TRANSCRIPTION

2 [Of transcriptions] The unnatural fury which
   possesses us to transplant even things written
   for the piano to string instruments, instruments
   so entirely opposed to each other, should
   certainly come to an end.
   Ludwig van Beethoven, Letter, 1802

3 To score a composition never intended for the
   orchestra, is an undesirable practice ... This is
   the lowest form of instrumentation, akin to
   tinted photographs, though of course the
   process may be well or badly done.
   Nikolay Rimsky-Korsakov, Preface to *Principles of
   Orchestration* (1896-1908)

4 Transcription occupies an important place in
   the literature of the piano, and looked at from
   the right point of view, every important piece is
   the reduction of a big thought to a practical
   instrument.
   Ferruccio Busoni, Letter to his wife, 1913

TRANSIENCE

See also SILENCE.

5 The audible sound of music flows away into the
   past and as it passes is impressed on the
   memory ... for except the sounds be retained in
   the memory of men they perish, for it is
   impossible to write them down.
   Isidore of Seville, *Etymologies*, III

6   Hark! the numbers, soft and clear,
       Gently steal upon the ear;
       Now louder, and yet louder rise,
       And fill with spreading sounds the skies;
   Exulting in triumph now swell the bold notes,
   In broken air, trembling, the wild music floats;
       Till, by degrees, remote and small,
           The strains decay,
           And melt away
       In a dying, dying fall.
   Alexander Pope, 'Ode for Musick, on St Cecilia's Day'
   (*c.* 1708)

7 The music in my heart I bore,
   Long after it was heard no more.
   William Wordsworth, 'The Solitary Reaper'

8 The harp that once thro' Tara's halls
       The soul of music shed,
   Now hangs as mute on Tara's walls
       As if that soul were fled.
   Thomas Moore, *Irish Melodies* (1807)

9 Music, when soft voices die,
   Vibrates in the memory.
   Percy Bysshe Shelley, 'To ——'

10 When the lute is broken,
        Sweet tones are remembered not;
    When the lips have spoken,
        Loved accents are soon forgot.
    Percy Bysshe Shelley, 'Lines: When the Lamp'

11 Perhaps it was owing to his own ignorance of
    music that he had been able to receive so
    confused an impression, one of those that are,
    notwithstanding, our only purely musical
    impressions, limited in their extent, entirely
    original and irreducible into any other kind ...
    Presumably, the notes which we hear at such
    moments tend to spread out before our eyes,
    over surfaces greater or smaller according to
    their pitch and volume; to trace arabesque
    designs, to give us the sensation of breadth or
    tenuity, stability or caprice. But the notes
    themselves have vanished before these
    sensations have developed sufficiently to
    escape submersion under those which the
    following, or even simultaneous, notes have
    already begun to awaken in us. And this
    indefinite perception would continue to
    smother in its molten liquidity the motifs which
    now and then emerge, barely discernible, to
    plunge again and disappear and drown;
    recognised only by the particular kind of
    pleasure which they instil, impossible to
    describe, to recollect, to name; ineffable ...
    Marcel Proust, *Swann's Way* (1913)

12 Pale tunes irresolute
    And traceries of old sounds
    Blown from a rotted flute
    Mingle with noise of cymbals rouged with rust.
    Max Beerbohm, 'Enoch Soames' (1919)

THE TROMBONE

13 The trombones are too sacred for frequent use.
    Felix Mendelssohn, attr.

14 Many a sinner has played himself into heaven
    on the trombone, thanks to the [Salvation]
    Army.
    (Barbara)
    George Bernard Shaw, *Major Barbara* (1907)

15 Never look at the trombones. It only
    encourages them.
    Richard Strauss, quoted by Sir Brian Young, BBC
    radio broadcast, 1983

16 Without question the most unpopular medium
    of musical sound in the world.
    Sir Thomas Beecham, *A Mingled Chime* (1944)

17 [To a bass trombonist] Mr Hoyland, are you
    producing as much sound as possible from the
    quaint and antique drainage system you are
    applying to your face? [Hoyland replied that he
    was.] Well, then, roll it about on the floor!
    Sir Thomas Beecham, quoted in Reid, *Thomas Beecham*
    (1961)

THE TRUMPET

See also MARTIAL MUSIC, HEAVENLY MUSIC.

1   It came to pass when the people heard the sound of the trumpet, and the people shouted with a great shout, that the wall fell down flat, so that the people went up into the city.
   Joshua 6:20

2   The Spirit of the Lord came upon Gideon, and he blew a trumpet.
   Judges 6:34

3   *At tuba terribili sonitu taratantara dixit.* And the trumpet with a terrible noise went 'taratantara'.
   Ennius, *Annals*

4   At the round earth's imagined corners, blow Your trumpets, angels.
   John Donne, *Holy Sonnets*, 7

5   Now had Fame's posterior trumpet blown.
   Alexander Pope, *The Dunciad*, IV (1742)

6   The silver, snarling trumpets 'gan to chide.
   John Keats, 'The Eve of St Agnes' (1819)

7   ——'s idea of heaven is, eating *pâtés de foie gras* to the sound of trumpets.
   Sydney Smith, quoted in Pearson, *The Smith of Smiths* (1934)

8   Against his pipping sounds a trumpet cried Celestial sneering boisterously.
   Wallace Stevens, 'The Comedian as the Letter C' (1924)

THE TUBA

9   The very lower bowel of music.
   Peter de Vries, *The Glory of the Hummingbird* (1974)

TWELVE-NOTE MUSIC

10   [Of his own experiments with a twelve-note system] It's an artificial process without strength, though it may sound busy & noisy. This wallpaper design music is not as big as a natural slushy ballad.
   Charles Ives, marginalia on the MS of *The Masses* (1915)

11   The introduction of my method of composing with twelve tones does not facilitate composing; on the contrary, it makes it more difficult.
   Arnold Schoenberg, quoted in Hughes and Van Thal, *The Music Lover's Companion* (1971)

12   Twelve-note technique . . . does not allow me to work swiftly.
   Alban Berg, Letter to Schoenberg, 1930

13   To limit oneself to home-made tonal systems of this sort seems to me a more doctrinaire proceeding than to follow the strictest diatonic rules of the most dried-up old academic.
   Paul Hindemith, *The Craft of Musical Composition* (1937)

14   It comes to a sort of composing before composition. The whole disposition and organisation of the material would have to be ready when the actual work should begin, and all one asks is: which is the actual work? (Zeitblom)
   Thomas Mann, *Doctor Faustus* (1947); trans. Lowe-Porter

15   When you have written ten notes of the chromatic scale, the temptation to add the remaining two is irresistible.
   Unnamed composer, quoted in Rosen, *Schoenberg* (1976)

16   [When told that young composers were employing his system] And do they put music in it?
   Arnold Schoenberg, quoted in Jacobson, *Reverberations* (1975)

17   That twelve-tone method — it was really six-plus-six.
   Arnold Schoenberg, quoted in Yates, *Twentieth Century Music* (1968)

18   There is little probability that the twelve-note scale will ever produce anything more than morbid or entirely cerebral growths. It might deal successfully with neuroses of various kinds, but I cannot imagine it associated with any healthy and happy concept such as young love or the coming of Spring.
   Sir Arnold Bax, *Music and Letters* (1951)

19   Other masters may conceivably write Even yet in C major, But we — we take the perhaps 'primrose path' To the dodecaphonic bonfire.
   Hugh MacDiarmid, *In Memoriam James Joyce* (1955)

20   [Of twelve-note music] I can see it taking no part in the music-lover's music-making.
   Benjamin Britten, quoted in Headington, *Britten* (1981)

21   Around 1950 . . . we went through a period of seeking our total control over music . . . What we were doing, by total serialization, was to annihilate the will of the composer in favour of a predetermining system.
   Pierre Boulez, in 1963, quoted in Jacobson, *Reverberations* (1975)

22   Any musician who has not felt . . . the necessity of the twelve-tone system is *superfluous*. For everything he writes will fall short of the imperatives of our time.
   Pierre Boulez, in 1969, quoted in Jacobson, *Reverberations* (1975)

23   With it [twelve-note music], music moved out of the world of Newton and into the world of

Einstein. The tonal idea was based on a universe defined by gravity and attraction. The serial idea is based on a universe that finds itself in perpetual expansion.

Pierre Boulez, quoted in Peyser, *Boulez* (1976)

1 An idea may suggest twelve-tone treatment perhaps, and then maybe it won't.

Aaron Copland, in 1970, quoted in Jacobson, *Reverberations* (1975)

2 It is ... no business of mine to say that an artificial treatment of twelve notes as if they were equidistant (which they cannot be) and of equal importance, would seem to be such a violation of the harmonic series (surely the basis of all music) that it cannot last for long ... I am not fitted to have much to do with this music.

Sir Adrian Boult, *My Own Trumpet* (1973)

3 Dodecaphony's mechanistic heresy.

Hans Werner Henze, *Music and Politics* (1982), 'German music in the 1940s and 1950s'

VARÈSE

4 My experimenting is done before I make the music. Afterwards, it is the listener who must experiment.

Edgar Varèse, quoted in Yates, *Twentieth Century Music* (1968)

5 Ever since I was a boy, most music sounded to me terribly enclosed, corseted, one might say. I liked music that explodes in space.

Edgar Varèse, quoted in Ewen, *American Composers* (1982)

6 Music is antiquated in the extreme in its medium of expression compared with the other arts. We are waiting for a new notation — a new Guido d'Arezzo — when music will move forward at a bound.

Edgar Varèse, quoted in Ewen, *American Composers* (1982)

7 It is a tremendous achievement to create a piece of music that incites riot ... to cause peaceful lovers of music to scream out their agony, to arouse angry emotions and to tempt men to retire to the back of the theatre and perform tympani concerts on each other's faces.

W.J. Henderson, reviewing Varèse's *Hyperprism*, in *The New York Herald Tribune*, 1923

8 That he fathered forth noise — that is to say, into twentieth-century music — makes him more relative to present musical necessity than even the Viennese masters.

John Cage, *Silence* (1961), 'Edgar Varèse' (1958)

VAUGHAN WILLIAMS

9 What we want in England is *real* music, even if it be only a music-hall song. Provided it possesses real feeling and real life, it will be worth all the off-scourings of the classics in the world.

Ralph Vaughan Williams, in *The Vocalist*, 1902

10 [Of his Symphony No. 4] I don't know whether I like it, but it's what I meant.

Ralph Vaughan Williams, quoted in Headington, *The Bodley Head History of Western Music* (1974)

11 [Of his Symphony No. 6] Malcolm [Sargent] says it needs another tune.

Ralph Vaughan Williams, quoted in Kennedy, *Barbirolli, Conductor Laureate* (1971)

12 [Vaughan Williams] looks like a farmer ... on his way to judge the shorthorns at an agricultural fair.

Stephen Williams, quoted in Machlis, *Introduction to Contemporary Music* (1963)

13 It is fairly safe to predict that Vaughan Williams will be the kind of local composer who stands for something great in the musical development of his own country but whose actual musical contributions cannot bear exportation ... His is the music of a gentleman-farmer, noble in inspiration, but dull.

Aaron Copland, in 1931, quoted in Kendall, *The Tender Tyrant: Nadia Boulanger* (1976)

14 [To the chorus at a rehearsal of *Sinfonia Antartica*] I want you to sound like 22 women having babies *without* chloroform.

Sir John Barbirolli, quoted in Kennedy, *Barbirolli, Conductor Laureate* (1971)

15 The Vaughan Williams world of half-lights, of melodies that seem to want to delay the unpleasant moment when they must sound as if they have arrived somewhere.

Colin Wilson, *Brandy of the Damned* (1964)

VERDI

16 I read with reluctance the librettos that are sent me. It is impossible, or almost impossible for someone else to divine what I want.

Giuseppe Verdi, Letter, 1853

17 The artist must yield himself to his own inspiration ... I should compose with utter confidence a subject that set my musical blood going, even though it were condemned by all other artists as anti-musical.

Giuseppe Verdi, Letter, 1854

18 I would be willing to set even a newspaper or a letter, etc. to music, but in the theatre the public will stand for anything except boredom.

Giuseppe Verdi, Letter to Antonio Somma, 1854

1 It may be a good thing to copy reality; but to invent reality is much, much better.

Giuseppe Verdi, Letter to Clarina Maffei, 1876

2 [Refusing to write memoirs] It is quite enough for the musical world to have put up with my music for such a long time! ... I will never condemn it to read my prose.

Giuseppe Verdi, Letter, 1895

3 If others say: 'He should have done thus and thus', I answer: 'That may well be so, but what I have done is the best I can do.'

Giuseppe Verdi, quoted in Bonavia, *Verdi* (1930)

4 [Of *Ernani*] It's organ grinder's stuff.

Charles Gounod, quoted in Harding, *Gounod* (1973)

5 Like Verdi, when, at his worst opera's end
(The thing they gave at Florence, what's its name?),
While the mad houseful's plaudits near outbang
His orchestra of salt-box, tongs, and bones,
He looks through all the roaring and the wreaths
Where sits Rossini patient in his stall.

Robert Browning, 'Bishop Blougram's Apology'

6 The music of *La Traviata* is trashy; the young Italian lady [Piccolomini] cannot do justice to the music, such as it is. Hence it follows that the opera and the lady can only establish themselves in proportion as Londoners rejoice in a prurient story prettily acted.

The Atheneum, 1856

7 Verdi ... has wonderful bursts of passion. His passion is brutal, it is true, but that is better than having no passion at all. His music exasperates sometimes, but it never bores.

Georges Bizet, Letter, 1859

8 His is a fine artistic nature ruined by negligence and cheap success.

Georges Bizet, quoted in Dean, *Bizet* (1975)

THE VIOL

9 We call 'viols' those instruments with which gentlemen, merchants, and other virtuous people pass their time. The other kind is called the 'violin', which is commonly used for dancing.

Philibert Jambe-de-Fer, in 1556, quoted in Mellers, *François Couperin* (1950)

10 Is it not strange that sheeps' guts should hale souls out of men's bodies?
(Benedick)

William Shakespeare, *Much Ado About Nothing*, II.iii

11 And from henceforth, the stateful instrument gambo viol shall with ease yield full various and as deviceful musics as the lute.

Tobias Hume, *The First Part of Ayres* (1605)

12 The gentlemen in private meeting ... played three, four and five parts with viols ... and they esteemed a violin to be an instrument only belonging to a common fiddler, and could not endure that it should come among them for fear of making their meetings to be vain and fiddling.

Anthony à Wood, *Antiquities* (1674)

THE VIOLA

13 The viola is commonly (with rare exceptions) played by infirm violinists, or by decrepit players of wind instruments who happen to have been acquainted with a string instrument once upon a time.

Richard Wagner, in 1869, quoted in Gattey, *Peacocks on the Podium* (1982)

14 That instrument of mixed sex ... this hermaphrodite of the orchestra.

Sir Thomas Beecham, *A Mingled Chime* (1944)

15 If you'd heard the violas when I was young, you'd take a bismuth tablet.

Sir John Barbirolli, quoted in Kennedy, *Barbirolli, Conductor Laureate* (1971)

THE VIOLIN

16 The Devil rides upon a fiddlestick.
(Prince Henry)

William Shakespeare, *Henry IV, Part One*, II.iv

17 A squeaking engine he applied
Unto his neck on north-east side ...
His grisly beard was long and thick,
With which he strung his fiddle-stick;
For he to horse tail scorned to owe,
For what he on his chin did grow.

Samuel Butler, *Hudibras* (1663-78)

18 Sharp violins proclaim
Their jealous pangs, and desperation,
Fury, frantic indignation,
Depths of pains, and height of passion,
For the fair, disdainful dame.

John Dryden, 'A Song for St Cecilia's Day' (1687)

19 When a man is not disposed to hear music, there is not a more disagreeable sound in harmony than that of a violin.

Richard Steele, in *The Tatler*, 1710

20 He was a fiddler, and consequently a rogue.

Jonathan Swift, Letter to Esther Johnson ('Stella'), 1711

21 Fiddlers, pipers, and *id genus omne*; most unedifying and unbecoming company for a man of fashion.

Lord Chesterfield, Letter to his son, 1751

22 Had I learned to fiddle, I should have done nothing else.

Samuel Johnson, quoted in Boswell, *Life* (1791)

1 In came a fiddler — and tuned like fifty
   stomach-aches.

   Charles Dickens, *A Christmas Carol* (1843)

2 A squeak's heard in the orchestra,
       The leader draws across
   The intestines of the agile cat
       The tail of the noble hoss.

   George T. Lanigan, 'The Amateur Orlando'

3 *Les sanglots longs*
   Des violons
   De l'automne
   Blessent mon coeur
   D'une langeur
   Monotone.
   The long sobbings of autumn violins wound my
   heart with a monotonous langour.

   Paul Verlaine, 'Chanson de l'automne'

4 Fiddle, n. An instrument to tickle human ears
   by friction of a horse's tail on the entrails of a
   cat.

   Ambrose Bierce, *The Devil's Dictionary* (1911)

5 It is not for nothing that the newly soulful tone
   of the violin counts among the great
   innovations of the age of Descartes.

   T.W. Adorno, *Versuch über Wagner* (1952)

VIRTUOSITY

See also PERFORMANCE.

6 The greatest strokes make not the best music.
   John Ray, *English Proverbs* (1670)

7 Today music is only the art of performing
   difficult things, but what is merely difficult
   ceases to please in the long run.

   Voltaire, *Candide* (1759)

8 [Of a celebrated violinist's performance]
   Difficult do you call it, Sir? I wish it were
   impossible.

   Samuel Johnson, quoted in *Johnsonian Miscellanies*
   (also attr. by Grétry, *Memoires*, to Baron Glucken)

9 [Of virtuoso sight-reading] The hearers ... can
   say nothing except that they have *seen* music
   and clavier-playing.

   Wolfgang Amadeus Mozart, Letter, 1778

10 Would to heaven that a race of freaks could
   arise in the race of artists, with one finger too
   many on each hand; then the dance of
   virtuosity would be at an end.

   Robert Schumann, *Aphorisms* (c. 1833)

11 We are tired of world-weary, pallid virtuoso
   faces.

   Robert Schumann, in *Neue Zeitschrift*

12 As you grow older, converse more frequently
   with scores than with virtuosi.

   Robert Schumann, quoted in Walker (ed.), *Robert
   Schumann; the Man and his Music* (1972)

13 The attraction of the virtuoso for the public is
   very like that of the circus for the crowd. There
   is always the hope that something dangerous
   may happen: M. Ysaÿe may play the violin with
   M. Colonne on his shoulders; or M. Pugno may
   conclude his piece by lifting the piano with his
   teeth.

   Claude Debussy, *Monsieur Croche, antidilettante* (1921)

14 In order to get beyond the virtuoso level, one
   must first be a virtuoso: one arrives at
   something more, not something different.

   Ferruccio Busoni, quoted in Stuckenschmidt, *Ferruccio
   Busoni* (1967)

15 There are limits to feats of skill, beyond which
   lie the realms of nonsense. Everything is quite
   difficult enough as it is, and what is simple
   actually comes hardest.

   Hans Werner Henze, *Music and Politics* (1982),
   'Instrumental Composition' (1963)

16 Nobody can *really* play the Mozart [Clarinet]
   Concerto yet, in spite of the fact that everyone
   can *almost* play it after four years of study.

   Jack Brymer, *From Where I Sit* (1979)

VIVALDI

17 An excellent violinist and a mediocre composer.

   Carlo Goldoni, quoted in Kendall, *Vivaldi* (1978)

18 [Vivaldi] is an old man, who has a prodigious
   fury for composition. I heard him undertake to
   compose a concerto, with all the parts, with
   greater dispatch than a copyist can copy it.

   Charles de Brosses, Letter, 1739

19 The peculiar characteristic of Vivaldi's music ...
   is, that it is wild and irregular.

   John Hawkins, *General History of the Science and
   Practice of Music* (1776)

20 If acute and rapid tones are evil, Vivaldi has
   much of the sin to answer for.

   Charles Burney, *A General History of Music* (1776-89)

21 Vivaldi is greatly overrated — a dull fellow who
   could compose the same form over and so
   many times over.

   Igor Stravinsky, quoted in Craft, *Conversations* (1958)

WAGNER

22 I know nothing at all about music.
   Richard Wagner, quoted by Hugo Wolf, Letter, 1875

23 By nature I am luxurious, prodigal, and
   extravagant, much more than Sardanapalus and
   all the other old emperors put together.

   Richard Wagner, quoted in Hadden, *Master Musicians*
   (1909)

24 Whatever my passions demand of me, I become
   for the time being — musician, poet, director,
   author, lecturer or anything else.

   Richard Wagner, Letter to Liszt

1 [Of *The Ring*] The whole will then become —
out with it! I am not ashamed to say so — the
greatest work of poetry ever written.
Richard Wagner, Letter to Theodor Uhlig

2 To me *Tristan* is and remains a wonder! I shall
never be able to understand how I could have
written anything like it.
Richard Wagner, quoted in Headington, *The Bodley
Head History of Western Music* (1974)

3 When I re-read my theoretical works, I can no
longer understand them.
Richard Wagner, quoted by Camille Saint-Saëns,
Portraits et Souvenirs (1903)

4 Were he as melodious a composer as he is an
intellectual one, he would be the man of our
time.
Robert Schumann, *Operatic Note-Book*, 1847

5 For me Wagner is impossible . . . he talks
without ever stopping. One just can't talk all
the time.
Robert Schumann, quoted in Gall, *Johannes Brahms*
(1961)

6 For our parts, we should prefer a state of
perpetual coma to a lively apprehension of Herr
Wagner, his doctrines and his music.
The Musical World (London), 1855

7 [Of Wagner's music] Brummagem Berlioz.
William Sterndale Bennett, attr.

8 I love Wagner; but the music I prefer is that of a
cat hung up by its tail outside a window, and
trying to stick to the panes of glass with its
claws.
Charles Baudelaire, quoted in Mencken, *Dictionary of
Quotations* (1942)

9 Wagnerian din — inspired by the riots of cats
scampering in the dark about an ironmonger's
shop.
Alexandre Dumas (père), quoted in Hadden, *Master
Musicians* (1909)

10 God give me a failure like that!
Charles Gounod, after the failure of the 'Paris version'
of *Tannhäuser*, 1861

11 Wagner's opera style recognizes only
superlatives; but a superlative has no future. It
is the end, not the beginning.
Eduard Hanslick, quoted in Lebrecht, *Discord* (1982)

12 The Prelude to *Tristan and Isolde* reminds me of
the old Italian painting of a martyr whose
intestines are slowly unwound from his body
on a reel.
Eduard Hanslick, quoted in Lebrecht, *Discord* (1982)

13 [Of *Tristan und Isolde*] A sort of chromatic moan.
Hector Berlioz, *A travers chants* (1862)

14 Wagner is Berlioz without the melody.
Daniel Auber, quoted in *Le Ménestrel*, 1863

15 Wagner is Verdi with the addition of style.
Georges Bizet, quoted in Dean, *Bizet* (1975)

16 I can only adore you . . . An earthly being
cannot requite a divine spirit.
Ludwig II of Bavaria, Letter to Wagner

17 Wagner has lovely moments but awful quarters
of an hour.
Gioacchino Rossini, in 1867, quoted in Naumann,
Italienische Tondichter (1883)

18 [Of *Die Meistersinger*] I listen to it as intently as
I can, i.e. as often as I can stand it.
Johannes Brahms, Letter to Clara Schumann, 1870

19 Happily for Wagner, he is endowed with a
temper so insolent that criticism cannot touch
his heart — even admitting that he has a heart,
which I doubt.
Georges Bizet, Letter to his mother-in-law, 1871

20 [Of *The Ring*] I look upon it as nothing short of
desecration to bring such a tremendous and
world-wide subject under the gaslights of an
opera: the most rococo and degraded of all
forms of art — the idea of a sandy-haired
German tenor tweedledeeing over the
unspeakable woes of Sigurd, which even the
simplest words are not typical enough to
express!
William Morris, Letter, 1873. (Morris was to publish
his version, *The Story of Sigurd the Volsung and the Fall
of the Niblungs*, in 1876.)

21 [Of *Das Rheingold*] This idea would be quite a
good one, were it not that the nixies resembled
bathing ladies of the *demi-monde* more than
figures of popular legend.
Otto Henne am Rhyn, in 1877, quoted in Blom, *The
Music Lover's Miscellany* (1935)

22 [Of *Siegfried*] The music is, taken all in all, an
endlessly ruminating monster afflicted with a
revolting eructation of leading motives.
Ludwig Speidel, in 1879, quoted in Blom, *The Music
Lover's Miscellany* (1935)

23 [Of *Götterdammerung*] How convenient is the
method of giving the same tinkling leading
theme to each reappearing person, each similar
situation and each returning trend of thought
— as though one were hanging a dog-licence
number round its neck.
Ludwig Speidel, in 1879, quoted in Blom, *The Music
Lover's Miscellany* (1935)

24 [Of the characters of *The Ring*] Thieves, liars
and blackguards.
Sir Arthur Sullivan, quoted in Lebrecht, *Discord* (1982)

1 [Of *Parsifal*] The first act of the three occupied three hours, and I enjoyed that in spite of the singing.

Mark Twain, *A Tramp Abroad* (1880)

2 You only have time to clamber up a tree and hold on like grim death. Your hair is blown about, your face streaked with blood, but when the storm dies off and recedes a little, you get down from your shelter, you shake yourself and you enjoy the pleasure of having escaped a great danger. The hurricane, my dear child, is Wagner and Wagnerism. It is fearsome but it passes on. The important thing is not to let yourself be carried away.

Charles Gounod, quoted in Harding, *Gounod* (1973)

3 [Of *Die Meistersinger*] German beer music.

Friedrich Nietzsche, quoted in Wilson, *Brandy of the Damned* (1964)

4 [Of *Die Meistersinger*] Of all the affected, sapless, soulless, beginningless, endless, topless, bottomless, topsy-turviest, tongs-and-boniest doggerel of sounds I ever endured the deadliness of, that eternity of nothing was the deadliest — as far as the sound went.

John Ruskin, Letter, 1882

5 I need hardly tell you that I fear the Wagnerians, and that they are capable of ruining my enjoyment of even the best of Wagner.

Johannes Brahms, Letter to von Bülow, 1882

6 If one has not heard Wagner at Bayreuth, one *has heard nothing!* Take lots of handerkchiefs because you will cry a great deal! Also take a sedative because you will be exalted to the point of delirium!

Gabriel Fauré, Letter to Marguerite Baugnies, 1884

7 [Of *Parsifal*] Christianity arranged for Wagnerians.

Friedrich Nietzsche, quoted in Headington, *The Bodley Head History of Western Music* (1974)

8 The old rattlesnake.

Friedrich Nietzsche, quoted in Cardus, *The Delights of Music* (1966)

9 [Of Wagner's style] The octopus in music ... 'endless melody'.

Friedrich Nietzsche, *Der Fall Wagner* (1888)

10 How terribly Wagnerian orchestration affects me! I call it the Sirocco. A disagreeable sweat breaks out all over me. All my fine weather vanishes.

Friedrich Nietszche, *Der Fall Wagner* (1888)

11 Is Wagner a human being at all? Is he not rather a disease? He contaminates everything he touches — he has made music sick ... Wagner's art is diseased.

Friedrich Nietzsche, *Der Fall Wagner* (1888)

12 [Of *Götterdämmerung*] It seems like a great deal of work over nothing.

Charles Ives, Letter to his father, 1894

13 That old poisoner.

Claude Debussy, Letter to Pierre Louÿs, 1896

14 [Of *The Ring*] Irresistible as the sea.

Claude Debussy, quoted in Lockspeiser, *Debussy* (1963)

15 A man, who, had he been but a little more human, would have been great for all time.

Claude Debussy, quoted in Lockspeiser, *Debussy* (1963)

16 I have been told that Wagner's music is better than it sounds.

Mark Twain, *Autobiography* (pub. 1924)

17 [*Götterdämmerung*] How sublimely classical.

Gabriel Fauré, in 1908, *Opinions musicales* (1930)

18 Wagner, thank the fates, is no hypocrite. He says out what he means, and he usually means something nasty.

James Huneker, *Old Fogy* (1913)

19 Richy Wagner is a soft-bodied sensualist — pussy.

Charles Ives, marginalia on the MS of his Violin Sonata No. 3 (1914)

20 The man's power outrages reason and decency; he draws men and women out of the tangible world of pleasure at the beginning of the London season.

Neville Cardus, in *The Manchester Guardian*, 1936

21 [Of a performance of *Parsifal*] The evening became tedious rather sooner than usual.

Neville Cardus, in *The Manchester Guardian*, 1939

22 [When rehearsing *Götterdämmerung*] We've been rehearsing for two hours — and we're still playing the same bloody tune!

Sir Thomas Beecham, quoted in Reid, *Thomas Beecham* (1961)

23 [Of Wagner in *The Ring*] He presented the mythology of music at the same time with that of the world; in that he bound the music to the things and made them express themselves in music.
(Kretschmar)

Thomas Mann, *Doctor Faustus* (1947); trans. Lowe-Porter

24 [Of *Tristan und Isolde*] The bull-fight character of a theatrical mysticism robust in its corruption.
(Leverkühn)

Thomas Mann, *Doctor Faustus* (1947); trans. Lowe-Porter

25 Wagner is not only the willing prophet and diligent lackey of imperialism and late-bourgeois terrorism. He also possesses the

neurotic's ability to contemplate his own decadence and to transcend it in an image that can withstand that all-consuming gaze.

T.W. Adorno, *In Search of Wagner* (trans. 1981)

1 Wagner is the Puccini of music.

J.B. Morton ('Beachcomber'), attr.

2 Once you know one Wagner opera thoroughly, there can be no fresh surprises from the others. There is great magnificence, but it is all of a kind, like the same mountain scenery going on for hundreds of miles.

Colin Wilson, *Brandy of the Damned* (1964)

3 The thrall of Wagner has abated for reasons as different as the shortage of Flagstads and the decline of the narcotic effects of the music, owing to the circulation of stronger drugs.

Igor Stravinsky, *Themes and Conclusions* (1972)

4 I refused to sing the young Siegfried, because I think he is a bore. I always call him a Wagnerian L'il Abner.

Jon Vickers, quoted in Jacobson, *Reverberations* (1975)

WALES

5 [The Welsh] do not sing in unison like the people of other lands, but sing in different parts.

Giraldus Cambrensis, *Topographia Hibernica* (c. 1185)

6 *Lady Percy:* Lie still, ye thief, and hear the lady sing in Welsh.
Hotspur: I had rather hear Lady my brach howl in Irish.

William Shakespeare, *Henry IV, Part One*, III.i

7 Please, no national music! To the devil with all this 'folksiness'! Here I am in Wales ... and a harper sits in the vestibule of every inn and never stops playing so-called folk-melodies, that is, infamous, common, faked stuff.

Felix Mendelssohn, Letter to Zelter, 1829

8 It is strange that, though they will burst into song on no provocation at all, the Welsh have produced so few eminent composers — with, of course, the exception of Johann Sebastian, Bach.

Anon., quoted in Ayre, *The Wit of Music* (1966)

WALTON

9 [Of a period in intensive care] It was all very quiet. Didn't see a soul, not even Ben Britten's. Then there was a fanfare, but it wasn't one of mine. Bliss, I suppose.

Sir William Walton, quoted in *The Observer*, 1983

10 [Of Walton's Symphony No.1] It has been pretty certain for some time that if Sibelius did

not hurry up and write his eighth symphony, somebody else would write it for him.

Neville Cardus, in *The Manchester Guardian*, 1935

WARLOCK (PHILIP HESELTINE)

11 To underline a poem word by word is the work of a misguided schoolmaster.

Peter Warlock, 'Aphorisms', in *The New Age*, 1917

12 He who has heard the cry of the curlew on a lone and desolate moor has heard the music of this richly gifted personality. It is the saddest music I know.

Eric Fenby, *Delius as I knew him* (1936)

13 This strange and gifted youth was born out of his time and suffered from a duality of nature whose two divisions were opposing and irreconcilable. One half of him looked wistfully back to the healthy naturalism of the sixteenth century while the other faced boldly the dawn of an age whose music shall have parted company with every element which for centuries we have believed to be the essence and justification of its existence. Such types have small part in the present.

Sir Thomas Beecham, *A Mingled Chime* (1944)

14 Heseltine was gentle and shy of women; Warlock roughly undressed them; Heseltine wrote dreamy and desolate songs to words by Yeats; Warlock wrote roistering songs about drink and sex.

Colin Wilson, *Brandy of the Damned* (1964)

WEBER

15 [After the first run-through of *Euryanthe* lasted four hours] My Euryanthe should be called Ennuyante.

Carl Maria von Weber, quoted in Saunders, *Weber* (1940)

16 [Of *Der Freischütz*] I never could have believed it of the poor weak little mannikin. Weber must write operas now; nothing but operas, one after another.

Ludwig van Beethoven, quoted in Saunders, *Weber* (1940)

17 The Briton does you justice, the Frenchman admires you, but only the German can love you. You are his own, a bright day in his life, a drop of his blood, a particle of his heart.

Richard Wagner, Funeral oration for Carl Maria von Weber's reburial, 1844

18 Weber, who seems to whisper in my ear like a familiar spirit, inhabiting a happy sphere where he awaits to console me.

Hector Berlioz, Letter to Ferdinand Hiller

WEBERN

1   Music is natural law as related to the sense of hearing.

    Anton von Webern, *The Path to the New Music* (trans. 1963)

2   [Of his own music] In fifty years one will find it obvious, children will understand it and sing it.

    Anton von Webern, quoted in Kolneder, *Anton Webern* (1968)

3   [Of the Symphony for Chamber Orchestra] The work had von Webern's cardinal merit of brevity.

    Oscar Thompson, in *The Evening Post* (New York), 1929

4   Webern can say more in two minutes than most other composers in ten.

    Humphrey Searle, *Twentieth Century Counterpoint* (1954)

5   I would very much like to know if Webern himself knew who Webern was.

    Igor Stravinsky, quoted in *Melos*, 1958

6   We must hail not only this great composer but a real hero. Doomed to a total failure in a deaf world of ignorance and indifference, he inexorably kept on cutting out his diamonds, his dazzling diamonds, the mines of which he knew to perfection.

    Igor Stravinsky, quoted in Kolneder, *Anton Webern* (1968)

7   A perpetual pentecost.

    Igor Stravinsky, quoted in Carner, *Alban Berg* (1983)

8   He seems to have almost no interest in communication: he plays music like a game of patience.

    Colin Wilson, *Brandy of the Damned* (1964)

9   [On hearing of the accidental shooting of Webern by an American soldier] Do you know what kind of myth *that's* going to make in a thousand years? The young barbarians coming in to murder the Last European, standing at the far end of what'd been going on since Bach, an expansion of music's polymorphous perversity till all the notes were truly equal at last ... Where was there to go after Webern? It was the moment of maximum freedom. It all had to come down. Another Götterdämmerung. (Gustav)

    Thomas Pynchon, *Gravity's Rainbow* (1973)

10 He shook the foundation of sound as discourse in favour of sound as sound.

    John Cage, quoted in Peyser, *Boulez* (1976)

WEELKES

11 Thomas Weelkes ... divers times and very often comes so disguised either from the tavern or alehouse into the choir as is much to be lamented, for in these humours he will both curse and swear most dreadfully.

    William Lawes, sub-chanter of Chichester Cathedral, quoted in Brown, *Thomas Weelkes* (1969)

WEILL

12 I am not struggling for new forms or new theories. I am struggling for a new public.

    Kurt Weill, quoted in Green, *The World of Musical Comedy* (1974)

13 I write for today. I don't care about posterity.

    Kurt Weill, quoted in Ewen, *American Composers* (1982)

14 I believe that the musical theatre is the highest, the most expressive and the most imaginative form of theatre, and that a composer who has a talent and a passion for the theatre can express himself completely in this branch of musical creativeness.

    Kurt Weill, quoted in Ewen, *American Composers* (1982)

15 [Of *The Threepenny Opera*] Brecht has torn language, and Weill music, from their isolation. Once more we listen to speech on stage that is neither literary nor shopworn, and music that no longer works with threadbare harmonies and rhythms.

    Herbert Ihering, in *Berliner Börsen Courier*, 1928

WOLF

16 What remains for me to do? He [Wagner] has left me no room, like a mighty tree that chokes with its shade the sprouting young growths under its widely spreading branches.

    Hugo Wolf, Letter, 1883

17 [After a performance of *Götterdämmerung*] Friends! One thing I can do, which Wagner could not. I can go hungry!

    Hugo Wolf, quoted in Walker, *Hugo Wolf* (1968)

18 Today two new songs ... have occurred to me, of which one sounds so weird and strange that I am quite afraid of it. God help the unfortunate people who will one day hear it!

    Hugo Wolf, Letter, 1888

19 I once sent him a song and asked him to mark a cross wherever he thought it was faulty. Brahms returned it untouched, saying, 'I don't want to make a cemetery of your composition.'

    Hugo Wolf, quoted in Lebrecht, *Discord* (1982)

20 [Answering a request for biographical details] My name is Hugo Wolf. I was born on March 13th 1860, and am still alive at the moment. That's biography enough.

    Hugo Wolf, quoted in Headington, *The Bodley History of Western Music* (1974)

1 If only I were Hugo Wolf.

Hugo Wolf, in his last days, quoted in Walker, *Hugo Wolf* (1968)

2 To think of his songs one by one is to see defiling before the eye a veritable pageant of humanity in epitome.

Ernest Newman, quoted in Cardus, *The Delights of Music* (1966)

WOMEN AND MUSIC

3 Consort not with a female musician lest thou be taken in by her snares.

Ben Sira, *The Book of Wisdom* (c. 190 BC)

4 Imagine with your self what an unsightly matter it were to see a woman play upon a tabor or drum, or blow in a flute or trumpet, or any like instrument: and this because the boisterousness of them doth both cover and take away that sweet mildness which setteth so forth every deed that a woman doth.

Baldassare Castiglione, *The Booke of the Courtyer* (1528); trans. Hoby (1561)

5 Like untuned golden strings all women are Which long time lie untouched, will harshly jar.

Christopher Marlowe, *Hero and Leander* (pub. 1598)

6 To live a barren sister all your life, Chanting faint hymns to the cold fruitless moon.
(Theseus)

William Shakespeare, *A Midsummer Night's Dream*, I.i

7 Not so young, sir, to love a woman for singing, nor so old to dote on her for anything.
(Kent)

William Shakespeare, *King Lear*, I.iv

8 There's no music when a woman's in the concert.

Thomas Dekker, *The Honest Whore, Part One*, II (1604)

9 Loud music is too harsh for ladies' heads, Since they love men in arms as well as beds.
(Simonides)

William Shakespeare, *Pericles*, II.iii

10 Our young women and wives, they that being maids took so much pains to sing, play and dance, with such cost and charge to their parents to get these graceful qualities, now being married will scarce touch an instrument, they care not for it.

Robert Burton, *Anatomy of Melancholy* (1621)

11 O! sir, I must not tell my age. They say women and music should never be dated.
(Miss Hardcastle)

Oliver Goldsmith, *She Stoops to Conquer* (1773)

12 [Visiting a Venetian women's conservatory] The sight of girls ... handling the double bass,

and blowing into the bassoon, did not much please me.

Mrs Hester Thrale, *Observations and Reflections* (1789)

13 No artist should ever marry ... if you ever do have to marry, marry a girl who is more in love with your art than with you.

Frederick Delius, quoted in Fenby, *Delius as I knew him* (1936)

14 The legend relates that one afternoon while Adam was asleep, Eve, anticipating the Great God Pan, bored holes in a hollow reed and began to do what is called 'pick out a tune'. Thereupon Adam awoke: 'Stop that horrible noise,' he roared, adding, after a pause, 'besides which, *if anyone's going to make it, it's not you but me.*'

Dame Ethel Smyth, *Female Pipings in Eden* (1933)

15 Oh I'm a martyr to music.
(Mrs Organ Morgan)

Dylan Thomas, *Under Milk Wood* (1954)

16 The man who is not thrilled to the bone by the sight of a woman playing the flute, blowing a clarinet or struggling with the intricacies of a trombone is no man.

Sir Malcolm Sargent, quoted in Gattey, *Peacocks on the Podium* (1982)

WOODWIND

See also individual instruments.

17 *Clown:* Why masters, have your instruments been in Naples, that they speak i' th' nose thus?
First Musician: How, sir, how?
Clown: Are these, I pray, called wind instruments?
First Musician: Ay, marry, are they, sir.
Clown: O, thereby hangs a tail.
First Musician: Whereby hangs a tale, sir?
Clown: Marry, sir, by many a wind instrument that I know.

William Shakespeare, *Othello*, III.i

18 'This is the way,' laughed the great god Pan
  (Laughed while he sat by the river),
'The only way since gods began
To make sweet music, they could not succeed.'
Then, dropping his mouth to a hole in the reed,
  He blew in power by the river.

Elizabeth Barrett Browning, 'A Musical Instrument'

WORDS AND MUSIC

See also CRITICS AND CRITICISM, LIBRETTI, OPERA, SONG.

19 For music any words are good enough.

Aristophanes, *The Birds*; trans. Planché

20 There will be no difference between the words that are and the words that are not set to music; both will conform to the same laws.

Plato, *The Republic*

1   A verse without music is a mill without water.

    Anon. troubadour, quoted in Burke, *Musical
    Landscapes* (1983)

2   For is it not as good to say playnly
    Gyf me a spade?
    As *Gyf me a spa, ve, va, ve, va, vade?*
    But yf thou wylt have a song that is gode,
    I have one of Robin Hode
    The best that ever was made.
    (Ygnoraunce)

    Interlude of the Four Elements (16th century)

3   Just as the soul is nobler than the body, so the
    words are nobler than the counterpoint.

    Giovanni de'Bardi, *Discourse on Ancient Music and Good
    Singing* (c. 1580)

4   Neither is there any tune or stroke which may
    be sung or played on instruments, which hath
    not some poetical ditties framed according to
    the numbers thereof.

    William Webbe, *Discourse of English Poetrie* (1586)

5   It will be a great absurdity to use a sad
    harmony to a merry matter, or a merry
    harmony to a sad, lamentable or tragical ditty.

    Thomas Morley, *A Plaine and Easie Introduction to
    Practicall Musicke* (1597)

6   So will it be counted great incongruity if a
    musician upon the words *he ascended into heaven*
    should cause his music descend, or by the
    contrary upon the descension should cause his
    music to ascend.

    Thomas Morley, *A Plaine and Easie Introduction to
    Practicall Musicke* (1597)

7   I love a ballad but even too well, if it be doleful
    matter merrily set down, or a very pleasant
    thing indeed and sung lamentably.
    (Clown)

    William Shakespeare, *The Winter's Tale*, IV.iv

8   Let the word be master of the melody, not its
    slave.

    Claudio Monteverdi, quoted in Morgenstern (ed.),
    Composers on Music (1958)

9   Let those which only warble long,
    And gargle in their throats a song,
    Content themselves with Ut, Re, Mi:
    Let words, and sense, be set by thee.

    Edmund Waller, 'To Mr Henry Lawes'

10 Blest pair of Sirens, pledge of Heaven's joy,
    Sphere-born harmonious sisters, Voice and
    Verse

    John Milton, 'At a Solemn Musick'

11 Music is the exaltation of poetry. Both of them
    may excel apart, but surely they are most
    excellent when they are joined, because nothing
    is then wanting to either of their proportions;

for thus they appear like wit and beauty in the
same person.

Henry Purcell, Preface to *Dioclesian* (1690)

12 But the numbers of poetry and music are
    sometimes so contrary that in many places I
    have been obliged to cramp my verses, and
    make them rugged to the reader, thus they
    might be harmonious to the hearer.

    John Dryden, Preface to *King Arthur* (1691)

13 Nothing is capable of being well set to music
    that is not nonsense.

    Joseph Addison, in *The Spectator*, 1711

14 To varnish nonsense with the charms of sound.

    Charles Churchill, 'The Apology'

15 Music, I have considered, should hold the same
    position with regard to poetry as brilliance of
    colouring and well-arranged chiaroscuro hold
    to a correct and satisfactory drawing, lending
    emphasis to the figures without altering their
    contours.

    Christoph Willibald von Gluck, Preface to *Alceste*
    (1767)

16 The vocal music of Italy can only be heard in
    perfection when sung to its own language and
    by its own natives, who give both the language
    and music their true accents and expressions.
    There is as much reason to wish to hear Italian
    music in this genuine manner, as for the lovers
    of painting to prefer an original picture of
    Raphael to a copy.

    Charles Burney, *The Present State of Music in France and
    Italy* (1773)

17 *Aujourd'hui ce que ne vaut pas le peine d'être dit, on
    le chante.* Today, what's not worth saying is
    sung instead.

    Pierre-Augustin Caron de Beaumarchais, *Le Barbier de
    Séville*, I.ii (1775)

18 Music begins where words end.

    Johann Wilhelm von Goethe, attr.

19 Why 'words for music' are almost invariably
    trash now, though the words of Elizabethan
    songs are better than any music, is a gloomy
    and difficult question.

    Walter Savage Landor, *Essays*, 'T.H. Bayly'

20 Johnson marched to kettle-drums and
                trumpets;
    Gibbon moved to flutes and hautboys.

    George Colman the Younger, *Random Records* (1830)

21 Where the speech of man stops short, then the
    art of music begins.

    Richard Wagner, *A Happy Evening* (1840)

22 Music is the vapour of art. It is to poetry what
    reverie is to thought, what fluid is to liquid,

what the ocean of clouds is to the ocean of waves.

Victor Hugo, *Les Rayons et les ombres* (1840)

1 *De la musique avant toute chose . . .*
De la musique encore et toujours!
Music before everything else . . . Music again and forever!

Paul Verlaine, *Art poétique* (1874)

2 Proceeding from the conviction that human speech is strictly controlled by musical laws, he considers the task of musical art to be the reproduction in musical sounds not merely of the mood of a feeling, but chiefly of the mood of human speech.

Modest Mussorgsky, statement prepared for Riemann's *Musik-Lexicon*, 1880

3 I seek above all to extricate the general feeling of a poem, rather than to concentrate on its details.

Gabriel Fauré, quoted in Orledge, *Gabriel Fauré* (1979)

4 The musician is perhaps the most modest of animals, but he is also the proudest. It is he who has invented the sublime art of ruining poetry.

Erik Satie, quoted in Templier, *Erik Satie* (1932)

5 If words are set to music, the music must be as independent an entity as the poem.

Peter Warlock, 'Aphorisms', in *The New Age*, 1917

6 Poetry is a comforting piece of fiction set to more or less lascivious music.

H.L. Mencken, *Prejudices* (1919-27)

7 What has been called Symbolism can be quite simply resumed in the desire common to several families of poets . . . to take back from music what they had given it. The secret of this movement is nothing other than this . . . We were fed on music and our literary minds only dreamt of extracting from language almost the same effects that music caused on our nervous beings.

Paul Valéry, Preface to Lucien Fabre's *La Connaissance de la Déesse* (1920)

8 Words created divergencies between beings, because their precise meanings put an opinion around the idea. Music only retains the highest and purest substance of the idea, since it has the privilege of expressing all, whilst excluding nothing.

Nadia Boulanger, in 1920, quoted in Kendall, *The Tender Tyrant: Nadia Boulanger* (1976)

9 I am certain that all melodic and rhythmical mysteries of music in general are to be explained solely from rhythmical and melodic points of view on the basis of the melodic curves of speech.

Leoš Janáček, Letter to Jan Mikota, 1926

10 When Satan makes impure verses, Allah sends a divine tune to cleanse them.

George Bernard Shaw, *Adventures of a Black Girl in Search of God* (1932)

11 Melody and speech belong together. I reject the idea of a pure music.

Carl Orff, quoted in Machlis, *Introduction to Contemporary Music* (1963)

12 A verbal art like poetry is reflective; it stops to think. Music is immediate; it goes on to become.

W.H. Auden, quoted in Copland, *Music and Imagination* (1953)

13 This has too many words.

Frank Sinatra, comment while singing Cole Porter's 'Don't Fence Me In', quoted in Whitcomb, *After the Ball* (1972)

14 Words are no longer searching for the accompaniment that music cannot give them. Not a decorative environment of sound, but unification: that new state in which they sacrifice their self-reliance, and gain a new force of conviction through music. And music is no longer looking for an insignificant text as a pretext, but for a hard currency language, a value against which it can prove its own.

Ingeborg Bachmann, in *Musica Viva*, 1959

15 [On setting words to music] If you wish to 'understand' the text, read it!

Pierre Boulez, quoted in Machlis, *Introduction to Contemporary Music* (1963)

16 The words of Mercury are harsh after the songs of Apollo.
(Armado)

William Shakespeare, *Love's Labour's Lost*, V.ii

AUTHOR INDEX

Note: Where authors have a topic heading to themselves, references to quotations by those authors under that heading are set in **bold** type.

SUBJECT INDEX

Note: The subject index mostly consists of musical terms, persons, works, etc., but a number of other keywords are also indexed. Where a keyword is also a topic heading in the text, the references to all quotations under that heading are set in **bold** type. The phrases in which the keyword occurs are arranged in alphabetical order beneath the keyword headings; indefinite and definite articles are generally omitted from the beginnings of phrases.